Martial Law Melodrama

Martial Law Melodrama

Lino Brocka's Cinema Politics

José B. Capino

UNIVERSITY OF CALIFORNIA PRESS

University of California Press
Oakland, California

© 2020 by José B. Capino

Library of Congress Cataloging-in-Publication Data

Names: Capino, José B., author.
Title: Martial law melodrama : Lino Brocka's cinema politics /
   José B. Capino.
Description: Oakland, California : University of California Press, [2020] |
   Includes bibliographical references and index.
Identifiers: LCCN 2019023489 (print) | LCCN 2019023490 (ebook) |
   ISBN 9780520314610 (cloth) | ISBN 9780520314634 (paperback) |
   ISBN 9780520974012 (ebook)
Subjects: LCSH: Brocka, Lino, 1939–1991—Criticism and interpretation. |
   Motion pictures—Political aspects—Philippines—20th century.
Classification: LCC PN1998.3.B7593 C37 2020 (print) |
   LCC PN1998.3.B7593 (ebook) | DDC 791.4302/33092—dc23
LC record available at https://lccn.loc.gov/2019023489
LC ebook record available at https://lccn.loc.gov/2019023490

Manufactured in the United States of America

28 27 26 25 24 23 22 21 20 19
10 9 8 7 6 5 4 3 2 1

CONTENTS

List of Illustrations   vii
Preface   xi
Acknowledgments   xxvii

1. The Country and the City: Social Melodrama and the Symptoms of Authoritarian Rule   1
2. "A Thoroughly Different Kind of Mother": Surrogate Autocrats, Restive Youth, and the Maternal Melodrama   42
3. The Melodramatics of Crime: Film Noir in the Twilight of Martial Law   74
4. Tales of Unrelenting Misfortunes: Family Melodrama and the 1980s Economic Crisis   108
5. Men in Revolt: Two Experiments in Political Cinema   128
6. A Dirty Affair: Political Melodramas of Democratization   161
7. Picturing "A Faggot's Dilemma": Sexuality, Politics, and a Commerce in Queer Movies   198

   Coda: Three Non-endings   237

Notes   247
Index   287

ILLUSTRATIONS

P.1. Bona (Nora Aunor) fetches water for her lover's bath, *Bona* xii
1.1. Posters from the political left loom behind Julio (Bembol Roco) in *Manila in the Claws of Light* 2
1.2. Berto (Mario O'Hara) watches helplessly as a woman pulls a child away from him, *Weighed but Found Wanting* 9
1.3. Junior (Christopher De Leon) joins two social outcasts (Mario O'Hara and Lolita Rodriguez), *Weighed but Found Wanting* 10
1.4. Milagros (Laurice Guillen) and Junior (Christopher De Leon) wait for the martial law-era curfew to pass, *Weighed but Found Wanting* 15
1.5. Junior (Christopher De Leon), holding Kuala's child, refuses his father Cesar's (Eddie Garcia) conciliatory gesture, *Weighed but Found Wanting* 17
1.6. Julio (Bembol Roco) and Pol (Tommy Abuel) behold the ruins of a shantytown fire, *Manila in the Claws of Light* 28
1.7. Scenes excised from the film's gay sequence, *Manila in the Claws of Light* 32
1.8. Julio (Bembol Roco) flees after stabbing Ah Tek (Tommy Chua), *Manila in the Claws of Light* 37
2.1. Tonia (Mona Lisa) complains about food expenses to her dependents, *Insiang* 46
2.2. Hilda Koronel plays the insurgent daughter to Mona Lisa's patriarchal mother, *Insiang* 48
2.3. Conrado Baltazar's cinematography and Fiel Zabat's production design create a vivid portrait of the slums, *Insiang* 52

2.4. Zita (Carmi Martin) lashes out at Pina (Mona Lisa), *Cain and Abel* 57
2.5. Zita (Carmi Martin) is murdered and her body disposed of, *Cain and Abel* 61
2.6. Ellis (Christopher De Leon) and Lorens (Phillip Salvador) are mortally wounded during a forest shoot-out, *Cain and Abel* 64
2.7. Renata (Lolita Rodriguez) avoids her daughter Ester (Nora Aunor), *Whore of a Mother* 68
2.8. Renata (Lolita Rodriguez) makes a final appeal to Ester (Nora Aunor) and Luis (Raoul Aragon), *Whore of a Mother* 71
3.1. Poldo (Phillip Salvador) scales the enormous landfill called Smokey Mountain, *Jaguar* 75
3.2. The well-groomed Poldo (Phillip Salvador) leaves his filthy environs for work, *Jaguar* 78
3.3. Police restrain Poldo (Phillip Salvador) after he attacks Sonny (Menggie Cobarubias), *Jaguar* 82
3.4. Police conduct a dragnet operation officially called a "saturation drive" but popularly known as "sona" (zoning), *Jaguar* 89
3.5. Cristy (Amy Austria) performs in an exploitation film, *Jaguar* 96
3.6. Angela (Hilda Koronel) is detained and gang-raped inside a cavernous warehouse, *Angela, the Marked One* 99
3.7. Angela's (Hilda Koronel) ordeal recalls acts of state violence against political prisoners, *Angela, the Marked One* 102
4.1. Aida (Vilma Santos) escapes poverty by becoming a mistress to a much older man (Mario Montenegro) in *Adultery* 112
4.2. Ricardo (Phillip Salvador) lashes out at Aida (Vilma Santos) in front of her son (Alvin Enriquez) in *Adultery* 115
4.3. Emma (Pilar Pilapil) consoles Melo (Ronaldo Valdez) after he loses his life's savings in *Such Pain, Brother Eddie* 120
4.4. Emma (Pilar Pilapil) and her children (Emily Loren and Aga Mulach) bid farewell to Melo (Ronaldo Valdez), *Such Pain, Brother Eddie* 124
5.1. Turing (Phillip Salvador) and his accomplices Lando (Raoul Aragon) and Boy the Shitter (Rez Cortez), *My Own Country* 135
5.2. Hospital employees restrain Turing (Phillip Salvador), *My Own Country* 137
5.3. Luz (Gina Alajar) cradles Turing (Phillip Salvador), *My Own Country* 140
5.4. Turing (Phillip Salvador) runs into his former coworker Willy (Ariosto Reyes), *My Own Country* 144
5.5. Miguelito (Aga Mulach) encounters his estranged birth mother Auring (Nida Blanca), *Miguelito* 152
5.6. Images of Ferdinand Marcos in Venancio's (Eddie Garcia) office, *Miguelito* 156

6.1. Commander Kontra's (Bembol Roco) militia, a composite of vigilante groups from the Marcos and Aquino regimes, *Orapronobis/Fight for Us*   165
6.2. Jimmy (Phillip Salvador) carries the remains of his son Camilo (R. R. Herrera), *Orapronobis/Fight for Us*   170
6.3. Images from the two censored depictions of cannibalism in *Orapronobis/Fight for Us*   175
6.4. Mayor Guatlo (Eddie Garcia) and wife Rowena (Charo Santos) mimic Ferdinand and Imelda Marcos in *A Dirty Affair*   183
6.5. Rachel (Dina Bonnevie) drops a bombshell during Mayor Guatlo's campaign sortie in *A Dirty Affair*   186
6.6. In *A Dirty Affair*, Rachel (Dina Bonnevie) and Levi (Christopher De Leon) appear as reimagined versions of Cristy and Poldo from *Jaguar*   188
6.7. Mayor Velasco (Ronaldo Valdez) and his wife Cresencia (Celeste Legaspi) console the bereaved family of a victim of their misdeeds, *Above Everything Else*   192
7.1. Benito (Eddie Garcia) romances a hustler who interrupts him to negotiate a higher fee, *Gold Plated*   204
7.2. Emma (Lolita Rodriguez) gets "picked up" at a party, *Gold Plated*   211
7.3. Benito (Eddie Garcia) kisses Diego (Mario O'Hara) "full on the lips" before turning the gun on himself, *Gold Plated*   213
7.4. Coring (Dolphy) tells a white lie about his cross-dressing to his foster child Nonoy (Niño Mulach) in *My Father, My Mother*   216
7.5. Coring (Dolphy) tends affectionately to Nonoy (Niño Mulach), *My Father, My Mother*   221
7.6. David (Mark Gil) offers moral support and a spare bedroom to Carissa (Dina Bonnevie), *Always Changing, Always Moving*   225
7.7. Carissa (Dina Bonnevie) renews her friendship with former suitor David (Mark Gil), *Always Changing, Always Moving*   229
8.1. Lino Brocka directs Allan Paule on the set of *Macho Dancer*   238
8.2. Dick (Gabby Concepcion) tends to his friend Nitoy (Christopher De Leon), *Sparkle in the Dark*   244

PREFACE

A young woman, puny and dark, is balancing heavy containers of water as she wends her way through a labyrinthine Manila slum. The scene is quite possibly one of the most unforgettable in Lino Brocka's melodramas from the martial law era. Bona, the young woman, is taking the water to her lover who waits atop a lofty staircase, indolent, impatient to bathe. Caught in a haze of fandom, Bona has dropped out of school and fled her lower-middle-class home. She has chosen to serve Gardo, a bit player and stuntman in cheap movies. Though he passively had sex with Bona once, this handsome nobody treats her like a slave more than a lover. Every so often he brings women home, rubbing his promiscuity in her face. He fools around with one of them in his room while Bona outside quietly seethes. When Gardo tells her to move out of his house, she finally snaps. Giving him a bath that same evening, she douses him with boiling water and watches him scream.

One of Brocka's most widely seen melodramas, *Bona* (1980) succeeded as a commercial outing and as a piece of socially relevant filmmaking. The psychology behind the heroine's enthrallment to an obviously flawed idol intrigued local critics. They also praised the staging of her feminist awakening.[1] Other reviewers approved of the film's self-reflexive commentary on the sexist fantasies purveyed by mass culture.[2] Ironically, the slavish devotion indicted by the film mirrored the adulation its star commanded in real life; Nora Aunor, who played Bona and produced the movie, enjoyed a massive nationwide fan base. Critics from abroad offered a different reading of Brocka's film. In France, where it played at the Cannes International Film Festival, Jacques Fieschi observed a powerful hidden gay subtext in *Bona*. Focusing on the single love scene between the lead characters, Fieschi compared Bona's furtive tryst with Gardo to a gay man's rape of another man.[3]

FIGURE P.1. Bona (Nora Aunor) fetches water for her lover's bath. *Bona*. Courtesy of Danilo Brocka/CCP Library/Lino O. Brocka Collection.

The scene depicts Gardo asking Bona for a massage, followed by wordless requests to fondle him and proceed even further. Gardo is actually fulfilling Bona's unspoken fantasies, but he also insists on making her feel degraded, both to feed his narcissism and to indulge her masochistic desires. Fieschi's highly counterintuitive but fascinating reading posits the woman as the subliminally coded male homosexual and Gardo as the masculine love object.

Years after the film's initial release, *Bona* continued to generate interpretation. Bienvenido Lumbera in a 1992 essay reframes the film as an allegory of Ferdinand Marcos's authoritarian hegemony as well as its inevitable undoing. Lumbera writes: "Defiance was not openly stated but it was definitely present in the images of incarceration, suppression, resistance, and struggle." The critic goes on to detect a political metaphor in the scalding of a bossy lothario: "Brocka was extolling in *Bona*, 1980, the act of revolt of the fanatical movie fan who decides to get back at her callous exploiter."[4] Scalding for Lumbera becomes nothing short of an insurgency.

Based on the film's critical reception alone, it would appear that Brocka's martial law melodrama registers not only the politics of antiauthoritarianism but also of gender and sexuality (that is, feminism and queerness) and culture (specifically, popular cinema). The critics' decoding of these divergent political meanings testifies to so much more than the richness of one particular film or the special talents of its director. The differing interpretations point to a film culture that engaged the pressing issues of the day. They also speak to a historical moment when popular cinema was still perceived by many—including the president—as a vital medium for sociopolitical representation. The chief executive, whose election was sealed by the release of a fawning biographical melodrama, used movies for propaganda and threatened or attempted to nationalize the film industry.[5] Numerous film artists, workers, and viewers resisted his designs, either by fashioning oppositional content or pursuing a vastly different agenda for the movies. *Martial Law Melodrama* is about this politically engaged cinema and its generative flux of meanings.

. . .

The Philippine strongman Ferdinand Marcos declared martial law in 1972. He wrested control of the mass media, censored political speech,[6] imprisoned or disappeared thousands of political enemies,[7] usurped private businesses,[8] and looted the nation's wealth and natural resources.[9] Despite its heavy strictures and immoderate use of violence, however, his was not a totalitarian regime. A brilliant politician-lawyer, Marcos devised a paradoxical form of dictatorship he billed as a "constitutional authoritarianism."[10] He upended democratic rule while seeking to maintain the fiction of legality and even benevolence. To do so, he created a constitution that granted him broad executive powers and installed a rubber-stamp legislature.[11] This façade of legitimacy allowed his autocratic rule to prevail for almost two decades. It also gave foreign governments and international creditors the excuse they needed to prop up his regime despite its appalling record of corruption and human rights violations.[12]

During martial law, the state's mechanisms for controlling the popular art of cinema reflected the same combination of blatant repression and a veneer of constitutionality.[13] The state placed additional restrictions on portrayals of sex, violence, crimes, and other acts it considered deviant or immoral.[14] It threatened to impose stiff penalties and jail time for films that "tend to incite rebellion, sedition or otherwise undermine the faith of the people in the government or in constituted authorities."[15] Motion pictures were censored twice over: first as story outlines or scripts and then as assembled motion pictures.[16] At whim, censors bowdlerized films, and pulled out prints already approved for screening.[17] They also refused permits for films to be exported.[18] One of Marcos's chief censors required producers to surrender the negatives of films submitted for review.[19] She ordered staff to deface or destroy strips of film containing scenes she did not like, making the censorship process irreversible. Multiple levels of appeal existed, however, to check the censor's powers—even if only for show.[20]

Surprisingly, the Philippine film industry was never more prolific than during authoritarian rule. Film production peaked in the 1970s, reportedly reaching an all-time high of 251 films in 1971.[21] The industry's output was quite diverse. It ranged from independently made prestige movies about sharecroppers and juvenile delinquents to avant-garde film poems—and from exploitation films about sexually deprived homemakers to big-budget genre films about mythical creatures. Citing quantity and especially quality, scholars and critics fondly look back on this period as the "Second Golden Age" of Philippine cinema[22] or the apex of a "New Wave in Tagalog Movies."[23] Such fondness, however, has a clear downside. Fascinated by the Second Golden Age, critics tend to dismiss the majority of commercial films made then as "escapist."[24] Almost in the same breath, they praise a small corpus—among them Brocka's films—as some of the most accomplished, progressive works in Philippine cinema's history.[25] While I agree with the critics about the stellar quality of the martial law–era films, I look askance at the impulse to draw sharp distinctions between socially relevant films and ostensibly escapist ones. The desire to form canons and to mount an ideological critique of films is indeed hard to resist. But the assumptions of value underpinning such efforts should give us pause. In light of heavy censorship during martial law, it simply makes no sense to place a high premium on a narrow corpus of overtly political works. The same may be said of valorizing iconoclastic works for their radical aesthetic innovation or superlative literary merits—traits found in all but a few works of commercial cinema. Edged into the shadows of the Second Golden Age and the era of dictatorship, the majority of Philippine movies no longer can be ignored.

My chief errand here is to demonstrate the significance of both popular and prestige films and upon reorienting our bearings, to come to grips with their valuable legacy. Rather than give all the credit to a small number of exceptional movies, I reconsider how mainstream films from the martial law era also undertake both mundane and exceptional practices of sociopolitical representation. The import of this neglected bulk, I further argue, consists in how it unsettles a widespread assumption. It challenges the notion that certain modes such as realism, certain filmmaking economies such as the independent circuit, or certain genre formations such as social problem films are uniquely suitable to cinema politics. Enthrallment to that assumption comes at a cost. It misrecognizes the fluidity of cinema history and the political uses of public memory.

The work of Lino Brocka presents a unique opportunity to examine cinema during the Marcos regime and to revisit the broader issue of politics in film. Brocka, like his movies, had plebian roots but inhabited the tension between high and low cultures. Born to poverty in the countryside in 1939, he won a scholarship to attend the prestigious state university in the nation's capital during the mid-1950s.[26] He dropped out after nine years and, in 1965, served as a Mormon missionary in Hawaii.[27] He left the church after clashing with his superiors and, by his own account, nearly starved to death busing tables and working at a nursing home in the San Francisco Bay Area.[28] He returned to the Philippines in the late 1960s and wrote press releases for a company that filmed American B-movies in the country.[29] He worked for a progressive theater group and directed episodes of a TV show produced by the same troupe.[30] In 1970, in the first year of Ferdinand Marcos's second term in office, Brocka launched his prolific movie career. It was a time of political upheaval inspired by antiestablishment protests and countercultural influences from the West.[31] The youthful dissidents who marched in the streets and stormed public venues condemned Marcos, in large part, for his coziness with American imperialists.[32] They also protested his looting the treasury to bankroll his recent campaign for reelection.[33] The president threw down the gauntlet a few years prior to the end of what should have been his final term in office. Declaring a state of emergency in 1972, he established a dictatorship and, as dissenters aptly put it, virtually made himself "President for Life."[34]

Brocka initially shied away from the sociopolitical in his filmmaking, building his career instead on commercial films. He imitated Hollywood blockbusters and made film adaptations of serial graphic novellas called *komiks*. In the succeeding years, he began producing a string of prestige and social realist films that would earn him the reputation of being his country's premier and most internationally recognized director. He financed or subsidized those innovative films with earnings from his commercial endeavors. His career see-sawed between mining box office gold and enduring a succession of flops.

Before his untimely death in a car accident in 1991, the prolific director had made over sixty-five films and numerous television programs. Life under the autocratic state lit up Brocka's screen with searing images. He explored spaces blighted by uneven economic development and state terror. His work made visible houses of prostitution, neighborhoods garrisoned by armed goons, and teeming shantytowns. He tracked the figures whom the dictatorship had marginalized: urban laborers branded as communist outlaws; rural folk terrorized by paramilitary groups; and gays oppressed by a patriarchal, homophobic society. Although Brocka made less than a handful of works of overt political criticism during the Marcos era, the filmmaker began to tangle with the dictatorship in the early 1970s because of censorship.[35] He turned to political activism in 1983, protesting new censorship policies, additional draconian laws, and government incursions into the lands of tribal peoples.[36] The assassination of Marcos's rival, Senator Benigno "Ninoy" Aquino Jr. that year brought further dissent.[37] For two weeks in 1985, Brocka was imprisoned, purportedly for taking part in a transport workers' strike but more likely for antagonizing the regime.[38] He continued his artistic and political battles long after Marcos lost power.

Critics like to separate the "good" Brocka films from the "bad" ones, the sociopolitical critiques from the potboilers.[39] This dichotomy is misleading. In Brocka's case, some of the most incisive critiques also occur in those oft-maligned commercial and minor works. To understand the cultural and political work of his melodramas, it is necessary to revise our notions of what counts as politics and where it lodges within popular cinema.

Jacques Rancière reminds us that politics does not pertain solely to the affairs of state. What constitutes politics, rather, is the action of challenging the established logics of inequality and exclusion. Political actors are those who with their deeds attempt to realize the outlines of a different, more equitable world. Addressed to a world foreseen only in outline, the politics of the possible is not always recognizable as such. Alain Badiou, who like Rancière writes on politics and cinema, observes that many films with a truly progressive charge "come at things obliquely."[40] Badiou contends that films with explicitly political topics should be scrutinized all the more carefully for their underlying "reactionary dimension."[41] There are as many kinds of action as there are actors differently moved by the possible. Hence, in appraising the politics of Brocka's movies, scholars and critics should consider a wider range of scenarios than the work dealing overtly with sociopolitical issues.

Martial Law Melodrama locates politics in both the obvious and least likely places within a single director's body of work. This book tracks how Philippine mainstream cinema from the 1970s to the early 1990s articulated the effects of authoritarianism while also channeling the insurgent energies that toppled the Marcos regime. My approach combines an attentive reading of the films with insights gleaned from extensive archival research and critical studies of cinema and culture. The archive is particularly useful in demonstrating how the sociopolitical traces in Brocka's films were taken up not only by the director and his collaborators but also by moviegoers, local and foreign critics, film festival programmers, and the officials of the Marcos regime. The latter proved to be astute readers, finding political significance in the visual details and narrative elements of the director's work.[42] Rancière's concept of "cinema politics" evocatively names the specific ways that politics crystallizes in the medium and cultural apparatus of cinema.[43] He uses the term to invoke the "politics in what a film is saying—the history of a movement or a conflict, exposure of a situation of suffering or injustice—and something more like 'policy,' meaning the specific strategy of an artistic approach: a way of accelerating or slowing time, shrinking or expanding space, harmonizing or de-harmonizing gaze and action, making or breaking the sequence of before and after, inside and outside."[44] As the following chapters delineate, Brocka's martial law melodramas inscribe politics and political statements on the film's surface, through the fabric and gaps of cinematic style and narrative, with and against genre conventions, and on the film's subtextual and allegorical registers.

The analysis found in the later chapters of this study revisits the concept of "political cinema." The term scarcely has circulated since the 1990s, when American and European film scholars largely abandoned Third Cinema and the political thrillers of auteurs such as Costa-Gavras. Notable exceptions include essays from

Rancière and Badiou as well as Mike Wayne and Martin O'Shaughnessy's books on political commitments in European and world cinema.[45] Analysis using the lens of political cinema, however, is deeply relevant to Brocka's oeuvre. Gilles Deleuze, who has authored the most influential philosophical volumes on film, named Brocka as a key figure in what he called "modern political cinema."[46] In spite of the filmmaker's prominence in France during the late 1970s and 1980s, the significance of Brocka's work to Deleuze's thinking remains unexamined. The later chapters fill in that gap.

MELODRAMA

"Melodrama" describes the films treated in this study. The elements that characterize these movies include formidable external conflicts and moral dilemmas, intricate plots, and stark contrasts between virtuous and malevolent characters. Linda Williams succinctly defines melodrama as an "art of strong pathos and action that recognizes the virtues of suffering victims."[47] Her definition invokes both the popular idea of melodrama as lachrymose female-centered narratives and the less familiar but historically accurate usage of the term to describe sensational, action-packed spectacles. Michael Walker notes that "action melodramas," which revolved around "heroes in conflict with the villains/the enemy/the bad guys/a hostile environment," were the "generic root" of Hollywood "swashbucklers, war stories, westerns, crime thrillers, adventure stories."[48] Both scholars have persuasively shown that mainstream American cinema is inextricably linked to melodrama. They are practically synonymous. This link casts a shaping force on Philippine cinema, whose mainstream emulates Hollywood's style and form. This inclusive notion of melodrama captures the diversity of Brocka's films, embracing both weepies and thrillers.

This study invokes alternate conceptions of melodrama that circulate in literary criticism, media scholarship, and other disciplines. In those fields, "melodrama" refers to a sensibility, a mode of representation and especially, as Ravi Vasudevan puts it, "a system of dramaturgy . . . displaying the characteristic ensemble of Manichaeism, bipolarity, the privileging of the moral over the psychological, and the deployment of coincidence."[49] He and other scholars note that this emotionally charged and sensational approach to storytelling is highly adaptable. It fuels the histrionic spectacles mentioned above as well as quiet observational works. Contrary to popular notions, melodrama is not antithetical to realism, for a work can be melodramatic even when its style and narrative aspire to stark verisimilitude.[50] As Williams avers: "If emotional and moral registers are sounded, if a work invites us to feel sympathy for the virtues of beset victims, if the narrative trajectory is the retrieval and staging of virtue through adversity and suffering, then the operative mode is melodrama."[51] In Brocka's case, the alternately seamless and contrapuntal juxtaposition of social realism and melodramatic sensibility represent an especially intriguing aspect of his art and cinema politics.

In elucidating the politics of Brocka's melodramas, I analyze the form of his work both close up and from a distance. The latter means examining structures and conventions that cut across individual movies. For instance, I aggregate Brocka's films into particular subgenres. Doing so allows me to show that the affordances of each subgenre are responsive to sociohistorical transformations. To cite one example, I contend that the family melodrama, with its emphasis on mundane conflicts, proved effective in illustrating the impact of the 1980s Philippine economic crisis on the various social classes. Just as productive as studying the use of genre conventions is paying close attention to the contours singular to each work. My analysis of Brocka's films reveals that much of their sociopolitical figurations and critiques are found in melodrama's assemblage of heterogeneous elements and details. The characteristically busy visual field of this cinematic mode presents numerous strategic openings for making political statements. Costumes and performances may satirize real-life figures. The blocking of actors and the staging of scenes may echo contemporaneous events. Pieces of décor may hold political significance. Allusions and double-meanings hidden in lines of dialogue function in similar ways. Narratives become vehicles for historically resonant characterizations or storylines. Subplots may play host to barbed political criticism.

While references to social problems abound in melodramas, films aimed at making overt political statements are infrequent even in the career of an activist such as Brocka. Politically charged images surface all the time in popular cinema, but not conspicuously enough to compel the viewer. On rare occasions, however, they flash in dense clusters, like points in a constellation through which a picture of society and politics at a specific historical juncture burns and elicits recognition. Such a constellation in Brocka's work, as well as in other martial law–era directors, is so prevalent it deserves its own category. I call it the "Marcosian moment." As explained later, the Marcosian moment is a scene of explosive violence inciting terror, precisely the fear of the autocratic state. Sociopolitical imagery saturates these brutal scenes. They are punctuated, moreover, by shots of characters looking straight or almost directly at the camera. These shots, these moments of arrest, telegraph a mute plea for signification on the audience's part. They impress on the viewer the need to take up the unsaid, to recognize what cannot be expressed in a climate of censorship and suppression.

Is the melodramatic sensibility ultimately inadequate to the task of representing such sociopolitical conditions? There are leading melodrama scholars who claim just that. Williams, for example, writes that while culturally preeminent in the United States, "melodrama cannot tell the story of the middle ground."[52] Elizabeth Anker, too, finds that melodrama's tendency to posit a singular cause or solution for complex sociopolitical problems hobbles the genre, although it is partially redeemed in that it "dramatically interrogates oppressive social structures and unequal relations of power."[53] What troubles Anker is "monocausality."[54] It is a trait found in melodrama's political rhetoric, which limits "its capacity to depict the distinct challenges and unintended effects of political life."[55] Filipino critics share similar views. Isagani Cruz writes of Brocka's tearjerker *Mother Dear* (1982): "The trouble is that the very genre itself—melodrama—is incapable of providing new insights into the Philippine situation."[56] Clodualdo Del Mundo Jr., Brocka's one-time collaborator, likewise faults the director for offering little more than political agitation: "I am a captured spectator, enrapt in Brocka's melodrama, and I respond emotionally to his endings. After some thought, however, I question what his melodramatic strategy has added to my understanding of the story of exploitation and oppression."[57]

The question of melodrama's efficacy qua sociopolitical discourse does not have to hinge on its fulfillment of any one or all of the things critics expect of it. Critics usually expect "socially relevant" films to include a coherent political position, a comprehensive analysis of sociopolitical issues, a measured critique, a transgressive ending, a well-articulated vision of the future, or a stab at overturning or self-consciously deconstructing the melodramatic form. In my view, no single aspect of a film can decisively mark the entire work as politically progressive or regressive. As critics have said of Hollywood movies, popular cinema is replete with contradictions and incoherence. A radical statement about proletarian activism may exist alongside a retrograde vision of gender equality. Moreover, happy endings routinely undermine otherwise complex treatments of sociopolitical dilemmas. The same is true of alterations either demanded by censors or made to satisfy their standards of morality.[58] The task of reading politics in melodrama, hence, entails a flexible, non-prescriptive approach. It calls for receptivity toward sporadic moments of lucidity and critique, tempering the bias for a comprehensive treatise. It requires a radical openness to the sociopolitical valence possible in any film and any work's discrete features. The point, as Bonnie Honig says in another context, is "not to press the cause of melodrama as the best genre for politics but rather to argue that there are things to be learned from it."[59]

The critic's habit of positing what melodramas ought to do for politics—and what method serves the ideal—valorizes the instrumentalization of art. Countering such a habit, Rancière urges artists, including filmmakers, not to aspire for "a straightforward relationship between political aims and artistic means."[60] They need not program their work, expecting to draw "a straight line between perception, affection, comprehension and action." Rancière goes on to say that images "do not supply weapons for battles." Instead, "They help sketch new configurations of what can be seen, what can be said and what can be thought and, consequently, a new landscape of the possible. But they do so on condition that their meaning or effect is not anticipated."[61] Just as the outcomes of a transformative politics cannot be programmed, so it is unproductive to circumscribe the political effects of an artwork. "Images change our gaze and the scape of the possible," Rancière writes, "if they are not anticipated by their meaning and do not anticipate their effects."[62] To preempt the incalculable is precisely to narrow the field of action.

In Brocka's case, the desire to represent the conditions suffered under authoritarian rule often did come with the hope of "opening the eyes of our countrymen,"[63] as the filmmaker himself said, and encouraging them to work toward bettering society. In spite of this desire to make art a midwife of social change, however, Brocka stopped short of prescribing its means and ends. Some of the most potent critiques and depictions of the autocracy in his melodramas appear to have been unconsciously formed or obliquely aimed.

Martial Law Melodrama studies Brocka's figurations of authoritarianism and its unraveling. That said, this book is neither a study encompassing the director's whole career nor an exhaustive account of film culture under the Marcos dictatorship. Several books, dissertations, and articles have accomplished such projects.[64] Though informed by those works, my study nonetheless avoids the detours they elicit into the thicket of interpretation and citation. This strategic avoidance makes for a fresh retelling of Brocka's politics in a length generally acceptable to publishers.

Given its focus on the work of a single filmmaker, some readers may characterize this book as an auteur study. I am aware of the risks of that designation, including the view that such endeavors are wrongheaded and passé. Unlike more conventional studies of film authorship, this book is not interested in making claims about Brocka's inimitable signature or the grand themes or central antinomies that structure his work. This study has two parallel concerns. One is to parse Brocka's work as a subset of mainstream cinema during Marcos's authoritarian rule. Another is to take stock of Brocka's role as a political actor who traversed the worlds of filmmaking and activism, whose aesthetics and politics altered in the course of his life, and whose triumphs and failures stem from his personal doings but also his emplacement within the film industry and the authoritarian state. Therefore, when I invoke the name Brocka, I also strongly imply his collaborative network whose contributions to the films are inseparable from those of the director. This network includes writers Jose Y. Dalisay Jr., Jose F. Lacaba, Ricardo Lee, cinematographer Conrado Baltazar, production designers Fiel Zabat and Benjie De Guzman, and musical composer Max Jocson, to name a few. As in the case of William Shakespeare or Orson Welles, it is misguided to distance Brocka the historical subject from his collaborators or the galvanizing force of his legend. My goal in describing Brocka's achievement is not to refurbish the monumentalizing notions of his genius. It is, rather, to account for crucial instances of his cinematic politics—critical interventions that recalled in sum may be seen to have helped subvert authoritarianism.

THE PLAN OF THE BOOK

The book is divided into seven chapters. Chapter 1 examines Brocka's attempts, in the early years of martial law, to create a new kind of cinema that was more "meaningful" and "relevant" than the commercial genre films of the time. His efforts resulted in two crucial works: *Weighed but Found Wanting* (*Tinimbang ka ngunit kulang*, 1974) and *Manila in the Claws of Light* (*Maynila: Sa mga kuko ng liwanag*, 1975). Both might be described as social melodramas—sensational and emotionally charged narratives proffering realistic analyses of social disruption or historical shift. To respond to contemporary issues without engaging in overt political discourse, the two films draw inspiration from the nineteenth-century panoramic social novel, particularly from the fiction of Philippine national hero José Rizal. Filled with veiled references and allegories, Rizal's novels were—even in the 1970s—the most influential and accessible tradition of Philippine sociopolitical representation. Like Rizal, Brocka employs multicharacter and picaresque narratives to depict a wide range of social maladies in his melodramas. *Weighed* follows a young man's rite of passage in a backwater community bound by superstition, hypocrisy, and antipathy toward nonconformists and the poor. It is a society vulnerable to abuse by authority figures, including wealthy business owners and lay church leaders. The young hero wises up to the defects of this community, which, much to his dismay, are shared by his own family. *Manila* follows a construction worker's quest to locate a woman who may have fallen into white slavery. The hero experiences the exploitation of laborers, the ramshackle lives of the urban poor, and the alienation of city dwellers. Brocka sets the film's unforgiving portrait of dog-eat-dog Manila two years before martial law and yet it comments on ongoing conditions. Although the two films owe their underlying sensibility to melodrama, their novel visual idioms—a combination of either gritty realism or observational naturalism and expressive stylization—represent a major departure from the romantic and fantastic movies of the period. True to Brocka's attempts to remake domestic cinema, these two social melodramas became landmarks of what came to be known as the "new Filipino cinema."[65]

The subject of chapter 2 is the conspicuous prevalence of horrible mothers in Brocka's films. His appropriation of the Hollywood subgenre of maternal melodramas famously eschews the normative image of the self-sacrificing matriarch. The maternal figure strategically functions as a stand-in for the paternal and, by extension, for the figure of Ferdinand Marcos. Substituting the monstrous mother for the autocratic father dissimulates the conventional link of patriarchs to dictators. The melodramas of the horrible mother are thus displaced allegories. They play out the metaphors of the political disputes that raged between the state and its dissident youth during the Marcos dictatorship. In *Insiang* (1976), the mother turns a blind eye when her boyfriend rapes her teenage daughter. The daughter, altered by her victimization, avenges herself by destroying the people who have wronged her. In *Whore of a Mother* (*Ina ka ng anak mo*, 1979), a woman seduces her son-in-law and bears his child. The mother's betrayal profoundly changes her daughter as it does with the heroine of *Insiang*. The daughter takes her mother to court and rejects her attempts at reconciliation. The inexplicably cruel matriarch in *Cain and Abel* (*Cain at Abel*, 1982) escalates the passionate rivalry between her children by willing the family's estate to her prodigal son. The brothers flee her domain and build small armies to wage war against each another. Set in hamlets and forests, their violent encounters recall Marcos's anticommunist campaigns resulting in the militarization of the countryside. What constitutes these maternal melodramas' political force are the fantasies of youthful insurgents deposing tyrannical parents and even denying them any chance at redemption.

Chapter 3 probes Brocka's crime melodramas and their more famous variant, film noir. The crime subgenre typically narrates the role of family, society, and the state in turning ordinary citizens into outlaws. More crucially, it lays bare the mechanisms of surveillance and repression in the name of state security. The eponymous protagonist of *Jaguar* (1979) is a bodyguard from the slums. After accidentally killing the man who attacked his boss, Jaguar runs afoul of both gangsters and cops. His boss abandons him in spite of their growing friendship. The sequence leading to the climax tracks Jaguar's futile attempts to dodge law enforcement. It ends in a dramatic face-off at a colossal landfill called Smokey Mountain, one of the Marcos era's most iconic spaces. *Angela, the Marked One* (*Angela markado*, 1980) reinterprets the 1970s American cycle of violent rape-revenge films, in which the victim of sexual assault becomes an avenger hunting down her male abductors. Worth noting here are two elements transgressive of martial law representation. First, *Angela* depicts torture, a practice of state violence the Marcos regime was known to use. Second, its protagonist is a female criminal who usurps the powers of the inept police, eludes state surveillance, and kills with impunity. The nighttime scenes in *Jaguar* and *Angela* are significant in that they register the lifting of the curfew imposed by the regime. Brocka made these films in the twilight of martial law, which ended formally in 1981.

Chapter 4 discusses films produced after the financial meltdown in the early 1980s Philippines. Marcos's plunder of the nation's coffers and resources, the political instability following former senator Ninoy Aquino's assassination, and panic among the nation's foreign creditors—all these triggered an economic cataclysm. Capital flight, the devaluation of the national currency, and hyperinflation dealt a severe blow to the poor and the middle class. Effects of the crisis are legible in Brocka's reworking of another subgenre inherited from Hollywood: the family melodrama. In *Adultery: Aida Macaraeg Case No. 7892* (1984), a waitress takes up with a "sugar daddy" after her husband goes to jail for transporting illegal drugs. *Such Pain, Brother Eddie* (*Napakasakit, kuya Eddie*, 1986) bears witness to a middle-class family's decline after the father loses his post at a manufacturing firm. Like many jobless Filipinos, he seeks work in the Middle East, but his long absence precipitates his family's unraveling. Though neither of these films blames the state for causing the financial crisis, they powerfully depict its social costs.

Chapter 5 examines films about young men who wage brave, if foolhardy, battles against the mighty. These male melodramas show the development of an expressly militant inflection in Brocka's work. They constitute important contributions to the political cinema that dawned in the Marcos regime's final years. *My Own Country: Gripping the Knife's Edge* (*Bayan ko: Kapit sa patalim*, 1984) draws parallels between the creation of a union at a printing press and the rise of political movements against Marcos. Amplifying Philippine melodrama's political content and radicalizing aspects of its form, *My Own Country* incorporates documentary footage of public demonstrations against the dictatorship. The film became the subject of a landmark Supreme Court case filed by the director. The censors sought to block the film's public exhibition in the Philippines due to its unauthorized screening at Cannes and Brocka's activism. *Miguelito: The Rebellious Child* (*Miguelito: Ang batang rebelde*, 1985) is about a son's disenchantment with his father, a corrupt and autocratic politician reminiscent of Marcos. Though more traditional in its form than *My Own Country*, the political content in *Miguelito* is just as progressive. The film, seething with civic anger, spins a thinly disguised parable of antiauthoritarian resistance. Brocka made it after his incarceration for joining a transport workers' rally. Due to its commercial packaging—as well as the chaos before Marcos's ouster—the censors were unable to contain the dissent writ large in the film.

Chapter 6 deals with Brocka's work after the "people power" uprising that deposed Marcos in 1986. During this period, his melodramas delved into his country's political culture. *Orapronobis* (*Fight for Us/Les insoumis*, 1989), Brocka's most incendiary film, is a slightly fictionalized account of gruesome killings by counterrevolutionary militias. These vigilante groups originated in the Marcos era. Ironically, however, the support of the new president Corazon Aquino allowed them to flourish beyond his two-decade rule. The protagonist of *Orapronobis* is a former communist guerilla and political prisoner. Rejoining mainstream society after President Aquino grants him amnesty, he starts a new family and volunteers for a human rights watchdog. But his dreams shatter when the vigilantes massacre his kin. Like the protagonist, Brocka witnessed firsthand the atrocities of paramilitary troops, causing him to lose faith in the new president, who once was his friend and political ally. Aquino's supporters branded Brocka's violent film as defamatory. With the help of a smear campaign and Marcos-era laws, Aquino's chief censor blocked the film from reaching Philippine theaters.

The director's subsequent political melodramas could not have been more different than *Orapronobis*. Aimed at the commercial market, *Dirty Affair* (*Gumapang ka sa lusak*, 1990) and *Above Everything Else* (*Sa kabila ng lahat*, 1991) are glossy serio-comic melodramas about the fickle games of politics and desire. Both movies fictionalize Marcos's dalliance with the American starlet Dovie Beams and use erotic intrigue to dramatize the nation's political culture. *Dirty Affair* offers an accessible postmortem on authoritarianism, while *Above Everything Else* diagnoses the blight of intractable government corruption. In a welcome development, the last two films were box office hits, achieving the commercial success and mass appeal once elusive for political cinema.

Chapter 7 trains the spotlight on queer protagonists in Brocka's work. It focuses on the overlap between his sociopolitical filmmaking and his other lifelong interest in depicting the lives of gay and bisexual men. The term "queer melodrama" aptly describes that overlap. *Gold Plated* (*Tubog sa ginto*, 1970) is a tragedy of a married man being blackmailed by his gay lover. Its portrayal of same-sex intimacy is ground-breaking in Filipino commercial cinema and more risqué than contemporaneous films from the West. *My Father, My Mother* (*Ang tatay kong nanay*, 1978) dramatizes the prejudice against effeminacy, cross-dressing, and gay parenthood. What distinguishes this movie is its clamorous politics of queer affirmation and its remarkable success at the box office. *Always Changing, Always Moving* (*Palipat-lipat, papalit-palit*, 1982) narrates the tangle of erotic desire involving a bisexual man and a married heterosexual couple. Apart from bisexuality, a rare subject on film, *Always Changing* offers self-reflexive commentary on the politics of representing nonnormative sexuality in mass entertainment. These pioneering queer melodramas are testimony to the capacious vision of the filmmaker, whose cinema politics includes that of gender and sexuality.

The coda discusses Lino Brocka's landmark queer film *Macho Dancer* (1989) as well as the projects he left unfinished before his death. The section also dwells on Brocka's continuing relevance to contemporary cinema. His melodramatic figurations of the sociopolitical world, his crossovers between prestige and commercial filmmaking, and his go-for-broke campaigns in show business and politics—all of these represent the enduring legacy of a particular historical figure in the era of Philippine melodrama's intense politicization.

Martial Law Melodrama, at once historiographic and interpretive, reckons with authoritarianism in the past tense. Unfortunately, in the wake of recent events, this project has gained urgency in ways I could not have anticipated when I began it in 2010. Authoritarianism has regained much of the ground it lost in the late 1980s, especially in the Philippines. The family of the late Ferdinand Marcos has steadily returned to power with the election of his wife, son, and one of their daughters to public office. In 2016 Rodrigo Duterte, an iron-fisted leader and self-avowed admirer of Marcos, was elected president. The late autocrat's daughter Imee Marcos allegedly helped finance the campaign that won Duterte the presidential seat.[66] The surprising resurgence of authoritarianism is due, in part, to the failings of the liberal democratic regimes that followed the dictatorship. Now as in the past, autocratic rule is a living nightmare for many but one that enjoys considerable popular support.

Marcos and Duterte, to be sure, are not identical strongmen. For example, while the Marcos presidency was often defensive about its imposition of martial law and its use of state-sanctioned violence, Duterte frequently brags about the same things in televised instances of political grandstanding. Amnesty International estimates that his so-called war on drugs racked up a body count of about three thousand just within the first hundred days of his presidency.[67] By 2018, the fatalities may have reached an astounding twenty thousand.[68] In such a brief span, the number has exceeded the 3,257 extra-judicial killings attributed to Marcos's two-decade rule.[69] Duterte stated early in his presidency that he would not hesitate to declare martial law under certain conditions.[70] He made good on this threat within the first year of his term, using terrorist activity in the southern island of Mindanao as justification. Cowed by his influence and popularity, Philippine lawmakers barely constrained him, defying legal procedure and recalling the days of Marcos's rubber-stamp legislature.[71]

Another stark contrast between the authoritarian eras of Marcos and Duterte is the current dearth of fearlessly outspoken directors. Protest or dissent certainly finds no advocate in Brilliante Mendoza, a Cannes award-winning director who extolled Duterte's ascendancy during the first state-of-the-nation address. Mendoza staged the televised event in the manner of Leni Riefenstahl's actuality films of the 1936 Berlin Olympics and the 1934 Nazi convention in Nuremberg. Duterte in Mendoza's production stands out not just as a noble statesman or idol of the masses but as a deified figure.[72] The question remains as to what kind of cinema still can help stem the tide of autocracy in the Philippines. The melodramas of another director now gone for a quarter of a century present themselves as an unexpected source of clarity for filmmakers, moviegoers, and scholars. A cinema politics, if not also a new political cinema, may yet emerge, inspired by Brocka's illustrious example.

ACKNOWLEDGMENTS

After a decade of working on this book, I am delighted to recall the moments of kindness that lit many crucial turns along the way.

Lino Brocka's brother Danilo deserves much credit for preserving the director's archive and for allowing me to share its riches here. Throughout this book, I will use the acronym LOBC (for "Lino O. Brocka Collection") to tag those materials, which are housed at the Cultural Center of the Philippines (CCP) library in Manila. Some of the press clippings and publicity materials may not contain full publication data but I use and cite them nonetheless because of the vital information they provide.

I am grateful to John Labella for plying me with essays on critical theory, listening to countless iterations of my arguments, encouraging revisions, and helping me write better. Jojo DeVera deserves special thanks as well for entertaining my weekly queries on 1970s and 1980s Philippine cinema, sharing his indispensable archive of rare movies, and enlisting his friends to assist me in my research needs. Benjamin Kahan, a dear friend in the trenches of academia, supplied the reading list that jump-started chapter 7.

Brocka's collaborators and friends gave interviews without hesitation. I treasure the conversations I had about the director with Butch Dalisay, Pete Lacaba, Doy Del Mundo, and the late Pierre Rissient.

Archivists and library staff at the CCP poured much of their time into this project, especially Vicky Belarmino and Alice M. Esteves, and also Richel Imperial, Danilo Nataba, Edna Nocum, Milagros Pasion, and Jovet Serrano. My gratitude extends as well to Arianna Turci, Giacomo Di Trapani, Jean-Paul Dorchain, and Francis Malfliet at Cinémathèque Royale de Belgique; Marion Langlois and Wafa Ghermani at Cinémathèque Française; Stephen Tollervey, Nina Bishop, and Kathleen Dickson at the British Film Institute; Pierrette Lemoigne and Daniel Brémaud at the Archives Françaisę du Film in Paris, Katja Wiederspahn at the Viennale, Ashley Swinnerton at MoMA, and the staff at the Margaret Herrick Library. At the University of Illinois, Megan Condis provided excellent research assistance while Deb Stauffer, Sandy Hardin, Amy Scott, and Gail Trent aided me in countless ways.

The late Cesar and Mario Hernando; Sonia Cenidoza of the MOWELFUND Film Institute; Juan Martin Magsanoc of Archivo 1984 Gallery; and Leo Katigbak, Pia De Leon, and Julie Galino of ABS-CBN provided film stills from their enviable collections.

This research was underwritten by a Helen Corley Petit scholarship, a Conrad Humanities scholarship, a Humanities Release Time grant, and a fellowship from the Illinois Program in Research and the Humanities—all from the University of Illinois. A Fulbright research fellowship, courtesy of the US Department of State and the Philippine-American Educational Foundation, funded my four-month archival work in Manila in 2016.

Friends in and out of academia have nourished this life of the mind and enabled a project of this scope. I only have space to name a few of those individuals here, but my debts of gratitude extend far and wide. Many thanks to Ian Aitken, Beth Austin, Edwin Avaness, Rob Barrett, Eric Benson, Nerissa Balce, the late Salvador Bernal, Chris Berry, Antoinette Burton, Eric Cady, Martin and Sandy Camargo, Lorenzo Castigniani, Ezra Claverie, Nancy Castro, Teddy Co, Bob Colucci, Ramona Curry, Nick Davis, Tim Dean, Pol Del Mundo, Rolando Dionisio, Audrey Evrard, the late Doreen G. Fernandez, Margaret Flynn, Andy Gaedtke, Lauren Goodlad, Dianne Harris, Chris Holmlund, Diana Jaher, L. S. Kim, Susan Koshy, Bliss Cua Lim, Julia Lesage, Jozon Lorenzana, Vicki Mahaffey, Gina Marchetti, Robert Markley, Bruce Michelson, Justine Murison, Gerry and Jim Nepomuceno, Tim and Lori Newcomb, Therese Ng, Abé Markus Nornes, Ellen Moodie, Kent Ono, Robert Dale Parker, Curtis Perry, Sarah Projansky, B. Ruby Rich, Richard T. Rodriguez, Michael Rothberg, Lindsay Rose Russell, Celine Parreñas-Shimizu, Robert Silberman, Jonathon Smith, Siobhan Sommerville, Ramon Soto-Crespo, Jasmine Trice, Marlu Vilches, the late Rene O. Villanueva, Tom Waugh, Gregory Wee, and Justin Wyatt; and special thanks to my former and present Filipino American peers at Illinois, Martin Manalansan IV and Augusto Espiritu. Jean-Jacques Poucel meticulously checked and revamped the translations of French-language material quoted here.

My late mentor, Chuck Kleinhans, sparked my interest in melodrama and lent his support to this project through most of its development. His commitment to authoring rigorous and accessible scholarship guided this writing. Memories of his generous spirit and the echoes of his inimitable belly laugh enliven my days in academia.

My mother, Linda Capino, spoke to me of her admiration of Brocka's work when I was in preschool, took me to his and other Filipino directors' films on weekends, and supported all my scholarly and creative endeavors. My late paternal grandparents, Professor Diosdado and Mrs. Gorgonia Capino, left a gift that started me out in graduate school and paid for the Laserdisc copy of Brocka's *Orapronobis* that served as the first research material for this project.

In the mid-1990s I was an advisor to an undergraduate thesis project on Brocka led by Mike Aquino and Kate Lacson. I recall being fascinated by their interviews with the director's associates, many of whom shared vivid details about the director's working style and hearty demeanor.

Few academics thrive without relatives who offer their hospitality during research travels. I am lucky to have enjoyed warm welcomes from Drs. Toni Capino and Connie Maileg, Dr. John and Madeline Capino, Tessie Elmido, and Elena and Mel Mistica.

Raina Polivka championed this volume from the start. Her guiding hand and recognition of Brocka's significance to world cinema have been instrumental in the realization of this project. The readers she enlisted for my manuscript could not have been more helpful and supportive. Working with Madison Wetzell, Jessica Moll, Dina Quan and their colleagues at the University of California Press has been a treat. Gary J. Hamel pulled off the daunting task of copyediting this hefty volume with aplomb, and Denise Carlson prepared the user-friendly index.

Earlier versions of a section of chapter 1 saw print in *The Routledge Encyclopedia of Films*, ed. Sabine Haenni, Sarah Barrow, and John White (New York: Routledge, 2014) and in the liner notes for the Criterion Collection's edition of *Manila in the Claws of Night*. I thank Sabine and Criterion's Anna Thorngate and Kim Hendrickson for their editorial guidance. A substantially different version of a section in chapter 2 appeared in *Film Comment* 42, no. 5 (September/October 2006).

I dedicate this book to my family: Linda T. Capino and the late Bernardo Capino; Joachim, Isabel, Nicole Clarisse, and José Joaquin Capino; Bernadette, Michael, Miguel Agustin, Jaime Lorenzo, and Javier Ignacio Dario; and Mary Lourdes, Danilo, Gianna, and Katelyn Besmonte.

1

The Country and the City

*Social Melodrama and the Symptoms
of Authoritarian Rule*

One of the most accomplished works of the new cinema that emerged in the Philippines in the early 1970s revolves around a scene of waiting, one in which little appears to be happening even though everything is actually at stake. The film, called *Maynila: Sa mga kuko ng liwanag* (*Manila in the Claws of Light*, 1975), returns intermittently to the image of a young man standing on a dingy corner of Chinatown. He has his eye on the window above an always-closed storefront. He waits for any signs of his lost sweetheart, a country lass who may have fallen prey to white slavery. Somewhere behind him, a fortune teller's sign reads: "Do you have a problem?" In an inconspicuous but visible corner of the movie screen, we might find the answer to that question. A snip of graffiti scrawled in blood-red paint on newsprint screams "Long Live the Workers!" Another handmade poster contains an image of a raised fist and the initials of a radical youth organization called Kabataang Makabayan (Nationalist Youth). A third poster, partially torn, alternately suggests the words *Junk* (*Ibasura*) and *Take Down* (*Ibagsak*), depending on which letters the man's body obscures and reveals as he moves around.

The political graffiti in Brocka's mise-en-scène are imprints of history. They are the traces of a political ferment that began in the West—in the antiestablishment and antiwar uprisings of the late 1960s—and spread, albeit not unchanged, to the third world country where the young man dwells. The First Quarter Storm was the name of the biggest salvo of the Philippine rebellion against "imperialism, feudalism, fascism" in the year 1970.[1] From January to April, thousands of angry college students, laborers, and political activists took to the streets to express displeasure at the reelection of President Ferdinand Marcos and to demand change in the country. They turned out in droves for the first state-of-the-nation address of his second

FIGURE 1.1. Posters from the political left loom behind Julio (Bembol Roco) in the opening sequence of *Manila in the Claws of Light* (Cinema Artists, 1975).

term and hurled rocks at the first couple as they exited the Congressional building.[2] The first lady bumped her head as she scurried into a car. Four days later, activists rammed a fire truck into one of the gates of Malacañang, the chief executive's residence.[3] Authorities went after protesters with batons, tear gas, and truncheons. Often, the youthful activists evaded capture with the help of Manila's sympathetic denizens, who popped open a door and pulled them in just seconds before the police turned a corner. Some of those events happened on the same streets where the film takes place. Yet in Brocka's movie, the images of this tumultuous period appear only in flashes, like the antiestablishment slogans glimpsed fleetingly behind the protagonist in the opening sequence.

In this and other chapters of the book, I venture a practice of closely reading such provocative inscriptions of politics and history in Brocka's martial law melodramas. The strict and inconsistent censorship of films during the Marcos regime demands that scholars pay attention to seemingly insignificant details. Such careful scrutiny is also necessary because of the abundance of both thinly veiled and subconsciously inscribed allegories in the director's work. As I hope to illustrate in this chapter, martial law melodramas follow a tradition of sociopolitical critique initiated in nineteenth-century Philippine letters. That tradition inscribes sociopolitical discourse overtly (through historical and political references) as well as indirectly (through allusions and metaphors). Central to it is the novel *Noli me tangere* (1887) by Philippine national hero José Rizal. Rizal's roman à clef inspired a nineteenth-century anti-colonial revolution against Spain.

Before I interpret Brocka's Marcos-era films through the prism of a critique inspired by Rizal, I wish to discuss the context in which his oeuvre emerged. The director articulated his desire to create a new kind of Filipino film in 1974, two years into martial law and the same number of years after he returned from a self-imposed hiatus from the film industry. Brocka's star was still on the rise when he took leave from filmmaking. He had directed nine genre pictures, six of them for an independent production outfit called LEA Productions. Several of his movies were box office successes, including his debut, *Wanted: Perfect Mother* (1970). His work also collected trophies for Best Picture and Best Director at awards ceremonies. Perhaps most notably, critics lauded *Tubog sa ginto* (*Gold Plated*, 1971) for its candid portrayal of homosexuality. Even the mediocre *Cadena de amor* (*Chain of Love*, 1971)—a romance that shows the leading man walking away from a small plane crash with only a reversible case of amnesia—took home seven prizes from the Manila Film Festival.[4] His career hit a low point with two commercial efforts that opened to scathing reviews: *Now* (1971), a youth-oriented musical with a subplot about political activism, and *Cherry Blossoms* (1972), a romance filmed partly in Japan and featuring American actor Nicholas Hammond.[5] Brocka shared the critics' poor opinion of his pictures and even told journalists to skip them.[6]

Brocka declined to explain his respite from the movies, claiming that his reasons were "personal."[7] One journalist speculated that a spat with LEA Productions prompted the hiatus. Rumors circulated that one of the outfit's proprietors bore a personal grudge against a star in *Gold Plated* and thus barred its exhibition at the Venice Film Festival.[8] Whatever the reason, Brocka diverted his energies to making quality television drama with members of the progressive-leaning theater group Philippine Educational Theater Association (PETA), which he joined in the late 1960s. He also planned his eventual return to filmmaking by trying to secure financing for a movie that would take Philippine cinema in a new direction. But, as the director would later recall, he came up empty-handed. "I wanted to work, but producers could not understand my desire to make films that can truly be considered meaningful [*may kahulugan*]," he told a reporter.[9] "Most of the producers that came to me wanted only action or fantasy movies." One of the board members of PETA created a scheme to fund the filmmaker's dream project. With the help of investors from the corporate world, the public sector, as well as film actors and creative personnel, Brocka scraped together enough money to found an outfit called CineManila. According to press releases, the company aimed to produce films "with a good story, good cast, that depicts Filipino values so that audiences can identify with them."[10] Brocka also expressed his desire to make "a complete breakaway from the trend for fantasies and slapstick comedy" that ruled popular cinema.[11] CineManila envisioned a transnational audience for its alternative pictures, identifying "Guam, Hawaii, Malaysia, Indonesia, Japan and California" as prospective markets because of their large overseas Filipino population.[12]

A project initially called *Buhay* (Life) served as the test case for Brocka's new cinema. Mario O'Hara wrote the screenplay, based in part upon stories from Brocka's youth.[13] The filmmakers changed the title to *Tinimbang ka ngunit kulang* (*Weighed but Found Wanting*), based upon a line from the Book of Daniel in the Old Testament. To obtain lush, bucolic scenery, Brocka filmed on location. As an article notes, he and cinematographer Joe Batac captured the rustic charm of the "hillsides of Tanay (Rizal), the heart of Sta. Rita (Pampanga), the pace and pulse of San Jose (Nueva Ecija) and the beautiful beaches of Nasugbu (Batangas)."[14] Brocka made his "dream project" with a shooting ratio of 4:1, considerably exceeding his usually slim allocation of film stock.[15]

The director remarked to a journalist that the film "is quite timely" ("*medyo ayon sa takbo ng panahon natin sa kasalukuyan.*") Quite tellingly, however, Brocka added in Filipino: "But it has nothing to do with Martial Law" ("*Pero walang kinalaman dito ang Martial Law.*")[16] Fear of drawing the censors' attention seems to underpin Brocka's equivocation. This attempt to downplay the film's political relevance was a calculated gambit. There would have been no means for Brocka's cinema politics to do its proper work if the censors blocked the film. Indeed, he took pains to avoid shaping the movie around resolute political statements. Only brief instances occur in the film that signal any link to martial law or Ferdinand Marcos. Set alongside these politically charged fragments, Brocka's insistence on de-politicizing his work generates a curious irony. The conscious erasure of the political all the more registers the moments when, however briefly, it becomes perceptible. The method I propose for reading the films in this chapter, hence, is that of seizing these moments as the distinct allegorical shards of sociopolitical critique.

Beginning with *Weighed*, Brocka devised a model for an alternative kind of sociopolitical representation on film. Focusing on Brocka's newly developed filmmaking, this chapter analyzes two landmark works in this vein. *Weighed* and *Manila* fall under the rubric of "social melodrama." John G. Cawleti characterizes the social melodrama as "an evolving complex of formulas" that tell intricate narratives of heightened feeling and moral dilemmas "with something that passes for a realistic social or historical setting."[17] Its purpose, he argues, is to give viewers a "detailed, intimate, and realistic analysis of major social or historical phenomena."[18] Cawleti's term is especially useful in describing the two Brocka films, both of which combine realism with the sensibility and features of melodrama but also differ from each other in several respects. Equally important, as I have mentioned earlier, the films draw from strategies of representation and critique that Rizal popularized. As in the latter's novel, the director's new social melodramas feature sprawling multicharacter narratives with a young male protagonist at their center. Whereas Rizal's *Noli* represented the conditions of Spain's decaying empire, Brocka's movies registered the state of affairs in the country and the city during the early years of martial law. In the balance of this section, I shall elucidate the workings of Brocka's social melodramas, trace their connections to Rizal's example, and map the relationship of his two most pioneering films to the politics of the Marcos regime.

WEIGHED BUT FOUND WANTING

After the cultural and political upheavals of the late 1960s and early 1970s, it might seem odd that Brocka looked back to Rizal's canonical nineteenth-century fiction in his attempt at devising a novel approach to Philippine cinema. That said, the national hero never lost his appeal to Filipino artists and intellectuals in search of social relevance. To cite just a few examples from the same decades, characters and subplots from Rizal's fiction inspired such landmark works of Philippine literature as Rogelio Sicat's short story "Old Selo" ("Tata Selo," 1962) and Paul Dumol's play *Barrio Captain Tales* (*Kabesang Tales*, 1975).[19] Rizal's influence on critical literature and the arts solidified many decades earlier. As Soledad Reyes notes, the pioneers of the twentieth-century Tagalog novel used his work as "the main sources not only of the realistic tradition but even as sources of realist techniques."[20] They emulated as well Rizal's project of using literature to engender social reform or, as he put it eloquently, "to expose the cancer of the body politic on the steps of the temple so that a cure may be offered."[21]

The influence of Rizal's vision of art and politics continued to spread with the help of legislation. Starting in the 1950s, the law mandated all Philippine schools to teach Rizal's writings, thereby informing the vision of artists of diverse political persuasions and various media. Philippine cinema from the start has celebrated Rizal's works and the hero himself. Its pioneers chose him as the subject of the first Philippine-produced movies. In the 1950s and '60s, the justly renowned Gerardo De Leon made film adaptations of Rizal's novels. De Leon was Brocka's idol, and it seems possible that his work inspired the latter's fascination with the national hero's legacy.

The influence of Riza's *Noli* on Brocka's *Weighed* is evident not only in the latter's approach to social criticism but also its narrative. Both stories begin with the young upper-class male protagonist trying to find his bearings in his provincial domicile. In *Noli*, Crisostomo Ibarra returns to the fictive town of San Diego (in Rizal's home province of Laguna) after seven years of studying and living in Europe. His homecoming is an unhappy occasion. He discovers that his father Don Rafael, one of the wealthiest men in town, died in prison after falling out with a Spanish priest named Damaso. In the Spanish-colonized Philippines, peninsular clergy such as Damaso were virtual sovereigns, more powerful and despotic than colonial administrators. Crisostomo eventually learns that Damaso not only put Rafael in jail but ordered the desecration of his corpse. Damaso's crusade against the Ibarras continues with his attempts to break up Crisostomo's engagement to his childhood sweetheart Maria Clara. The young woman is very dear to the friar. As it turns out, Damaso is Maria Clara's biological father.

Damaso makes snide remarks about Crisostomo's father on several occasions. Rather than minding such provocations, Crisostomo takes the high road and busies himself with charitable work. He finances the building of a modern public schoolhouse in his father's memory. Damaso and his fellow clerics ensure, however, that those plans never materialize. They attempt to kill Crisostomo through a staged accident at the school's construction site. When the scheme fails, one of the Spanish priests, driven by lust for Maria Clara, successfully frames Crisostomo as the leader and financier of a fictitious uprising against the Spaniards in town.

Damaso, who epitomizes the malevolence of theocracy and the colonial system, is but one of many broadly sketched characters that represent society's ills. He and other clerics prey on citizens from various social classes. The victims of this theocracy include the peasant Sisa and her two young sons. Sisa's boys earn a pittance as bell ringers at the church. Their supervisor, an ill-tempered sexton, frequently docks their pay and beats them up. In a series of tragic events, Sisa's children disappear (the younger likely killed by the sexton), and she loses her sanity as a result. Crisostomo, who learns about the family's troubles from a mysterious boatman named Elias, comes to their aid on several occasions.

Elias, witnessing Crisostomo's empathy for Sisa's family, reveals himself as an outlaw and dissident. Although Elias's family has a history of conflicts with the Ibarras, he recognizes Crisostomo's virtue and rescues him twice from the schemes of Damaso and his conspirators. On the second of those rescues, Elias heroically sacrifices his life to save Ibarra. He does so in the belief that a reformer from the upper crust would be better equipped to change society than a poor worker like himself. Rizal's novel concludes with many of the other virtuous characters—including Crisostomo, Maria Clara, Sisa and her older son Basilio—devastated, injured or dead. The faint glimmer of hope from Elias's sacrifice and Crisostomo's political awakening reappears in the novel's sequel, *El filibusterismo* (1891). In that work, Crisostomo returns under the guise of a Cuban jeweler named Simoun and uses his influence and wealth to gather the forces of dissent in a violent rebellion against the colonial order.

Like Crisostomo, the protagonist of *Weighed* belongs to a landed family. Junior (played by first-time actor Christopher De Leon) is the child of a couple with a rice plantation and business interests in rice milling and operating gas stations. As with *Noli*, the narrative of his development also proceeds along two lines of action that frequently converge. The first is a coming-of-age story. In the months between summer and Christmastime, Junior falls in and out of love with his first girlfriend, Evangeline (Hilda Koronel). Their relationship deteriorates, and she ends up getting impregnated by and marrying their mutual friend Nitoy (Joseph Siytangco), the mayor's son. All is not lost for Junior, however, as he experiences sex for the first time with an older woman named Milagros (Laurice Guillen). The latter, a college student from Manila, happens to be Nitoy's illegitimate half-sister. Amid these bittersweet events, Junior discovers a terrible family secret. The revelation changes his life.

The second line of action focuses on Junior's relationship to the provincial society in which he grew up. As a corollary to his sexual coming of age, the teenager matures as a social being in the span of a few months. Venturing away from his family and fellow teenagers, Junior gains an awareness of society's inequities, its prejudices, and even its violence. His development hastens in the course of an unlikely friendship with a mentally impaired homeless woman named Kuala (played by Lolita Rodriguez) and a leper named Berto (played by O'Hara). As Noel Vera correctly points out, Brocka's Kuala is the counterpart of Rizal's madwoman Sisa, while Junior is the substitute for Crisostomo.[22] Brocka claims in an interview that he patterned the character of Berto after a resident of the leper colony at Molokai, the Hawaiian island where the director once lived as a Mormon missionary. That said, *Noli* also features a minor but haunting character afflicted with leprosy. Epifanio San Juan describes the latter as an allegorical figure "of the degrading and dehumanizing essence of the [colonial] system."[23]

While Rizal's novel made for good entertainment, both its content and the reputation of its author cued readers to interpret the work's sociopolitical significance. To be sure, the sociopolitical valences of Brocka's film were more opaque than those of Rizal's fiction, and the director did not yet have the reputation of being politically minded like the nineteenth-century writer and intellectual. As I mentioned earlier, Brocka was even careful not to call attention to the film's politics during an interview. Apart from emphasizing that *Weighed* "has nothing to do with Martial Law," he characterized it as a simple film about a young man's rites of passage. He stated: "My main purpose is to show how and what the boy learns about life and love, about values from his town; the people in his town, and more important, the town's outcasts—mainly Berto and Kuala."[24] That said, the allusions to Rizal's novel and the positioning of *Weighed* as a "meaningful" picture encouraged viewers to expect valences similar to those found in *Noli*.

While *Weighed* uses the narrative of Junior's development to revisit some of Rizal's concerns about class relations and secularism, I venture that *Weighed* also yields a powerful but rarely elucidated allegory of the Philippines under Marcos. As I shall explain later, one of the keys to this allegory is the film's rendition of patriarchal figures, some of whom are linked implicitly to the authoritarian state.

A Panorama of Social Maladies

As in *Noli*, *Weighed* introduces social issues in the course of a picaresque movement about town by the hero and other pivotal characters. In both works, the narrative's examination of social geography reveals both the dilemmas that individuals face and the systemic issues affecting the community. *Noli* portrays the machinations of imperialism, the opportunism of native compradors, and the plight of subalterns in a decaying colonial society. In contrast, Brocka's film depicts the rural Philippines under martial law. As in *Noli*, the regressive forces in Junior's backwater society include religious zealots, heartless capitalists, and a docile and self-serving citizenry.

Among the different social maladies that the film critiques, two stand out as the most common. The first is sexual perversity. The narrative portrays several of the young adults in town as "fornicators." Their parents, no better at controlling their urges, take part in adulterous liaisons. The teachers—typically figures of respectability—likewise commit sexual transgressions. One of them, a gay man (played by Orlando Nadres), openly flirts with his underage male students. The other perverse educator is a young woman who consorts with married men. Apart from these teachers, many of the film's significant characters engage in acts considered depraved by the town's morally conservative inhabitants. As I shall discuss later, the perverse tendencies of these characters point to a deep-seated flaw that ultimately has little to do with sexual morality. Not merely a form of concupiscence or state of moral fallenness, such perversities represent a culpable weakness and malign predilections among the populace.

The other social ill depicted in the film is a pervasive antipathy toward others, especially those at the margins of society. The narrative demonstrates the consequences of such widespread social antagonism through the journeys of Junior, Kuala, and Berto. Only the last two, however, suffer their neighbors' hostility due to their lowly station in life.

Early in the film, the owner of a kitchenette tries to drive Kuala away when he notices her feeding on leftovers at a vacated table. The man also callously upbraids her for smelling bad. Too famished to mind his harsh words, Kuala even scoops up the scraps that have fallen to the ground. Sadly, the other townsfolk are no less cruel to her than the petty capitalist. For instance, children invite her to play, only to mock and pelt her with stones. Similarly, the adults ply her with drinks to the point of inebriation, the better to make her dance saucily so they can make fun of her.

Berto's encounters with the townsfolk are often worse than Kuala's. Because of his illness, they do not even regard him as human. The woman who runs the *kabaret* refuses him admission, telling him to relieve his sexual urges by "rubbing [himself] against an electric post" instead of visiting with her hospitality girls. The men are harsher: without reason or provocation, they slaughter Berto's dog and laugh in his face as he unknowingly consumes a dish made of its flesh.

The church women make a show of being charitable, but the effect of their actions is no more benign. As in Rizal's fiction, the Catholic women act like harpies toward their neighbors. One pious woman, for instance, a member of the lay sorority La Asociacion de las Obreras Cristianas, belittles the leper Berto's act of kind-

FIGURE 1.2. Berto (Mario O'Hara) watches helplessly as a woman pulls a child away from him. *Weighed but Found Wanting*. Courtesy of Danilo Brocka/CCP Library.

ness. When a boy trips on a rough road, just as soon as Berto rushes to help him, the lay sister yanks the kid away, leaving Berto abashed. The scene recalls the title of Rizal's novel: "touch me not!" Several months later, when the church women discover that Kuala is with child, they detain her to prevent further sexual contact with the leper. Their cruelty toward the two outcasts extends to other indigents. For example, the sorority members propose to demolish shanties by the railroad tracks, simply because one of its residents is known to engage in sex work occasionally. The irony of such antipathy toward prostitutes and lepers—precisely the social types Jesus Christ urged his followers to treat kindly—is lost on the unthinking bullies.

Junior bears witness to some of the indignities heaped upon the two outcasts. The experience of seeing the abjection of others alters the way he sees his community, makes him aware of his class privilege and pushes him to discover how else to be in society. Through the use of camera distance and editing, the film dramatizes the formation of a critical subjectivity in the young man. In a series of eyeline matches and switchbacks, the camera lingers on close-ups of Junior's face as it registers his response to the privations of his townsfolk. This pattern of shots occurs numerous times, as when Junior shows disappointment at his friends after they dunk Kuala in a canal or when they belittle Milagros behind her back for

FIGURE 1.3. Junior (Christopher De Leon, top right) joins two social outcasts (Mario O'Hara and Lolita Rodriguez) in the hills outside town. *Weighed but Found Wanting*. Courtesy of Danilo Brocka/CCP Library.

being born out of wedlock (and, Nitoy adds, "to a whore at that"). The same visual devices likewise recur when Junior observes Evangeline (then still his girlfriend) flirting with Nitoy or when Junior witnesses his parents trading insults and criticizing other people. By isolating Junior from other characters, this visual pattern represents, with bold simplicity, his growing disaffection with family and the town.

As Junior distances himself from his kin and friends, the film's social geography moves to the edge of town. There he and the misfits form an alternative community. Berto and Kuala were already a couple when Junior befriended them. The couple's relationship began after Berto lured her to his ramshackle dwelling, a hut symbolically placed at the margins of town and its cemetery (that is, in a liminal area between virtual exile and death). The leper bathed, fed, and then romanced the mentally impaired woman. Kuala latched on to him despite his appearance. Berto, afraid of scandalizing the town, tried to hide the affair from the townsfolk by putting her out in the street during the day, only taking her back into his hut at dusk or when no one else was around. Junior accidentally discovered their arrangement while trailing Kuala one day. The leper panicked when he noticed Junior spying on them. Berto pled for discretion, which Junior granted, and they became pals.

To escape the prying eyes of the townsfolk, Junior and the couple retreat to the hills during the day and play like children. In one memorable shot, we see Junior perched high up on the limbs of a tree, blissfully relaxing as Kuala and Berto frolic in the grass below him. This pastoral idyll conjures a vision of a free and harmonious society so different from the one that exists in their small town.

In his study of *Noli*, Epifanio San Juan Jr. describes the goal of Rizal's novel as one of enabling the "attainment of ethico-political awareness among his readers."[25] Through realist fiction replete with allegories, Rizal "conveys the ideological as well as economic structures underlying or subsuming the relations among individuals," thus opening the viewer's eyes to social injustice and the repressiveness of the colonial order.[26] To accomplish his goal, Rizal appeals to the intellect as well as to the emotions. *Noli* features lucid conversations about social issues between the protagonist and the other characters. Some of those discussions are couched in allegory, while less sensitive issues are treated plainly. The topics include public education, the separation of church and state, freedom of speech, and the future of the Spanish empire. Alongside these cerebral moments are episodes of stirring melodrama, including the persecution of Sisa's family, Elias's final sacrifice for Crisostomo and their country, and Maria Clara's compassion for the unnamed leper. Recognizing that the colonial system benefits from fostering social inequality and infighting among the natives, Rizal uses emotionally charged episodes of social injustice to "exorcise the specter of putschist individualism which he knows as the endemic malady of his class."[27] Rizal thus writes Crisostomo, his alter-ego, as a bourgeois obsessed with redeeming himself through civic engagement.

Brocka's film appropriates *Noli*'s penchant for didacticism and melodrama, as well as Rizal's message about the urgency of reforming society. However, *Weighed* resists overt criticism of authority figures and institutions. The film's nod to Rizal's veiled critiques explains why, at first glance, *Weighed* appears to limit its concerns to humanitarian issues and common civic problems. As I mentioned earlier, Brocka himself even stated that *Weighed* had "nothing to do with Martial Law" and thus with politics. But even if one were to take him at his word, it still would be a mistake to disregard the sociopolitical valences of the film. As Fredric Jameson points out, film artists unwittingly inscribe ideas, signs, and meanings from their historical moment into the movies they make.[28] I have been proposing here that one finds evocative figurations of authoritarianism in some of *Weighed*'s surface details as well as in its subtextual layers.

The Specters of Martial Law

There are three passing but arguably significant references in the film to either Marcos or martial law. As Brocka noted, the allusions serve the practical purpose of indicating that the film unfolds in the contemporary moment. At the same time, the allusions to the national leader and political matters invite viewers to think of

Junior's dysfunctional community as a microcosm of the Philippines under authoritarian rule. It is important to note that the film's production script makes no mention of Marcos or martial law, suggesting that the references were introduced into the film during preproduction or in principal photography.[29] I do not wish to speculate on the reasons behind their addition to the film but shall venture an interpretation of their significance.

The first of the political references occurs near the beginning of the film, at the wake of a man named Clemente. We learn from an earlier scene that he was involved in politics and that he had reneged on a promise to campaign for Junior's father Cesar during an unsuccessful bid for the mayor's seat. Clemente was apparently a fan of Ferdinand Marcos, as indicated by the poster of the strongman that hangs prominently in his home. The portrait shows Marcos dressed in Philippine finery, while behind him loom the Philippine flag and the presidential seal.

The visitors at Clemente's wake resemble the town's population in miniature. The wake is, not insignificantly, one of four scenes in which virtually all the major and minor characters appear together. (The other scenes include his burial ceremony, a religious procession, and a public killing.) Junior and his parents arrive at the wake later than the other townsfolk, including the mayor and his wife. His parents, rancorous as ever, proceed to backbite the politico and his spouse just moments after exchanging pleasantries with them. We learn that Cesar is still sore at the mayor for defeating him at the polls while Cesar's wife Carolina (Lilia Dizon) complains about the uppity behavior of the town's first lady. Later, in front of the Marcos portrait, Cesar holds court. He shows Junior off to the men, taking credit for his son's good looks and virility. When the effeminate school teacher Mr. Del Mundo (Orlando Nadres) acknowledges—with matching googly eyes—that Junior is indeed "all grown up and handsome," Cesar makes another reference to his own manliness, boasting of his quickness with women and advising Junior to emulate him.

Elsewhere at the wake, the church ladies scold the teenage girls—including Evangeline and the daughter of Clemente—for spying on Junior while he was urinating in the bushes. Outside the house, the young men behave inappropriately as well, getting Kuala drunk and goading her to dance for them. They proceed to mock her, and she retaliates by wetting her shorts and splashing urine on the hecklers.

The second reference to something associated with the nation occurs just moments after the Marcos portrait appears onscreen. Evangeline's mother Amor Ortega (Anita Linda) excuses herself from the wake, saying she could no longer wait for her husband to arrive because she needs to beat "the [impending] curfew." She is referencing the same curfew that Marcos initiated when he imposed martial law. It prohibited residents of the country from leaving their homes between midnight and four o'clock in the morning.[30]

At face value, these allusions to Marcos or his autocratic policies seem like throwaway references. However, embedded as these details are in a sequence critiquing social malady, they cannot but form part of a political interpretation of the film. Brocka's gambit here is to rely on the fact that Rizal's novels have long established the practice of allegorical reading among Philippine audiences, and that some viewers would use the same approach to interpret his film.

I read the scene of Clemente's wake as a metaphor for Philippine society under martial law. The visual reference to Marcos and the dialogue about the curfew place the film's characters within the time and space of authoritarian rule. I say this despite—and especially because—of the fact that most of the characters seem oblivious to the implications of autocratic rule. For instance, even as the severe threat of breaking curfew looms for all the persons at the wake, only one of them (Mrs. Ortega) appears to be concerned. Some church women depart at the same time but the rest pick at each other, drink irresponsibly and distract themselves with cheap amusements. Like the visitors at Clemente's wake, citizens who actively or passively support dictatorships forget the pernicious consequences of living in a police state.

Marcos used the term "New Society" to characterize the docile citizenry he envisioned cultivating through authoritarian rule. His slogan—"to achieve national development, discipline is required"—justified the cost of social repression by making a slew of lofty promises to the people.[31] The autocrat sowed fear and dispensed violence in his ambitious remaking of the nation. He also relied on fascistic rituals to distract the public from the brutality of his regime.

Apart from drawing attention to the complacency of the townsfolk, Brocka's film also slyly makes fun of their intellect and political choices. As mentioned earlier, the poster of Marcos at Clemente's home suggests that the deceased was a supporter of the president. While viewing Clemente's coffined remains, his widow tells a fellow churchwoman that he died from "eating too many ripe mangoes." The purported manner of his demise thus characterizes the autocrat's follower as a glutton and idiot. The widow who accepts the ridiculous account of her husband's misadventure is no wiser than him.

Significant Father Issues

The presence of three fathers in the scene of the wake—Cesar, the deceased Clemente, and the national paterfamilias Marcos—links the patriarchy to authoritarianism. What should we make of this connection? Critics have rarely examined the film's Oedipal plot, perhaps because it seems unremarkable. Although Father-son rivalries are generic to melodramas, they may be imbued with metaphorical significance. Both *Weighed* and Rizal's novel trace their youthful protagonists' disenchantment with paternal figures. In *Noli*, Crisostomo uncovers the history of his grandfather's misdeeds. He learns that his ancestor built the family fortune through land grabbing and Elias's grandfather was one of the victims. The bourgeois hero's encounters with Elias thus open his eyes to the role of his family and class in perpetuating oppression. The novel features other malevolent or failed patriarchs, including Damaso and Maria Clara's (legal) parent, Capitan Tiago, both of whom also represent corruption in the colonial regime. In *Weighed*, Junior's coming into manhood overlaps with the discovery of his father's role in Kuala's troubles. Cesar becomes the figure of an unseemly form of masculinity that Junior will struggle to disavow.

Near the start of the film, Junior overhears from one of his parents' frequent quarrels that Cesar recently bedded their housemaid, causing her dismissal. On another occasion, Junior's mother catches her spouse escorting one of their son's teachers in public. That evening, she berates Cesar for the incident within earshot of Junior. Things take a turn for the worse when the teen discovers that his father is not just an adulterer and rabid sexist but also a hebephile. One day after mass, Junior overhears his father speaking to pals about the thirteen-year old hostess he regularly hires at the *kabaret*. Cesar brags about satisfying her and other lovers with his "long-playing" and "long-eating" sexual techniques. Much to Junior's embarrassment, he and his friends spot his father inside the drinking joint one night where, as the other teenagers point out, Cesar is carousing with "an awfully young companion."

Junior tries to grapple with his father's depravity while dealing with his own sexual urges. In another of the film's key moments, the young man strays into a bowling alley late at night and loses his virginity to a woman he barely knows. He had just walked out of a religious parade called Santacruzan after seeing his ex-girlfriend being escorted by a movie actor at the procession. Junior tries to deal with his jealousy by ordering a beer from the concession stand. Milagros, who works the closing shift, declines to serve alcohol because he is underage. She also reminds him to start for home to beat the curfew. He stays put, and they make small talk about their mutual disdain for the self-righteous townsfolk. Junior professes, to Milagros's delight, that: "Everyone in this town is a member of La Asociacion de Obreras Cristianas, all of them gossipmongers, and nosy wretches!" Milagros then shutters the bowling alley and, without saying a word, offers herself to Junior. Brocka described the love scene as "a case of two lonely souls communicating with each other,"[32] but the reference to authoritarianism in the dialogue charges the episode with political significance. As with the teenage women's voyeurism at Clemente's wake, Junior and Milagros commit a perverse act in the same scene where a character invokes the strictures of martial law. Because Junior and Milagros have sex while passing the curfew, their intimacy is defined in part by the fear of transgressing the edict of the nation's authoritarian patriarch.

The furtive sexual encounter is similar to Kuala and Junior's trysts. In both cases, the woman is a social outcast and the assignation is both morally transgres-

FIGURE 1.4. Milagros (Laurice Guillen) and Junior (Christopher De Leon) wait for the martial law-era curfew to pass. *Weighed but Found Wanting.* Courtesy of Danilo Brocka/CCP Library.

sive (because it occurs out of wedlock) and mutually affirming. Additionally, both couples engage in sexual relations amid the threat of constant surveillance by the self-righteous townsfolk and, in Milagros and Junior's case, by the police state (the curfew's enforcer). These couplings—both ill-fated—cast the authoritarian regime as an entity so oppressive as to place intimacy under duress. Indeed, how benevolent could the autocracy be when even the most private moments of its citizens are tainted with the fear of heavy-handed social control?

Due to his sexual awakening, Junior regains some empathy for his libidinous father. He even turns to Cesar for advice on being with women. The bond frays quickly, however, and the contours of an Oedipal conflict sharpen as Junior learns of Cesar's culpability for Kuala's trauma. The last quarter of the film stages the public unmasking of Cesar as the killer of her unborn child and the person most deeply responsible for her miseries. Junior's response to this discovery is crucial to my reading of the film's antiauthoritarian politics.

Disappointment follows Junior's sexual initiation. He loses Milagros after their tryst. She refuses to see him again without explanation and leaves town for good. (Unfilmed scenes from the script have her dying of an unspecified cause, but this is not the case in the assembled film.)[33] In the meantime, Berto and Kuala also experience an abrupt parting. The church ladies discover that Kuala has become pregnant with Berto's child. They remove her from his shack and take her to the home of a sorority member. Out of pity for his friends, Junior seeks his father's help in reuniting the couple, but he catches his father in the middle of an afternoon "quickie" inside the family-owned rice mill. Even more upsetting to Junior than witnessing his father's indiscretion is the latter's refusal to lift a finger for Kuala and Berto. The episode foreshadows the impending confirmation of Junior's worst fears about Cesar. "You are selfish!" he cries to his old man. "How do I know you're not the Cesar Kuala mutters?" The question is probably rhetorical. One assumes that it has been difficult all along for Junior to repress the suspicion that his father is indeed the person whose name Kuala invokes in her fits of traumatic reminiscence.

True to a convention in melodrama of vindicating the persecuted heroine and rebuking her tormentors, the film exposes the depths of Kuala's suffering and the worst of Cesar's misdeeds in an emotional highlight. The climactic sequence begins with Berto and Junior liberating Kuala from the church women and taking her back to Berto's place. Kuala goes into labor later that evening. The leper fetches the town's doctor—Evangeline's father, Dr. Ortega—but he refuses to help. Berto, in desperation, drags him by knifepoint across town, creating a hostage situation. The cops shoot Berto to death in front of the townsfolk at the first opportunity. Moments after the killing, the crowd turns to Kuala, who has just given birth inside the leper's shack. In a lucid moment, Kuala frees up a repressed memory and addresses Cesar, who happens to be one of the onlookers at the scene. "Cesar, our child is alive!" she proudly declares. Her joy instantly vanishes, however, when another repressed memory takes over. She begins to relive the moment in which she begs Cesar to stop the abortionist from terminating her pregnancy. The revelation of Cesar's role in the forced abortion and causing Kuala's madness brings tears to Junior's eyes. Kuala, who has been bleeding out, takes comfort in another reminiscence—that of Berto tenderly combing her hair—before handing off her child to Junior and breathing her last.

The film ends in a grand Hollywood-style tableau vivant that, as one reviewer correctly notes, is straight out of Nicholas Ray's *Rebel without a Cause*,[34] a film that made a strong impression on Brocka.[35] The scene depicts Junior filing out of the cemetery with the child in his arms, heading toward Berto's corpse. The townsfolk watch as Cesar reaches out to Junior, who rebuffs him. Junior's gesture of refusal—"touch me not!"—makes another allusion to the title of Rizal's novel. Without any need for words, Junior disavows Cesar's malign paternalism and becomes a father to Kuala's child, if only temporarily.

The contrast between Junior's movement and the crowd's stillness emphasizes his act of protest, his turning away not just from his father but from the malignant social order that has caused the death of his beloved friends. A wide overhead shot

FIGURE 1.5. Junior (Christopher De Leon, center), holding Kuala's child, refuses his father Cesar's (Eddie Garcia, left) conciliatory gesture. *Weighed but Found Wanting*. Courtesy of Danilo Brocka/CCP Library.

captures the spread of the crowd at the cemetery while also suggesting an omniscient perspective. The framing indicates a reversal in Kuala's situation. For much of the film, the townsfolk judged and treated her harshly, but the ending signals that now it is society that has been "weighed but found wanting" by an all-seeing divinity and, more subtly, by her as well.

As the film closes, the theme song plays, with Kuala reciting its lyrics. There is a hint of anger in her voice. Gone from her speech is the childish affectation that has signaled her mental impairment throughout the film. The application of a reverb effect on her voice suggests that she is addressing the viewers from the hereafter or some other place bereft of malign patriarchs such as Cesar. "When the flame is extinguished," she warns, "my blood will come flooding" (*"Kung apoy ay mawala / Dugo ko'y babaha."*)[36] The lyric alludes to the snuffing out of the fetus's life and the bleeding that results from its abortion. Alternatively, the ominous words suggest the fierce, if also fatal struggle of the oppressed. Extra-textual information about the lyric's authorship bolsters the latter interpretation. The words belong to Emmanuel Lacaba, a former member of Brocka's theater group who died as a revolutionary just ten months after the film's release.[37]

I interpret the ending as a gathering of the film's antiauthoritarian energies. It features a young man's public defiance of a patriarchal figure and a heartrending dirge for the fallen innocents. Although the cruel paterfamilias lives on, his sins are exposed, and the townsfolk will likely shun him. Hope lives on in Junior as well as in Kuala's child. But the ending is not as optimistic as one might think. Berto and Kuala's deaths visibly affect the crowd but do not spur constructive action. Like the citizens of an authoritarian state, the townsfolk have become passive, transfixed by the distractions organized by, or for the benefit of, the fascist establishment.[38] Those distractions range from the spectacles of mass incarceration and public killings (such as that of Berto in Brocka's film) to various rituals (such as the flag-raising ceremonies and historical pageants that the Marcos regime fancied).

Even as the film presents the symbols described above, it offers few clues to their political significance. Moreover, the film does not suggest an alternative way of interpreting the central motif of perversity, beyond the obvious valence of moral corruption. Cesar's characterization as a rotten paterfamilias is never again linked to the nation's authoritarian father beyond the one instance at Clemente's wake. As mentioned earlier, I venture that the perversity of the characters is allegorical of the desire of many Filipinos to be disciplined and ruled by an autocrat. Amid the era's dramatic upheavals—political, countercultural, and economic—authoritarianism represented the taming of the insurgent forces that were drastically reordering society. Authoritarianism offered a reassuring solution to the anxieties of a beleaguered social order, even if the remedy exacted a heavy price from its citizens. The impulse to surrender one's liberties in exchange for a promised social transformation that is probably unattainable and unbearably stifling is nothing if not perverse. Regrettably enough, a broad swath of Philippine society desired and supported authoritarian control even when faced with its most deleterious effects. Filipinos gave Marcos license to rule for over two decades. If *Weighed* allegorizes the desire for autocratic rule as a form of perversity, then many in Junior's town harbored such perversion.

Because so much of *Weighed*'s political meanings remained veiled or obscure, it was also one of but a few Brocka films before the 1986 uprising that features an allegory of Marcos as the malign patriarch of an ethically wayward people. Not insignificantly, the most effective iteration of this allegory occurs in *Miguelito: The Rebellious Child* (*Miguelito: Batang rebelde*, 1985), a strident reimagining of *Weighed* that Brocka completed just before the fall of the autocracy. I shall discuss that film in the fifth chapter of this book.

Reception

In an auspicious turn for Philippine cinema, Brocka's first attempt at creating a new, "meaningful" kind of Filipino movie enjoyed an enthusiastic reception at the box office. Shortly after *Weighed* premiered at the upscale Magallanes Theater,

CineManila ran newspaper ads boasting that the "damn movie is making money."[39] The press reported that the picture, which cost 400–500,000 pesos "made 369,539 in 34 days" of its theatrical run.[40] Apart from touting the film's quality, the marketing campaign made pioneering efforts to engage students and cultivate them as an audience for innovative movies.[41] Following the theatrical release, CineManila held screenings and talkbacks with the cast and filmmakers at educational institutions and similar venues. Thanks to those efforts, *Weighed*'s earnings reportedly hit the 2 million-peso mark, an impressive number for a prestige film.[42]

Amelia Lapeña Bonifacio, a playwright and professor at the University of the Philippines, filed a lawsuit against the film. But the complaint had little, if any, impact on robust theatrical and nontheatrical sales. Bonifacio alleged that the makers of *Weighed* plagiarized *Sepang loca* (1957), her one-act play in English. Bonifacio's script is about a mentally impaired woman whom the men in a rural village use for sex. The mayor abuses and impregnates her. Alone in a hut, Sepa delivers their child but loses the newborn just moments later in a freak accident. Weakened by childbirth and the trauma of killing her child, Sepa expires as well.[43] Brocka vigorously defended himself against Bonifacio's claim that he stole the "spine of her story," pointing to the fact that O'Hara modeled Kuala after a real person from his hometown.[44] Save for the plot elements mentioned above, O'Hara's screenplay bears little resemblance to Bonifacio's lyrical and expressionistic drama. Brocka also refuted an allegation, made in a letter to the entertainment journalist Joe Quirino, that *Weighed* drew inspiration from *Johnny Belinda* (Jean Negulesco, 1948), a Hollywood small-town melodrama about a doctor who teaches sign language to a deaf-mute woman but is accused by townsfolk of molesting and impregnating her. Brocka denied ever having seen the film.[45] If there is an aspect of *Weighed* that is uncannily reminiscent of the Hollywood picture, it would be the shot of the male lead perched on the limbs of an enormous tree. Both allegations of plagiarism also did not prevent the film from winning six trophies at the prestigious FAMAS (Filipino Academy of Movie Arts and Sciences) Awards, including the prizes for Best Picture, Best Director, Best Actress, Best Theme Song, and an unexpected Best Actor plum for seventeen-year-old Christopher De Leon.

Most critics praised the quality of Brocka's work. Billy Balbastro called it "a milestone, a major achievement, an intelligent movie worth seeing."[46] He credited Brocka for "capturing local life, its trimmings and its stark realities with such intensity that cannot be ignored." He linked the rendition of "stark realities" to a paring down of style or narrative or, as he put it, storytelling with "No gimmicks. No exaggerations." Along the same lines, Jesselynn L. Garcia called attention to the fact that the film's "story is woven from a simple yet intricate loom."[47] M. N. Cruz lauded the movie's rendition of "life's everydayness," while Jorge Arago opined that filmmakers had previously explored some of the film's concerns, "but not, if we are correct, with such rawness."[48] Gino Dormiendo, who effusively called the film the "future of the industry," also compared it to the finest works of postwar Philippine cinema. "And for us," he writes, "*Tinimbang* means a trip back to reality, to quality filmmaking that characterized some local movies of the fifties." He likened Brocka's picture to those of Brocka's idol Gerardo De Leon. The comparison is apt, for De Leon crafted melodramas that also stood out for their attention to social concerns, casting of non-stars as protagonists, realistic production and costume designs, and lifelike rendition of rural landscapes through deep-space mise-en-scène.[49] For instance, De Leon's American-sponsored features *Dawn of A New Day* (*Ang bagong umaga*, 1952) and *The New Teacher* (*Ang bagong maestra*, 1953), dealt with pressing issues such as agrarian labor while also offering exceptionally vivid pictures of small-town life. However, Dormiendo did not note the substantial differences between the realism of the 1950s and that of the contemporary moment. For instance, *Weighed* differed from De Leon's work in its persistent forays into naturalism, including the use of contemporary dialogue, individualized performances, as well as the incorporation of uneventful passages to simulate the rhythms of small-town life.

Brocka's fresh approach to realism and social critique also prompted comparisons to foreign art films, including those screened by European embassies in Manila. In an article about "The New Wave in Tagalog Movies," Jessie Garcia likened Brocka to "Italian neorealist auteur Victor DeSica [sic]" and touted *Weighed* as "just about the best film ever to come out from this informal new group of local film-makers."[50] The resounding praise for verisimilitude may have encouraged Brocka and other pioneers of the new Philippine cinema to devise even more richly detailed renditions of character psychology, mundane experiences, and the sociopolitical milieu than are found in *Weighed*.

Not all critics regarded the film and its version of realism as superlative. Writing from the Filipino diaspora in the United States, Luis Francia described Brocka's picture as "not revolutionary" but instead "moderately good." *Weighed*, he opined, "avoids, for the most part, that penchant for melodramatization which constitutes the single deadliest bane of Filipino films."[51] He cited the following as undesirable elements of Philippine filmmaking: "an excess of subplots," the "oftentimes overbearing presence of the music," the "leaden weight of half-hatched subplots," "one-dimensional" characterizations, and "stagey" scenes "so obviously manipulative of the audience's emotions."[52] Although he was right in saying that *Weighed* was still a melodrama despite the infusion of a captivating realism, his gloss on "melodramatization" needlessly denigrated some of Philippine cinema's most common features. Moreover, by pitting those elements against "revolutionary" filmmaking, he implicitly set a narrow criterion for cinematic innovation that few works in the Philippine film industry would ever satisfy. Francia would later come to realize that melodrama was not incompatible with the realist aesthetic he and other critics admired. (In chapter 6, I quote his words of praise for two Brocka films he calls melodramas.)

Some critics made a point of discussing the merits of the film's narrative and insights. Their reviews mostly touched on the film's themes or what David Bordwell and Kristin Thompson call its "implicit meaning."[53] Echoing Brocka's description of the film in interviews, Balbastro stated: "A young boy discovers life. This is the gist of the movie. It seeks to present a fruitful search of a lost soul for ideals and social and personal values."[54] Jesselynn Garcia opted to highlight the contrast between Junior's virtue and the flaws of his community. She wrote: "He alone, with hands unsoiled and dreams untrammeled, has the right to set on trial and weigh the lives of the people."[55]

None of the reviews discussed the film's references to martial law and Marcos. Neither did they venture an interpretation of the film's relevance to contemporary events. As was often the case in Philippine evaluations of Brocka's oeuvre before his turn to political activism in 1983, the critics rarely touched on the political valences of movies. Apart from taking their cue from Brocka's restraint in signifying politics, one might attribute the critics' silence to self-censorship and a resistance to "over-reading." Moreover, flagging a film's political content would have created problems for both the filmmaker and the critic. Apart from bowdlerizing films, the Marcos regime suppressed free speech by imprisoning hundreds of writers and media professionals, often just long enough to scare them into silence. In such an environment, even those who escaped persecution were careful not to make trouble for themselves or the subjects of their writing.

Critics began to write more candidly about the film's progressive aspects in the years following its release, although they used the word "social" rather than "political" in their assessments. Dormiendo pointed out that *Weighed* "paved the way for other directors to treat their materials as social commentaries."[56] Jerry Sussman opined that the film had "relevance" and that its "allegorical value for almost every small town dweller in the Philippines is what drew the excited interest of the whole nation."[57]

The most illuminating readings of the film dwelled on its representation of sexuality and its sociopolitical critique. Arago emphasized the thematization of the "elusive and improbable ways of desire"[58] in *Weighed*. He praised the film for daring to "take a dig at the artificiality of the family unit, as we have come to know it, to start with." Charles Tesson similarly touched on the film's representation of unorthodox intimacies and perverse desires, including Junior's replacement of his traditional family with an alternative one in which he becomes "as it were, both a 'parent' and a 'child' to the pair [that is, Kuala and Berto]."[59] However, neither critic marshals his observations of the characters' perverse desires into a political reading.

In an important essay on Brocka, Gina Marchetti traces the links between politics and bodily matters in *Weighed* as well as in his later films. She argues: "On one level, these films dealing with the loss of control over the body function as political allegories."[60] She cites as an example the scene in which "the wealthy landlord" Cesar forces Kuala to abort their child despite her desperate pleas. Marchetti ventures that in that particular instance and in similar ones that underline the power differential between women and the patriarchy in Brocka's films, the dynamic of oppression was as follows: "The roles of lover, wife, mother, mistress, and the like blend together and become tantamount to prostitution. Economic desperation and political oppression underlie all these roles."[61] The ruthless patriarchy that effects these and other forms of "prostitution" of women is thus a versatile allegorical figure for the dictatorship and the entities that support it. Marchetti goes on to say that: "Here, the father or lover or boss stands in for the government or church or American business, and these texts insist that these neocolonial institutions must be eliminated."[62] This astute reading of the film—and the Brocka canon more generally—has inspired my interpretation of *Weighed* as a dissimulated allegory of Marcosian authoritarianism. Allegory does not refer here to a precise correspondence between objects or a purposeful or intentional use of metaphor in a veiled reference. As Walter Benjamin suggests, an allegorical image is similar to a rune, an inscription that has become partly or fully unreadable over time.[63] Movies encode allegories of politics either intentionally or unwittingly. Those allegories are, in addition to being polyvalent, legible to some audiences but not to others.

The reception of *Weighed* showed that Brocka's immediate viewers could only partially access the allegory of authoritarianism. But the variance in legibility diminished none of the film's capacity to renew the social uses of melodrama and the Rizalian tradition of critical art. The prominent writer Celso Al Carunungan confirmed the film's debt to that tradition in one of the newspaper advertisements for the film. He stated: "*Tinimbang Ka Ngunit Kulang* is, simply, one of the finest Filipino pictures I have ever seen. It has a searing social force that humbles the proud and exalts the weak. I'm sure that if Rizal were alive today—and if he were a film-maker—this is the kind of picture he would have loved to make."[64] The quote, which I discovered after completing a draft of this chapter, indicates that some of the film's original audiences read Brocka's work as an homage to the national hero's inscription of history, politics, and society.

It is not the nature of Rizal's novels or Brocka's film allegories to yield their meanings—including their political valences—easily. As Brocka understood well, "to be able to make the kind of movies I [he] wanted to make, I [he would] have to help develop my [his] audience first."[65] To further train his audience in the art of critical engagement with cinema and reality, Brocka had to continue in his practice of remaking the social melodrama in the course of his career. He would reach another milestone in his ambitious quest just a year later, with *Manila in the Claws of Light*.

MANILA IN THE CLAWS OF LIGHT

While promoting *Weighed* on the nontheatrical circuit, Brocka told a reporter of his desire to continue making substantial films. He said: "There's too much fantasy in the movies, too much escapism, too much of things that make people forget [their problems]. Filipino films are wanting in content; they need more realism."[66] The same reporter asked him to comment on Imelda Marcos's claim that a "cultural renaissance" was occurring in the midst of martial law. Brocka did not mince words, betraying his contempt for the president's wife. He said: "There is no cultural revival in the cinema and the First Lady's attendance of [a film awards ceremony] ... should not be cited as proof of cultural renaissance.... What we are experiencing is cultural retrogression."[67] This tone of defiance echoes in his next attempt at creating a panoramic social melodrama.

That new film was an adaptation of a social realist novel called *Sa mga kuko ng liwanag (In the Claws of Light)*, which was itself drawn from author Edgardo M. Reyes's experiences as a construction worker and a gofer at a Chinatown brothel. Brocka reportedly suggested the addition of "Manila" to the film's title.[68] Reyes's novel won a contest sponsored by the literary magazine *Liwayway* (Sunshine). Its 1967–1968 serialization in that mass-market periodical was a success. Mike (credited as Miguel) De Leon secured the rights to the film version after reading an adapted screenplay by Clodualdo del Mundo Jr. De Leon was a budding filmmaker and the scion of a landed family that also owned LVN Pictures, one of three big movie studios of the postwar era. Having just returned from studying art history and film processing abroad, De Leon was looking to make his mark in the local entertainment industry with a prestige film. Impressed by the success of *Weighed*,[69] he offered Brocka the necessary resources to make the picture. *Manila* was to be the first venture of De Leon's newly founded Cinema Artists production outfit, and he would serve in a dual capacity as cinematographer and producer.

As in the case of *Weighed*, *Manila* uses dialogue and visuals to make overt and discreet references to contemporary political events. Most significantly, the film transposes the novel's setting from the 1960s to the year 1970. This alteration sets the narrative two years before the declaration of martial law and five years before the film's release. It is unclear if the censors demanded this change or if the filmmakers just wanted to make the adaptation less dated than its source. As expected, the apparent provocation of changing the setting to a time of political turbulence did not go unnoticed. De Leon recalled in 2018 that the censors required the addition of "a title card that said [the narrative begins in the year] 1970, thereby informing the audience that the story took place before Martial Law was declared in 1972."[70]

Whatever its rationale, the change in setting had an ambivalent effect on the film's critique of authoritarianism. On the one hand, the altered setting implied that the dire sociopolitical conditions represented in the film belonged to what Marcos called the "old society" rather than the so-called New Society he sought to realize through martial law. Marcos was himself critical of the national situation before 1972, even though he was already a second-term president at that time, citing the "deteriorating economy" and "increasing social injustice."[71] Indeed, he used some of the very problems his government exacerbated as the pretext for putting the country under authoritarian rule. On the other hand, the grim social conditions the film attributes to the year 1970 still prevailed when the film opened in 1975, under martial law. The similarities suggest that authoritarianism, even after three years, left the country's social problems unresolved.

Apart from the graffiti described at the beginning of this chapter, the other conspicuous reference to the country's political climate is the depiction of a rally late in the film. Youthful participants in this scene are shown bearing placards and streamers that read "Down with imperialism and fascism!" Mindful of the Marcos regime's paranoia about subversive content in movies, the director described the scene of civil unrest as mere "background, purely as background." After uttering those words in the behind-the-scenes documentary for the film, the director nervously added: "I do hope the Board of Censors . . . would see the point of why these things are used . . . because, as I've said, we're trying to make a realistic movie."[72] In spite of Brocka's disclaimer, it is unlikely that *Manila*'s original viewers would have regarded the image of a political protest—an activity strictly prohibited by the regime—as insignificant.

Following Rizal's model of sociopolitical critique, Brocka's *Manila* conjures a panoramic vision of Philippine society. Moreover, as in the case of Rizal's *Noli* and Brocka's *Weighed*, Del Mundo structures the film's narrative as a picaresque. The film tackles an array of social concerns in the course of the hero's peregrinations across the grimy metropolis. Compared to *Weighed*, however, *Manila* deals overtly with issues that the state considered sensitive, such as labor relations and poverty.

Manila tells the story of a young village fisherman named Julio Madiaga (Rafael Roco Jr. a.k.a. Bembol Roco) who follows his girlfriend, Ligaya Paraiso (Hilda Koronel), to Manila, where she has gone missing shortly after being recruited as a housemaid. Their names are both symbolic: Julio Madiaga translates as "Julius Patience" while Ligaya Paraiso means "Joyful Paradise." As in *Weighed*, the narrative of *Manila* appropriates Rizal's use of social types, veiled historical references, and allegory. Ligaya is the modern equivalent of Rizal's Maria Clara, the country lass who becomes the object of a friar's lust in *Noli*. Julio is the counterpart of Elias, the underclass figure who later reveals himself as a revolutionary.

Manila opens with black-and-white footage of the derelict Chinese enclave stirring to life. As horse-drawn carriages, cars, and people begin to fill the streets, and color gradually saturates the images. At the corner of Misericordia and Ongpin Streets, Julio waits for any signs of his missing sweetheart. The passage from monochromatic to polychromatic images marks the temporal setting as the recent past. With greater subtlety, the scene of waiting triggers a lengthy flashback that traces Julio's quest.

In its final quarter, the film goes back to this same moment. Nested within this long recollection is another layer of brief flashbacks and hallucinations that represent Julio's memories of Ligaya at their fishing village in Marinduque province. In contrast to the gritty realism employed in much of the film, these recollections are markedly stylized. Each picture-perfect memory of their village, bathed in golden sunshine, conjures an Eden that seems paradoxically lost and unattainable.

The narrative begins late in the protagonist's search. Seven months pass before Julio stumbles on Mrs. Cruz (Juling Bagabaldo), the woman who recruited Ligaya into domestic service. He tails Mrs. Cruz and observes her entering a typical Chinatown dwelling with a storefront on the ground floor and private quarters above.[73] The sign hanging above the storefront reads "Chua Tek Trading Company." It becomes clear later on that Chua Tek (Tommy Yap) is another one of the narrative's allegorical figures, something that is reinforced by the fact that he is usually called Ah Tek, a name that sounds like *atik*, which is Filipino slang for money. Julio spends his free time keeping watch outside the dwelling until he finally spots Ligaya walking to church. They catch up while hiding inside a movie theater and after making love in a motel. She reveals that she survived forced prostitution but is now the kept woman of Ah Tek, who still treats her like a prisoner even though she has just borne him a daughter. Julio persuades Ligaya to attempt an escape despite her warning that Ah Tek has threatened to kill her if she tries to flee. She misses their appointed meeting time. That same night, she dies under mysterious circumstances. Julio exacts revenge on the Chinese businessman, fatally stabbing him with an ice pick. Running from the murder scene, Julio attracts a mob that corners him in an alley and presumably lynches him.

The Laboring Class

The story Brocka is actually telling through his urban fable of star-crossed lovers is a sociopolitical one, about the plight of Manila's expendable working class. The hero's quest for his girlfriend cuts a path through the various contemporary guises of slavery, the dire conditions in Manila's hovels, and other pressing indications of social inequality. The film depicts the Philippine capital, in Raymond Williams's borrowed words, as "a city of death in life,"[74] offering its laborers no more than a hand-to-mouth existence, terrible working conditions, and soul-crushing alienation. The exploitation of workers takes many forms. Right after the film's opening credits, Julio is shown applying for a job and getting hired at a construction site for a building called La Madrid. The foreman, Mr. Balajadia (Pancho Pelagio), offers Julio a salary much lower than the going rate. He additionally docks 30 percent from the amount indicated in the paymaster's ledger. Not content with the wage theft, the foreman tells workers that the construction firm has no funds to pay them on time, but he could front the money for a fee. Omeng (Joonee Gamboa), Julio's emaciated coworker refers to this predatory loan as "Taiwan," and its effect is to drive the workers to near starvation. The foreman carries out this unconscionable scheme every payday, threatening to fire anyone who complains. When

Julio's friend Atong (Lou Salvador Jr.) dares to stand up to the foreman, he is thrown in jail and killed there by Balajadia's men. In spite of the foreman's immense power over the workers, however, the film shows that he is just another cog in the wheel of capitalist exploitation. Balajadia reports to another character named Mr. Manabat who appears to be the brains behind the "Taiwan" racket.

The association of foreign places such as Taiwan and Madrid with insidious forms of exploitation registers the outsize role played by transnational capital during the Marcos regime. A deluge of foreign monies propped up his government. These include IMF and World Bank loans to fund the autocrat's development projects, sweetheart deals between the president's cronies and foreign corporations, money from overseas for military assistance, and earnings from sex tourism and illegal arms trading. By and large, these forms of global capital had a negative impact on the lives of workers during the Marcos years. Gavin Shatkin points out, for instance, that "the development of an export-oriented economy has [had] led to downward pressure on wages, environmental destruction and the dislocation of communities of the poor."[75]

In the two instances I have just mentioned, the film delivers social analysis both directly (for instance, Omeng's lecture about wage theft) as well as through metaphor (for example, the use of symbols such as La Madrid, the capital of the first colonial power to turn Filipinos into vassals). In keeping with Brocka's cinema politics, *Manila* employs a range of filmic devices in advancing its critique. Stark images of the unfinished building floors—dusty, sun-bleached, littered with protruding rebar—evoke the hazards of construction work with the effective plainness of documentary-style cinematography. The film supplements this realist aesthetic with touches of expressionism. *Manila* conveys the physical and psychic toll of the peons' backbreaking labor by introducing bits of stylized sounds and images. Canted or off-kilter shots emphasize the immensity of structures tackled by a small troop of workers with few hard hats and no safety harnesses. Some of the construction noises are over-modulated, conveying the relentless pace of work. The alternation of quick editing and repetitious actions dramatize tedium. These expressive devices are employed in scenes of Julio collapsing due to hunger, Omeng experiencing terrible coughing fits from inhaling cement dust, and Benny (Danilo Posadas), another of Julio's fellow peons, meeting an accident. In that last scene, wooden bars get dislodged and hit Benny, who fails to duck, causing him to plunge several floors to his death. His coworkers take him all the way across town to a free hospital because their employer would not foot his medical bill. Benny does not survive the journey. One of his friends predicts that his body will end up as a cadaver for purchase by medical students. In a characteristically didactic bit of melodrama, the scene punctuates Benny's death with an insert shot of the music magazine (a type of publication called "song hits") he left behind. He loved using the slim booklet, which contains lyrics and guitar arrangements, to aid him in belting out love songs at break time. The shot implies that Benny died not only due to workplace hazards but also because he was distracted by the mass culture fantasies he had been using to escape his alienation. In Reyes's novel, powdered cement with clumps of Benny's blood are scooped up and incorporated into the concrete mix by his coworkers. They hesitate out of respect for him but proceed anyway, fearing they might get sacked for wasting construction supplies.

Marcos pledged to uplift the lives of the "poorest of the working people"[76] after he imposed martial law, but much of his economic policies were inconsistent with this rhetoric. His government intervened in labor negotiations and, as mentioned earlier, contributed to the depression of wages. Such policies aimed to enrich the autocrat and his cronies and encourage foreign companies to manufacture their goods in the country. While creating a "good business climate" and the trappings of economic development, those policies took a heavy toll on the underclass. When Julio's coworker Imo (Pio de Castro III) lands a job at an advertising agency after years of juggling night school and daytime construction work, the film shows the great disparity between their two social classes. Imo, a beneficiary of Marcos's economic policies, treats Julio to an impromptu blow-out at a diner. In an attempt to show off, he orders more dishes than they could consume. But even as Julio gorges himself on Imo's food, he does not know where he might find his next meal.

Unsettled and Disoriented

Lopsided property relations, the second social problem represented by *Manila*, are not central to Julio's mission. He is hardly interested in acquisition or ownership. For most of the film, his possessions amount to no more than a change of clothes and a pocket-sized diary. Literally homeless, Julio seeks shelter at the construction sites where he works and occasionally crashes with friends. It is his fellow construction worker Atong who puts a face to the inequities tied to property relations. Midway through the film, Atong takes Julio in for a few days when the latter loses his job at the construction site. Atong and his family live in a squatter's area (informal settlements) along a polluted canal called Sunog-Apog (Burnt lime). Atong, his sister Perla (Lily Gamboa-Mendoza), and their mute and paralyzed father (Abelardo Reyes) moved to the area after being kicked off their suburban homestead by a land grabber. Their story recalls the plight of Old Selo, his son Barrio Captain Tales, and Tales's daughter Juli, the subalterns in Rizal's *El filibusterismo*, although land grabbing cases were still prevalent at the time of the film's making.

Sunog-Apog turns out to be an unreliable refuge for Atong's family. Months later, after Atong dies in jail from being assaulted by Balajadia's men, the shanties catch fire. The mysterious conflagration reduces the jam-packed informal settlements to smoking debris and tattered iron sheets. The flames reportedly engulf Atong's father, while his sister, who was away during the fire, ends up in the streets, and later, in a brothel. The total dispossession and ruination of Atong's family thus

FIGURE 1.6. Julio (Bembol Roco, right) and Pol (Tommy Abuel) behold the ruins of a shantytown fire that left their friends homeless. *Manila in the Claws of Light.* Courtesy of Danilo Brocka/CCP Library.

prefigure Julio and Ligaya's fates. It also portrays Manila as a proletarian inferno, one whose circles of despair go deeper than Julio can fathom.

Julio's homelessness and Atong's housing problems reflected real-life property relations before and during the Marcos regime. Manila was already receiving a heavy influx of migrants from all over the Philippines even before World War II. Informal settlements sprouted all over the capital, reaching 37.4 percent of the population by 1968.[77] A so-called "primate city" with an intense concentration of the nation's jobs, schools, businesses, government offices, and leisure spaces, Manila's resident population stood at 7.5 million in 1976, possibly a half-million more with daytime traffic.[78] The high population density created a shortage of affordable housing and overtaxed the city's infrastructure and resources.

As part of the regime's attempts to beautify the capital region and its unstated aim of controlling "grassroots mobilisation by the Left,"[79] the government evicted "a few thousand" informal settlers. In Imelda Marcos's harsh words, the displaced were among those who had been "privileged to usurp the esteros and inconvenience the lives of millions."[80] It is worth citing some examples. The government razed the homes of more than one hundred thousand persons in preparation for hosting the 1974 Miss Universe Pageant.[81] Twice that number were evicted the following year for US President Gerald Ford's visit. Just a month after *Manila* hit theaters, Marcos's Presidential Decree Number 272 criminalized squatting and authorized the demolition of all illegal constructions, including the "buildings on and along esteros [canals],"[82] the type of dwelling where Atong and his family lived. Demolitions continued after 1976 when Marcos appointed his wife as governor of the entire Metropolitan Manila area.[83] She identified "continued rural migration to the city" as one of the significant challenges to her vision of remaking the "decaying" metropolis into an "egalitarian" and picturesque "City of Man."[84] Mrs. Marcos failed to acknowledge the main reason behind the movement of rural folk into the capital and their determination to stay there against the government's wishes. "The continuing rural-urban migration," writes Manuel Caoili, "is a product of the country's overall underdevelopment,"[85] especially in "the rural countryside, where 70 percent of Filipinos reside."[86] In other words, the government's unsound economic policies were partly responsible for the continued overcrowding of Manila.

Brocka portrays the living conditions of Manila's underclass with images of unforgiving bleakness. Cinematographer Mike De Leon frames an abundance of long shots to capture the squalor of the slum dwellings. Even in scenes of intimate conversations, the foreground and background of shots teem with slovenly faces and dilapidated structures. This detailed visual treatment is reminiscent of Italian neorealism, an aesthetic that, in André Bazin's words, sought "to reveal social reality, to transform into spectacle the human world that surrounds us and that we nevertheless ignore."[87] By shooting on location, seamlessly blending professional and nonprofessional actors, and emphasizing mundane details, the neorealist approach obtained quasi-documentary images with the quality of "brute representation."[88] It was the raw output of the camera's basic recording function. In the best works of neorealism, the scene appeared to be a "fragment of reality,"[89] possessing a "concrete density" of details on its surface while also evoking a sense of "totality in its [very] simplicity."[90] Brocka, who counted Federico Fellini's *Nights of Cabiria* (1957) as one of his favorite films, began to appropriate neorealism's unvarnished visual style and humanitarian sentimentality in the slum settings of his earlier works, especially in *Three, Two, One* (*Tatlo, Dalawa, Isa*, 1974). He employed the aesthetic more extensively in *Manila* to depict crippling poverty and project an image of the city that flew in the face of the Marcos regime's beautification campaigns. Brocka would go on to harness neorealism's expressive possibilities throughout his career, making it a distinctive feature of his cinema politics. The resulting visual statements, both eye-catching and provocative, inspired praise and derision from conservative and progressive elements. The latter faulted the director trafficking in exoticized images of poverty.[91] The former, including presidential daughter Imee Marcos, condescendingly referred to his work as "slum movies."[92]

It is also worth noting that photojournalism appears to have supplemented neorealism as one of the film's aesthetic touchstones. Brocka kept gritty black-and-white photographs of various waterside slum dwellings in his archive for *Manila*. It is unclear if he used the pictures in location scouting, as studies for the cinematography or as publicity material, but they testify to his and De Leon's interest in using various modes of "brute representation" to telegraph socioeconomic conditions. As mentioned earlier, the film yields interesting results by juxtaposing this neorealist aesthetic with conspicuous stylization. First, the artful cinematography unfolds in jarring contrast to the city's ugliest sights, thus dramatizing the tension between the city's appeal and its repulsiveness. Secondly, the alternation between realism and stylization captures the wavering of Julio's point of view between exteriority and inwardness, as well as between the oppressive realities of his existence and the fantasies of transcendence that prevent his psyche from collapsing. Because Julio is deliriously hungry, exhausted, terrified, and hopeful, the harshness and beauty of Manila as he sees it clash and blend in unpredictable ways. In this regard, the pairing of various aesthetic modes deepens characterization and achieves a textured representation of the proletariat's experience.

Traded Flesh and Alienated Love

Brocka portrays yet another social problem, human trafficking and prostitution, as both real and symbolic conditions. The system of trafficking is laid out like a puzzle. Julio, uneducated and new to the city, must rely on the help of his friends to search for Ligaya based on the information contained in the only letter she sent him. Julio's fellow workers—especially Pol (Tommy Abuel)—speculate that Ligaya's recruiter used a false name and sold her to a brothel. It is also part of Julio's friends' theory that Ligaya has ended up in nearby Chinatown where the seediest bordellos are located.

When Julio reunites with Ligaya, she confirms that the peons' assumptions about her ordeal were entirely correct. She further explains why she has not attempted to escape despite recently being allowed to venture outside Ah Tek's apartment on her own. While Ligaya still dislikes being with Ah Tek, she gives him credit for sparing her from the worst of the flesh trade. By paying the madam to make Ligaya exclusively his, Ah Tek "saved" her from being forced to perform in live sex shows and engage in group sex while high on dope. To Julio, however, Ligaya seems to have lost everything in spite of having fled the world of prostitution. She looks pale and gaunt, and she erupts in fits of hysteria. Her gaze is empty, and her spirit, broken. His own experiences in the flesh trade inform Julio's view of Ligaya's emotional state. He engaged in prostitution during a spell of joblessness. A gigolo named Bobby (Jojo Abella) recruited him to work at a male brothel owned by a Filipino-Spanish mestizo named Cesar (Chiqui Xerex-Burgos). There, in a walk-up apartment somewhat resembling the structure of Ah Tek and Ligaya's dwelling, the brothel's attendants pimped him to middle-class clients as a "Mexican beauty." Julio left the flesh trade after a client (played by fashion designer Rikki

Jimenez) insisted on romancing him in the presence of a pet dog and complained about his unwillingness to "sing and dance" (that is, perform oral and receptive anal sex).

The "gay" sequence generated controversy. Brocka asked the screenwriter to create the subplot, not found in the novel, of Julio's recourse to hustling. The director believed it was necessary for bringing symmetry to the hero and heroine's fates and delivering a more realistic social "exposé."[93]. *Manila*'s portrayal of male prostitution achieved some of that desired verisimilitude by filming the city's gay haunts. For example, the scenes at the male brothel were filmed on location at a "massage parlor" on the edge of Chinatown. The receptionists played themselves on film and even improvised parts of their dialogue.

De Leon had serious reservations about the episode, however, and with Brocka's consent, trimmed the section before releasing the film abroad. De Leon offered the following rationale for the alterations: "I told him [Brocka] that in my opinion, the extended male prostitute sequences could be shortened because they 'stopped the story.' These were the words I used (but in Tagalog). The whole point of the novel and the film was the search by the main character (Julio) for his provincial sweetheart Ligaya. I further explained that all Julio needed was [to earn some] money and after that traumatic incident at the gay brothel, the story had to return to the search for Ligaya."[94]

I have not seen a detailed account of the issue from Brocka's perspective. He only mentioned in passing that he was sorry to have left out scenes from that episode, including a few that centered on Bobby.[95] The deletions are not among the film elements of *Manila* preserved by the British Film Institute, the Asian Film Archive, the Cineteca di Bologna, and the *Cinémathèque française*. De Leon maintains that the material no longer exists.[96] If he is correct, the deletions survive only in the form of still photographs, the pages of the production script, and the recollections of film critics.[97] One of those scenes shows the call boys extorting money from a gay college student who sits next to Julio at a movie theater where homosexual encounters are known to take place. The hustlers' racket involves using Julio as bait to lure gay movie patrons into a restroom where Bobby and his friends, pretending to be undercover cops, threaten to arrest them unless bribed.[98] The scene is reminiscent of the 1969 Oscar-winning film *Midnight Cowboy*. Another scene takes place at a disco with backrooms that rent by the hour. In the production script's likely unfilmed version of the scene, Julio and Bobby come to the venue hoping to get hired by a foreigner they call "Kano" (short for "Amerikano" or "white man"). He is known for paying a tidy sum for bondage play with multiple partners. Julio is engaged instead by a local who asks him to perform fellatio and leaves in a huff when he refuses. The production script also includes scenes that develop Julio's friendship with Bobby. The latter becomes infatuated with Julio and, in a moment of tenderness, steals a kiss from him. Julio punches Bobby and

FIGURE 1.7. This composite image represents scenes excised from the film's gay sequence. *Manila in the Claws of Light*. Courtesy of Danilo Brocka/CCP Library.

ends his stint in the flesh trade.[99] Had this last scene been retained, it might have offered more insight on why Julio abandoned the lucrative sex work and settles for starvation wages as a construction worker.

The film's allegorical motif of fatal brightness—referencing the "light" in the title—underscores the parallelism between the hero and heroine's sexual exploitation. Depicting Ligaya's confinement in Ah Tek's house, Brocka frames her as a silhouette enclosed in a flash of light seeping through translucent window panes. Likewise, when Julio enters the flesh trade, neon signs burn in the night sky, looming over the park where a call boy recruits him. The motif recurs when Julio sets foot in a male brothel ablaze with tacky lighting and when Ligaya's corpse is waked at a brightly lit funeral parlor. In keeping with a popular metaphor, the two provincials are the moths lured and obliterated by the dazzling city.

Manila suggests that even Ligaya and Julio's terrible ordeals in the flesh trade are not the worst cases imaginable. Earlier in the film, a pimp brings a sex worker to the construction site. The peons make a beeline and take turns mounting her in a nearby shed. She fetches a respectable sum, but only after servicing a dozen men. The worst case of prostitution is brought up during Julio and Pol's search for Ligaya. A man approaches them, flashing a photograph and offering to set them up with a "very young one." The camera does not show the picture, but the dialogue establishes that the man is trafficking an underage female.

The Emblem of Autocracy

Early in this chapter, I described two scenes from *Manila* that invoked the history of the Marcos regime. The first uses the film's visuals—particularly signs and graffiti—to reference the political agitation that gripped the country in the first quarter of 1970. The second overt reference to the autocrat's tenure was the brief scene of an anti-establishment rally that Julio encounters but does not join. There is a third example, but unlike in the two earlier scenes, it figures authoritarianism opaquely.

I venture that in *Manila*, the most powerful emblem of Marcos's autocracy is the one that bears neither resemblance to the president nor directly references the history of his tenure. This allegorical emblem appears in the sequence leading up to Julio's death at the hands of a lynch mob. After Julio secretly attends Ligaya's burial with his friend Pol, he parts ways with him, buys an ice pick, and heads to Ah Tek's quarters. There he stabs the Chinese businessman repeatedly in the neck. (Later in his career, Brocka described this moment as "the most violent scene" he had ever filmed.)[100] The bloodcurdling screams of Ah Tek's maid punctuate the attack. People on the street heed her call, their voices floating over the film's tense images: "What has he done? He killed a Chinese! Teach him a lesson! Beat him up!" A mob forms as Julio runs along Avenida Rizal (Rizal Avenue), the city's commercial and entertainment district. Visibly winded and confused, Julio turns a corner and rushes into a dead-end alley, its concrete walls extended to an unrealistic height with rusty sheets of galvanized iron. One look at the soaring enclosures around him and Julio realizes he is doomed. The mob picks up stones, sticks, and discarded lumber. For a second there is a détente, as the members of the crowd look at each other to see if they should proceed. As they tighten their grip on their weapons, we see their shadows advance. The screen then fills up with the image of Julio's terrified expression, his eyes looking almost directly at the camera, begging for mercy. As the image of his silent scream freezes, a dreamlike vision of Ligaya—shrouded in blinding light, as if she were already in heaven—briefly appears onscreen.

The flash of explosive and unstoppable violence befalling a youthful person, the victim's direct appeal to the camera, the suggestive mise-en-scène—these are the elements of what I call the "Marcosian moment." This emblem registers the historical trace of authoritarianism and flashes across Brocka's films and those of other directors from that era. The Marcosian moment is alternately a product of intent (a mise-en-scène purposely charged with political meanings) and of unconscious processes (the historical situation of authoritarianism writing itself into popular narratives and collectively produced images). In *Manila*'s Marcosian moment, the violence of the mob suggests the influence of a larger, more formidable force crushing hapless individuals. The murderous crowd is summoned not just by the cries of Ah Tek's maid but the city folk's instinctive loyalty to those who hold power in society. Ah Tek, a capitalist, is one such influential person. As the instrument of a fearsome propensity for violence that originates in and is sanctioned by the collective, the lynch mob serves as the proxy for authoritarian rule.

Julio's facial expression inscribes the terror unleashed by the collective. His direct appeal to the viewer suggests a desire to make a statement about the contemporary situation that the state and its censors would likely disallow. Moreover, his lynching in a Manila alley is evocative of the authoritarian regime's heavy-handed suppression of youthful activists, among other acts of ubiquitous state violence. A precursor to this Marcosian moment had already emerged in the scene of two deaths that closes *Weighed*, Brocka's social melodrama from the previous year. The ending of that film contained some of the elements of a Marcosian moment. They include the fatal shooting of the young leper Berto as well as the image of Kuala gazing at the camera before her demise (and in the presence of her longtime oppressor, Cesar). The only element lacking in the film's climax is a cold-blooded murder, something that is particularly suggestive of the autocrat's sovereign power to kill and let live.

Julio ironically perishes at the hands of his fellow proletariat. Lacking class consciousness, the working-class mob does not even bother hearing Julio out before attacking him. As is the case in much of Brocka's film, the Marcosian moment of Julio's lynching suggests a relation of substitutability between the violence inflicted by capitalism and that which is wrought by the autocracy. While authoritarianism and capitalism should not be conflated, they have much in common. Often, authoritarianism maintains itself not simply by brute force but by inflicting economic violence upon its subjects. For instance, it is by keeping the masses in the grip of poverty that strongmen amass wealth and curtail the people's means of organizing resistance.[101]

The censors did not object to the scene of vigilantism that ends the film; to the violence of Ah Tek's murder; or, perhaps most surprisingly, to the political rally. Thanks to "a film critic in the Board of Censors who supported the film," *Manila* was passed without deletions and received a favorable "General Patronage" rating.[102] For whatever reason, it was the short documentary about the making of the film that reportedly displeased the media gatekeepers.[103]

The film premiered at the Delta Theater on July 16, 1975.[104] In just fifteen days at cinemas, *Manila* reportedly grossed almost half a million pesos and surpassed the first month's revenue of *Weighed*.[105] As with Brocka's previous social melodrama, *Manila*'s producers targeted students and financed an encore run the following year to capitalize on the film's critical acclaim.[106] Despite strong business, however,

De Leon estimated that the 700,000-peso film—expensive by the standards of the time[107]—only managed to break even.[108] At the awards night of the Filipino Academy of Movie Arts and Sciences (FAMAS), Brocka's entry fetched nine trophies, including the prizes for Best Picture, Best Director, Best Screenplay, Best Cinematography, Best Sound, Best Editing, and Best Actor for Roco's first starring role.

Brocka's film earned mostly rave notices from local critics. In a review titled "Goodbye to Fantasyland," Maria Socorro Garcia Roque gushed that "Philippine cinema will never be the same" after Brocka's film.[109] Cristina Pantoja-Hidalgo described the film as "clearly superior to any other Filipino production" and "the brightest spot in the local cinema scene."[110] Comparing the two social melodramas studied in this chapter, Hidalgo opined that: "If *'Tinimbang Ka Ngunit Kulang'* announced the coming of age of Philippine cinema, then *'Maynila . . . Sa Mga Kuko ng Liwanag'* pronounces its firm establishment as an art form." Matching Garcia and Hidalgo's enthusiasm, Mario Hernando called *Manila* "an uncompromisingly great film, the best and the most truthful in several years."[111]

Also reminiscent of *Weighed* was the critics' enthusiasm for *Manila*'s realist aesthetic. Dormiendo observed that the film "opened a new path of realism." Hidalgo averred that the film "takes us literally deeper into reality than any local film before it, deep into the heart of Manila—its *estero* slums, its construction sites, its gay bars—deep into the heart of poverty and exploitation, which is the only reality for most of the city's people." She ascribed the film's "verism" to its "on-location shooting," "the inclusion of details which contribute to the film's authenticity," as well as to "the acting, which is so natural it does not give the impression of acting at all." For Nieves Epistola, the film's realism served a clear purpose. She wrote: "This is the first movie though that projects realistically the plight of the working class. Its description of the working class is the most powerful part of the movie."[112]

M. R. Avena faulted the director for leaning too much on visuals to mount his social critique. He opined: "Images, in other words, are substituted for insights, leaving the viewer unenriched in his feeling for humanity."[113] While it is true that Brocka plies social critique through images, his heavy reliance on visuals is endemic to both melodrama and cinematic storytelling more generally.[114] His approach is reminiscent of Rizal's use of vivid imagery to create allegories and heighten emotions in his writing. For instance, in the opening passages of *Noli*, he sketches the architecture and human geography of Maria Clara's home as an objective correlative for the structure of Spanish colonial society. Rizal likewise treats the most sensitive political matters through visual metaphors, famously using a conversation about horticulture between Ibarra and the eccentric philosopher Tasio to allude to strategies for reforming the colonial system.[115] The novel's most unabashedly melodramatic sections render the depths of Sisa's poverty and torment by making readers visualize the meager contents of her pantry (for example, three sardines and rice "which she herself gathered from the threshing room floor")[116] and the violence of her child's beating ("The priest . . . thrashes him, but he no longer defends himself. . . . He is rolling about the floor like an inert mass, leaving a wet trail behind him").[117]

Avena's critique of *Manila*'s visual rhetoric did not exemplify the negative responses to the film. So much of the carping about *Manila* focused on comparisons to the novel. Several reviewers, driven by unexamined or blatant homophobia, disapproved of the gay sequence. Dormiendo claimed that it was extraneous to the plot and was "simply a box office attraction."[118] In an essay that Reyes selected to preface the second edition of his novel, fellow writer and friend Ava Perez Jacob concludes with the homophobic charge that Brocka "tried but failed to sissify a manly novel about an ever masculine city."[119] Perez Jacob does not care to say when and how Manila became "ever masculine." It was Epistola, an academic, who voiced the most incisive defense of the gay sequence, pointing out that homosexuals "are very much a part of contemporary Manila."[120] In addition, she offered a theory of how gayness fits within the grid of social relations drawn by the film. She said: "In my opinion, the homosexuals may be seen as buffers—a buffer between the oppressor and the oppressed. So, in this system, you have the oppressed below and the oppressor up there, and we have the homosexuals in between."[121]

Reflecting the productive dialogue about identity politics from the 1970s onward, some reviewers charged Brocka with anti-Chinese racism. The film's portrayal of Ah Tek was the subject of bitter criticism. Valerio Nofuente objected to "the very drastic way Ah Tek was killed."[122] Randolf David expressed the following reservations in a roundtable with other scholars: "I consider the focus on the Chinese minority in Ongpin [Chinatown] as a bit unfortunate. The greater majority of these people themselves suffer from the oppression and exploitation of their wealthier brethren, i.e., the ones who control the distribution of prime commodities in our country."[123]

The flat characterization of Ah Tek and his vilification originated in Reyes's novel, but it was not altered in the film adaptation, even when the opportunity presented itself to the screenwriter and the director. Unfortunately, Brocka responded to criticism from the Chinese Filipino community without the cultural sensitivity warranted by the situation. He said in an interview: "It could have been an Indian national or an American [character]. But in the Philippines, the Chinese have servants whom they turn into their concubines. I have nothing against the Chinese. A year after the film was shown, they were still protesting."[124] Writing long after Brocka's death, Caroline S. Hau described *Manila* as "an anti-Chinese film," the most prominent, she says, of many such cultural works that propped up Filipino nationalism and identity by denigrating the Chinese minority. In the novel and film of *Manila*, so much hatred "is directed against the Chinese who is both an alien and instrument of capitalist alienation."[125] She goes on to say that characters like Ah Tek dehumanize Chinese Filipinos and the Chinese in the Philippines, casting them in the role of the "abject alien."[126]

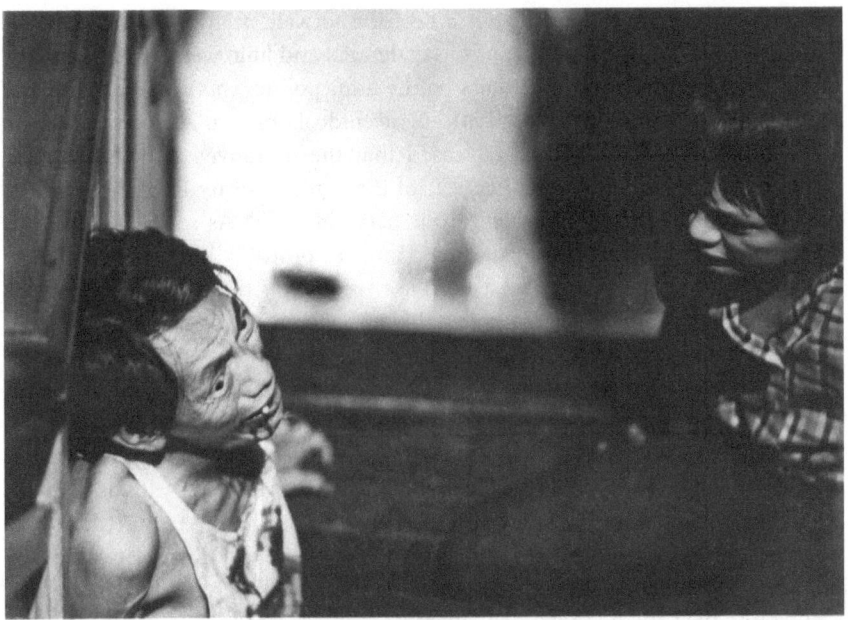

FIGURE 1.8. Julio (Bembol Roco, right) flees after stabbing Ah Tek (Tommy Chua). *Manila in the Claws of Light*. Courtesy of Danilo Brocka/CCP Library.

It is possible to accept Hau's critique of the film and novel's anti-Chinese discourse without denying the history that the film condenses in the Ah Tek subplot. That history, which is also what Brocka references in the interview quoted above, is that of the fraught class and race conflicts between Filipino workers and Chinese or Chinese Filipino capitalists.[127] In attending to the specificity of *Manila*, it is useful to note that Ah Tek is not the sole character that embodies capitalism in the film, yet he alone is scapegoated for all of its sins. As regards the critique of the film's racism, Gina Marchetti helpfully clarifies that "although Ligaya's captor may fit the stereotypes associated with Chinese villains in Philippine cinema, *Manila* emphasizes that his power over Ligaya comes from wealth rather than some sort of ethnic degeneracy."[128] These qualifications notwithstanding, the film's racialized characterization of Ah Tek (and his double, the store owner who physically abuses his Filipina employee) remains one of the film's most problematic elements.

Critical Appraisal

Critics took note of *Manila*'s overt political references, but their responses varied. Mario Hernando observed that by resetting the story "to the activist days of 1970," the film gave Julio "another choice before he charges his opponent."[129] Hernando did not elaborate on the protagonist's decision to walk away from the "activist-demonstrators," going only so far as to say that Pol and Julio were "equally apolitical."[130] The same reticence for discussing the film's politics was evident in the first of two reviews written by leftist critic Bienvenido Lumbera. At the time of the film's initial release, he sounded pleased that the narrative's setting had been changed "to the turbulent opening year of the 1970s in order to underscore the pertinence of the novel's message to our national life."[131] As someone who was jailed by Marcos for his ties to the left, Lumbera probably knew better than to expound on that "pertinence," lest he cause trouble for the film. After Marcos's ouster, however, Lumbera revisited the film and offered a less sanguine view of its politics. Writing in 1987, he noted: "1970 was the year when social movements in the Philippines were politicized, but it appeared that politics played no role in Julio's quest for justice."[132] Lumbera's complaint is understandable; for a film set during such a momentous period, its treatment of history and politics is conspicuously limited. It seems odd, however, that Lumbera did not qualify his assessment by taking stock of what he knew about censorship during the regime. In a 1982 interview, Brocka spoke of the challenges he faced in the mid-1970s. He said: "The film was difficult to make in the context of the government campaign to turn Manila into the City of Lights. Also, there was martial law."[133]

Lumbera did give Reyes's novel and Brocka's film some credit for "traveling the path cleared by Rizal's *Noli* and *Fili*," but he lamented "the hazy delineation of social forces carried over from the novel into the film."[134] He added that while the film succeeded in "concretizing the social forces that ensnared Julio and Ligaya," it failed in "crystallizing the true nature of the conflict that was playing out in Philippine society." The "victims," he argued, "are unable to comprehend the forces that have led them astray" and are thus "also unable to fight or resolve them."[135] Lumbera did not specify which truths, conflicts, or forces he believed the film should have represented. His reading does not acknowledge, for instance, the insightful account that *Manila* provides of the hierarchies that operate within the rapacious economies of developing nations. At the bottom of the heap—even lower than wage laborers like Julio—are the subalterns, the beggars as well as the victims of human trafficking. Above Julio are middle-class folks, who exploit the underclass with impunity. They include the foreman Balajadia and Mrs. Cruz. Small-time capitalists such as Ah Tek and the gay brothel owner Cesar occupy a higher social station than the petty bourgeois. The oligarchs, too high up to be visible to the underclass, fittingly appear in the film only by proxy. Throughout, images of commercial signage and the sights and sounds of foreign popular culture suggest the culpability of domestic plutocrats and global capitalists for the hardscrabble existence of Manila's underclass.[136] The film could have used dialogue to explain plainly the workings of those various forces, rather than simply invoking them through images, words, and sounds. The advancement of patently discursive forms of sociopolitical critique was not, however, the project of Brocka's film or even Reyes's novel.

Additionally, by the 1960s and 1970s, the political and economic processes shaping the city of Manila and the lives of its working class may have already become so complex as to resist adequate representation in a work of art.[137] Fredric Jameson wisely observed that in late capitalism "the truth of our social life as a whole ... is increasingly irreconcilable with the possibilities of aesthetic expression or articulation available to us."[138] Put differently, works of modern literature and culture tend to encode politics more densely in subtextual and allegorical registers than in surface details. Unlike Lumbera, Jameson would not clamor for straightforward depictions of "social forces" in contemporary films. He regards cinematic scenarios and images not as explanatory tracts but as partial and often obscure allegories of an unimaginably vast and intricate social system.

That said, Lumbera and others who remain critical of the film's treatment of politics might appreciate the fact that both Reyes's novel and Brocka's adaptation contain highly legible features that are also present in radical political tracts, particularly Fredrich Engels's *The Condition of the Working Class in England*. As with *Manila*, Engels's portrait of Manchester's proletariat tells a picaresque narrative and abounds with vivid descriptions that lend insight into their situation. Engels's analysis benefits from rich illustrations of the lumpen's dwellings, their leisure spaces and practices, their social and intimate lives, and their systemic exploitation and immiseration. Moreover, Engels's socialist tract is, like Brocka's film, melodramatic in its sensibility, beginning with what one scholar calls a "ludicrously idyllic picture of pre-Industrial England."[139] The author then contrasts it with the horrendous filth, starvation, and loneliness of life under capitalist industrialization. Brocka's account of class and political oppression in *Manila* arguably resonates with these and other aspects of Engels's nineteenth-century socialist portrait of the industrial town, in addition to sharing its progressive spirit.

CONCLUSION

Brocka's attempts at devising a new kind of Philippine cinema produced two innovative renditions of the social melodrama. These films were shaped, among other things, by an influential mode of sociopolitical critique begun in the late nineteenth century by José Rizal. As with the national hero's panoramic social novels, Brocka's films employ a series of interlocking narratives of individuals and their immediate milieu to treat much broader concerns.

In his study of social melodramas in the West, John G. Cawleti admits to the form's problematic tendencies. For instance, he takes issue with the pat resolutions common to such works. He notes that often even the most ambitious social melodramas conclude with "the triumph of the good and the punishment of the wicked."[140] Such endings, he says, rehearse "the basic melodramatic principle that things are as they should be." Cawleti's misgivings about simplistic resolutions are irrelevant to *Weighed* and *Manila*. Although *Weighed* leads to a hopeful ending in which a youthful surrogate father rescues an orphaned child, it does not suggest the continuity of a paternalistic social order. Indeed, the finale stages the downfall of the abusive patriarch and criticizes the society that condoned his misdeeds. The conclusion of *Manila* is even grimmer than that of *Weighed*. Brocka's film about the Philippine capital ends by dispatching its pivotal characters in senseless deaths.

Cawleti also points to the dubious quality of the insights purveyed by many social melodramas. "The social melodramatist," he writes, "tends to take advantage of anything that can give his tale the appearance of deep social significance and truth."[141] This impression of substance and verisimilitude usually is achieved through what he describes as "techniques of simplification and intensification."[142] He avers that many social melodramas use "masses of information and analysis" but to little effect.[143] Some relentlessly appeal to the viewer's emotions to disguise an otherwise superficial treatment of social concerns. *Weighed* and *Manila* arguably do not suffer from those deficiencies even if both films deliver their sharpest sociopolitical critiques indirectly. For example, *Weighed* offers an early (and rare) figuration of a malign paternalism that registers the national patriarch's autocratic character and moral bankruptcy. Additionally, the film conjures an allegorical image of social decay under martial law. *Manila*, for its part, uses sounds and images to register the socioeconomic conditions that were causing unrest in the 1970s.

Some Filipino critics praised various aspects of *Weighed* and *Manila* but were particularly dissatisfied with the content of Brocka's social melodramas. Most of them expressed a preference for overt and systematic analysis instead of the director's recourse to images, metaphors, and allusions. One of those critics, Bienvenido Lumbera, suggested not only that *Manila* was deficient but, more provocatively, that Philippine filmmaking had been remiss for never having produced a veritable "social cinema" (*pelikulang sosyal*) in nearly a century of existence.[144] However, he did not define the terms of such a cinema, only saying that it was a type of filmmaking that other countries had already accomplished and that Filipino directors would do well to emulate.

Brocka did not comment specifically on Lumbera's reappraisal of *Manila* or the critic's notion of a "social cinema" that has so far eluded all Filipinos directors. In another context, however, Brocka expressed concern over the discrepancy between his filmmaking praxis and the expectations of critics such as Lumbera (whom he respected). "I won't let myself be imprisoned by other people's expectations of me," Brocka insisted during an interview. "Like Bien Lumbera, he's always looking for social relevance. Can't a director make small films anymore?"[145] By "small films," Brocka probably meant lower-budget independent films and commercial films with modest artistic and sociopolitical statements.

The director's reference to the unsustainable practice of only making prestige films with social themes is useful in understanding the direction that he took following his efforts in remaking Philippine cinema. Largely because of economic imperatives, Brocka seldom found the opportunity to work with the same degree of creative freedom and on the grand scale of his two social melodramas from the mid-1970s. His production outfit CineManila shuttered after a series of flops and accruing debt that burdened him for over a decade. He continued to explore various possibilities of sociopolitical representation in popular cinema, but much of those subsequent efforts were commercial films instilled with varying amounts of "social relevance."

In the 1980s, however, Brocka revisited and vastly reimagined the scenarios of *Manila* and *Weighed* in the form of smaller, independently financed commercial films such as *Miguelito* and *Macho Dancer* (1989). In returning to his pioneering works, Brocka demonstrated that social melodrama continued to hold the promise of a historically responsive and adaptable long-term project for Philippine filmmaking and cinema politics.

2

"A Thoroughly Different Kind of Mother"

Surrogate Autocrats, Restive Youth, and the Maternal Melodrama

Lino Brocka launched his career with a maternal melodrama called *Wanted Perfect Mother* (1970). Lifting plot elements from *The Sound of Music* (Robert Wise, 1965), Brocka's debut picture follows the plight of a young woman who, employed as a governess, helps an affluent family move past their grief over losing the mother to a car mishap. The subgenre of maternal melodrama preoccupied Brocka throughout the two decades of his filmmaking. Interestingly, from the mid-1970s to the early 1980s, his movies in this subgenre lacked the heartwarming glow of his debut picture. Instead, at the center of these later films, lies the figure of the virulently authoritarian matriarch. This chapter dwells on the significance of the hostile mother across three of Brocka's most acclaimed films: *Insiang* (1976), *Whore of a Mother* (*Ina ka ng anak mo*, 1979), and *Cain and Abel* (*Cain at Abel*, 1982).

Maternal melodramas, according to Mary Ann Doane, "play out all the permutations of the mother-child relation."[1] This kind of picture, paradigmatic of the woman's film in 1930s–1940s Hollywood, became a staple in Philippine cinema. Part of what explains its popularity to this day is America's irrevocable cultural influence. Film critic Noel Vera observes another key factor: "Philippine cinema is dominated by the twin themes of love of mother and survival of the family."[2] Eliciting popular response, Vera suggests, is the *amor mati* inscribed in Filipino movies' deep affective formations.

It is important to note that in the Philippines—a country where the cult of motherhood never waned—"monstrous mothers"[3] similar to those in Hollywood films rarely appeared in domestic movies and television shows, except perhaps as the *madrasta*, the cruel stepmother.[4] The recurrence of this aberrant figure in the martial law era is oddly surprising, given the usual characterization of strongmen leaders as overbearing national fathers. Logical expectation points to those types of patriarchs as Marcos stand-ins. Surprisingly, with the exception of such figures as the incestuous father in Mike de Leon's *In the Blink of an Eye* (*Kisapmata*, 1981) and the controlling paterfamilias in *Wildflower* (*Ligaw na bulaklak*, 1976), the monstrous patriarch was largely absent in the era's most accomplished works. The domineering mother, in contrast, kept recurring not only in several of Brocka's melodramas but also in other films and television programs.

Brocka's maternal melodramas appear to set up two simultaneous levels of substitution. On one level, which remains entirely subtextual, the harsh father doubles for the tyrannical leader while the defiant but virtuous son stands in for the political revolutionary. On another level, which the films dramatize, domineering mothers and their clashing (often female) offspring embody, respectively, the two male figures noted earlier. The melodramas of hostile mothering, in other words, allegorize Marcos's dictatorship and his antagonism toward the nation's restive youth. The maternal relation in these films substitutes for the paternal. These allegories, however, do not detail the exact workings of the authoritarian regime. They render only the broad dynamics of dominance, submission, and resistance. Historically speaking, this apparent limitation had its advantage. The displacement of the paternal dissimulated the enmity toward the Marcos regime. This occlusion may have helped the films avoid extreme censorship.

Alongside the figure of hostile matriarchy in Brocka's films stands its counterpoint: the self-abnegating mother. This contrapuntal figure harkens back to the martyrs in Hollywood classics such as *Imitation of Life* (Douglas Sirk, 1959) and indeed in much of Philippine cinema. This other figure of benevolent mothering constitutes the afterimage of dictatorship's victims (including their loved ones) in real life. Following a tradition in Philippine art, the virtuous matriarch may also represent Inang Bayan or Mother Country.[5]

The idea that hostile mothers can double for the male tyrant sounds extravagant, but it has precedent in film historiography. In Spanish melodramas produced during Francisco Franco's autocratic regime, according to Marsha Kinder, "the father is usually absent, idealized and sometimes replaced by an ineffectual surrogate."[6] Kinder adds that in those films "mothers frequently stand in for the missing father as the embodiment of patriarchal law and an obstacle both to the erotic desire of the daughter and to the mimetic desire of the son."[7] The rebellious offspring's desire to defy the harsh patriarch manifests through "perverse displacements between the mother and the father." For Kinder, the Oedipal conflicts of the Franco era resulted in matricidal fantasies.[8] The historical and cultural links between the Philippines and Spain likely account for the maternal melodrama's similar functions in both national cinemas.

Notwithstanding the Spanish precedent, I realize that one limitation the maternal melodrama suffers is its typical emphasis on the nobility of female sacrifice.[9] This limitation makes the subgenre an unlikely vehicle for sociopolitical critique.[10]

Further, some might say that my argument about the maternal substitution of paternal autocracy warrants an ethnographic, historical study of reception. It is not my claim, however, that viewers of Brocka's films actually interpreted his hostile matriarchs as Marcos surrogates. My argument is largely speculative, and its starting point is not a piece of historical evidence but rather a strange lacuna. I was astonished by the virtual absence of the tyrannical patriarch in the films of the period. Such absence has prompted me to look for this figure in its proximate other, that is, to see through the visage of the maternal.

To call a father or mother *authoritarian* is not to say that the parent champions political authoritarianism. In this chapter, however, it makes sense to conserve both the domestic and political registers of the term. In Brocka's melodramas, the harsh mother possesses what Max Horkheimer describes as an "authoritarian character."[11] Referring to the same trait, Theodor Adorno along with his colleagues uses the phrase "authoritarian personality."[12] Adorno's original conception makes no distinction between individual authoritarianism and state authoritarianism. The term "authoritarian personality," moreover, points to an entire sociopolitical formation: the "nondemocratic," the "antidemocratic," and the "fascist mentality" informing racism as well as totalitarianism.[13] The earliest studies of the authoritarian personality illuminated the family's role in shaping attitudes of reverence or defiance to authority, whether at home or in larger collectives such as nations and ethnic groups. As Franz Samelson writes: "In a patriarchal society, the family became the place where the state's structure and ideology were molded. By embedding sexual inhibition and fear in the child, the family produced identification with the authoritarian imperialism of the state."[14]

While Marcos refused to see himself as an overbearing father of the nation, he behaved as such. After declaring martial law in 1972, he instituted a curfew, ordered the mass incarceration of political rivals, and enabled the torture and killing of dissidents. Contrasting the president's rigid stance, his wife Imelda presented herself as a nurturer. The first lady, acting both as the minister of human settlements and governor of the Manila Metropolitan Development Authority beginning in the late 1970s, launched ambitious programs aimed at caring for the bodies of Filipino citizens. She created mass housing projects, built hospitals, and established feeding programs for indigent youth. In the 1980s, as Ferdinand's health declined due to lupus and kidney disease, he positioned Imelda to succeed him.[15] Because Imelda tirelessly cast herself in the role of benevolent mothering, however, the substitution at work in the maternal melodramas stops short of assimilating her into the image of the hostile matriarch.

INSIANG

The opening scene of *Insiang* shoves viewers rudely into a dark, steamy abattoir. Pigs hang on a conveyor belt that drags them through the stages of slaughter. Dado the *matadero* (Ruel Vernal) stabs each animal and slits its neck. The carcasses plunge into a vat of boiling water. The belt then carries them to an automated apparatus that removes their hair. The slaughtering machines roar. The pigs, still kicking, squeal. The cries are disproportionately loud, as though the dead animals, too, continued to emit sounds, creating a phantom chorus. The slaughterhouse, Brocka suggests, is an uncanny image both of the hellish slums and the nation writhing in the grip of violence.

Dado turns out to be less fearsome than his lover, a middle-aged fishmonger named Tonia (1930s star Mona Lisa, in a casting coup).[16] Tonia's scowl only begins to suggest her appetite for destruction. The fishmonger is the mother of the eponymous Insiang, short for Potenciana. Along with the relatives of Tonia's estranged husband, all thirteen or so of them cram into a one-room shack where they inevitably see each other's bodily functions. The household's large size and composition are typical in Manila shantytowns. According to ethnographer F. Landa Jocano, whose work Brocka cited while promoting *Insiang*,[17] the multifamily household of "slum social organization has become matricentric." The fathers have gone to jail or simply abandoned the family.[18]

Tonia deserves credit for taking on freeloaders and protecting them from the perils of slum life. But the melodrama positions her as a loathsome villain. To borrow Kinder's phrase, Tonia is a "repressive patriarchal mother."[19] She also embodies the traits that Adorno identifies with the authoritarian personality. She is cold, stern, domineering, overly strict, compulsive and highly punitive.[20]

Tonia's authoritarian personality is evident in the way she runs her household. While the iron fist is the common trope for autocratic rule, the mouth is the true locus of Tonia's control. She wields tremendous power by regulating her lodgers' access to food. Beyond their need for shelter, their dependence on the sustenance Tonia provides is what ensures her control. The matriarch carps about her food expenses often when her dependents are eating. Tonia's words also hold extraordinary power. When she commands, her dependents obey, acquiescing to her every whim. If they ignore her, she cuts them down with rapid-fire insults. Even Insiang suffers from her mother's nagging. Tonia insists on collecting her daughter's earnings and at one point, asks Insiang to repay her for "everything I've fed you since you were born."

Tonia cultivates her power through other means beyond verbal abuse. Like a true autocrat, she punishes those who cross her with severe measures, such as expulsion from her realm. The freeloading relatives witness her sovereign wrath when, after a spat, Tonia wastes no time evicting them. Part of the scene's cruel absurdity is that on the street, Tonia demands from two evicted children the clothes she once gave them and asks the kids to undress right there. She collects their clothing even if it is of no use to her. This display of power is also implicitly addressed to Insiang. The patriarchal mother is using the threat of eviction to strike fear in her daughter's heart.

FIGURE 2.1. Tonia (Mona Lisa) complains about food expenses to her dependents. *Insiang.* Courtesy of Danilo Brocka/CCP Library.

Tonia, in fact, has been scheming to make room for Dado in her house all along. Her display of power forces Insiang to accept her scandalous affair with the strapping young man. The mother's sexual satisfaction comes at high cost, however, incurring her daughter's resentment. Ronald Wintrobe notes that within the politics of authoritarianism, flagrant acts of repression occasionally backfire. They increase the likelihood of revolt stripping the dictator of power.[21] The threat of being deposed consequently breeds paranoia in the autocrat. In Brocka's melodrama, the patriarchal mother develops precisely that fear when it dawns on her that Dado is infatuated with Insiang.

From the first time Dado and Insiang share a scene, it is clear that the slaughterhouse worker only has eyes for the fishmonger's daughter. Insiang is an exceptional beauty, radiant against the backdrop of Tondo, Manila's worst slum. Dado leers at her from the window of a motorcycle cab. Simulating his point-of-view, the camera zooms lurching at Insiang amid the squalor that litters the field of vision. The *matadero* is not the only guy caught under the spell of his lover's daughter. The belle of Tondo entertains two suitors: the mechanic Bebot (Rez Cortez) and the storekeeper's son Narding (Marlon Ramirez).

The blossoming of Insiang grates at her mother's ego. The autocratic parent grows more repressive than ever, and the meek heroine turns into an angry rebel. This scenario is hardly surprising in light of Adorno's observation that the child of an authoritarian is not always "broken" into lifelong submission to other authority figures. "Instead of identification with parental authority, 'insurrection' may take place."[22] Adorno's text persuades me to advance a symptomatic reading linking *Insiang* to its contemporaneous political reality. Insiang exudes a sexual power that destabilizes Tonia's control and weakens her composure. Paranoia, as a result, grips the authoritarian matriarch, fuels a bitter contest with her own child, and foments revolt. The daughter's insurrection reflects the young political activists' defiance of Marcos in the late 1960s and 1970s.

Tonia's rivalry with Insiang worsens the very night Dado starts living with them. At bedtime, the matriarch wastes no time cozying up with her lover even though only a flimsy curtain separates them from Insiang. Tonia feigns some concern for privacy. She asks Insiang to let the faucet drip so that the steel drum can fill up overnight. The sound of dripping water offers little distraction from the lovemaking noises. With Dado's encouragement, Tonia quickly overcomes her concerns about behaving amorously toward him in front of Insiang. The mother even giggles and coos loudly when he touches her, perhaps to flaunt her virility to her daughter. As if overhearing Tonia's canoodling and coital exertions were not enough, Insiang ends up having to fend off Dado's sexual advances.

Late one night, Dado sneaks away from Tonia's side. He grabs Insiang as she returns from turning off the faucet. He clamps her mouth shut, punches her gut, and rapes her just within earshot of her mother. The film abbreviates this scene of pseudo-incestuous sexual violation, and the victim takes only a short period to grieve it. A scholar of family life in the Philippines sheds light on the strangeness of this episode. Belen Medina notes that incestuous rape in the country often goes unreported because "it is sometimes seen by the mother as a private matter, and kept within the family."[23] This habit of secrecy partly explains Tonia's reaction when she learns about the rape from Insiang. The mother initially believes her daughter but takes no action. Dado confronts the accusation and tells Tonia that it was Insiang who seduced him. Choosing to believe the lie, Tonia takes her lover's side.

Insiang flees her mother's house. She heads straight to the garage where Bebot works, asking him if he still wished to run away with her. They spend a night at a Chinatown motel. Waking up alone in a seedy room the next morning, Insiang figures out that all Bebot wanted was to bed her. She heads back home and alters for the worse, but the film encourages viewers to identify with her metamorphosis. The once-hapless daughter turns into something like the mother she scorns. She even comes to exceed her mother's licentiousness and vindictiveness. A recurring image suggests that Insiang's brimming sexuality is both a source of power and a

FIGURE 2.2. Hilda Koronel (left) plays the insurgent daughter to Mona Lisa's patriarchal mother. *Insiang*. Courtesy of Danilo Brocka/CCP Library.

danger to her. Juxtaposed with the steel drum overflowing, faucet unattended, are shots of her sleeping in a mosquito net as if under water. An erotic surplus occurs alongside the risk of drowning. Insiang realizes that her beauty can be used to right the wrongs she has suffered. Learning to wrest control of her sexual currency and to profit with revenge, she first takes aim at Bebot and Dado. Manipulating Dado, she then tears down the matriarch.

Intent on vengeance, the scarred heroine rejects a respectable marriage proposal. Narding seeks her hand despite rumors that Bebot and Dado have despoiled her. Marrying Narding is likely to purge her tarnished honor. Insiang also stands to gain a better economic future with him because his family owns a convenience store attached to their house. Marriage prospects, however, mean nothing to the woman who has disavowed the patriarchy. Rejecting the chance at maternal bliss, Insiang hastens to plot her enemies' destruction. She trades in sexual favors and lures others to mete out punishment on her behalf. She convinces Dado to assault Bebot. Dado and his hooligan friends drag Bebot to a secluded corner of a landfill where one goon brandishes a scavenger's pick made of wood and rusty nails. The film does not show the beating. Viewers only learn of Bebot's fate later when neighbors gossip about the loss of all his teeth.

After dispatching Bebot, Insiang goes after Dado and her mother. She heats up her seduction of Dado when Tonia is nearby. Desperate to keep the *matadero* and Insiang apart, Tonia takes her daughter with her to work at the fish stall. Her attempts at control fail miserably, and jealousy consumes the matriarch. She eavesdrops on Insiang flirting with her lover. She wakes up at night to check if he has left her side to lie with her daughter. Insiang feeds this paranoia, making sure that Tonia is within earshot when Dado asks her to run away with him. Mad with rage, Tonia stabs Dado in the back and chest. The image of the bleeding *matadero*—hands upraised, stare frozen—recalls the film's title scene.

The dramatic opening was a notably late addition. Brocka and his crew found the abattoir "while on location hunting."[24] The filmmaker decided to use it as Dado's workplace, drawing a parallel between the slaughterhouse and the murder scene. The teleplay by Mario O'Hara that served as the basis for his and Lamberto Antonio's screenplay rendered Dado's character originally as a menial laborer at the market where Tonia sells fish.[25] Brocka likewise switched one detail in the murder. While the teleplay indicates a pair of scissors as Tonia's weapon, the film shows her using a knife as though to expunge the difference between the butcher and the pigs stabbed at the beginning.[26]

The daughter's scheme of reprisal pays off. The matriarch loses not just her authority but her very freedom. The extreme rupture of the filial bond here is anomalous even by the standards of maternal melodrama. Typically, in Hollywood and European renditions, maternal melodramas see at least one of the women walking away with a modicum of happiness after the struggle. A famous example is the bittersweet ending of *Stella Dallas* (King Vidor, 1937). It shows its eponymous heroine (played by Barbara Stanwyck) watching her daughter's wedding secretly from afar. The scene tugs at heartstrings because it comes after Stella's decision to fall away from her daughter's life. The mother's self-exile enables the daughter to marry well and ascend the social ranks. Such sacrifice is also the stuff of maternal melodramas in the Philippines.[27]

The severity of maternal conflict in *Insiang* drew the ire of the censors. They prevailed upon Brocka to change the ending. For them, sheer common sense dictated that "in the Philippines, a daughter cannot hate her mother."[28] The issue the censors took with Insiang's defiance is significant. In the climate of distrust that the regime created, ambiguity in films stirred paranoia. *Insiang* gives no full account of either the matriarch's belligerence or the daughter's lethal resolve. Hostility occurs from the start—even before the male object triangulates conflict and turns it into a rivalry. The hostility's apparent lack of origin opens the themes of domination and reprisal to treacherously multiple readings. Scorn for the matriarch appears to encourage hatred of authority itself—a stance that for obvious reasons, no dictatorship can tolerate.

Acquiescing to the censors, Brocka revised the conclusion. In O'Hara's teleplay—and in one of the story outlines prepared for the censors—the ending depicts Insiang gloating before she leaves Tonia to rot in jail.[29] "No, mother, I never loved Dado," Insiang crows. "I loathed him. You and I have now changed places, and I am finally avenged."[30] The teleplay's final sequence shows Insiang taking over her mother's stall at the wet market, "looking very pleased at her job, smiling at every customer who approaches." In contrast, the assembled film shows Insiang begging forgiveness, which Tonia denies her. Another version of the story outline, possibly incorporating the censors' recommendations, specifies that "Insiang leaves the prison in tears" after her mother's rejection.[31] Downplaying Insiang's defiance, this ending represents the matriarch's imprisonment as a pyrrhic victory for the daughter.

Brocka executes the censors' preferred conclusion—but in a richly ambiguous way. In his assembled film, the daughter's lachrymose reaction seems contrived. Koronel, the actor playing Insiang, performs a well-calibrated shift in her expression. After wiping her tears, she goes into complete emotional withdrawal. Her remorse suddenly feels insincere. By the time Insiang leaves the prison in the final shot, she looks drained of affect. A reporter quotes Brocka describing the ending as "neither yes or no," which is also an apt description of what her face signifies. "That's the nice thing about cinema," the director adds. "You don't even have to state it. Because if you do, you rob your audience of participation."[32]

An impassive mask indeed provokes variant readings. Vanquishing the mother, the daughter takes her place. She either has managed to "liquidate"[33] authoritarian traits or simply has internalized them. Paradoxically thus, the daughter's triumph may also have broken her spirit. Insiang's emotional withdrawal may indicate the continuing effects of brutalization. Alternatively, it may point to utter recoil from the actions and rhetoric of autocratic figures. Such recoil may be regarded as a novel defense against tyranny, a passive act of civil disobedience, or even a passive support of treason. While the authoritarian state anxiously holds vigil over insurgency, it often lacks the power and imagination to deal with peculiar forms of resistance.

"Slum Movie" Politics

Exactly how the Marcos regime interpreted the sociopolitical critique and antiauthoritarian provocation of *Insiang* remains in shadow. The dearth of government records prevents me from further inquiry. The unease *Insiang* generated among censors, nonetheless, supports my reading of its provocation. Months after its domestic premiere, Brocka tangled with another division of the censorship board. The regime tasked this division to issue so-called export permits for local films to be shown abroad. The division initially denied *Insiang* a permit when the Cannes International Film Festival organizers selected it for their Director's Fortnight.[34] The censors took issue with its portrayal of the slums. "I tried to explain to the Board that a squatter area which is the setting of *Insiang* can be found all over the land," Brocka said. "I asked for the intercession of Undersecretary [of Defense] Carmelo Barbero who didn't see anything wrong with my movie. Barbero I think advised the board that ghettos are all over the world." The censors ruled, however, that slums do not represent "a true image of the country."[35] The regime certainly was not the first to politicize the image of destitution in the movies. Its language echoed what cinema scholars recall as the Andreotti Law of 1949. That law in Italy blocked from exportation any film that "might give an erroneous view of the true nature of our [that] country."[36]

The fracas over the slums is a critical moment in Philippine cinema history and the Marcos regime's cultural politics. Jo-Ann Maglipon, a journalist close to Brocka, reported that Imelda Marcos loathed his film's slumland panoramas.[37] The first lady, after all, was obsessed with beautifying Manila. The transformation of the capital was meant to showcase the regime's purported successes in economic development, humanitarianism, and the arts. Expensive beautification projects required the clearing of the very places Brocka featured. The persistence of slums—both on and off screen—undermined Imelda's attempts to dazzle foreign dignitaries and international visitors with historical conservation projects and modern architecture.

It is easy to understand why Imelda fretted over the use of shantytown backdrops. As in Brocka's *Manila in the Claws of Light* (*Maynila: Sa mga kuko ng liwanag*, 1975), the spatial motifs of *Insiang* blasted open what the regime built to hide: abjection. Heaps of garbage ringed the place where Brocka shot much of the film. The landfill at Barrio Magsaysay in Tondo (later known as Smokey Mountain) gave scavengers a livelihood, but its toxic fumes and landslides endangered the community. The depiction of these precarious lives predates the film adaptation. O'Hara's teleplay describes the slum setting as "a place that is inundated with knee-deep flooding during the rainy season but is still muddy year-round."[38] To realize the space O'Hara described, production designer Fiel Zabat converted a waterside shack used for unloading the fishing yield, into the set of Tonia's home for the film.[39]

Through the storyline, production design, and cinematography of *Insiang*, the slum became metonymic of the regime's intolerable conditions. The excessive presence of trash in the film heightens the impression of squalor. The spatiality peculiar to informal settlements comes alive in the film's cinematography by Conrado Baltazar. There is an abundance of panoramic establishing shots and deep-space compositions. Baltazar's camera work meanders deftly through the arteries where bodies circulate and clot. The dense urban fabric leads viewers to infer that the physical and social environment shapes the vicious conflicts there. The slum folk in *Insiang* have neither heart nor hope. They seem to have few redeeming qualities beyond an instinctive will to live. Nosy, envious, spiteful, and hypocritical, they turn out to be as rotten as the trash heaps that surround them.

FIGURE 2.3. Conrado Baltazar's deep-focus cinematography and Fiel Zabat's production design create a vivid portrait of the slums. *Insiang.* Courtesy of Danilo Brocka/CCP Library.

In a different way, the squatter (informal settlements) issue concerned another Marcos family member: the president's daughter Imee. Brocka "actually toyed with the idea of casting Imee in the title role of Insiang," Maglipon relates.[40] A budding actress on the legitimate stage, Imee had already appeared in Bertolt Brecht's *Mother Courage and Her Children* in a theater her mother built. No record documents why Brocka considered the president's daughter for the role of a slum lass. Brocka's friendship with Imee before he became politically active in 1983 may have been a key factor. While he confided his disdain for Imelda to friends, he socialized with Imee and even visited the presidential residence. Brocka relates in a little-known interview that he used to watch movies in Malacañang with Imee and her siblings, Ferdinand Jr., and Irene. "We used to laugh a lot," Brocka says, recalling their discussions on the movies. "Good times, you know."[41]

Brocka's casting coup fell through. Despite that, Imee sponsored the fundraising premiere of *Insiang.* Proceeds went to the Philippine General Hospital's burn unit and the outreach program run by Assumption College for squatter families resettled in Sapang Palay. Imee's involvement, however, seemed not at all benign. The presidential family tried to co-opt the meaning of what Imee called one of Brocka's "slum movies."[42] Three articles, printed three days in succession, shed light on the clever tactic. The name "Imee R. Marcos" gains prominence in one press release calling her "the over-all chairman for the premiere presentation."[43] Another article, printed in a Marcos-controlled newspaper, makes a preposterous claim. "The basic message of the movie," this second article states, is that "the problems of slum living can be solved by intelligent resettlement."[44] A third press release likewise frames the slum problem in terms of "the crying need for people in such areas to be relocated and offered a better future." Such is ostensibly "the message Director Lino Brocka imparts through '*Insiang*.'"[45]

With Imee in the spotlight, the film's first exhibition turned into a publicity stunt for the Marcos family. As noted earlier, the "chairman" of the premiere allocated part of its funds to a resettlement community. Sapang Palay was a creation of the previous administration, but the Marcos regime was eager to appropriate it and project the image of success for its own relocation efforts. In 1975, a year before *Insiang*'s release, Presidential Decree Number 772 criminalized squatting. It authorized the demolition of all illegal constructions, including the "buildings on and along *esteros*," that is, along canals and other interstitial sites.[46] Demolitions continued after 1976, the year *Insiang* reached theaters, when Imee's mother Imelda assumed the post of governor for the entire metropolitan Manila area. The first lady's architectural enthusiasms produced an ironic reversal. Relocation projects were only "successful in freeing particular sites for real estate development by legally recognized owners," writes Michael Pinches. But the "large numbers of relocated squatters, who were predictably unable to make a living away from the city, simply returned to squat elsewhere."[47] Manila's beautification relied on the cheap labor of the destitute who were pulled back to the city. Thus, even with formidable legislation and coercion, the Marcoses failed to halt the proliferation of slums. Resettlement could not solve the problem of housing the urban poor.

No part of Brocka's melodrama alludes to squatter resettlement. Remarkably, one of the story outlines of the movie includes an epilogue featuring the government's efforts at slum-clearing and relocation. Insiang in this unfilmed epilogue watches "the demolition of their slum house in preparation for relocation to another area, and hopefully, another life, a new future."[48] Demolition and resettlement present a better alternative to "the 'violence' of congested areas," the synopsis suggests, "and the loss of human dignity." The film's production script, however, omits this final scene. Whether or not the filmmakers only added that section in the story outline to please the censors is unverifiable. What cannot be disputed, however, is the regime's impact on both the making and reception of *Insiang*.

The Transnational Flux of Meaning

Brocka made *Insiang* on a tight shooting schedule and with scarce resources.[49] To meet the deadline for the Manila Film Festival, he filmed in "16 days and exposed only 27,000 footage where he would sometimes use up [to] 50,000."⁵⁰ CineManila, the director's production outfit, ran out of funds to complete the picture. With additional financing from the young businesswoman and restauranteur Ruby Tiong Tan, Brocka reportedly delivered the picture under its projected 600,000-peso budget.[51] According to Tan, *Insiang* broke even at the tills.[52] Its box office draw was attributable to the director and his star. Brocka enjoyed a following among critics and viewers who appreciated the quality of his commercial films. Once a popular teen starlet, Koronel was building her reputation as a dramatic actress after starring in high-quality television serials directed by Brocka.

Most of the domestic reviewers praised *Insiang*'s bold "experimentation in realism,"[53] its unusually vivid but "simple description" of "real life"[54] and "slum life."[55] Echoing the reception of Brocka's earlier "serious" and "prestige" films, various critics praised the maternal melodrama's "social relevance" and "social commentaries."[56] Billy Balbastro called *Insiang* the "one relevant film in the festival . . . simply because it is now." He added: "It pulses with today's problems. It is a slice of truth."[57] Pio de Castro III gushed with mixed metaphors in assessing the film, regarding it as a "lacerating surgical examination" and as "Brocka's vision of the Slum as Wasteland and crucible for the spirit," which the filmmaker "deftly painted stroke by stroke." Interestingly, de Castro states that the film's "main flaw seems to lie in the characterization of Insiang," who "remains cold and remote" largely "because the audience does not know what she wants." As a result, "Dado and Tonya appear to be more sympathetic."[58] De Castro's reservations are worth probing. A degree of cognitive dissonance appears to be at work in his perception of Insiang's inscrutable affect. What appears to have repelled the critic was Insiang's embodiment of youthful rebellion so fierce, novel, and perplexing as to seem unreal. The nation's young activists, in reality, were becoming frighteningly mercurial. At one moment, they contented themselves with peaceful street protest, demanding social justice and freedom from tyranny. At the next, they were resorting to violence—hurling Molotov cocktails at the police, hatching schemes to storm the palace, and killing soldiers involved in counterinsurgency operations.

The 1978 Cannes International Film Festival exhibited *Insiang* in the Director's Fortnight. After a stupendous festival outing, the film gained theatrical release in France later that year.[59] Pierre Rissient, an advisor to the festival's director, picked *Insiang* for Cannes while scouting for new work in South and Southeast Asia. Dealing Brocka a great service, Rissient described the film to the press in ways both familiar and appealing to the continental audience of world cinema. With huge clout in Cannes, bearing the moniker of "éminence grise of French cinema"[60] and having been Jean-Luc Godard's assistant director in the legendary new wave film *Breathless* (À bout de souffle, 1960), Rissient confidently declared before the festival that Brocka was standing "on the threshold of an international career."[61] He was right. *Insiang* earned Brocka a loyal following in Europe.

The French raved about the melodrama. Quibbles were minor and few. Brocka's "trés beau cinéma"[62] earned high praise for its masterful direction, performance, and cinematography. One critic described it as "truly revelatory."[63] Another regarded its resistance to Hollywood convention as an example of a "renewed Philippine cinema."[64] Critics looking for an Asian precedent pondered the influence of Yasujiro Ozu[65] and Akira Kurosawa's "great universal cinema," recalling, in particular, a very similar everyday scene in *Dodes'ka-den* (Kurosawa, 1970).[66] There were critics citing Luis Buñuel *Los olvidados* (1950) as a touchstone for the portrayal of derelict youth.[67] The images of dispossession in *Insiang* also earned comparisons to Italian neorealism, linking the film to Vittorio De Sica's *Bicycle Thieves*.[68] Not surprisingly, most critics traced the film's sensibility to "*la tradition des grands mélodrames amércains*."[69] The apt if not always flattering comparison calls to mind the Philippines' colonial relationship to the United States.

Reviews praised the unflinching look at the Philippine condition. The critic for *L'Humanité* assured readers that "social ills fester just beneath the melodrama."[70] A writer for *Rouge* noted that: "The film puts underdevelopment on trial."[71] Another wrote that even though its depiction of "a population suffering from unemployment, wallowing in promiscuity, and living hand-to-mouth in filthy slums" remains rhetorically neutral, *Insiang* gathers and presents all the facts to mount an "indictment" of Philippine society.[72]

There were also assessments specifying the film's political implications. Brocka related to journalists in Cannes that the Marcos regime had censored *Insiang*. Taking up this fact, French critics came to dwell on the film's antiestablishment stance.[73] A capsule review in *L'Express* stated that the film "is above all a fascinating political radioscopy" that enables a deep and objective perception of working-class life.[74] M. Dumas, writing in *Le Quotidien de Paris,* wondered about the film's relation to the "authoritarian political system" in the Philippines, which the "European spectator" would find of special interest.[75] An unnamed reviewer in *Le Canard Enchaîné* praised the film for "offering the dictator, Ferdinand Marcos, a scathing social critique."[76] Eugène Guillevic, who traveled with Rissient in Manila, also named Marcos in an article promoting the French theatrical release of *Insiang*. Guillevic's article situated *Insiang* and three other Brocka films (*Manila; Weighed but Found Wanting*; and *One, Two, Three*) in relation to political unrest. Guillevic was alluding to the national referendum Marcos called—and rigged—in 1977 to legitimize yet another unconstitutional extension of his term in office.[77]

Most remarkable in these early responses is the way they described Tonia. The critic for *Le Canard Enchaîné* regarded Insiang as a "ravishing laundress [who is] tyrannized by [her own] mother and solicited by her mother's lover." Another reviewer, writing for *Le Point*, also links Tonia to "tyranny."[78] Even more telling, the critic for *L'Humanité-Dimanche* called the matriarch "authoritarian and violent."[79]

The language used by the French critics validates my account of her as a hostile mother and a Marcosian double.

CAIN AND ABEL

Another Brocka film six years after *Insiang* brought back the "tyrannical mother."[80] Played by Mona Lisa—the same actress in *Insiang*—the matriarch of *Cain and Abel* (*Cain at Abel*) manages her rice plantation and her manor like an authoritarian. Brocka invites viewers to infer that competing in the patriarchal world of rice cartels and *hacienderos* or plantation owners forced the señora to cultivate a tough persona. Widowed at a young age, Señora Pina Lorente built her fortune through hard work.

Like the protagonists of Hollywood maternal melodramas, Pina engages in "excessive mothering."[81] She interferes in the lives of her two sons, both grown men. Although her firstborn Lorens (Phillip Salvador) has taken over the farm operations, Pina insists on having the final say on major business decisions. She also tries to run Lorens's domestic affairs, often criticizing his marriage with Becky (Baby Delgado), their parenting, and their financial investments. She orders Lorens, for instance, to divest himself of his stake in a *kabaret*, a small beer garden run by his friend Jumbo (Ruel Vernal). Frowning upon her son's association with the drinking spot, calling it *sanggano* or "gangsterish," Pina deems it a blemish on "the Lorente family name."

Another mother-son dyad obtains between Pina and her younger son Ellis (Christopher De Leon). The Oedipal script of eroticism and power marks Pina's relationship more legibly with Ellis than with Lorens.[82] Apart from pampering Ellis, Pina's meddling in his life focuses inordinately on his sexual affairs. Expository dialogue reveals how Pina used to keep tabs on her son's indiscretions with lower-class women, usually the daughters of plantation workers. To prevent scandal, the matriarch gave enraged parents hush money and even paid for their daughters' abortions. Among these country women, Pina makes an exception for Rina (Cecille Castillo), the daughter of her most trusted farmhand Pilo (Venchito Galvez). Longing for a grandchild before dying, the old señora insists on having the peasant lass carry her pregnancy to term. Pina offers her work as a housemaid and promises to subsidize Pilo's household.

Even when Ellis returns with his girlfriend Zita (Carmi Martin) after quitting music studies in Manila, Pina continues to smother him. Ellis seems to enjoy it, referring to his mother as his "sweetheart" and showering her with gifts and kisses. These excessive displays of affection, bordering on the improper, are a form of emotional bribery. Ellis convinces his mother to take Zita into the family. On the first night of living with Zita under his mother's roof, the son insists on having sex. Ellis knows that only a plywood wall divides the rooms and his mother's bedroom

FIGURE 2.4. Zita (Carmi Martin, left) lashes out at Pina (Mona Lisa, right), her fiancée's overbearing mother. Rina (Cecile Castillo, center) looks on. *Cain and Abel*. Courtesy of ABS-CBN Film Restoration.

is right next to his. Zita tells Ellis that the bed's creaking bothers her and they have sex on the floor. The son, however, makes no effort to tone down the coital noises.

Ellis eventually declares his plan to marry Zita, but Pina disapproves of her. The mother speaks privately with Ellis and later confronts his new girlfriend. Pina accuses her of being a loose woman—someone her son just happened to pick up at a movie theater, take "to a motel just last week," and call his fiancée out of whim. Pina mocks her for wearing a miniskirt, implying that it reflected her looseness, and commands her to dress modestly. Zita refuses, savvy enough to read the signs of Pina's maternal jealousy as being sexually fraught, and to recognize her wish to determine her son's object choices. The new woman in the family romance quickly reveals herself to be as fierce as the rebel of *Insiang*. Challenging the patriarchal mother of *Cain and Abel*, Zita understands that defeating Pina entails shaking off her psychic grip on her sons.

Overestimating her power, Pina makes a rash decision about her estate. The matriarch grants Ellis the privilege of declaring which properties he wants for himself. What motivates Pina is a recognizable symptom of the authoritarian's fear.

As Milan Svolik reminds us, uncertainty over who either succeeds or ousts the autocrat destabilizes the leader's hold on power. The nagging question of "leadership succession," according to Svolik, is "a perennial source of authoritarian instability."[83] In *Cain*, the crisis of succession occurs most traditionally, hinging on property transfer. Ellis chooses to claim sole rights to the plantation despite having no experience in running it. The choice is no shock to the matriarch. Since childhood, Ellis has been playing a nasty game of one-upmanship with his elder brother. Their romantic competition over Becky, a contest of virility, is part of an unelaborated backstory. Becky eventually marries Lorens after rejecting the younger brother's sexual advances. The film never fully reveals the origins of the fraternal conflict which mounts with Pina's choice for succession. The matriarch initially balks at her indolent son's claim on the plantation but wills it entirely to him, leaving only "a small amount of money to be spent on Lorens's children." Predictably, the apportioning of the estate upsets Lorens and his wife Becky. It even disturbs Zita. The older son's disinheritance fits a lifelong pattern of favoritism and cruelty, which included corporal punishment with a rattan cane when Lorens was a child. When the Lorente patriarch died of a heart attack after witnessing the brothers fight, Pina incorrectly blamed the older son. Threatened with disinheritance, Lorens reveals that he took the blame for starting the fight and that he did so to protect Ellis. The matriarch, however, doubles down on her prerogative. Pina gathers the servants and farm workers for an ad hoc succession ceremony.

The ceremony is remarkable in its depiction of the harsh mother as a substitute for the dead patriarch. To create the symbolic and material force needed to effect succession, Pina mobilizes the memory of her late husband. The ceremony honoring him involves the distribution of money as gifts. What Pina enacts, however, is less the nonreciprocity of true gift-giving than "the political economy of a dictatorship," as described by Ronald Wintrobe.[84] The so-called gifts are in fact bribes for loyalty. At a symbolic register, they forge a continuity between the señora and the dead patriarch. Appropriately enough, the screenplay, using the language of patriarchy, describes Pina as "*babaing padre de pamilya*" or a "female paterfamilias."[85] The ceremony reminds the community that the late Señor Lorente's authority survives through her person, coursing through the material circulation she controls and through her words. The mother thus arrogates to herself the power of the dead to transfer leadership and property to the favored son. When Pina tells her audience that "from now on Ellis will take charge of the plantation," sheer utterance becomes law.

Scholars of the authoritarian personality note that fathers—"stern and distant" and "domineering" fathers—are responsible for their children's authoritarian dispositions.[86] These scholars note further that heavy-handed exercise of paternal authority breeds sadomasochistic tendencies, forming subjects who take "pleasure in obedience and subordination."[87] The children learn to take pleasure in submitting to authority but also in seeing others dominated.⁸⁸ In some cases, however, scholars observe that "henpecking mothers" perform the same function as domineering fathers.⁸⁹ Pina is such a mother, having raised a fellow authoritarian in Ellis and a submissive offspring in Lorens. Paradoxically, however, the dominant son also enjoys submission more than his older brother, while the dominated son enjoys more purchase in masculine virility than his younger sibling. Caught between the nodes of sadomasochistic formation, both similarity and difference between the two brothers fuel their enmity.

The crisis of succession Pina sets into motion not only provokes greed in Ellis. It also costs her the loyalty of Lorens. Clashes with the matriarch quickly ensue following the disinheritance of the older son. Lorens quickly moves his family out of the house overnight, giving Pina no word of his departure. The slighted mother tells her household that Lorens and his family are no longer welcome at the manor. Because Pina has underpaid Lorens over the years, he can afford only a drab small house to shelter his family, one just slightly better than the kind of dwelling plantation workers occupy.

Zita criticizes Pina's treatment of Lorens. Far from the bimbo Pina takes her to be, Zita poses one challenge after another to the patriarchal mother. Although Zita stands to gain from Lorens's estrangement, she brokers peace between the brothers. She pressures Ellis to meet Lorens and begs the older brother to return to the manor. What Zita pursues is no longer simply the attempt to keep the mother's power at bay. Zita ends up trying to reconfigure fraternity past rivalry, to affirm a kind of relation maintained along equalizing horizontal vectors. The patriarchal mother, hence, finds in Zita a rebel much like Insiang. Zita's insurgency, however, is subtle and nonviolent in bypassing the hierarchical, vertical relations that the autocrat zealously maintains.

Zita's refutation of autocratic power emerges in another scene, when she takes Rina aside and tells her gently about the engagement with Ellis. The dialogue generates an unspoken bond of sisterhood, undoing the conventional narrative of women fighting over the same male object. It may be true that the vertical relations of patriarchy do not wholly collapse in this encounter between women, which maintains the allure that the heteronormative prospect of marriage holds. Nonetheless, what Zita brings to the fore is the possibility of self-other relations no longer dependent on the logic of domination and submission found in patriarchal motherhood.

Unfortunately, the mother's actions have already borne serious consequences. Even with no prompting from Lorens, Jumbo and his thugs launch a vendetta against Pina and her favored son. When Ellis and Zita search for Lorens at Jumbo's *kabaret*, Jumbo harasses them, and Ellis hyperventilates, apparently lacking virile courage as a result of excessive mothering. At the beer garden, a place reeking of violent masculinity, panic triggers the weak son's asthma and unmans him. Retaliating for Ellis's humiliation, Pina removes Lorens's children from her will. A pregnant Becky implores her husband to protect his children's future, but he opts to hold back. Frustrated by his cowardice, Becky storms Pina's home and berates her mother-in-law. The odd gender reversal—with women waging battles on behalf of men—testifies to the patriarchal mother's emasculation of her sons. Rage unchecked, Becky grabs a cup of coffee and throws its contents at her mother-in-law. Ellis comes to the matriarch's defense and slaps his sister-in-law. Lorens joins the fray and attacks his brother. Ellis accidentally shoves Becky during the scuffle, hurling her into a corner. She hits her swollen belly against a console table and starts to hemorrhage. As if to expose manhood as being more destructive than sisterhood—and fraternity, more destructible—Zita rushes to Becky's aid while the brothers continue to fight. When Lorens comes to his senses, he rushes his wife to the hospital, but Becky expires en route, cradled in Zita's arms. Lorens stops the vehicle, pulls his wife out, and kneeling by the road, gathers her lifeless body and weeps. Stepping back, Zita leaves him to his grief. The scene, composed like a pieta, recurs in many of Brocka's films. The camera takes up Zita's point of view, turning the film's audience into witnesses of the torment the hostile mother has wreaked.

Pina, Ellis, and Zita pay their respects at Becky's wake, but a fuming Lorens drives them away. This public repudiation of Pina sets off an all-out assault on her matriarchy. In the subsequent episodes, Brocka draws out implicit parallels between the explosive family feud and the state growing increasingly violent with autocratic rule. Pina loses her harvest when unseen men torch her freshly bundled rice stalks. The farmhands—among them, Rina's father—rush to stomp out the flames but fail. The estranged son looks on, lurking in shadow, and flits away from the burning fields. In a more brazen attack, unseen persons (most likely Lorens, Jumbo, and his fellow thugs) strike Pina's house with gunfire. While Ellis runs to hide in terror, the matriarch dashes out, weapon ablaze, her twelve-gauge pump action shotgun firing at the enemies. Pina's show of hostility is absolute, needing no further comment in light of my argument about substitution. As for Lorens, his aggression calls to mind the insurgency raging beyond the city. The assault on parental authority reflects the militancy of Filipino youth activists against the Marcosian state. Brocka stages the crossfire at the plantation as a scene metonymic of "the people's revolution" in the countryside.

The political significance of the clash between mother and sons rings loud as a volley of bullets. Such meaning is more evident in the second instance of a tragic death in the family. Zita confronts Pina about the way the matriarch has pitted her sons against each other. "The mother is a gangster," Zita says: "*Sanggano ang ina*." Escalating the violence, Zita warns, is likely to destroy both sons. Zita once more tries to broker peace, but she crosses paths with Jumbo's men as they hunt down Ellis. Abducting Zita, they shove her into a cluttered storage room. A thug assaults

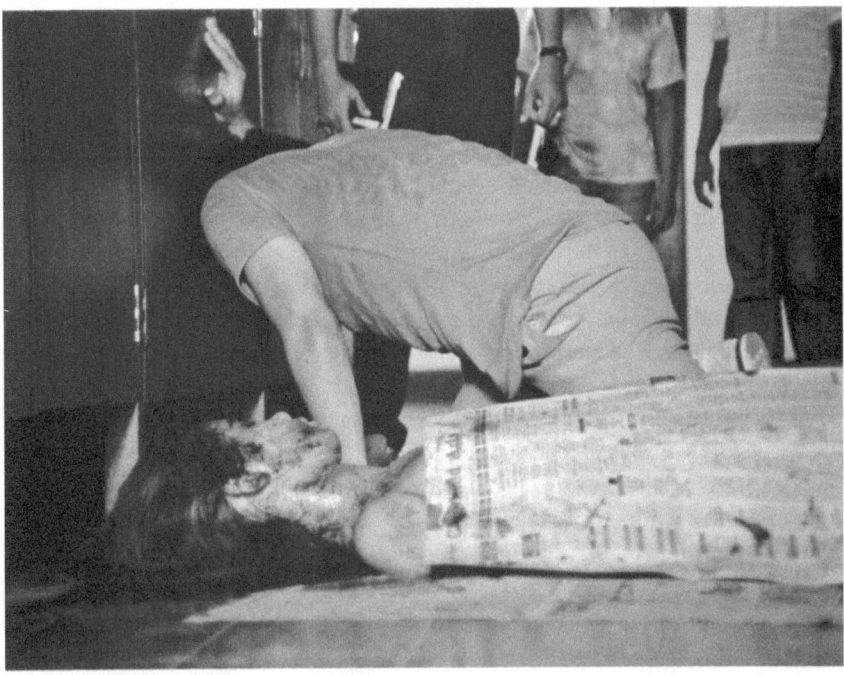

FIGURE 2.5. Zita (Carmi Martin, foreground) is murdered and her body disposed of in a manner reminiscent of political killings during the Marcos regime. *Cain and Abel.* Courtesy of ABS-CBN Film Restoration.

her below the waist. Brocka does not show what goes on down there, but Zita's horror is enough to convey the brutality.

In the next scene, Ellis rushes to the town hall where people are crowding around Zita's lifeless body partially wrapped in newspaper. The scene of death occurring in a town hall, a place saturated with state power, is an emphatic reminder of the Marcos regime's summary executions. The regime was notorious for using state agents to liquidate its political enemies and dump their corpses in places that ensured discovery. There was an element of spectacle in these killings. Ironically called "salvaging," they functioned as a gruesome warning against dissent, keeping citizens fearful and docile.[90] In Brocka's film, the bloodied corpse wrapped in newspaper strains the capacity for human recognition. When Ellis sees Zita's body, disgust overwhelms his recollection of the living image. The sight of the dead loved one makes Ellis vomit. Interestingly, Brocka revised this scene's elements during the making of the film. The script originally called for Zita to be found dead in her car, apparently strangled with a pair of stockings.[91] Whereas the script visualized the effects of a rape-slay motivated by personal conflicts, the scene as filmed calls attention to the visual tropes of state-sanctioned murder. The town hall setting points to the deep constraints that the regime placed on redeeming the memory of persons who were victims of so-called salvaging.

Within days, Zita's brother Robert (Michael Sandico) escalates the conflict. He arrives from Manila with high-powered M-4 and M-16 military grade rifles, plenty of ammunition, and trigger-happy friends. Robert notes gleefully that his buddies are rich hooligans from Dasmariñas, a posh gated community. He boasts about their heinous crimes in the big city. One crime involved "raping a woman crippled by polio." Robert brags about one of his friends taking the hapless woman "right there in her wheelchair!" He also describes their wild shooting sprees after getting high on drugs. Armed with sophisticated weapons and identified with the urban elite, Robert and his friends call to mind two kinds of figures associated with Marcosian violence. First were the public officials' sons and daughters—vicious spawn infamous for their drug use and high-profile crimes including the rape and killing of celebrities. Second were the members of the military and internal security forces, many of whom turned gun-crazy and abused their legal monopoly on firearms. In the company of such hooligans, Ellis finds a means to prop up his weak masculinity and quickly adopts their violent ways. The once-cowardly son forms a vigilante squad with Robert and his friends, acting with military precision in killing off Jumbo's men. These scenes in *Cain and Abel* are disturbingly reminiscent of the state agents tasked with the "salvage" operations mentioned earlier.

As the armed conflict between the brothers heats up, Pina passes away in her sleep. Pina's lack of remorse marks a contrast between her and her son Lorens. The portrayal of her death scene significantly departs from the story outline presumably submitted to the censors. The outline reads: "Pina prayed all day and all night, not only for the sins of her warring sons but most especially for her own because she had caused all these [sic] bloodshed."[92] Given Lorens's response to the death of Zita, the outline's insertion of remorse would not have been ill-conceived. Lorens did not premeditate Zita's abduction and murder. Upon learning of it, he starts to claim responsibility for the way the war, spinning out of control, has racked up casualties. Unlike Lorens, however, Pina in the filmed version performs no act of contrition before dying. Brocka leaves her unredeemed, an authoritarian to the very end.

After the death of the matriarch, *Cain and Abel* winds down to a didactic finale. Scenes of vigil briskly give way to the staging of Pina's legacy of destruction. First, mowed by gunfire from Jumbo's men, Rina and her child die in front of Ellis just a few hours after he sneaks into the manor to visit them. News of their demise moves Lorens to make one last try at resolving the conflict. He seeks Rina's father, Pilo, and asks him to arrange a meeting between him and his brother. Ellis, despite his rage, warms to the idea. Weary of losing his loved ones, he, too, has come to question his row with Lorens. "What else are we fighting for?" he asks Robert.

Ellis agrees to meet Lorens at an appointed place in the forest. Just as Lorens thanks Ellis for showing up, the hooligan Robert, hiding in foliage, yells that Lorens is reaching for a concealed gun. Ellis shoots Lorens, who is actually unarmed, and instantly regrets it. Jumbo, also lurking nearby, fires back at Ellis. The gunshot proves fatal. With his dying breath, Ellis addresses Lorens as *kuya*, "older brother." Lorens glances at his younger brother to acknowledge the gesture, and also expires. After several bursts of gunfire, the forest falls silent. The camera zooms out and frames the two brothers' corpses, Ellis in a military jacket with a patch bearing the phrase "U.S. Army," a clipped reference to the state's repressive power. The final image harks back to the movie's first shot showing a spider fight, a traditional Filipino game that involves placing a pair of spiders on a stick and forcing them to duel. Implicit in this parallelism is Brocka's tragic vision of the longstanding ideological conflict between the militant Left and the Marcos regime. No victor emerges in the end.

Cain and Abel concludes with the image of death in the heartland to index the militarization of the countryside and spaces close to the wild. Strewn with the dead, the forest emerges as a place metonymic of unrestrained hostility, calling to mind the sites of real-life clashes between the military and the Communist insurgents.[93] The film's press kit even highlights the import of the setting, intriguing the reader with the idea of a "fateful meeting between the two brothers in the forest."[94] The image of young men engaged in armed struggle summons the era's popular notion of youthful political activists and underground revolutionaries.[95] To quash these enemies, the dictatorship's anti-insurgency campaigns altered the plains and hinterland into places of widespread brutality.[96] In the film, the obstacle to peace is group violence that culminates in the forest bloodbath. In reality, rigid ideological positions and a habit of war making prolonged the armed conflict in the countryside. The left dubbed it the "protracted people's war," and the state, its "counterinsurgency operations."[97] But neither term registers the savagery that ensued with the militarization of rural and wild environs. Both sides of hostility, *Cain and Abel* suggests, contributed to the havoc claiming numerous lives. The heartland is not by itself savage but, as Brocka depicts it, is made so by human violence. Like the forest battle in the film, the wars in the countryside far exceeded the scope their instigators had imagined.

The rhetoric of dictatorship, ironically, thrived on the public's fear of a society pushed back into a chaotic ideological wilderness. In his rationale for martial law, Marcos warned of the "bloody Jacobin revolution"[98] that might result from "the unrest and the violence,"[99] casting blame on political opponents and dissidents. While Marcos did not characterize them in terms of age, the dissidents included youths taking part in mass actions, occupying the state university, and even storming the presidential palace.[100] The visibility of young people identified them with action that severely needed taming, as William Rempel notes: "Political allies were

FIGURE 2.6. Ellis (Christopher De Leon, left) and Lorens (Phillip Salvador) are mortally wounded during a forest shoot-out that recalls real-life encounters between the military and leftist insurgents. *Cain and Abel*. Courtesy of ABS-CBN Film Restoration.

pressing Marcos to take sterner measures against the student activists."[101] The dictator calculated that the leftist youth would join forces with "the reactionary right."[102] Apparently, they were also ready to cast their lot with Muslim secessionists, private armies, political warlords, and criminal elements.[103] Marcos posited that all these state enemies would figure "in a fratricidal clash of arms, a bloody social revolution."[104] This idea of collaboration among sworn enemies was absurd. Deteriorating social conditions during and after martial law were, in truth, what led to a "fratricidal clash of arms" between insurgents and the authorities.

An image of ideological differences crystalizes in the conclusion of *Cain and Abel*. While the brothers resolve their feud and recognize that their hostility has contaminated an entire community, their goons refuse to give up fighting. This plot point draws an implicit distinction between familial and ideological conflicts. The ending prevents the film from rehearsing what critics of melodrama lament in the genre—namely, its tendency to reduce political conflict to psychological tensions, or to conflate them.[105] Quite the contrary, what *Cain and Abel* portrays is a decisive split between the resumption of a fraternal bond and the perpetuation of hostilities at the group level. The goons' refusal to back down is symptomatic of the ideological rigidity with which both dissidents and the state pursued their battles. What the split between brothers and their hooligan friends reveals is the turmoil into which martial law plunged the nation. Brocka thus inscribes the toxic family romance with the signifiers of political allegory.

A plethora of overt symbols signals the film's allegorical thrust. Among them are figures of the subhuman, the dueling spiders already mentioned as well as the termites infesting the manor—termites being a common metaphor of moral and social decay. The manor itself is figured as a matrix of perverse desire, jealousy, and revenge. Parallelism and repetition contribute to the proliferation of symbols, which at times recur all too neatly. Examples worth noting include the parallel deaths of the two young women, the brothers' separate visits to their mother's tomb, the equal ruthlessness of the brothers' friends, and the similarities between the sons of Lorens and their father and uncle, both of whom are caught in a fractious relationship. These allegorical cues belie the filmmakers' description of the film to the censors as a simple story of enemy brothers. Of the brothers' conflict and the proposed ending, the story outline says: "It was all a mistake. Somewhere in the past in their lives, the mistake had begun, but now it was too late, and they all had to pay."[106] The word *mistake* courts the notion that ideology played no part in the fratricidal war. The outline takes for granted the origins of conflict in an archetypal flaw, as if the filmmakers' chief interest were merely to update a biblical tale.

Like the filmmakers, journalists tiptoed around the allegorical cues. An unidentified writer, though bungling the film's title, quipped that "*Abel at Cain* implies something. The title alone suggests that there is a message in there about two different directions and beliefs in life."[107] Based on the entertainment press' coverage, *Cain and Abel* was received as a "serious" and "important" work.[108] Critics welcomed it as the polar opposite of the "sex comedies" and other commercial movies the director had been making at that time.[109] As one piece remarked of Brocka's latest opus: "After eight years, this is his first movie with the depth (of emotion) and breadth (of intelligence) of *You Were Weighed and Found Wanting*."[110] Perhaps most intriguing is the way journalist Zenaida LaTorre describes Zita's brother Robert as her "revolutionary brother."[111] LaTorre, however, does not expound on her use of a term synonymous with the insurgency. Such reticence over potentially touchy aspects of the film is not surprising in the journalistic and critical writings on Brocka's work. It usually dovetails charged innuendo on social relevance. Some of the writers simply lacked the intellectual curiosity to track the sociopolitical valences of these films, while others sought to protect them from government scrutiny.

The most explicitly political statements about *Cain and Abel* focused on its unusual gender politics. Isagani Cruz found the "strong women characters" to be "most memorable."[112] He went on to say, "These are portraits of the Filipina radically different from the long-suffering, weak, virginal, religious stereotype of conventional productions." The government's newly formed Film Ratings Board (FRB) similarly noted "the presence of the four strong female characters" in its rationale for giving the film a second-best quality rating of "B."[113] Although Imee Marcos controlled the agency to which the FRB belonged, it appeared that she exerted no influence on the decision concerning *Cain and Abel*. The film became the "first ever to be awarded a rebate" in taxes by the board. The FRB citation traced the weakening of "the film's earlier tight structure" to "the escalation of the brothers' feud."[114] The citation tellingly offered no comment on the tyrannical parent as the sower of hostility. To suggest that the FRB actively policed content on behalf of the government is perhaps to go too far. The independent minds on the board—comprised of film industry types and critics—famously granted "A" and "B" ratings to more overtly political films such as Mike De Leon's *Batch '81* (1982) and Brocka's *My Own Country: Gripping the Knife's Edge* (*Bayan ko: Kapit sa patalim*, 1984). The FRB's interpretation of *Cain and Abel* may be viewed accurately, rather, as the state's attempt to shape reception and to depoliticize the cinema.

Predictably, nonetheless, several articles registered public fascination with the hostile matriarch in the film. Pina was variously described as "dominant," "tough, intimidating," reeking of "viciousness," and an "irascible mother" with an "unmotherly attitude."[115] Writers also commented on how her cruelty caused "great misery" and how she seemed "hard-hearted not only to her family members but also her workers."[116] Beyond remarking on traits that seem aberrant in a mother, the entertainment press did not dwell on the implications of her villainy. They left unsaid the strange familiarity of her authoritarian streak and its destructive effects.

WHORE OF A MOTHER

In 1979, between *Insiang* and *Cain at Abel* (*Cain and Abel*), Brocka made two maternal melodramas worth examining. *Heat Wave* (*Init*) and *Whore of a Mother* (*Ina ka ng anak mo*) pivot on the conflict between the patriarchal mother and her rebellious children. *Heat Wave* is a racy adult melodrama set in a remote seaside village in Curimao, Ilocos Norte, whose townsfolk produce sea salt. Osa (Charito Solis), the matriarch in *Heat Wave*, exceeds *Insiang*'s Tonia in cruelty and sexual depravity. Years ago, when Osa's lover forced her into prostitution in Manila, she murdered him but never spent a day in jail. Osa fled to an island where she gave birth to and raised her daughter Bayang (Rio Locsin). One day, a man from Manila is cast ashore. An attractive fellow in his twenties, Emil (*Cain and Abel*'s Phillip Salvador), sparks a sexual rivalry between mother and daughter. Emil turns out to be a shady entrepreneur who betrayed his fellow thugs. They are now hunting him. While Emil desires Bayang, he relies on the food and shelter that Osa trades for sexual favors. Osa's sexual hunger is as intense as her acid tongue and her desire to control everyone around her. Bayang, meanwhile, loses her virginity to Emil. Discovering that Bayang yielded to Emil's advances enrages Osa, and the mother accidentally kills her daughter. After hiding the body, Osa has sex with Emil one last time, frames him for Bayang's murder, and feeds him to a lynch mob.

As with *Insiang*, Marcos's censors brought down the hammer on *Heat Wave*. Objecting to its sexual content, they recalled the permit for *Heat Wave* after its premiere. They required all the board members to review the picture and demanded another round of cuts.[117] Even promotional material for the film was altered. For instance, a silhouette of embracing lovers replaced a newspaper ad showing Locsin pleasuring herself on the sand.[118] Although the film was an exaggerated rehash of *Insiang*—and perhaps Nagisa Oshima's *In the Realm of the Senses* (1976)—the way *Heat Wave* portrayed the hostile mother lacked political resonance. Its island fantasy seemed to cast into watery depths the historical references, allegorical cues, and Marcosian tropes and emblems proliferating in the two films discussed earlier.

In contrast to *Heat Wave*, it is Brocka's other 1979 melodrama that takes up the cinema politics found in *Insiang* as well as *Cain and Abel*. The authoritarian figure in *Whore of a Mother* is the patriarchal mother Renata (Lolita Rodriguez). The conflict at the outset hinges on a problem of mourning the loss of the *paterfamilias*. The mother is at odds with her daughter Ester (Nora Aunor) over the death of her father, Renata's late husband. Ester, a social worker, blames Renata for the loss. Ester claims that her mother's materialism drove her father to seek greener pastures in the United States and work himself to death there. Renata insists that he died of a workplace accident. One fateful night, while Ester is away on a provincial assignment, an inebriated Renata virtually seduces Ester's husband Luis (Raoul Aragon). The one-night stand results in a pregnancy. Renata, a devout Catholic despite her sexual errancy, refuses abortion. The mother and her son-in-law hatch a plot to conceal the pregnancy, but Ester discovers it. The scene in which she confronts the adulterers is unforgettable. Ester finds Renata, who has just given birth, resting in bed with her child while Luis and his friends watch over them. After quietly surveying the room, she stares directly at her mother and exclaims "*hayop!*" ("filthy animal!") The devastated expression and restrained cry of Nora Aunor, channeling Ester, mortifies Renata. Aunor reduced ten words of dialogue to just one, and yet still managed to covey the depth of the character's pain and rancor at her mother.[119]

The daughter sues them for concubinage. When they appear in court, however, she withdraws the charges after seeing them shamed in public. As with the hysterical mother in Brian De Palma's *Carrie* (1976)—a popular film in the Philippines at that time—Renata slips into religious insanity. She becomes a recluse, desperate to atone for her sins. She prays incessantly and stops eating. On her deathbed, she begs her daughter's forgiveness, but Ester withholds it. Denying a person's last wish—especially that of a loved one, however estranged—is deemed a transgression in the

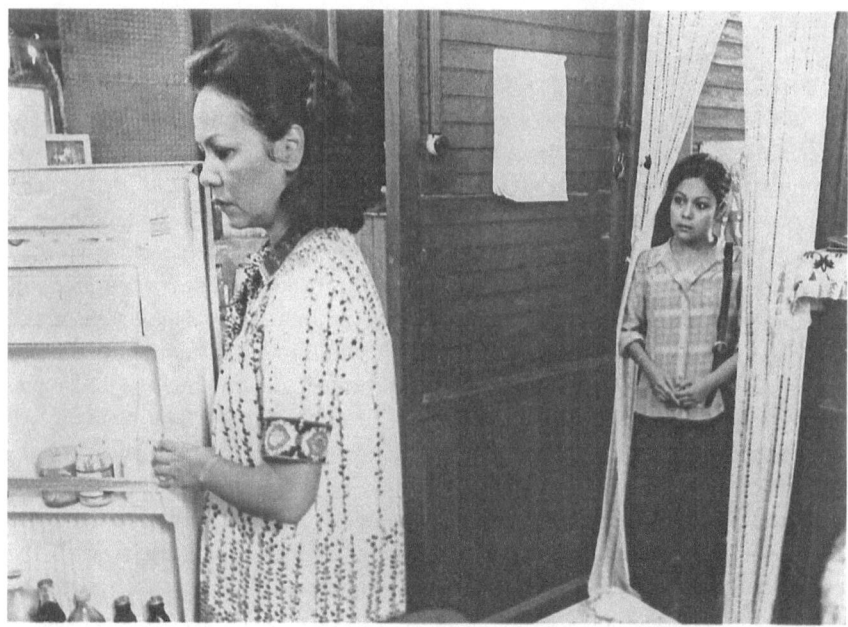

FIGURE 2.7. Renata (Lolita Rodriguez), wracked with guilt over her transgressions, avoids her daughter Ester (Nora Aunor). *Whore of a Mother.* Courtesy of Mario and Cesar Hernando.

Philippines. But when Renata dies, Ester casually leaves her mother's side and asks Luis to deal with funeral arrangements. Like Insiang at the end of her travails with Tonia, Ester steels herself, visage bereft of feeling. The rebellious daughter practically gloats over the authoritarian parent's demise. *Whore of a Mother* adds a coda to mitigate this bleak denouement. A perfunctory happy ending shows Ester fetching from Luis's rooming house the baby who, as a reviewer writes, "is curiously enough, both her brother and her son."[120] Ester takes the infant just before Luis, preparing to leave for work in Saudi Arabia, gives up the child for adoption. Although the marriage is irreparable, the innocent child is saved.

Alongside the daughter's rebellion against her authoritarian parent, several elements in the film harbor signs of civil unrest (and also political grievance). Two motifs are worth noting as features of the living conditions associated with the Marcos era: the recurring power outages, and the labor migration that poverty spurred. These elements were not lost on one reviewer. Mario Bautista took note of Luis's "desire to work in Saudi Arabia to improve their lot in life." Bautista also remarked that the pseudo-incestuous encounter between Luis and his mother-in-law occurred "in the midst of darkness caused by a brownout" ("*sa gitna ng karimlang dulot ng* brownout").[121] Referring to a power outage, the "brown-out" was a constant feature of everyday life under Marcos. They stemmed from an energy crisis that began in the postwar era. In spite of the Marcos regime's lofty promises of development, its botched energy policies and other factors beyond its control deepened the crisis.[122] The problem worsened with insufficient fuel imports, international oil price hikes, and the regime's monopolization and nationalization of the energy sector. Scheduled "brown-outs" in factories halted industrial activity. But unplanned outages also occurred, affecting work sites as much as homes. A short-term solution the regime devised in 1971 was an "energy conservation" campaign. The so-called Enercon program appealed for civic participation in keeping the nation afloat. Its rhetoric was so ubiquitous that a comic-strip parody of *Insiang* criticized Tonia's household for wasting tap water, a resource considered as precious as electricity.[123] The prolonged and "massive" Enercon campaign was actually the regime's attempt to downplay its failed energy policy.[124]

At many instances in *Whore*, the characters grumble about the power outages in Renata's household. These gripes often occur alongside talk about the increasing discomfort of their lives, implicitly venting dissatisfaction with the regime's broken promises of modernization and development. This motif was not initially in Leticia Fariñas's story outline of the film. Fariñas indicated thunderstorms. In the process of adapting the storyline, however, the screenwriter Jose Y. Dalisay Jr. used another motif instead of retaining the imagery of nature. Dalisay opted for historically specific detail, calling attention to a crisis that the regime failed to solve.[125] The "brown-outs" in the assembled film—both the scheduled and random outages—either precipitate or intensify conflicts. Initial scenes portray the three main characters caught up in petty fights in which angry complaints about "increasingly frequent" and "exasperating brownouts" punctuate their bickering. During one of these scenes, a power outage is featured at length, occurring while Renata delivers a tirade against her son-in-law and daughter. The mother reveals her tyrannical streak as she undercuts Luis's masculinity and berates Ester for skipping mass. Attributing Ester's childlessness to spiritual laziness, Renata scolds her for refusing to venerate a saint known for performing miracles of fertility. This scene snuffs out whatever goodwill remains between mother and daughter, and their intergenerational conflict escalates. Another power outage later in the film gives occasion to the pseudo-incestuous tryst in which Luis and his drunk mother-in-law end up having sex.

Throughout *Whore*, Luis dreams of working in Saudi Arabia. He tells Ester early in the film: "I want to get ahead. Lift us out of poverty. There's nothing for us here. I am fed up." What is most compelling in this recurring talk of leaving the country is the avoidance of naming it. During a conversation with his mother-in-law, Luis once again associates the deixis "here" (*dito*) with the country as a dead-end: "If we were to depend on what I'm earning here, we would never get ahead." Each time Luis contemplates life elsewhere, he bemoans the constraints of living in the Philippines, the impossibility of succeeding "here" or much less, getting by. At his most irate, Luis tells a coworker that he cannot wait to leave for Saudi Arabia because: "I can put up with anything, just to get far away from here!" As before, Luis uses the deixis in referring to the country whose name he repeatedly withholds. "Here" places him in a land stripped of economic prospect and shot through with domestic conflict. Quite literally, given its power outages, it is a benighted country. Luis's implied migration when the film ends can be viewed as a form of protest against the unbearable living conditions that martial law produced. The regime, ironically, coopted the subversive act of fleeing. Turning the pathos that spurred migration into a form of currency, it encouraged its citizens to seek jobs abroad and remit their income back home. It is no surprise, then, that the nation Luis wishes to flee is left unnamed. "Here" locates the intolerable in an unspeakable homeland.

When *Whore of a Mother* hit the cinemas, the problems with the censors were few. Fariñas, the author of the film's storyline, was "a writer at the Ministry of Information,"[126] but nothing in the historical record indicates that this factor helped the film pass censorship. Additionally, unlike the storyline for *Insiang*, that of *Whore* ends with a reconciliation between mother and daughter, a scene eventually omitted in the assembled film. Censors apparently demanded a revision in the film's initial title, *You Are Your Mother's Child!* (*Anak ka ng ina mo!*). Most likely, with its exclamation point at the end, the titled jarred because it echoed the Tagalog curse phrase "*Putang ina mo!*" (Your mother is a whore!). The title was altered to *You Are the Mother of Your Child!* (*Ina ka ng anak mo!*).[127] The exclamation point was eventually dropped. In a notice of approval, the censors' "Committee on Storyline Review" raised no objections to the proposed film. A surprisingly preserved rare document, the notice asks the producers to ensure that "the portion depicting the moment of weakness between Renata and her son-in-law be merely implied" and that the story be filmed in "an aesthetic and somber way."[128]

The few reviewers who ventured anything beyond a superficial reading of the film located its subversive energies in a "trenchant criticism of the failure of Christian morality to equip individuals with enough strength [to resist temptations]."[129] None of the critiques or publicity alluded to sensitive political topics. Several articles took note, however, of the matriarch's aberrant personality and the daughter's unusual toughness. Renata struck one writer as "a thoroughly different kind of mother," and as "a strong woman who becomes a weak and remorseful person after she realizes the gravity of the mistake she committed."[130] Another critic, riveted by Aunor's performance, described her character as "willful, rebellious and 'practical' . . . everything her mother is not."[131] Importantly, the same writer, despite being no fan of Brocka's work, observes the popularity of maternal melodramas not only on film but also on television. He made that observation while faulting the director for picking "this same plot in the soap opera [which I have seen] so

FIGURE 2.8. Renata (Lolita Rodriguez, left) makes a final appeal to Ester (Nora Aunor) and Luis (Raoul Aragon). *Whore of a Mother*. Courtesy of Mario and Cesar Hernando.

many times I've lost count." Another writer expressed a similar comment, though in more neutral terms, pointing out the fact that two of the ten films competing in the same festival were about "mother-daughter relationships."[132] While Brocka's film was about "a mother and a daughter riven by several problems," the critic writes, Cirio Santiago's *Bronze Model* (*Modelong tanso*) features Aunor's professional rival Vilma Santos essaying the role of "a daughter overshadowed by her mother's success." These comments about the maternal melodrama's ubiquity indicate the subgenre's popularity and perhaps also, its peculiar timeliness during the Marcos regime.

CONCLUSION

Cutting across the melodramas examined here is the atypical image of the hostile mother. The correspondences organized around this image collectively produce an allegory of the tyrant met with rebellion. The subgenre of maternal melodrama allows Brocka to erase the patriarchal figure in the authoritarian position conventionally assigned to men. This erasure has prompted my account of these films as allegories, with hostile mothers doubling as the father of the authoritarian state. The outraged children, in turn, call to mind the revolutionaries during martial law. Enemy brothers in *Cain and Abel* undermine the hostile mother. The women in

Insiang and *Whore of a Mother* assume the role of both authoritarian parents and their vengeful offspring.

The allegorical thrust in these melodramas of authoritarianism present contradictory directions. On the one hand, Brocka's tactic of substituting matriarchs for patriarchs forestalls direct confrontation with the autocratic state and its censors. On the other hand, there is the more urgent task of cinema politics: that of providing the mass audience a language for grappling with the volatile economy of the authoritarian psyche—with its greed, its paranoia, and its unpredictably wrathful affects. That task falls to the idiom of maternal melodrama, which Brocka made his own.

Substituting the maternal for the paternal, however, is not without retrograde tendencies. As my preface cautions, no matter what good faith any recuperative interpretation holds, the melodramas themselves do not consistently serve the ends of progressive critique. From a feminist standpoint, the figure of the hostile matriarch in Brocka's maternal melodramas is deeply problematic. These narratives vilify women and even toy with the notion that emancipation requires virtual matricide. Marsha Kinder rightly points out that the fantasy of killing the mother is a revenge fantasy directed at the wrong object. "Matricide frequently functions," Kinder writes, "to deny the father's responsibility for violence against mothers and children."[133] The matricidal revenge fantasy harbors a compensatory Oedipal logic. Getting the father off the hook and pinning the blame on the mother, it misses the proper object of just rage.

Brocka's maternal melodramas are indeed Oedipal. Their subversive reference to the male dictator exists right alongside a dubious gender politics. As toxic family romances, they risk perpetuating the misrecognition Kinder decries. The mother in Brocka's melodramas, however, is never entirely herself. Patriarchal violence never ceases to haunt—within the place of power that she occupies—an unaccountable excess, which her extreme hostility can index but cannot adequately substitute. The object of revenge, as a result, stubbornly remains unsettled, and the violence attributed to the harsh mother implicates that of the patriarch. It is a paradox of Brocka's maternal melodramas that they never quite obscure *paternal* tyranny as the object of just rage. The patriarchal state remains unnamed, however, precisely for being more fearsome than matriarchy.

Querying Brocka's gender politics offers yet another interpretive opening beyond the scope of this chapter. It is possible to argue against the reading I have pursued here, that *Insiang* and *Whore* both reject melodrama's Oedipal scenario in favor of what Amber Jacobs calls an "Oresteian" script. In the family romance, both the drama of parent-child bonding and the child's identity formation occur "under the aegis of a symbolic law which the father incarnates."[134] The patriarch's looming influence characterizes the Oedipal script as the "master myth" of Western narratives.[135] The Oresteian script, however, focuses on the mother-daughter bond and more crucially, on the problem of matricide. In the classical tale to which

Jacobs refers, the daughter Electra leads her brother Orestes to kill the queen Clytemnestra. The queen's murder appears merely to terminate a filial bond. Jacobs observes that the loss of the mother is "neither mourned nor avenged."[136] What the Oresteian script tracks, thus, is less the representation of women as monsters than the hostility toward the maternal itself. This other script exposes the pervasive antipathy toward matriarchal figures.

Read as Oresteian scenarios, Brocka's maternal melodramas make visible the antipathy elicited by female power under the Marcosian regime. Whether as state figures or as youths resisting authoritarian rule, powerful women seemed suspect in a political climate in which power was confused with violence, and dissent, with anarchy. Perhaps reflecting such confusion in the films, rebellious daughters serve ambivalent functions. Rehearsing a retrograde gender politics, they stand in for male revolutionaries. But they also embody the young women in real life who took part in the revolution. The autocratic mothers, in turn, provoke hostility not only because their bodies veil an allegorical tie with the male tyrant, but also because their effigies are supercharged with cognitive dissonance in the face of the regime's overwhelmingly patriarchal violence.

The idea of Oresteian melodrama requires another occasion to develop. My point here is simply that portrayals of belligerent young men were more likely to get suppressed because they raised the specter of revolution. Activists and dissidents were often—but not exclusively—represented as male in the popular imaginary. Brocka's maternal melodramas countered the hypervisibility of men in real-life clashes between an oppressive state and revolutionary agency. Allegorizing the struggle against the dictatorship through a story with female protagonists is a boon for both feminist assertion and cinema politics. There is much to explore, as Bonnie Honig notes, beyond the trope of politics as father-son conflict.[137] Breaking with convention—in genres as in gender roles—holds the potential of renewing our vision of emancipatory politics.[138]

In 1983, the assassination of Marcos's rival Ninoy Aquino and the economic crisis that followed altered the gendering of the autocratic parent in some of Brocka's subsequent melodramas. Brocka continued to use the maternal trope in films that registered the disasters that martial law precipitated. Mothers remained prominent as flawed benevolent characters, unlike the matriarchs in the films discussed here. When Marcos's political fortunes took a turn for the worse, Brocka seized upon the male melodrama, specifically its paternal variant, as the preferred subgenre for his increasingly militant works. In one such film, the overbearing paterfamilias and the autocratic politician merge as one figure. This change obviates the need for the authoritarian mother to serve as the dictator's allegorical double. Alongside other developments, this transformation in melodrama's gendered representations of the Marcos regime preoccupy the next two chapters.

3

The Melodramatics of Crime

Film Noir in the Twilight of Martial Law

JAGUAR

At the foot of a mountainous garbage heap, cops are chasing a handsome young man through a shantytown. The pursuers hop nimbly on wooden planks to avoid the muck of excrement and industrial waste. The pursued, a creature of the slums, leaps onto the giant landfill and up its slope in a matter of seconds. The quick succession of shots alternates between the hero in panic and the cops out of breath. The sequence culminates in a series of panoramic high- and low-angle shots. The hero is dwarfed in the frame of these images, as if in the eye of a ruthless god surveying a third world inferno, a dumpsite dotted with small fires, while city lights flicker at a distance. After a brief pause, the camera picks up speed again. It follows the hero as he scampers down the other side where the garbage spills into a river. The cops are nowhere in sight. Suddenly, in the final shot of the sequence, light beams on the young man, picking him out of the darkness. A cop's voice, booming through a megaphone, tells him to stop. The sequence ends with the fugitive's hands raised, his face taut with a look of terror and defeat. This gripping sequence is from *Jaguar*, a 1979 film about a security guard from a Manila slum who accidentally kills a wealthy man while defending his employer's son.

The famous American critic Andrew Sarris, reporting from the Cannes International Film Festival, had the following words of praise for the movie: "The most pleasant surprise of the Festival so far has been Lino Brocka's *Jaguar*, a socially conscious *film noir* from, of all places, the Philippines."[1] The implicit comparison to American crime movies is particularly apt because, among other reasons, *Jaguar*'s climax is reminiscent of the famous uphill chase between cops and the villain of Joseph Losey's film noir *The Prowler* (1951).

FIGURE 3.1. Poldo (Phillip Salvador) scales the enormous landfill called Smokey Mountain, an icon of the Marcos regime. *Jaguar*. Courtesy of Danilo Brocka/CCP Library.

Despite its similarities to US crime films, and although Brocka lavished the attention and funding reserved for a prestige picture on *Jaguar*, his film shared common features with the commercial action-dramas regularly shown on local screens. Those elements include empathy for the poor, a heterosexual romance, and sensational fight scenes. Unlike most action films, however, *Jaguar* offered a heavy dose of social criticism, and for that reason it drew the ire of censors and, reportedly, First Lady Imelda Marcos as well.[2]

As Sarris notes, *Jaguar* contains the elements of film noir, a type of filmmaking often centered on tales of crime and injustice. Film noir features gritty and dreamlike images of cities or small towns, a tone of "pessimism and existential anguish," and such bleak narrative tropes as "eroticized violence, instrumental surveillance, and social and psychological malaise."[3] Film noir did not originate as a genre but rather as a set of stylistic and narrative conventions associated with crime movies and many non-comedic American films from the 1940s to the late 1950s. As James Naremore reminds us, film noir "did not become a true Hollywood genre until the Vietnam years, when productions such as [Martin Scorsese's 1976 film] *Taxi Driver* appeared with some regularity."[4] Post-1950s noir and its trappings—often referred to as "neo-noir"—gained favor among filmmakers worldwide and continue to function "like an international genre."[5] Philippine cinema, which closely follows Hollywood filmmaking, began producing crime films and emulating aspects of the noir style long before the revival that Naremore mentions. That said, the influence of American neo-noir is suggested by the pervasive use of noir stylistics in Brocka's work and the popularity of films such as *Taxi Driver* suggest the influence of American neo-noir.

The preoccupation of crime and noir films with violence, illicit activities, and urban blight makes them especially amenable to the figuration of social reality and politics. Contrary to popular belief, many of those films do not revolve around detectives and gangsters but ordinary persons who are forced to commit crimes or are falsely accused of doing so.[6] Scholars have written of film noir's "obsession with social justice,"[7] its interest in depicting "malevolent capitalism,"[8] and its portrayal of political corruption.[9] They have also found in these movies a capacity to allegorize "the moral issues of the period,"[10] to expose "the process of criminalization,"[11] and to "examine the price of social repression as imposed by the criminal justice system."[12] During the cold war era, left-leaning US directors, scriptwriters, and actors realized film noir's potential for sociopolitical criticism through mise-en-scène and narratives that dealt overtly or metaphorically with fascism, social inequality, and racial prejudice. To cite some examples, the last two issues are treated, respectively, by *The Prowler* and *Body and Soul* (Robert Rossen, 1947). Several scholars have applied the term *film gris* (gray film) to about a dozen works with a "greater focus on social realism" than the bulk of film noirs made between 1946 and 1951.[13] These progressive crime movies were created by filmmakers who were blacklisted from Hollywood or shunned due to their association with Left politics.

Scholars have described film noir—with its narratives of wayward or beleaguered men—as a form of male melodrama.[14] This admittedly counterintuitive notion is grounded in history, for as Elizabeth Cowie points out, "films later considered *films noirs* were [previously] described as 'crime melodramas.'"[15] The term *melodrama* originally denoted a sensational form of storytelling while *drama* more narrowly corresponded to stories centered on women and the domestic sphere. Steve Neale notes that up to the 1960s, the US film industry's trade journals labeled as melodramas "war films, adventure films, horror films, and thrillers, genres traditionally thought of as, if anything, 'male.'"[16] Even in their more recent iterations, noir and crime films contain elements that betray their roots in melodrama. These include an expressive mise-en-scène, stark contrasts between good and evil, plots that feature coincidences and multiple threads of action, an all-consuming quest for justice, and a moralistic ending.[17] Raymond Durgnat elegantly sums up the crime film's relation to melodrama in a much-cited quote. "The American film noir," he writes, "paraphrases its social undertones by the melodramatics of crime and the underworld."[18] The cultural work of such sensational and absorbing tales lies in parsing troubles with the law.

In this chapter, I shall discuss the political valences of three noir films by Brocka. I am particularly concerned with their figuration of Philippine society under the authoritarian rule of Ferdinand Marcos. The films appeared during the so-called period of "normalization," the three-year transition phase of graduated political liberalization that led to the conclusion of martial law. It was during this period, which stretched between 1977 and 1981, that the dictatorship ended the curfew barring Filipinos from leaving their homes between midnight and four o' clock in the morning.[19] The gradual lifting of curfew starting in the first year of "normalization" registered, if only implicitly, in the extensive nighttime ventures of the characters in Brocka's films.

I shall devote much of this section to *Jaguar*, the most accomplished of Brocka's noir films and the one that famously grated on the Marcos regime. I offer a condensed treatment of *Angela markado* (1980) and briefly reference *Caught in the Act* (1981) to enrich the discussion. Former political dissidents scripted the first two films, Jose F. Lacaba and Ricardo Lee writing *Jaguar*; Lacaba independently penning *Angela*'s screenplay.

It is worth noting that Brocka was already savvy with the elements of noir even before making *Jaguar* and *Angela*. To cite just one example, *Manila in the Claws of Light* (*Maynila: Sa mga kuko ng liwanag*, 1975) featured images of urban blight and oneiric nighttime scenes reminiscent of film noir. He continued to draw inspiration from this type of filmmaking after directing *Manila* and the films discussed here. *Jaguar* and *Angela*, however, embody his fullest engagement with noir. To track the dark pursuits of these two films is to gain deeper insight into noir's sociopolitical functions in a country under authoritarian rule. I venture that Brocka's fascination with noir aesthetics is linked to the problem of vicious class striation and the practices of surveillance and torture during the Marcos dictatorship.

Noir's Class Melodrama

Social mobility, Paula Rabinovitz argues, is one of the "central tropes of film noir."[20] She goes on to say that a "class melodrama"[21] animates many such films. Along similar lines, Kristen Moana Thompson identifies an entire subset of crime movies particularly concerned with social mobility. She calls them "aspirational crime films" and writes that their narratives typically "understand crime as an act of free will, motivated by an ambitious desire to rise or escape from poverty or class."[22] Another scholar notes that in noir films' grim, class-inflected tales, rapid social mobility amounts to a "punishable deviation from one's assigned place," and often ends tragically.[23]

The opening moments of *Jaguar* telegraph the recurring idea that Leopoldo Miranda (Phillip Salvador), the film's hero, desires to escape the slums at all costs. To make himself presentable to the world beyond the shantytown, he grooms himself like a middle-class urbanite: he wears deodorant and cologne, a big watch,

FIGURE 3.2. The well-groomed Poldo (Phillip Salvador) leaves his filthy environs for work. *Jaguar.* Courtesy of Danilo Brocka/CCP Library.

shiny leather shoes, well-pressed pants, and perfectly combed hair. He abhors the disheveled alcoholics loitering at the store and chastises his sisters for socializing with other slum kids. On his daily commute to work, he squeezes through an opening in a tall, white wall neatly separating the informal settlements from the rest of the city. Such barriers were a Marcos-era commonplace, designed to beautify the metropolis for tourists and the upper crust.[24] This part of the protagonist's routine is emblematic of his status as an interloper between social worlds.

Poldo—short for Leopoldo—works as a security guard at a publishing firm that issues entertainment magazines and comic books. His post at the building's reception area is within earshot of a room where the publisher's heir, Sonny, entertains a parade of female companions. One evening, Poldo comes to Sonny's aid by breaking up one of the latter's tussles with his longtime friend Direk (Johnny Delgado). Poldo subdues both Direk and his lackey, which Sonny finds impressive. Direk (Filipino slang for "director") got his nickname after making a sexploitation film with his father's money. He and Sonny fight over women—and male buddies—all the time.

The incident shows Sonny that, like Direk, he also needs a lackey if he is to survive his troublemaking ways. It may even be the case that he develops a crush on Poldo.

This is not farfetched: indeed, one of Sonny's friends makes fun of his homoeroticism with Direk. "Direk and Sonny are like spouses," he says. "Always fighting and then quickly making-up." Moreover, one of Sonny's women later intimates that he might be queer, referring to him behind his back as "*silahis*" or bisexual. Sexual tension between men is not unusual in Brocka's work and crime films more generally.[25] As Durgnat suggests of film noir, "intimations of non-effeminate homosexuality are laid on thick," and "homosexual and heterosexual sadism are everyday conditions."[26] Among male figures in film noir, perversities—including gayness—often signal moral corruption. More complicatedly in *Jaguar*, Sonny's homoerotic yearnings indicate an attraction to men while also being symptomatic of a capitalist heir's megalomaniacal desire to accumulate beautiful possessions, especially people.

Soon after the brawl at Sonny's office, Sonny and Direk reconcile, and they ask Poldo and Direk's lackey to do the same. Sonny then announces Poldo's entry into their clique. Direk suggests that they also give him a nickname: "Jaguar" (an anagram of "guwardiya," meaning "security guard" in Filipino). The next day, Sonny gives Poldo a lift in his flashy sports car, driving his employee all the way to the Tondo slums. The kind gesture moves Poldo and encourages his fantasies of social mobility. Poldo begins to tag along with Sonny and his friends at discos and runs with them in the middle of the street while high on drugs. His feeling of oneness with his boss and his boss's friends deepens into what Paul Arthur calls a "slippage in class identification."[27] The latter typically occurs in film noir when criminals from the lower classes suddenly come into money or when affluent fugitives from the city go into hiding with rural folk. For Poldo, sustaining the fantasy of class mobility entails financial sacrifices. Performing unwaged work for Sonny, Poldo furthers his exploitation. Typically, workers like Poldo resist their employers' attempts to lengthen the workday without recompense, but Poldo happily serves as Sonny's bodyguard in between shifts guarding the press. Poldo also increases his spending on clothes and grooming, using up his meager earnings to keep up with Sonny and his friends.

Not surprisingly, Sonny appreciates Poldo's obsequiousness. He tests Poldo's loyalty by commanding him to do progressively riskier things on his behalf. For instance, Sonny asks Poldo to buy him an unlicensed firearm. The scene in which the latter delivers the gun illustrates both the lopsided relationship and the mutual attraction that binds them. Poldo is visibly dazzled when he enters Sonny's room. He quietly scans the place, marveling at Sonny's possessions. Sonny takes notice and offers him an unworn long-sleeved shirt from his closet, along with a couple of hand-me-downs. Sonny rather tenderly asks Poldo to join him in front of the mirror and try on one of the garments. Sonny tugs at the fabric to make it drape better on Poldo and beams proudly while gazing at their reflection. The gesture impresses Poldo. One can tell from his expression that he is prepared to offer virtually everything he has to Sonny in gratitude for such small acts of kindness. Indeed, Poldo has already broken the law by procuring the weapon.

Poldo emulates the boss's gesture by presenting the shiny firearm as if it were a gift. This time, it is Poldo who beams as Sonny admires the weapon. Poldo gently reminds him to be careful because the gun is loaded. Sonny responds—tenderly, as before—by assuring him that he knows what he is doing, even if he clearly does not.

Following the conventions of film noir, *Jaguar*'s class melodrama grows more complex with the entrance of a strong and enigmatic woman. Direk introduces Cristy (Amy Austria) the featured go-go dancer at his club to Sonny and their other friends. Once again, the acquisitive Sonny covets one of Direk's possessions. Within a matter of days, Sonny enlists his factotum to locate Cristy in one of Manila's shantytowns. Sonny lures her away from Direk by putting her on the cover of a magazine and promising to introduce her to "real" filmmakers. Incensed by the betrayal, Direk breaks into Sonny and Cristy's love nest and trashes the place. He also makes an implicit death threat by leaving behind a funeral wreath bearing Sonny's name. Sonny assigns Poldo to watch over her after the break-in. Cristy tries to get over her fears by throwing herself at Poldo. He only briefly resists the temptation, thrilled by the idea of romancing his master's woman.

Michael Walker notes that films noir often contain not one but "three interlocking sexual triangles."[28] There are at least that many in *Jaguar*, such as the love triangle of Sonny, Poldo, and Cristy or, less obviously, the all-male threesome of Sonny, Poldo, and Direk. These triadic relationships thrive on a peculiar mix of attraction and friction among members of disparate social classes—and also, to a lesser extent, on repressed homoeroticism. Late in the film, Sonny tries to salvage one of his dysfunctional relationships. Accompanied by Poldo and Cristy, Sonny heads to a disco that Direk frequents to make peace with his oldest friend. Instead of making amends as planned, however, Sonny changes his mind and does the opposite. He sneaks up on Direk and punches him. Fisticuffs ensue between the feckless scions' gangs. Sonny, Cristy and his rich friends dash out of the club, leaving Poldo to fight Direk and his three goons by himself. Poldo aims Sonny's gun at Direk but begs him and his men to step back so he does not have to fire at them. Direk does not comply. Although Direk is unarmed, Poldo still pulls the trigger, hitting him in the head. Discovering that Sonny and his crew have left him behind, Poldo escapes on foot. He learns while in hiding that the shot he fired was fatal.

Some extra-textual information is useful here. Although Poldo committed manslaughter rather than murder, a Marcos-era law practically conflated the two felonies, making "killings done with unlicensed firearms automatically punishable by death."[29] When Poldo shows up later at Cristy and Sonny's apartment, Sonny offers him pocket money and tells him to go into hiding. Poldo realizes—and tells his boss—that he has nowhere else to go. Having been born into the urban working class he is, to borrow Amy Wendling's words, "precariously removed from kinship structures" enjoyed by the bourgeois and by country folk.[30]

Taking pity on Poldo, Cristy secretly arranges for him to board with a couple at the house in the slums where she used to reside. She later informs Poldo that Sonny's and Direk's fathers—longtime friends, like their sons—had reached a truce. Direk's father has promised not to harm Sonny if he hands Poldo over to the cops. The news devastates Poldo, who was still clinging to Sonny's pledge of assistance. Cristy severs her ties with Sonny and further aids Poldo by arranging for his escape to a distant island where he might assume a new identity and start over. On his last night in the slums, the police conduct a surprise dragnet operation popularly known as "*sona*" (zoning). Poldo, afraid that the cops are running a *sona* expressly to root him out, sneaks out of the house and escapes into the dimly lit periphery of the slums. He makes the mistake of brandishing a gun at some male bystanders, who proceed to gang up on him. He accidentally fires the weapon, attracting cops who, it turns out, were not searching for him in the first place. The police corner him after the chase described at the beginning of this chapter.

Cristy and Poldo's family come to see him at the police station. She brings presents and relates that her movie career is taking off. Sonny turns up unannounced to visit Poldo, prompting the other visitors to leave. He begs Poldo to take all the blame for Direk's killing, promising to foot the bill for a good lawyer. Poldo, who has been relentlessly flicking his lighter to contain his anger, finally snaps. He leaps at Sonny and strangles him. The cops restrain Poldo and throw him back in jail. An officer carps at him, but he does not say a word. Poldo stares obliquely at the camera and, in a succession of close-ups and zooms, his still-seething but also vacuous expression fills the screen. The images telegraph the devastating effects of his ordeal. The episode's jailhouse setting suggests that Poldo is not simply a victim of class antipathy but also of state repression.

The scenes of his arrest and jailing constitute what I have been calling in this book a "Marcosian moment." Through specifically cinematic means, such wordless depictions of violence expose a crisis in social relations wrought by authoritarianism. The paroxysm of fear that grips the characters, the abrupt welling and waning of their affective capacities, the supercharging of the mise-en-scène with sociopolitical meaning—these elements register the violence of autocracy, albeit without direct reference to the Marcos regime. By looking almost directly at the camera, the character onscreen establishes a rapport with the film's viewers, stirring their emotions and telegraphing statements that could not be openly expressed or shown. This powerful motif of state violence is found in many Brocka movies and is carried over into the aftermath of the dictatorship.

Apart from the melodramatic effects orchestrating its Marcosian moment, *Jaguar* makes other statements about the tyranny of class and state domination through cinematic elements associated with crime and noir films. One example is

FIGURE 3.3. Police restrain Poldo (Phillip Salvador, right) after he attacks Sonny (Menggie Cobarubias). *Jaguar.* Courtesy of Danilo Brocka/CCP Library.

the nighttime scene in which Poldo finds shelter in a partially burned-down dwelling. This moment comes after he loses his remaining places of refuge, namely: his mother's home, which the cops surround, and Sonny's place, where he is no longer welcome. In this moment of painful solitude, Poldo recalls a conversation he once had with his mother, when he giddily told her of his deepening friendship with Sonny. The memory returns through a sound flashback that plays over the image of our despondent hero. The exchange goes like this:

Poldo: Wouldn't you know it, I have a boss who treats me like a friend? And he's rich too. Finished college. I, on the other hand, only got to high school—and poorer than a mouse. Still, he treats me like an equal—like, uh, like a brother!
Mother: A brother?! I think he treats you like a servant!

Poldo tears up as he recalls the dialogue, realizing that his much-vaunted friendship with the boss's son was not what he thought it was. The scene dramatizes a process called "demystification." Robert Stam, following Karl Marx, characterizes demystification as a means of "stripping the conditions under which we live of their drapery of legalistic and moralistic concepts by confronting society's self-image, its schemes of representation, its mystifications, and idealizations, with its real-life processes."[31] The memory of the conversation undoes Poldo's delusional identification with Sonny and the upper crust. The fragments of sonic flashback evince the shattering of Poldo's cherished fantasies of inter-class friendship and social mobility. At this late moment—and in melodrama, it is often "too late"[32]—he becomes acutely conscious of the depths of his exploitation and alienation.

The substance of the film's "moral lesson," and even the image of the protagonist seeking refuge in an abandoned building, derive from the true-to-life story upon which the film's screenplay was loosely based. In the 1961 nonfiction story "The Boy Who Wanted to Become 'Society,'" the renowned author Nick Joaquin (writing as Quijano de Manila) weaves a narrative of class conflict around the fatal shooting of an upper-middle-class teen. Joaquin describes the killing at a restaurant in a Manila suburb, for which a teenage slum kid named Napoleon Nocedal (better known by the moniker Boy Nap) was responsible, as the tragedy of "an upstart, a social climber, who was intent on gaining status at any price, of crashing the old society of purple titles and blue blood."[33] Like Poldo, the criminal in Joaquin's story is a young man who "came in contact with moneyed, flashy teenagers and began to rebel against his lot." Invested in a fantasy of sudden class mobility, Nocedal "was living beyond all his means—financial, physical, and emotional."[34] Like Poldo, Boy Nap was the type of person who "in spite of the heat, is always fully dressed, in trousers and shirt." He "envied all the boys who were so reckless and audacious," mirroring Poldo's fascination with the bad-boy behavior of his rich friends.[35] Brocka's film and Joaquin's story present the deadly confrontation as a flashpoint of class antipathy. Joaquin concludes his story by invoking a famous American class melodrama: F. Scott Fitzgerald's *The Great Gatsby*, which he describes as "a novel about another poor boy whom the rich used and discarded."[36] Brocka, in turn, references *Gatsby* in interviews he gave to French journalists during *Jaguar*'s Cannes screening.[37]

The broken promise of social equality in Joaquin's story and Brocka's *Jaguar* resonate with Marcos's vow to heal class divisions through the social and economic policies of martial law. In *Notes on the New Society of the Philippines*, Marcos characterizes pre-martial law Philippines (what he calls "the old society") in melodramatic terms, as "a sick society of privilege and irresponsibility" controlled and nearly burned to the ground by the "rich minority."[38] The elite, says Marcos, enjoys the "extravagances of the 'high life,' while the majority of the people are virtually ill-fed, ill-clothed and ill-educated."[39] He promises that martial law will usher in a "New Society," a "community of equals" where "the needs of the poorest of the working people take precedence over those of the rest."[40] "Equality," Marcos asserts, "should be the ideological force behind the New Society."[41] Embracing populist rhetoric, he defines equality in terms that an ordinary citizen would find comprehensible and appealing: namely, that every Filipino will have access to "three square meals, a roof over his head, efficient public transport, schooling for his children, and medical care for his family."[42] Marcos adds that the nation could only attain true social equality through the "regulation and distribution of wealth" and the internalization of "national discipline" under martial rule.[43]

True to his pledge, Marcos aggressively seized wealth from oligarchs but redistributed the spoils mainly to his family and cronies. He also harshly disciplined the citizenry but never delivered on his promise of equality. As the economist James Boyce reports, the "increase in inequality [during the Marcos regime] was so great that many people experienced an absolute decline in their standard of living."[44] He adds that: "Between 1971 and 1985, both rich and poor experienced real income declines, but in percentage terms the incomes of the poor fell more than the incomes of the rich. Hence inequality continued to widen."[45] The result was "strong polarization" in which the rich became "absolutely richer, and the poor absolutely poorer."[46] Martial law's failed promise to relieve social inequality resulted in the intensification of class struggle in the Philippines. The crime rate returned to pre-martial law levels in the late 1970s and membership in the socialist revolutionary movement grew steadily.[47] *Jaguar*'s class melodrama registers both the making of the promise of equality and the disappointment that followed when the pledge was broken.

Censorship and Defiance

The explosion of class antagonism in *Jaguar*—the film's movement from the utopia of inter-class friendship to the dystopia of class warfare—caught the attention of the regime. According to a journalist close to Brocka, the film upset Imelda Marcos: "Now she considered him downright subversive, for he had characters in there getting back at their masters. . . . As expected, she had him brought to her. 'I don't like your films, Lino,' she gave it to him straight. 'They're pessimistic, hopeless.'"[48] Brocka recalled the conversation a decade later in an interview: "She found my movie *Jaguar* very depressing. . . . I told her that she didn't understand it. 'I am not advocating violence,' I said. 'What I am saying is when things don't change it seems there is only one option left for these poor people and that is violence.'"

Brocka's reference to violence likely pertains to Poldo strangling his boss near the end of the film. The director goes on to say: "He's not a dog, that's what he [Poldo] was saying through the last act. I don't have to state it. And you know what she said, 'Yes, I understand that but how many of us intellectuals understand that?' I am quoting her!"[49]

In an interview given during *Jaguar*'s Cannes premiere, Brocka related that other government officials shared Mrs. Marcos's misgivings about the film. The censors also despised its resolution as well as the pattern in his oeuvre of protagonists turning violent. He recalls that the censors pointedly questioned how "characters, so different from each other, with dissimilar occupations, somehow end up behaving the same way."[50] Brocka justifies Poldo's outburst at the jail by comparing him to the protagonists of *Manila in the Claws of Light* and *Insiang*. "They accept everything, they suffer without flinching, but as soon as you take away something dear to them, they are ready for anything." Later in the interview, he adds: "*Jaguar* is maybe only a small contribution to the awakening of the spectators; yet, as with *Manila*, I was blamed strongly for its tragic conclusion."[51]

Brocka was more forthcoming about his sociopolitical critique in the press kit for the film's international release. Confirming the note of defiance in the ending, he said: "People say that there was no fight in 'Jaguar.' I beg to disagree. In the end, he has fully realized the stupidity of his servitude. The ending is [actually] the beginning. He is now a man."[52] In light of Poldo's outburst, Brocka's references to an "awakening," a "fight," and a new "beginning" indicate his awareness of the film's progressive valences. To be sure, it would have been unwise of him to acknowledge that tendentiousness explicitly, even to foreign critics and journalists who raised the issue. Given the strictures of martial law, it became the duty of those foreign critics and journalists to explicate the politics of Brocka's films without getting him into too much trouble with the Philippine government. Let me cite a few examples. In *Revue du Cinéma*, Max Tessier describes Poldo's assault on Sonny as a "violent revolt" that comes after the hero finally snaps out of his "blind obedience" and "stupefaction."[53] Tessier seems to imply a political allegory, one in which "naïve and blind obedience" and "stupefaction" under capitalism correspond to the citizen's subservience to the authoritarian state. In *Variety*, Gene Moskowitz describes Poldo as eventually "running amok" after failing to contain his "restrained rage."[54] Michel Ciment describes a similar flashpoint in his review for *L'Express*. "*Jaguar*," he writes, "speaks of a country on the brink of exploding."[55] In another French publication—*Cinématographe*—Jacques Fieschi refers to the film's "political bitterness."[56] His term reinforces Mrs. Marcos's characterization of Brocka's film as "depressing."

The censors had other problems with the film besides the message of its ending. In interviews with French critics and journalists, Brocka reported that the censors mandated the deletion of certain elements. He said: "In *Jaguar* they cut the crude language, the sex scenes, the [shots of] flies on meat."[57] The strictures on love scenes are unremarkable. By the time of *Jaguar*'s release, Marcos and his censors had already ended their late 1960s–early 1970s reprieve on the censorship of graphic nudity on film and erotic magazines.[58] The censors' objection to the flies was, on the other hand, quite intriguing. It is likely that the image is from the scene in which Poldo travels to a nearby slum to locate Cristy. Poldo and a child named Azon pass by a wet market stall that sells fish, some of which are swarming with flies. The Philippine home video release registers an abrupt cut at the end of the scene while the 35 mm print of the film's international version (held at the Cinémathèque Royale de Belgique) continues into a few more shots where Poldo complains about the neighborhood's foul smell. The child blames it on the nearby "rubbish dump."

Students and lovers of cinema will recall a comparable, justly notorious, image of insect-laden food in Sergei Eisenstein's *The Battleship Potemkin* (1915). In Eisenstein's film, a mutiny ensues after the ship's medic dismisses the sailors' complaints about their putrefying rations. Close-ups of maggots swarming on a carcass of beef punctuate the start of the sailors' uprising.[59] From the perspective of Marcos's censors, the flies on the meat may have evoked any number of symbolic and superficial associations with social reality, including the unsanitary conditions in shantytowns and the unwholesome food in the nation's capital. Christian Espiritu, coincidentally one of Mrs. Marcos's couturiers, noted the significance of the flies in an admiring review of the film. He wrote: "Brocka succeeded in painting a landscape oozing with slime, dirt, stagnant water and those ubiquitous flies with the optimum of effectivity."[60] The objection to the "flies on the meat" remind us once more that Marcos's censors were wise to the figurative and allegorical meanings contained in films.

Censorship might have also impacted the film's opening moments. As if to placate the censors, *Jaguar* begins with a title card discouraging viewers from reading the film as a piece of sociopolitical commentary. Composed in stilted English, it says: "This is the story of a young man who dreams of joining the world of bigshot and high class and longs to escape from the world of poverty and deprivation, only to realize in a moment of crisis that it is in his own world that he can find love and sympathy. The screenplay was inspired by a news story from the book *Reportage on Crime* by Nick Joaquin, National Artist. The original article was written in 1961."

The title card mentions Joaquin and his National Artist award because President Marcos himself conferred the distinction and it was Imelda's brainchild. The reference to the 1960s implies that the material that inspired the film is neither subversive nor a commentary on present conditions. Immediately after the title card, Brocka inserts a rejoinder of sorts. It is a shot of a poster with diagrams of weightlifting exercises. The poster touts the physical fitness campaign of the Marcos regime. It reads: "Mass calisthenics *sa* Bagong Lipunan [in the New Society]. An exercise for people of all ages and physique [sic]. 14 daily exercises for longer, zestier life." The next shot shows Poldo exercising at home, with the poster displayed nearby. The sequence suggests that he is a compliant subject of the authoritarian state, one who embraces the New Society's vision of a physically vigorous citizenry. Alternatively, the visuals might be poking fun at the regime's exercise program and the myth of the New Society.

Noir Squalor and the Police State

An article in *Daily Variety* reported that censors thrice denied *Jaguar* an export permit for its exhibition at the Cannes International Film Festival.[61] They only relented after hearing that Brocka's friends from abroad (especially Pierre Rissient, who prepared the film's international version, and director John Boorman) had tapped Sean Connery to write a letter of support for Brocka. They chose the James Bond actor because, apart from his stature, he had played golf with Marcos. Afraid of upsetting the president, the censors speedily issued the permit, perhaps even before Connery drafted the note.[62]

Brocka learned that the censors' most serious objections concerned the film's portrayal of the slums, which was the same reason they initially declined to issue an export permit for *Insiang* (1976). He conjectured that they were following the first lady's lead on the matter. He said: "Mrs. Marcos . . . does not want to have the world see the slums of Manila, which she herself does not see."[63] The filmmaker added, "I went to the appeals committee and said, 'What you are seeing is the physical city, and it embarrasses you. You are not trying to see the *humanity* that is in my films. . . . You are missing the soul of the film.'"[64] He was right about Imelda's disdain for images of poverty. Two years after *Jaguar* opened in Philippine theaters—and several months after the release of yet another Brocka "slum movie," *Bona*—Imelda declared the Tondo shanties off-limits to filmmakers.[65] The director easily found other slums to film.

Mrs. Marcos's moratorium on filming in the Tondo slums was repressive but not unprecedented. As mentioned in the previous chapter, other autocrats issued similar orders. For instance, the Spanish dictator Francisco Franco proscribed images of poverty and hovels.[66] The Marcos regime's notion that films might influence the spectator's perception of their physical and social environment was likewise not farfetched. As Raymond Durgnat notes in an essay on film noir, "A crime [narrative] takes us through a variety of settings and types and implies an anguished view of society as a whole."[67] Similarly, Edward Dimendberg observes that "The film noir cycle articulates fantasies about public space." Film noirs generate such myths or impressions through images of squalid cityscapes and rural poverty seen in the "wayfinding, peregrinations, and strolls of characters."[68] The trope of "passage through the metropolis," Dimendberg goes on to say, is not only "the veritable cornerstone of the literature of detection" but crime films as well.[69] He finds in film noir and its scenes of urban passage a typical "cinematic excoriation of the polluted and mechanized metropolis."[70] Metropolitan squalor in noir is, for Dimendberg, not just a symbol but rather the "symptom and critique of the spatiality that it represents."[71] Cinematic images of urban blight, even when endemic to genres such as the crime film, affect how moviegoers perceive and experience a city.

Brocka rationalized his use of slum imagery in the following terms: "It is less expensive to make crime films. My set is the slums. I don't have to buy costumes, [and] my actors can wear what they like. And then the genre is favorable to action, sex, chase scenes. I also liked the atmosphere of wet streets in American film noir, so there is often a street lamp in my own movies. And then I can speak at the same time of my country's social reality."[72] *Jaguar* demonstrates that Brocka especially valued the risky but important cultural work of depicting the national situation. To create verisimilitude, he put his cast and crew through a long, grueling shoot in the crime-ridden Tondo district as well as in the dingy fishing port of Navotas.[73]

Jaguar not only explores the informal settlements but also maps their relationship to the bourgeois world. As Alain Garsault notes, "We are brought from the world of misery to a display of luxury with just a few steps or a few shots."[74] During Poldo's misadventures in social climbing, he strays into mansions where the rich hoard their possessions and into spaces of leisure (such as pizza parlors, amusement parks, and discos) where they squander their wealth. The film then returns periodically to the slums, where Sonny's objects of desire (i.e., a lackey, a woman, a gun) are extracted and then discarded. The film depicts such journeys between the melodramatically polarized worlds of the rich and the poor as fraught with tension if not animosity.

Apart from sketching the social totality and plotting areas of inequality and class conflict, scenes of urban passage in noir films register what Edward Dimendberg calls the "mapping and surveillance procedures" practiced in the city.[75] In *Jaguar*, the spectator vicariously joins Poldo in his futile attempts to evade the law. Moreover, they are made to share his overwhelming fear of being captured. Paranoia is endemic to film noir,[76] but in *Jaguar* the hero's psychosis reflects the public attitude toward the police state. Marcos established a formidable intelligence apparatus with secret police, plenty of willing and coerced civilian informants, and no less than "three intelligence groups acting independently and competing with one another."[77] They inspired such fear that Poldo finds no comfort in the assurances of the couple he is rooming with that slum denizens are tight-lipped with cops, including those who might be coming after him. Moreover, he worries that even the remote island of Mindoro, where Cristy has arranged lodgings for him, is not far enough to evade the authorities. Alfred McCoy suspects that the Marcos regime actually "lacked the skilled manpower and information systems to effect a blanket repression"[78] but Poldo's acute paranoia shows that the climate of fear made up for such logistical deficiencies.

The film depicts one of the authoritarian regime's surveillance procedures in the climactic sequence. *Sona*, the police operation that accidentally lures Poldo out of hiding, was a much-despised feature of the Marcos era. William Chapman describes the practice, which originated during the Japanese occupation of the Philippines in World War II, as "dead-of-night zonings" in which military units "surrounded a neighborhood, roused residents from their homes, and made house-to-house searches, hauling suspects before a hooded informer for identification."[79] In the absence of informants, the persons rounded up were presented to police and other government agents. When not used for counterinsurgency opera-

FIGURE 3.4. Police conduct a dragnet operation officially called a "saturation drive" but popularly known as "sona" (zoning). *Jaguar.* Courtesy of Danilo Brocka/CCP Library.

tions, zonings were conducted—as in the film—to "flush out suspected 'bad elements' and to confiscate 'loose' firearms."[80]

The spectacle of this aggressive practice of surveillance and social control is especially disturbing because the film prompts its viewers to identify with the targets of the raid. The film does so by amplifying the thud and rustle of feet as well as the interminable barking of dogs. The policeman's script, read over the megaphone, goes like this: "My countrymen, listen carefully. We are agents of the law. All males, aged fifteen and higher, should please come out of their homes. Gather in the center [of the neighborhood]." Dozens of uniformed and undercover cops, many of them armed, bang on doors and search houses at will. The young and old men of the community are herded away from their homes and ordered to shed their T-shirts and expose their legs. They are made to raise their arms for a prolonged period as the cops pat their trousers or shorts and aim their flashlight at body parts in search of gang and prison tattoos.

Brocka mentions that he recruited actual police officers for the *sona* scene and the chase up the landfill. He related: "I simply asked the police to dramatize how they usually apprehend criminals in the area. The outlaws are usually allowed to run to the top of the garbage heap when they are cornered and captured. Sometimes a very dangerous criminal would just disappear."[81] The ability of the police to penetrate the slum's darkness with flashlights and floodlights, and to shatter the silence of the small hours with megaphone speeches, suggests the fearsome power of the authoritarian government. The film's nocturnal illumination of the slums—an astounding technical feat by cinematographer Conrado Baltazar, given the size of the area—is itself a homology for the *sona* and the police state. With its exotic setting, the chase sequence is at once hyperrealistic and oneiric.[82] Poldo quickly discovers that, like the autocratic regime in which he lives, the colossal landfill offers no escape. In a bit of cruel irony, the man who has always dreamed of fleeing the slums ends up trapped in an impossibly enormous garbage dump.

It is worth dwelling further on the location of the film's climactic moment. Both Joaquin's story and one of Lacaba's storylines for the film ends the narrative in a faraway province.[83] Brocka asked the scriptwriters to change the setting to the landfill near the shantytown where he had filmed his maternal melodrama *Insiang* (1976). The garbage heap later became known as Smokey Mountain, a quintessential icon of Marcos-era Philippines. The setting, he notes, evokes "Dante's hell." He continues: "And then, in the background, you can see [the city of] Manila."[84] The garbage heap, too real to be considered as a mere symbol of the Philippine capital, marks one of the points where the semiotic excess of melodramatic representation coincides with the extreme poverty that the Marcos regime created. This final instance of urban passage in *Jaguar* testifies to film noir's capacity for signifying politics through the power of evocative images.

Fantasies of Subversion

In the process of adapting Nick Joaquin's 1956 true crime story into *Jaguar*, Brocka and his screenwriters added—and then later took out—elements that I consider politically significant. As Isagani Cruz notes, the writers "correctly decided to strip the story of [Joaquin's protagonist] Napoleon Nocedal to its two basic elements: the shooting at the restaurant and the slum origins of the killer."[85] In addition to bits of trenchant sociopolitical critique, screenwriters Lacaba and Lee introduced new subplots and action scenes to Joaquin's material. By the third draft of the storyline, *Jaguar's* plot began to loosely resemble the structure of John Farrow's *The Big Clock* (1948). Farrow's crime movie is set like *Jaguar* in a publishing firm and pits its hero (played by Ray Milland), a journalist, against his boss, a publishing magnate. The capitalist (played by Charles Laughton) bludgeons his mistress in a fit of rage. Trying to mask his guilt, he uses one of his serials—a magazine specializing in true crime stories—to launch a public hunt for her killer. He enlists the protagonist, a star correspondent and editor, to write an investigative report about the killing. Unbeknownst to the boss, the hero coincidentally met the victim on the night of her death and was also the last person seen in public with her. The protagonist races to find the killer (not knowing it was his boss) and also cover his own tracks to avoid being pinned for the crime. As with *Jaguar*, *Clock*'s protagonist lands in deep trouble because of his employer's misdeeds. The similarities between Farrow and Brocka's films might be purely coincidental, but they are remarkable enough to merit brief mention here. It is worth noting as well that Lacaba does not remember having seen *Clock* or using any specific film as a model for *Jaguar*.[86]

More compelling than the tale of *Jaguar*'s Philippine and American influences is the behind-the-scenes story about the evolution of the film's sociopolitical commentary. Archival materials—drafts of story outlines and script materials—help tell that narrative. One version of the story outline depicts Poldo and his shantytown friends as antiestablishment figures.[87] Poldo, a widower, has a seven-year-old daughter named Azon. They live in the house of his cousin Quintin and his wife, Elena. The husband and wife are leaders in the slum community. They help the community draw up petitions in support of the rights of informal settlers. They also organize patrols to fend off the goons whom the landlord sends to raze their dwellings. The couple's knowledge of petitions and the rights of informal settlers ("squatters") alludes to the radicalization of the poor. During the Marcos regime, left-leaning organizations engaged with indigent communities, educating them about the workings of capitalist oppression and informing them of their legal rights.[88] In this particular version of *Jaguar*'s story outline, Cristy is not a go-go dancer-turned-actress as she is in the film, but rather the heiress of an affluent family. Her family, bearing the allegorical name of Europa, runs a construction firm and "does business in Africa and the Mideast."[89] They own the land on which Poldo's cousin squats and also the mansion where Poldo works as a security guard. The story outline describes Cristy as "a rebellious college student in her early thirties" who "regularly appears in socially conscious college plays." She and her theater friends go on "immersion trips" in the slums "to better internalize their roles." On one such occasion, security guards from her father's company—including Poldo—receive orders to demolish the shantytown. Racked with guilt, Poldo turns against his employer and persuades his coworkers to back off. The Europas retaliate by sacking Poldo and dispatching goons to beat Quintin to death. At the latter's wake, a demolition crew swoops in with "three bulldozers and a bigger contingent of security guards, along with a troop of goons wielding hammers." The fracas ends with Quintin's coffin "on the ground, battered and overturned" and with Azon "in a mud puddle, shaking with the cold, one of her legs crushed under a fallen beam." The child (whose physical impairment somewhat recalls that of "Tiny Tim" Cratchit from Charles Dickens's *A Christmas Carol*) eventually dies. Despite its histrionics, the eviction sequence is not wide of the mark in portraying the state's treatment of informal settlers. Robert Youngblood notes that the Marcos regime demolished numerous shanties to make way for public and private development projects. Moreover, "squatter leaders were jailed or forced underground for speaking out against the evictions."[90]

Poldo turns into a vigilante after the death of his child. He stalks and kills some of Europa's goons before turning against Mrs. Europa and Cristy. Filled with rage, he grabs the boss's wife "by her well-coiffed hair, and drags her as he smashes her antiques with a swinging carbine." He takes both women to a basketball court in the middle of the slums. There, in front of the squatters, he tries Mrs. Europa in a kangaroo court. The police attempt to rescue the Europas. They shoot at Poldo but Cristy, "moved by a sudden, inexplicable compassion," takes the bullet for him. The scenario ends, like the film, with Poldo's incarceration and a close-up of him "looking lost, a wild animal caught in a trap from which there is no escape."

This early iteration of the film's scenario portrays social relations in a manner reminiscent of the "class analysis" or "social investigation" exercises that communists taught to impoverished communities during the martial law era. As William Chapman relates, the revolutionaries' pedagogy involved the use of "Marxist categorization" to finger "who in the barrio was exploiting whom."[91] Through these applications of socialist ideas, the communists helped the townsfolk "identify with precision those forces, institutions, trends, etc., which promote the interests of the people and the revolution." Both of *Jaguar's* screenwriters would have been familiar with socialist discourse, if not specifically with Marxist analysis, from their time in the underground.

In the draft of the scenario mentioned above, the "class analysis" begins with the squatter's ground-level struggles and goes all the way up to the global dimensions of the Europas' business interests. The screenwriters show that the Europa family's habits of class oppression in Manila are coextensive with their exploitative ventures in other third world countries. Even if the writers' Marxist-inspired "class analysis" may have been too high-minded for an action film, the references to the Marcoses would have probably been more legible to audiences at that time and also more politically incendiary than I have as yet acknowledged. Cristy, the dilettante interested in theater and helping the poor, is a veiled reference to the presidential daughter Ma. Imelda (Imee). Imee dabbled in theater; befriended Lino Brocka; and, as I note in chapter 2, was briefly considered for the lead role in *Insiang* (1976), a film set in the slums.[92] While Cristy turns "inexplicably" heroic at the end, much of the narrative portrays her as a spoiled brat. Moreover, her concern for the poor is mercenary. The overage college student only hangs around with slum folk to feed her acting hobby. Moreover, she seduces Poldo and beds him in her father's house not out of love but to satisfy her lust and secretly rebel against her parents.

Cristy's parents are not-so-thinly veiled stand-ins for the president and the first lady. The characterization of her mother as "well-coiffed" is a reference to Mrs. Marcos's iconic bouffant hairdo. Mr. Europa, Cristy's absent but influential father, brings to mind the Philippine dictator. Poldo's fantasy of vengeance against these Marcos stand-ins is both uproarious and subversive. Not content with showing the film's hero pulling the first lady's iconic "well-coiffed hair" and smashing her opulent home décor, Lee and Lacaba also put her in a scene of public humiliation. The Imeldific figure's impromptu trial references the "people's courts" held by communist insurgents for "enemies of the people" (e.g., thieves, crooked cops and politicos, usurers, rapists).[93] Such trials "usually but not always" resulted in public executions. One can imagine the delight of the screenwriters in conjuring such punishment for the Marcoses, whose government had jailed and tortured them.

Predictably enough, the next version of the storyline scraps the revenge fantasy, likely because of self-censorship on the part of the filmmakers. Poldo's vigilante spell is excised as well. The narrative of a killer haunting Manila's streets would have constituted a depiction of lawlessness, something technically prohibited by the censors. However, as I will show later in the chapter, the figure of the urban vigilante returns—albeit in a less threatening female form—in Brocka's next crime film.

The writers deleted other incendiary events in subsequent drafts of the story outline. They initially retained a considerable amount of political content in the course of making revisions but ended up removing or burying them deep in the narrative. The presence of the radical poor is one of the political elements they sought to keep. Quintin, the squatter's rights leader in the first draft of the storyline, turns into a union leader at a factory by the third version of the narrative. In that iteration, the character is renamed and implicitly described as something of a Marxist. The draft reads: "Berting, the visionary unionist, speaks of his dream of seeing a world where all men will be equal."[94] The completed film, however, only references Berting's labor activism in passing. The laborer tells Poldo near the end of the film that the corrugated box factory where he worked until recently has shut down because of an extended labor dispute in which he was involved. Concerns over censorship likely prompted the scriptwriters to excise other references to labor activism as well. As Francisco Nemenzo reminds us, Marcos banned strikes and stifled trade union activities during martial law, thus making their depictions in the media a touchy matter.[95]

My goal in discussing these suppressed elements is to demonstrate the writers' attempts at making their script relevant to the political situation in 1979. Along with censored and self-censored elements, these alternate plots and characterizations arguably haunt the versions realized in the assembled film. They offer a valuable glimpse into the possibilities generated by the film's political-artistic project, before and after censorship. When possible, the study of cinema politics should include not only the actual elements found in the completed movie but also what was "virtually" in the picture before being withdrawn by the filmmakers or excised by the censors.[96]

The Liberated Noir Woman

No discussion of *Jaguar*'s or film noir's politics would be complete without considering the woman's story. In an essay on women in film noir, Elizabeth Cowie points to the tendency of scholars and critics to overemphasize male narratives in such movies. Film noir, she reminds us, "afforded women roles which are active, adventurous and driven by sexual desire."[97] In Brocka's film, the woman's story offers a striking counternarrative to the hero's struggles.

If one were to trace the trajectory of Cristy's narrative alongside Poldo's, two things become evident. First, their stories are quite similar. Second, Cristy succeeds or escapes every time Poldo fails. *Jaguar* establishes the parallelism between their tales at various moments. For instance, the movie shows both of them departing their respective shantytowns in elaborately filmed scenes of picturesque squalor. The opening sequence shows Poldo leaving the slums for the day's work. A parallel scene depicts Cristy exiting the squatter's area. Her departure is permanent, however, for unlike Poldo, she never resides there again. To cite another example, Cristy and Poldo both become Sonny's playthings. But while Poldo's relationship with Sonny turns into blind devotion, Cristy wisely keeps her distance. Indeed, she dumps Sonny after landing her first movie role. Mindful of Poldo's naivete, she constantly reminds him that Sonny does not have his best interests at heart.

Finally, Poldo and Cristy share a melancholic streak. On one occasion, she speaks regretfully to Poldo of dating certain men to get ahead in life. She says something that invites the viewer to think of her too—not just Poldo—as the creature that the film's title references. While speaking about one of her ex-lovers, Cristy reinforces the motif of her animalism. She says: "My first ... friend, he turned me into a go-go girl, a sexy dancer ... a *cage* dancer." Indeed, she first appears in Brocka's film dancing on a go-go bar stage with a cage-like set. Days later, she moves in with Sonny and, as one of the film's reviews points out, becomes "a captive occupant of their love nest."[98] Nocturnal, sly, and opportunistic, Cristy draws comparison to the predatory feline named in the film's title. Her fierceness shines through when Poldo begs her to run away with him. Although clearly smitten by the handsome fugitive, Cristy not only resists getting carried away by her feelings but also musters the courage to give him the unadorned truth. "I can't go back to a quiet life," she tells him. "You know I've done everything I can to become a famous actress. I'm almost there. I can't quit now." When she visits Poldo at the police station, she promises to use her newfound fame to help him out. She also offers him a meaningful gift: a lighter and a pack of imported cigarettes. The gift recalls a moment they shared earlier in their friendship. On that occasion, she asked Poldo for a cigarette and a light, but he only had the former. To save him from losing face, she told him that she was better off not smoking anyway because it causes cancer. By gifting him with a lighter during his incarceration and invoking happier times, Cristy conveys a message of hope to Poldo. If not "I will stand by you, as always" the gift says, "someone you know escaped the slums for good, and you can too." In the end, while Jaguar returns to his prison cell, Cristy slinks her way out of the police station and into a promising movie career. Brocka acknowledged her tenacity. He said: "She knows what she is getting into. In a way, she is tougher than Jaguar."[99]

A Filipino reviewer named Mario Bautista found parts of Cristy's star-on-the-rise subplot to be superfluous to the film.[100] While I do not agree with his opinion, his criticism seems to locate a crucial seam in the film. Cristy's story, insofar as it imagines a successful, alternative version of Poldo's quest for social mobility, may appear redundant. To flesh out her character, *Jaguar* tries to sustain a dual-focus narrative in which the woman's tale parallels the central male story. Her presence also adds commercial appeal and a feminist angle to the film. Equally important, *Jaguar* utilizes Cristy's story to encode a commentary on cinema under Marcosian authoritarianism.

A scene that Bautista particularly disliked is actually a rich moment of cinematic reflexivity. More than halfway into the film, with Poldo already in hiding, Cristy lands a role in a "bold" (sexy) movie. Her role requires her to shoot a rape scene set in a scenic but polluted river. The film's effeminate director loudly complains to his crew about the stench and filth of the chosen location while dousing himself in rubbing alcohol. He complains that directors like Lino Brocka manage to get better locations than he does. The director then sets up the scene, reminding Cristy to "look pretty" and "stay in the water" while vigorously struggling against her attacker. As the shoot progresses, the rationale for the riverine setting and the director's instructions becomes clear. The objective is to artfully drench Cristy's sheer white dress so that her breasts show through the fabric. The peekaboo method is called the "wet look," a tactic prevalent during the Marcos era to circumvent restrictions on nudity on film. The satirical moment exposes both the shallowness of martial law–era entertainment and the absurdity of the censors' restrictions. Through the likely improvised line that mentions his name, Brocka pokes fun at his complicity in this system of filmmaking. Like Cristy's flamboyant director, Brocka peddles a combination of sex and scenic poverty in his films. He also makes his share of "bold" movies and is not above having his actors do laughable things to skirt censorship laws.

According to Brocka, the local audience appreciated the satirical humor in the "wet look" scene, which ran longer in the film's local version than in its foreign release.[101] The scene also caught the attention of foreign critics. In his review for *October*, Joël Magny suggests that the scene is "not so much a critique of Philippine cinema as it is a metaphor of the situation of the protagonist and even the filmmaker himself."[102] I agree that Cristy's objectification in the skin flick parallels

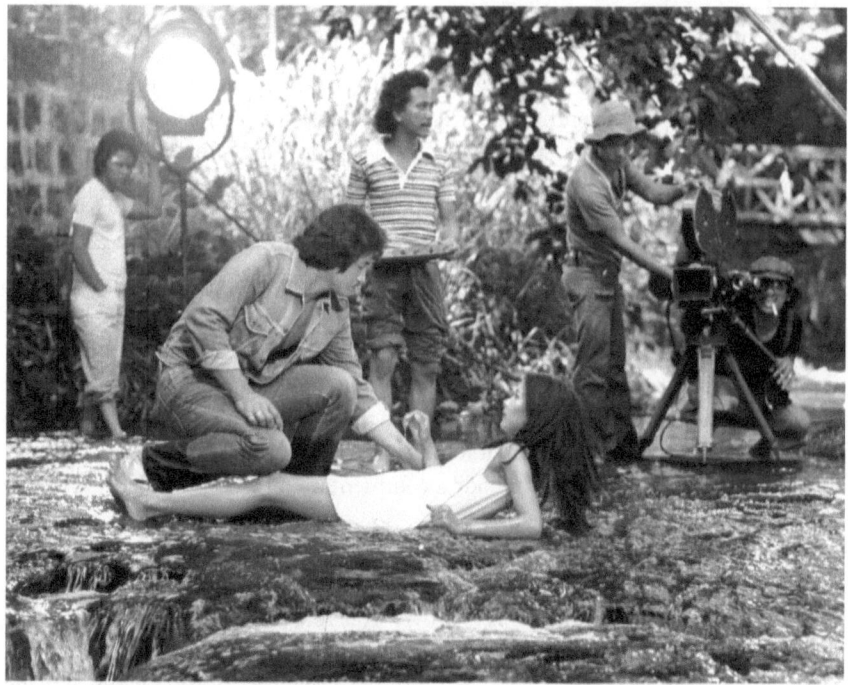

FIGURE 3.5. Cristy (Amy Austria, front center) performs in an exploitation film. *Jaguar.* Courtesy of Danilo Brocka/CCP Library.

Sonny's exploitation of Poldo. But I do not think that the scene's insight on Brocka's predicament as a filmmaker cannot also be extended, as Magny suggests, to the general situation of Philippine cinema. Under the regime of Marcos's paradoxically labeled "constitutional authoritarianism," the proposition that a wet fabric can mark the difference between a licit image and an illicit one is as flimsy as the veil of constitutionality legitimizing Marcos's unseemly dictatorship. For Brocka and other directors, any attempt to represent sociopolitical conditions on film had to proceed through a similar peekaboo tactic, which entailed shrouding provocative imagery and smuggling sociopolitical critique into seemingly innocuous genre films. The censors, for their part, separated the permissible from the forbidden using the slightest of distinctions. Regarding its cultural work, cinema under authoritarianism functioned like the wet see-through fabric of Cristy's garment: it is a thin layer of fantasy at once exposing and occluding the real sociopolitical conditions lying underneath.

As I have shown in the preceding discussion, Cristy's story is vital to an analysis of the relays between cinema and politics in *Jaguar*. The noir woman's story traces lines of flight[103]—possible routes of escape—from abjection within a culture industry and society under a patriarchal autocracy.

ANGELA, THE MARKED ONE

During an interview at the Cannes screening of *Jaguar*, Brocka mentioned that his latest crime film also ran afoul of censors. That picture—*Angela, the Marked One* (*Angela markado*, 1980)—is, in his words, about "a woman who kills the five men who raped her." Brocka said that the film "was banned by the censors because it supposedly had no redeeming moral value."[104] As in the case of *Jaguar*, they later reversed the embargo.

Brocka did not think much of his film, dismissing it as a "commercial project"[105] even after it won two international prizes, one at a festival in Nantes and another in Pesaro. He pointed out that the movie was based on a Filipino *komiks* (serial graphic novella) and was also derivative of François Truffaut's *The Bride Wore Black* (1968). He added: "But let's face it, the movie may have certain merits but [did it truly deserve] the Grand Prix at Nantes?"

While *Jaguar* was decidedly superior to *Angela*, the latter deserved a better appraisal than what it received from Brocka. Isagani Cruz, a critic who often tangled with the director, was presumably being sincere when he declared *Angela* "one of Brocka's best films ... a masterpiece in cinematography, acting, editing, and screenwriting."[106] Brocka's friend, film historian Agustin Sotto, had a theory on why the director misprized *Angela*. He wrote: "Having no formal schooling in film, he was largely unaware of the contributions of his ace cinematographer, Conrado Baltazar.... Reevaluated a decade later, *Angela markado* is an underrated film. It may have impressed some critics as too much of a genre film in the Hitchcockian tradition, but its storytelling is undeniably engrossing and visually exciting."[107]

Beyond its impressive visuals, *Angela's* significance to the director's body of work lies in its continuation of the project he began in *Jaguar*. That project centered on his figuration of Philippine sociopolitical conditions—including the effects of Marcosian authoritarianism—through the affordances of film noir and the crime genre.

Like Poldo in *Jaguar*, the protagonist of *Angela markado* (played by Hilda Koronel) is working class, while her antagonists belong to a higher station. Similar to the hero of *Jaguar*, Angela turns into a criminal and roams Manila's nocturnal world. Additionally, the movie represents the police state's mechanisms of surveillance and control or uses them as a structuring absence to the protagonist's criminal doings. Furthermore, the heroine ends up—much like Poldo—trying to evade capture in the film's spectacular climactic sequence. Lastly, both pictures feature the gritty and sometimes dreamlike mise-en-scène of noir films, resulting in images that allegorize the characters' psyches and their sociopolitical milieu.

Angela differs markedly from *Jaguar* in its extreme depiction of violence and the protagonist's belligerent response to her oppressors. These differences are rooted in the former's sub-generic configuration as a rape-revenge film. Rape-revenge films, according to Sarah Projansky, are "feminist narratives in which women face rape, recognize that the law will neither protect nor avenge them and then take the law into their own hands."[108] As with the larger category of crime films to which it belongs, the rape-revenge film is a form of melodrama, one fueled by female suffering at the hands of cruel men. I venture that the heroine's ordeal in *Angela markado* indexes state violence under authoritarian rule while her revenge represents a metaphorical act of rebellion.

Less than fifteen minutes into the 140-minute narrative, five of Angela's customers kidnap her outside the beer garden where she waits tables. The men drag her into a Land Cruiser and take her to a warehouse. Over five days, and more than a tenth of the film's running time, they take turns assaulting her in front of each another. The mise-en-scène and the staging of the victim's assault evoke a scenario of military-style torture, the kind inflicted on actual and suspected dissidents during the Marcos regime. The setting—an empty warehouse seemingly located in the middle of nowhere but probably not too far from the city—brings to mind the secluded dwellings that the authorities used for their illicit activities. An Amnesty International report describes those places—ironically named "safehouses"—as "undisclosed and unauthorized interrogation centres ... [where] interrogation was commonly accompanied by torture involving electric shocks, sexual abuse, and beatings."[109] Moreover, the vehicle of the heroine's abductors resembles a military jeep. When the youthful kidnappers sit on its hood and bumper or lean on its side, they resemble forces stationed at roadside checkpoints that proliferated during the Marcos regime.

What does it mean to say that the five abductors inflict "military-style" physical, psychological, and sexual torture on Angela? We see them point a gun at her, jeer at her, force her to dance, pull her hair, rip her clothes off and inflict other indignities. They hold her down while taking turns forcing their genitals into her mouth, her vagina, and when she is nearly passed out, into her rectum as well. They douse her with beer to revive her, making sure she witnesses everything they are doing to her. These forms of cruelty were either evocative of or comparable to the methods employed by the authoritarian regime. Consider, for instance, the following description of a female political prisoner's torture and killing. Amnesty reports that she was "kept sleepless for eight days and nights, made to stand for several hours naked before a full-blast air conditioner and was slapped hard."[110] She was also "forced to undergo 'unwanted caresses.'" Days later the woman was found "sprawled on the cement floor, saliva frothing out of her mouth and acidic smoke rising around her body."[111] The government insisted that she chugged on muriatic acid because she was depressed. Save for her gruesome

FIGURE 3.6. Angela (Hilda Koronel, foreground) is detained and gang-raped inside a cavernous warehouse. *Angela, the Marked One.* Courtesy of Danilo Brocka/CCP Library.

death and the use of an air conditioner to torture her, the prisoner's fate resembles Angela's ordeal.

The Amnesty reports—generated mainly through interviews with prisoners—do not cite cases of sexual intercourse between captors and prisoners. They mention, however, that some of the prisoners complained of being "threatened with rape" or, in the case of male prisoners, were told that the authorities would rape their spouses. Accounts of female rape appear in other sources. A recent anthology of writings by martial law activists notes that many female prisoners experienced sexual abuse. A contributor to the anthology relates a story that circulated among activists about a torture session in which the assailant inserted an "eggplant dipped in a crushed chili pepper" into a prisoner's vagina.[112]

The combination of sexual and psychological cruelty was not reserved for women. Another Amnesty report describes an incident involving a male victim who was "ordered to perform a dance, was beaten about the ears and chest, had a cigarette extinguished on his chest and had bullets placed between his fingers which were then crushed together."[113] Angela had to endure the first two indignities as well in Brocka's film. Amnesty tells of other forms of violence directed at the sexual organs of male captives. One interrogator supposedly "applied the flame of a gas lighter" to a victim's "pubic hair and penis."[114] Another victim testified that an interrogator yanked a piece of palm leaf midrib from a broom and inserted it into "the uterus [sic] of my penis."[115]

How else does the vicious and spectacular conduct of torture in *Angela* register aspects of its real-life counterparts during the Marcos regime? In a large section of the torture scene, Angela's captors place her in front of the jeep with the headlights turned up on full beam. The blinding light hits her body and casts tall shadows upon the wall behind her. Later, some of the captors join her "in the spotlight," and continue abusing her with theatrical cruelty. When viewed up close, the torture scene resembles a marionette show. When the camera pulls back for a wider view, the frame captures a different kind of spectacle. The gigantic animated shadows of Angela and her tormentors perform a violent kind of shadow theater. Finally, as did the assailants in *Angela*, the Marcos regime concealed the spectacle of torture from public view. The real-life authorities, however, dumped mangled corpses in conspicuous places or set tortured victims free to sow fear among the public.

For those unfortunate enough to have suffered or witnessed the regime's atrocities, torture sessions played out as flamboyant displays of cruelty, no matter how few the spectators. Amnesty reported the case of two sisters tortured in "a beach house beside the bachelor officers' quarters." They "were subjected to electric shock for about 45 minutes each, one sister watching the other."[116] Kept awake for "for almost two nights running," the spectacle of one sister's torture intensified the other's suffering. In a similar case, a woman reports that she "was forced to watch my husband, wearing his briefs only, bound on the chair, beaten on his head, his chest, his arms, his shoulder blades, his stomach, with guns, long guns and pistols, and with fists."[117] Alfred McCoy characterizes such forms of abuse as "theatrical torture."[118] He avers that it endowed its practitioners, especially those who victimized prominent citizens or their social superiors, with "a superman sense that they could remake the social order at will."[119] Performed repeatedly for years on end—on an estimated thirty-five thousand citizens during the Marcos regime—torture became, in McCoy's words, a "theory of social action founded on an inflated belief in the efficacy of violence."[120] This practice of state violence, which an entire generation of cops and military personnel embraced, persisted well beyond the strongman's reign. It haunts Philippine democracy to this day.

In reference to a term I used earlier, I posit *Angela*'s torture sequence as a "Marcosian moment" writ large. The sequence is replete with violence and cruelty, with visuals that evoke the brutality of the authoritarian state. It also contains numerous shots of the heroine's pained appeals to the camera (and, by extension, to the film's viewers) for compassion. Lacaba, the screenwriter of *Angela*, understood the mechanics of ritualized violence under Marcos only too well. He was imprisoned for nearly two years during martial law and endured repeated torture. In harrowing accounts of his time in the strongman's Grand Guignol, he recalls his abuse in terms rife with theatrical imagery. He writes: "My tormentors and interrogators sat in chairs or stood before me, hitting me each time a question was asked or an answer was unsatisfactory. Troopers passing by, on their way to their lockers or wherever, felt free to hit my nape or the back of my head with open palms or karate chops."[121] Lacaba's torturers also directed him to perform self-injuring acts as part of their sessions. In the following excerpt, he describes a form of theatrical torture with an unmistakable Marcosian signature:

> At another point, I was made to lie down with the back of my head resting on the edge of one steel cot, both my feet resting on the edge of another cot, my arms straight at my sides, and my stiffened body hanging in midair. This was the torture they called *higa sa hangin* (lying down in air), also known as the San Juanico Bridge, named after the country's longest bridge, built during martial law and dedicated by Marcos to his wife, Imelda.... "Lying down in air" is difficult enough, since you have to contend with the pull of gravity. But even before gravity could take its toll, somebody standing close by would give me a kick in the stomach and bring my body down to the floor. The steel cot scraped the skin off my nape as I slid down.

Lacaba also recalls small details about his seven-month ordeal which may have unconsciously ended up in the film's torture scenes. He writes about suffering through marathon torture sessions (one lasting eight hours), "shivering uncontrollably" in front of his laughing tormentors, being "made to board a jeep" and taken to another place of suffering, losing consciousness, and being "half-carried" by his captors after being abused. The rest of the details in the scenes of Angela's torture probably came from other sources besides Lacaba's experience, including fictional details from Carlo Caparas's graphic novella and possibly Truffaut's film. Film scholar Richard Allen, who wrote a scathing review of *Angela* after seeing it in Pesaro, cites another possible source for the film, noting that the "structure of the narrative mirrors Michael Winner's *Death Wish* [1974]."[122] It is difficult to establish Winner's movie as an inspiration for *Angela*. Lacaba was already a political prisoner when *Death Wish* opened in July 1974 (the state detained him from April 1974 to March 1976). Lacaba's storyline for the film is dated March 1980. It is unclear if Lacaba had seen Winner's vigilante movie in the intervening years or if some of its details were, along with material from Truffaut and rape-revenge films such as *I Spit on Your Grave* (Meir Zarchi, 1978), already folded into Caparas's novella.

Whatever its inspiration, the violence of the torture scenes was less intense in the finished movie than in Lacaba's story outlines and production script. The script details two scenes of psychological and sexual abuse that Brocka changed in the assembled film. In the first of these scenes, one of the rapists pulls out his comb,

FIGURE 3.7. Angela's (Hilda Koronel, foreground) ordeal recalls acts of state violence against political prisoners. *Angela, the Marked One.* Courtesy of Danilo Brocka/CCP Library.

runs it through his hair, and then blows off the accumulated dandruff. The description then continues: "Through his succeeding actions, we can infer that he is combing Angela's pubic hair. He laughs uncontrollably, clearly enjoying his actions. He raises the comb and removes curly strands of hair. He inhales the comb."[123] In another unused scene, one of the rapists, also gleeful in inflicting violence, shows off a "big ring-shaped object wrapped in fur ... a 'sexual device.'"[124] In the assembled film, Brocka replaced the scene involving the pubic hair with a shot of one of the rapists inhaling Angela's blouse after taking his turn raping her. The director dropped the risqué scene depicting the use of a "sexual device" (presumably a cock ring) altogether. These changes tamed the sexual content and harshness of the torture scenes, likely in a desire to preempt problems with the censors.

While the creative labor on *Angela* required Lacaba to tap into traumatic memories of his ordeal, it also spurred him once more (as he and Ricardo Lee had done in an omitted scene from *Jaguar*) to engage in the possibly cathartic enterprise of conjuring scenarios of retribution against those who commit such heinous acts. But that is not the only explanation for the violence of Angela's reprisals. In rape-revenge films, the severity of the victim's trauma implicitly entitles her to seek vigilante justice through premeditated killings. The exceptionally cruel finale to Angela's ordeal motivates her recourse to serial murder. After her rape and torture, one of her captors tattoos all of their first names on her back. Pleased with the results, they assign her the moniker "Markado," meaning "the marked [or tattooed] one." They then sell her to a sex trafficker. Fortunately for Angela, cops raid the brothel before the transaction was completed, and she is set free. The depiction of the raid implicitly criticizes Philippine authorities; the madam at the brothel receives a phone call from law enforcers forewarning her of the sting.

Angela escapes during the melee and rushes home to her bedridden mother, only to find that the latter has died. Angela's neighbors castigate her for abandoning her parent. Distraught by the turn of events, Angela flees her home and wanders about the city. A kind, over-the-hill bar hostess named Rona (Celia Rodriguez) takes her in after seeing her in distress. Angela uses Rona's wardrobe to launch her revenge plot. When the latter leaves home for her nightly trade at the Red Velvet Club, Angela helps herself to her host's collection of wigs and outfits. Sporting disco-era fashions—including an afro wig and oversize sunglasses—Angela goes incognito and hunts down her former captors in the precise sequence in which their names appear on her tattoo. She eliminates three of them in short order. If, as Paula Rabinovitz puts it, the "femme fatale possesses a power offered by the street," Angela uses the physical and social disarray of the city to commit and hide her crimes.[125]

A law student named Celso (Raoul Aragon), brother to one of Angela's now-deceased rapists, eventually detects a pattern in her killings and teams up with the two surviving rapists to foil her revenge plot. They confront her outside the suggestively named Big Mouth bar. The film directly confronts the moral dilemma behind Angela's quest for vigilante justice when Celso accidentally exposes the tattoo in the act of restraining her. Following a trope of melodrama, the suffering woman confirms her identity and asserts her righteousness at the narrative's high point. Peter Brooks describes such moments within melodrama as instances of "self-nomination," "self-assertion," and the revelation of virtue.[126] Angela tells Celso that his late brother was a vicious rapist and "pimp" who wronged her terribly. Celso empathizes with her but asserts that she should not have taken the law into her hands. She replies with a rhetorical question: "I am poor. Do you think the law cares about me?" Two of Angela's rapists interrupt the conversation to pounce on her, but she dashes off to a nearby lumberyard. A thrilling chase scene ensues, so highly reminiscent of the Smokey Mountain pursuit in *Jaguar* that the film scholar Paul Willemen confused one scene for the other.[127] The setting, with its massive stacks of weathered logs, invokes pillaged natural resources and stalled development projects. Both happen to be hallmarks of Marcos's authoritarian regime, which famously decimated the nation's forests[128] and abandoned several flashy infrastructure projects it could no longer fund.[129]

Angela nimbly wends her way through the ill-lighted and obstacle-filled space. One of her pursuers, Bobby (Johnny Delgado, who plays Direk in *Jaguar*), shoots the other rapist by mistake, leaving only Celso and himself on her trail. Celso tries to end the chase, announcing he had already called the police. Bobby tells him to back off. Bobby climbs up a pile of logs to reach Angela, but she stabs his hand with a knife and turns his gun at him. Celso tries to stop Angela from pulling the trigger, but she fires twice, putting the second bullet through Bobby's head. She hands the gun to Celso after dispensing what one scholar might call "restorative justice."[130]

Like Poldo at the end of *Jaguar*, Angela wears a blank facial expression at the film's conclusion, as if drained of spirit. As Celso leads her away, a disclaimer appears in crawling titles. The crawling text is an excerpt from a fictitious court decision finding Angela guilty of five counts of murder. Following advice he received earlier in his career, Brocka invokes the Bible to justify his use of censorable material in the film. He adds two famous biblical passages to the text of the disclaimer: "an eye for an eye, a tooth for a tooth" and "vengeance is mine, says the Lord." The graphic likewise explains the significance of those passages, to wit: "The injustice she suffered at the hands of her victims has not given her the right to seek justice in extra-legal means. The end does not justify the means, and the end is justice, not revenge."

Brocka recalled adding the disclaimer to comply with the censors' wishes.[131] Isagani Cruz disputes his account, albeit without offering proof.[132] The absence of censorship records makes it impossible to say who is right. Archival finds make it possible, however, to comment on another aspect of the film's ending and the impact the disclaimer may have had on the film. A comparison between the assembled film and the story outline presumably submitted to the censors shows that the finished product omits the depiction of Angela's capture. The storyline reads: "The final scene is in a hospital, where Celso visits Angela, now under police guard. He tells her he holds no grudge against her: although he cannot agree with her methods, he understands the desperation that led her to become the avenging angel. She smiles at him gratefully, at the same time steeling herself for the inevitable punishment that society has in store for her."[133] Brocka dropped this scene altogether, ending the film shortly after Angela kills Bobby. The police, whom Celso had reportedly called, fail to show up before the film ends. Without the disclaimer, the film would not have concluded with the assurance that the state would punish the heroine. The absence of a disclaimer would have also left open the possibility that Celso would take pity on her and let her go before the cops arrived.

Carlos Clarence suggests in his famous book on crime films that "violence reaches the audience as an all-purpose metaphor."[134] Foreign critics offered a variety of interpretations of *Angela* and its depictions of violence.[135] Except for Richard Allen, those critics viewed the film as superior to typical exploitation fare from the

Global South. For instance, Hubert Niogret praised the film for its non-gratuitous portrayal of violence and making powerful statements about the horrors of sexual abuse and the silencing of rape victims.[136] Most of the Filipino reviewers similarly appreciated the film's message about the abuse of women.[137] One reviewer even linked the violent scenes to the film's critique of the Philippine situation, although he was careful not to cause trouble for the director. He noted that *Angela* portrayed violence reminiscent of the "old society"[138] instead of the present. Marcos used this term to denote the state of affairs that justified his imposition of martial law. Although he was already president during the last years of the "old society," Marcos characterized the period as one gripped by unrest and violence.[139]

Due in part to the popular conception of rape as a crime against individuals, and to the film's genre coding as a rape-revenge movie, neither critics nor the censors appear to have considered the allegorical relationship between Angela's rape and the Marcos regime's use of torture. The same reasons, in addition to Angela's gender, probably discouraged the censors from interpreting the subversive implications of her crusade. I venture that, as with the revenge fantasy excised from *Jaguar*, Angela's urban vigilantism warrants a strong reading. If we were to conceive of *Jaguar* and *Angela* as related projects, we might find significance in the fact that the urban vigilante character migrates from one narrative to the other. Excised from an early storyline of *Jaguar*, the figure of the urban vigilante stealthily hunting down violent men resurfaces in female form in *Angela*. Superficially less threatening than her male counterpart, the avenging woman roams the noir-like Manila environs in martial law's twilight, taking down one vicious armed thug after another.

The urban vigilante prefigures the rise of so-called "sparrow units," small communist hit squads that operated in Philippine cities beginning around 1980, the year when the film was made and released.[140] Assigned to liquidate the enemies of communists and to seize weapons from the military, the sparrows worked stealthily, their lone gunmen plugging "one shot in the back of the [target's] skull" before disappearing back into the crowd.[141] Apart from advancing party interests, the revolutionaries engaged in targeted killings as a form of political propaganda. Like Angela, the vigilantes responded to a climate of [state-sanctioned] terror by striking fear in the hearts of dirty cops, politicians, capitalists, and other persons who inflicted violence with virtual impunity. The heroine's vigilantism also figures or prefigures other forms of urban guerrilla warfare. In 1979, the "Light a Fire Movement" bombed the floating casino that Imelda Marcos built.[142] The following year, another entity called the April Six Liberation Movement also used explosives to disrupt a conference of American travel agents held at Imelda's Philippine International Convention Center. Because of her gender, Angela the "avenging angel" might have come across as an unlikely figure of political insurgency. In this regard, she is similar to the rebellious daughters who rise against their oppressive parents in Brocka's maternal melodramas, only more fearless and deadly. The censors tolerated subversive female figures whose insurgency appeared to be merely personal or domestic.

CONCLUSION

On August 22, 1977, Marcos used an international conference on seeking "World Peace through Law" as the venue for yet another attempt at legitimizing his dictatorship to international observers. He announced measures to end martial law in three years. "We are moving irretrievably toward normalcy," he said, "as we come closer to a solution of the southern [that is, Moro] secessionist movement as well as the leftist-rightist rebellion and the economic crisis."[143] The autocrat made good on his promise in 1981, just in time for the visit of Pope John Paul II. Marcos declared amnesty for certain "subversive" detainees and also outlined plans for the first local elections since martial law.[144] As was his style, the much-touted liberalization was partial and, in most cases, merely apparitional.[145] For example, he only freed a specific class of political detainees and kept draconian laws in force.

The extensive nocturnal journeys in *Jaguar* and *Angela* indexed the lifting of the curfew over Metro Manila in 1977. A government publication gave the regime's account of the curfew and its ostensible benefits. It said: "Curfew reduced the capability of the subversives and insurgents to carry on their activities under cover of darkness. It has also helped stabilize the peace and order situation by preventing criminal elements from availing of the night hours to pursue their activities."[146] Both *Jaguar* and *Angela* treated the reopening of that sequestered nocturnal time and space with ambivalence. Night gave cover to the transgressions of dissident figures, but it was not, as the films suggested, impervious to the authoritarian state's vast powers of surveillance and social control.

As was true of American cases in which crime movies indexed fluctuations in the national crime rate, Brocka's film noirs appeared in the wake of surging criminality. While, as Raymond Bonner points out, the "crime rate plummeted ... and murders in Manila dropped 90 percent in the first weeks" of martial law, the former increased by 17.5 percent in 1976.[147] Even the government's propaganda machine saw it fit to acknowledge that "from 1976 onwards, an upward trend has been noticeable in the crime rate."[148] In the first two years of "normalization," the number of murder cases in Metro Manila almost tripled from 210 (in 1976) to 593 (in 1979), while the homicide rate climbed from 1,245 to 1,945.[149] The government blamed the surging criminality on such factors as "population growth, rural-urban migration, rapid industrialization, [and] the economic difficulties being experienced by some sectors of society as a result of inflation brought about by the increase in oil prices." More dubiously, the government posited that the rise in crime was also a "consequence of the [three-year] normalization process."[150]

Manila's rampant criminality registered in the narratives and mise-en-scène of *Jaguar* and *Angela*. But if the causes behind the protagonists' criminalization did not reflect the reasons the authoritarian state gave for the uptick in crime, it was because both films were trafficking in allegories and offering a different perspective on social issues. One could say the same things about the opaque motivation for (and political significance of) the protagonists' nefariousness in Brocka's *Caught in the Act* (1981), a film noir released two months after the lifting of martial law. In the film, a sexually promiscuous woman named Bea (Lorna Tolentino) sneaks out on her older husband to have casual sex with men from the lower classes. The anti-heroine meets and becomes obsessed with Leo (Phillip Salvador, the star of *Jaguar*), a small-time peddler of smuggled electronics and, like her, a married person with multiple lovers. Impelled by lust and a raging antipathy that the film never explains, Bea and Leo engage in illicit acts and deliberately hurt their loved ones. Bea, for instance, splurges on home furnishings with her husband's money before heading straight to a motel to tryst with Leo. As for Leo, he sells electronics in the black market before coming home to beat his wife senseless or ordering his other paramour to have an abortion.

In an implicit critique of lawlessness under Marcos, the goons of powerful capitalists serve as the forces of social control, casting aside an inept police. Out of nowhere, thugs begin to trail the adulterous couple. Some days later, Bea's husband randomly asks her to wear a beautiful cocktail dress and go with him on a date. He takes her to a warehouse where she finds Leo hogtied and beaten by the goons who had been trailing them. The husband orders his men to blow Leo's brains out. The sequence captures the gunshot, Leo's grimace, and the adulterous wife's terror all in slow motion. With sadistic laughter, the husband looks on at the horrendous violence.

In this iteration of the Marcosian moment, lines of force converge, indeterminately traceable to larger structural conflicts. Inscribed here, as in similar instances in *Jaguar* and *Angela*, are the vectors of class hostility, the violations of state-sanctioned torture and surveillance, and the ruthlessness of the patriarchy. Brocka suggests that the individual predilection for evil cannot quite account for the unbearable excess of the Marcosian moment. The surplus of violence it displays seems so pervasive or generalized it takes on the character of an enigma external to humans. Lurking in *Jaguar*, *Angela*, and *Caught in the Act* is something inchoate, something malevolent—like the dark abyss of authoritarianism's violence—which Brocka limns as much as shrouds with the desolate light of cinematic noir.

4

Tales of Unrelenting Misfortunes

Family Melodrama and the 1980s Economic Crisis

Authoritarian leaders engage in various forms of repression and bribery to preserve their monopoly on power. As Ronald Wintrobe points out in his study of the political and economic underpinnings of autocracies, these two instruments of authoritarian rule cost enormous sums of money. The price of repression includes, among other things, purchasing weapons and paying handsome salary increases to security forces and mercenaries. Fostering loyalty to a dictatorship also entails granting exclusive privileges to the autocrat's inner circle.[1] It might also entail sponsoring public works projects for the masses.[2] Milan Svolik adds that, apart from building infrastructure, autocrats co-opt their citizens by "redistributing land, subsidizing basic goods, or even distributing cash."[3]

The expenditures for repression and loyalty incur "a deadweight loss to the economy," putting many autocratic states in debt.[4] Ferdinand Marcos's dictatorship depended heavily upon foreign and domestic creditors to keep up with its pay-offs. Emmanuel de Dios reports that the Philippine strongman increased the nation's external public debt at the rate of 25 percent annually between 1970 and 1981.[5] James K. Boyce offers a broader picture of those foreign borrowings. In 1962, three years before Marcos first took office, the country's external debt stood at $360 million. By 1986, the year he was deposed, the debt had ballooned to $28.3 billion, "making the Philippines one of the most heavily indebted countries in Asia, Africa, and Latin America."[6] A substantial portion of those loans was "on-lent to private banks," which in turn extended credit to favored private companies "at the express instructions of President or Mrs. Marcos."[7] Those guaranteed or "behest loans" circumvented government procedures that would have ensured greater odds of repayment. The loans were, at bottom, oversized pay-offs to Marcos's cabal.

Foreign creditors lent heavily to the dictatorship with the encouragement of transnational entities such as the World Bank and the International Monetary Fund (IMF). The two entities backed or made loans even when the strongman was at his most repressive and in the face of reports that about a third of government spending "was being diverted to corrupt purposes, most of it sent abroad."[8] These entities' support of authoritarian rule was due mainly to the influence of the United States, whose strategic interests (including access to military bases in the Philippines) were served by keeping Marcos in power.[9]

In the early 1980s, the combination of indebtedness and other internal and external pressures led to an unprecedented economic catastrophe. Scholars from the University of the Philippines identified several reasons for the crisis. First, "two oil price shocks" (in 1973 and 1978), increased the country's oil import bills from $187 million in 1973 to more than $2 billion in 1982, immensely straining the country's dollar supply. Second, two recessions (in 1974–1975 and 1980–1982) hit developed economies. Those nations imposed new tariffs on imports, which reduced their demand for Philippine products. Third, the Philippines experienced low economic growth—the "lowest per-capita GDP growth rates" in Southeast Asia between 1950 and 1980. The dismal performance was due, among other things, to flawed economic development policies. Fourth, the deepening political and economic instability in the Philippines resulted in capital flight. The losses eventually reached an amount "equivalent to 70 percent of the country's external debt outstanding."[10] Fifth, the assassination of Marcos's political opponent Benigno "Ninoy" S. Aquino Jr. on August 21, 1983, triggered a "crisis of confidence" among foreign creditors, including nations that supported the authoritarian regime.[11]

In October 1983, the Philippine government copped to the virtual depletion of its foreign currency reserves and declared a ninety-day moratorium on paying the principal amounts of its external debts. It subsequently extended the holding pattern four more times.[12] The IMF still offered loans, but they came with steep demands on the country's economic policy, such as allowing the devaluation of the Philippine currency to almost half its value before the crisis. The economic downturn and the policies aimed at reversing it visited great hardship on Filipino citizens, many of whom were already in dire straits.

In this chapter, I examine two films made in the wake of the economic crisis. Brocka and his writers configured both works as family melodramas, a subgenre featuring narratives of marital woes, intergenerational conflict, and other intangible and material concerns related to domestic life. *Adultery: Aida Macaraeg Case No. 7892* (1984) and *Napakasakit, kuya Eddie* (*Such Pain, Brother Eddie*, 1986) both tell stories of families facing chronic or sudden impoverishment. I wish to illumine how these films transmuted the reality of the financial catastrophe into melodramatic scenarios and images. More specifically, I aim to examine the particularity with which Brocka's films inscribed Philippine socioeconomic conditions during the 1980s. I will also show how these films linked the financial devastation of their protagonists to the policies and actions of the authoritarian regime.

ADULTERY: AIDA MACARAEG CASE NO. 7892

Adultery bears witness to a lower-middle-class woman's attempts to escape her deepening impoverishment. Jose Javier Reyes based his script upon journalist Aida Sevilla Mendoza's essay about an actual legal dispute. The film begins with the travails of a Manila waitress, also named Aida (played by superstar Vilma Santos).[13] Aida, we learn, is the sole breadwinner of an extended family that includes elderly parents and siblings, including a younger brother and his growing family. The brother has been unable to find a job since getting laid off some time ago. They have a sister, Miriam (Deborah Sun), who does not live with them. She volunteers to help with expenses but their mother refuses to let her. The old lady has virtually disowned Miriam for taking up with a married man.

Aida worries aloud to her mother and brother about ending up as an "invalid" from overworking herself. The film demonstrates that she is not exaggerating. Scenes depict Aida working long shifts at a Chinese restaurant. At the end of the night, when she is finally relieved of her tight cheongsam and the burden of running around the vast dining room in high-heels, Aida is so exhausted she can hardly speak. She also lacks the energy to touch the plate of noodles Ricardo "Carding" Bautista (Phillip Salvador) orders for her. As Karl Marx might have put it, she is virtually bereft of labor power and lacks the means to reproduce herself for the next grueling workday.[14]

Aida reaches the end of her rope after learning that her brother's wife is pregnant with their second child. The thought of feeding another mouth sends her reeling. "I can't go back to that house.... They will work me to death!" she tells Ricardo despondently. Ricardo tries to comfort her with a proposal of elopement, which she accepts. Aida returns home one last time, but only to chide her "irresponsible" brother for breeding again and then to blame their mother for enabling his freeloading ways. The latter calls Aida "greedy" ("*sakim*"), proving she is oblivious to the financial burden her daughter has been carrying.

Out of love and machismo, Ricardo asks Aida to quit her job after their elopement. He works as a drug runner to provide for both of them. He rationalizes his illicit trade by pointing to the unrealistically low wages in Manila. Historical records show that he was right about the abysmal pay. Marcos's economic policy resulted in a steep decline in the value of wages. As de Dios reports: "The real wage of skilled laborers in Manila in 1980 was only 63.7 percent of its level in 1972 [the year martial law was declared] while that of the unskilled was even lower, 53.4 percent."[15]

In a brief episode of domestic contentment, Ricardo uses his earnings to lease a home for himself and Aida and to put down payments on some appliances. Their domestic life crumbles, however, when the authorities capture Ricardo while moving drugs. Not insignificantly, both the drug trafficker for whom he works and their client have foreign-sounding names. Ricardo's superior goes by the moniker of "the Bombay man" while their new client responds to the name of "Mr. Tan." Both speak Filipino and are likely citizens, but their names and appearance mark them as foreign. Both conform to stereotypes of the Chinese and Indians in the Philippines as ruthless capitalists.

Those ethnic stereotypes link East Asians to drug trafficking, hoarding, and white slavery while casting South Asians as usurious lenders. Tan and Bombay are but two of several foreign persons and things referenced in the film. The other indices of foreignness include Aida's cheongsam and Chinese restaurant job, her and Ricardo's consumption of Kentucky Fried Chicken in one scene, Ricardo's craving for chocolate cake, and the mostly foreign goods sold at the boutique of Aida's sister Miriam. Apart from serving as emblems of the middle-class life to which the characters aspire, these signs of foreignness collectively register the international dimension of the Philippine economic catastrophe. Without exonerating Filipinos such as Ricardo from their role in their financial troubles, the film uses these markers of the foreign to suggest that the economic crisis is not reducible to Filipino doings or issues. The crisis is, rather, the result of a confluence of domestic forces, detrimental foreign activities in the local economy, and an entrenched desire among Filipinos for foreign things. Images of foreign persons and objects similarly appear in the other film discussed in this chapter.

Aida returns to waitressing during Ricardo's imprisonment. She visits him almost weekly and gathers resources for his defense. On one occasion, he notices the toll such burdens have taken on Aida's already slight frame. "You've lost so much weight," he tells her worriedly. Despite appreciating her predicament, he continues to use her as a financial and emotional lifeline. Their conjugal visits result in pregnancy, complicating their situation even more. When Aida breaks the news that she is with child, Carding pressures her into marrying him "right this very moment." She concedes, unable to think of an excuse quickly enough. Aida only pries herself loose after he is sentenced to fifteen years in prison and transferred to a far-flung penal colony. Just before his sentencing, Aida obtains an abortion secretly, knowing she would not be able to provide for a child. Miriam covers for Aida while she recuperates from the procedure, telling Ricardo that Aida had a miscarriage. Aida stops communicating with him altogether after his transfer.

Finally relieved of carrying the financial burdens of others, Aida seizes the opportunity to improve her lot. At a new restaurant job, which she obtains with Miriam's help, Aida meets a much older man who immediately takes a liking to her. Tito Pangilinan (Mario Montenegro) is the proverbial "rich geezer with one foot in the grave" ("*matandang mayamang madaling mamatay*"), the type that Philippine films and sitcoms touted as the salvation of every hard-up woman.[16] On

FIGURE 4.1. Aida (Vilma Santos) escapes poverty by becoming a mistress to a much older man (Mario Montenegro, left) and having his child (Alvin Enriquez, center) in *Adultery*. Courtesy of the MOWELFUND Film Institute (MOWELFUND).

their first date at a classy restaurant, Tito frankly lays out his plan to recruit Aida as his mistress. The old man's transactional pitch unnerves her at first, but then she realizes that she is not above selling herself. She shares this epiphany with her sister, saying: "If I were to go wild, I might as well do it for someone who can be of use to me. What do I have to lose anyway? Whatever there is to lose, I'd lost long ago." After a narrative ellipsis that spans a few years, the film's visuals reveal the price of her companionship: namely, a large but not extravagant house, a car and chauffeur, and maids for the household and their son Alvin (Alvin Enriquez).

Interestingly enough, the film does not take a moralistic view of Aida's decision to commodify herself. Thanks to Tito's wealth, the formerly bedraggled waitress turns into a cheerful suburban matron who wears fashionable clothes and speaks in English when doting on her boy. The sympathetic portrayal of someone who might be considered a female gold digger suggests, among other things, a relaxation of society's moral standards in the wake of the recent economic cataclysm.

The motif of commodifying persons recurs after Ricardo obtains early parole. He spends only seven out of fifteen years in prison due to good behavior. He tracks Aida down through Miriam, who runs a boutique in an upscale mall. He turns up at Aida's home and watches as her car pulls into the driveway with a young boy in the backseat. Aida invites Ricardo into the house and nervously feeds him lies about her current life, before suggesting that they repair elsewhere for dinner. To further placate him, she sleeps with him at a motel.

Ricardo becomes suspicious of Aida's excuses for not taking him in. He spies on her and learns of her relationship with Tito. Ricardo demands that she abandon the older man and move in with him, presumably in the house of his aunt, his closest relative with property. When needling Aida, Ricardo talks as if her new life and possessions were ill-gotten, obtained by bartering the erotic privileges and affection that still rightly belonged to him. Erroneously thinking that Alvin is his son, Ricardo tries to claim him as well.

Tito puts up a fight, but not with Ricardo. He berates Aida for lying about her relationship with Ricardo and for dragging him and his other (legitimate) family into scandal. Moreover, Tito abandons their love nest and takes Alvin away from her. Ricardo eventually withdraws his claim on Alvin, however, after getting Aida to confess that she had aborted the earlier pregnancy.

With the help of his aunt's lawyer friend, Ricardo brings suit against Aida. While Aida's prospective liability mainly involves jail time and separation from her child, the punishment he seeks is also an economic one, in keeping with the film's narrative of financial ruin. Ricardo's suit deprives Aida of Tito's support. The attorney's fees and court costs will also deplete her (and her generous sister's) financial resources. A judgment in Ricardo's favor will thus virtually erase the advantages she had earned over the years as he was languishing in prison. "You traded me for an old man . . . [and] now you have a house and a car!" he cries on one occasion, calling out what he saw as Aida's opportunism. She tries to settle the case by offering to move in with Ricardo, for as long as she can keep her child. "Alvin is all I have," she confesses. Now shorn of all her upper-middle-class trappings and powerless before him and the law, the woman volunteers to surrender all she has left to give: her dignity, herself. Peter Brooks describes such pathos-filled articulations of one's virtuous suffering as the melodrama's trope of "self-nomination."[17] As is commonly the case in such instances, Aida's self-nomination as a fully dispossessed woman softens Ricardo's heart. Moreover, he balks at the harshness of causing Aida to lose her only reason for living.

In the final court scene, the film generates tension by playing up the likelihood of Aida's conviction. With Alvin as the living proof of her transgression and in light of legal statutes that punish women more severely than men for marital infidelity, Aida's lawyer reluctantly admits that their defense is weak and that she might be facing jail time. Out of pity, Ricardo withdraws his suit at the eleventh hour, in a dramatic reversal characteristic of trial scenes in melodramas.[18]

The film closes on an epilogue after the happy resolution at court. The scene, steeped in melodramatic excess unlike much of the rest of the film, shows Aida and Ricardo reuniting at the dock of a picturesque man-made lagoon. The setting sun baldly symbolizes the demise of their relationship. Ricardo brings Alvin with him, the result of a bargain he had struck with Tito on her behalf. Such gentlemen's agreements are inherently sexist because they exclude women from making life-changing decisions, but the deal Ricardo struck was exceptionally favorable to Aida.

Before they part ways, Ricardo volunteers that he will be moving south once more, this time to work in the farmlands of Cebu, in the country's not-so-fertile midsection. His modest ambition shows the limited economic opportunities then available to the urban poor. The scene concludes on a melancholy note, as Aida tenderly inquires: "Whatever happened to the two of us, Carding?" He replies: "Don't ask anymore. The answer might be too painful to consider." Posing that question would force them to recall the bitter truth that they both mortgaged their hearts and futures to stave off crippling poverty. The finale is doubly sad for Aida. Not only does she lose Carding forever but it is unclear if Tito will take her back. Both losses are punishment for her transgressions.

I have attempted thus far to highlight the film's references to financial matters and its depiction of economic adversity, both of which I view as indices of the 1980s economic crisis. The crime of adultery is a fitting subject not only for a narrative of economic desperation but, more broadly, for dramatizing the state's intrusion into the personal and financial affairs of its citizens. As Friedrich Engels has noted in his treatise on the family under capitalism, the state maintains an interest in promoting monogamous marriages chiefly for economic reasons. The capitalist state institutionalized and continues to privilege monogamy to ensure the smooth transfer of property and wealth in society, from private owners to their "natural heirs."[19] Reproduction outside of marriage casts doubt on paternity and also complicates the determination of legal inheritance. Engels also found that sexism was endemic to the "patriarchal form of the family," because only "the monogamy of the woman was required, not that of the man."[20] The "right of conjugal infidelity" was reserved for the man while "adulterous" wives faced "grave legal and social consequences" for the same transgression.[21] Equally important, monogamous unions legitimized the "domestic slavery" of women, devaluing their labors (including household chores and sexual acts) as menial and uncompensated work.[22]

The narrative of Brocka's film resonates with Engels's ideas about the chauvinism of the patriarchal family and society's opportunistic rationale for valorizing monogamy. For instance, Ricardo invokes the material and intangible losses he has borne due to Aida's infidelity. He blames Aida for depriving him of the blissful family life he had envisioned upon his release from prison. The film challenges his tale of male dispossession, however, by depicting his earlier insistence on a prison wedding as a ploy to trap Aida and oblige her to continue visiting him and help fund his defense. The film also supports the view that Aida was right to seek a new

FIGURE 4.2. Ricardo (Phillip Salvador, center) lashes out at Aida (Vilma Santos) in front of her son (Alvin Enriquez, left) in *Adultery*. Courtesy of MOWELFUND.

life during Ricardo's imprisonment, if only to save herself from destitution. In both instances, the film questions the legal and cultural mechanisms that enforce monogamy in Philippine society.

Adultery links the predicament of its characters to the Marcos regime, albeit indirectly. In keeping with a pattern in Brocka's earlier films such as *Weighed but Found Wanting*, conspicuously placed images of Marcos comprise the most specific references to his dictatorship. In several of *Adultery*'s court scenes, a poster of the strongman appears to be both purposely and incidentally placed in the background. I say "incidentally" because images of the president normally abound in public buildings. I also say "purposely" because the large, faded poster of the Filipino dictator looms in the frame at particularly significant moments in the courtroom scenes. I might as well add "not insignificantly" to this list of qualifications, since Marcos, whose image appears as a symbol of the law during the trial of an adultery case, was, in fact, a well-known womanizer himself. Among his affairs was a sordid liaison with the American B-movie actress Dovie Beams, which became a cause célèbre of the late 1960s.

I can think of two instances when the Marcos poster appears to invoke the relation between the melodrama of private lives and the adverse socioeconomic doings of the authoritarian state. In the first example, Marcos's portrait looms behind Ricardo's lawyer as the latter grills Aida about her infidelity. Aida looks away from him (and the image of Marcos) at one point. She then turns her gaze directly at Ricardo and offers her explanation to him rather than to the court. Ricardo acknowledges the gesture and, as he and Aida lock eyes, they momentarily and symbolically shut the overbearing government out of their private affairs.

The opposition between domestic lives and state interference recurs in the next example. It is Ricardo's turn on the stand. Aida's lawyer grills him about his criminal activities to show that he had failed to support Aida with an honest living. Like her, Ricardo failed to live up to the obligations of a married individual and had broken the law as well. As with Aida's interrogation, the camera occasionally frames him with the same picture of Marcos in the background. In both scenes, the film associates the autocrat's image with the heavy-handed punishment of crimes committed out of economic desperation.

The critics and reviewers of *Adultery* did not comment on the significance of the Marcos posters but picked up on the film's resonances to the contemporary socioeconomic situation. Mario Bautista touched on the broader implications of Aida's financial struggles in his review. He wrote: "There are plenty of women like Aida in our society today. Finding themselves in dire straits, they reach for something that might keep them from falling into the abyss. Do they sin by trying to solve their problems in a practical manner? From a moral standpoint, they do. That said, it is easy to pass judgment when one does not face such grave problems." Bautista heaped praise on the film's "highly realistic situations and characterizations" that, although delivered in a "melodramatic narrative," are nevertheless faithful to "real life."[23] Another entertainment journalist, Anselle Belluso, was "impressed" by the "vivid and starkly real" treatment of the material and "the intense truth that the film conveys to its viewers." He also expressed appreciation for the film's social commentary, writing: "Obliquely, the film comments on contemporary social attitudes as it builds up the story-telling, utilizing very real human elements entangled in genuine dilemmas of present times."[24] The phrase "genuine dilemmas of present times" seems to reference the problems wrought by the economic crisis.

Brocka described *Adultery* as another one of his commercial "[love] triangle films."[25] Some reporters, however, framed the work as his "first serious movie . . . in a long time."[26] It was supposedly quite "unlike the romance and tearful quickies" the director had been making of late.[27] One journalist added that "the old Brocka is back."[28] Some thought he was likely to regain "his reputation as a director of sensible films."[29] Another reporter emphasized that Brocka made the film "in the midst of his political involvements" and quotes leading man Phillip Salvador as saying that the director's work has benefitted from "all his political involvements."[30] One reporter even joked that the director had been feverishly making films like

Adultery to make hay "before he is captured upon the orders of you-know-who"[31] (i.e., President Marcos).

It is unlikely that such talk about social and political relevance contributed substantially to the film's impressive box office showing. It was rather Santos's star power, her pairing with Salvador, and her previous successes in pictures about marital infidelity that resulted in box office gold. The film reportedly raked in 1.3 million pesos "on its opening day" and reached a "4 million take on its first three days."[32] At a loss for superlatives, Ricardo Lo described the film as "a big, big hit" and "a giant hit."[33] Indeed, those earnings were impressive when measured against the 700,000-peso budget of low-end independent films in the early 1980s.[34]

The government weighed in on *Adultery* both through the censors and an entity called the Film Ratings Board (FRB). I cannot find any traces of the censors' findings but have seen the latter's report. The FRB, which offered tax rebates to quality films and belonged to a different agency than the censors, awarded the film its highest rating of "A," its first for 1984.[35] The report lauded the film's "general fidelity to real-life situations" and the "highly believable drama" that emerges from the "potentially maudlin material." The report commended the film's "particularly remarkable" ending in which "democratic justice triumphs."[36] The latter, however, is a convenient misreading of the film's resolution. The flawed heroine narrowly avoids harsh punishment, but not because of the fairness of the criminal justice system. It was instead Ricardo's act of love, compassion, and—in recognition of his and Aida's shared economic vulnerability—class solidarity that ultimately kept her from prison. When Ricardo walks away from mother and child at the film's conclusion, he repeats his earlier gesture at the courthouse of surrendering all his claims to Aida. His generous concession would have fully liberated the woman, were she not still beholden to that "old man" with the "house and the car," the decrepit, opportunistic capitalist and wayward patriarch whose patronage she could not afford to lose in such hard times. To be sure, there is no triumph of "democratic justice" here.

SUCH PAIN, BROTHER EDDIE

Such Pain, Brother Eddie (1986) bears witness to a middle-class family's precipitous decline after a series of financial setbacks. It was released shortly after the February 1986 uprising that ousted Ferdinand Marcos but was already in development by May of the previous year[37] and in principal photography by August.[38] The project's conceptualization and filming thus occurred in the midst of the economic catastrophe hastening the regime's demise.

Such Pain is not only Brocka's most detailed representation of the 1980s financial crisis but also a key work in the first cycle of melodramas about the lives of Filipino overseas workers. The film was mostly ignored by critics, perhaps due in part to the cloying eponymous theme song that inspired the film's narrative. The ditty (composed by Jerico Rimas) revolves around a letter sent by a migrant worker in Saudi Arabia to "Brother" Eddie Ilarde, a popular host of confessional programs on radio and TV. The letter writer vents to Brother Eddie about his toils in the oil fields and the family troubles caused by his absence. Sung by Roel Cortez in the twangy manner of American country music, *Such Pain* was a phenomenal hit in the Philippines. The song's popularity did not, however, translate into box office success for the film adaptation. In a column published before the film's release, one of the producers seemed to question whether a song that had already become the butt of jokes on television was even appropriate for the soundtrack of a dramatic film.[39] It also did not help that the script pokes fun at the song, which blares on the radio twice and, in one scene, kills the mood for a couple about to make love.[40]

Such Pain registers the economic crisis both overtly and indirectly. The direct references to the crisis begin with the film's opening image, which shows a long queue of men standing outside an unidentified office, many of them clutching or filling out job applications. The film's original viewers likely would have connected this opening image to the economic and unemployment crisis that began three years earlier. Broad notes that "Millions of workers were laid off during the first half of the 1980s.... Three million people (15 percent of the workforce) lost their jobs between January 1984 and January 1985."[41]

The treatment of the economic crisis continues in the next scene, as the film listens in on employees at an unspecified firm who are worrying aloud about their slipping economic security. For example, a middle-aged man wonders how long his retirement pay will last "in these [hard] times." He was right to be concerned. In the first year of the economic crisis, the consumer price index for food prices rose by 54 percent, greatly diminishing the buying power of Philippine wages.[42] In another scene close to the beginning of the film, several women discuss applying for jobs at other firms, second-guessing their bosses who could not be relied upon to tell the truth about the company's finances. Elsewhere in the same office, a manager waits nervously for the approval of a "letter of credit" that would allow their firm to purchase the raw materials needed to stay in business.

The film quickly initiates a pattern of moving between the broader social context of the economic crisis and its particular effects on one family's financial and personal affairs. Early in the narrative, Carmelo/Melo (Ronaldo Valdez), the father of two teenagers, is laid off from his managerial position at a manufacturing firm. The boss relates that a surge in the cost of raw materials "almost tripled the cost of production" at their factory, thus necessitating substantial cutbacks on operating expenses. More specifically, as one of his coworkers later explains over drinks, their firm could no longer obtain "imported chemicals" without "any dollars left" for doing business.

The employees' dialogue about the steep increase in the cost of imported goods and the dearth of universal currency directly reference the nation's disastrous balance-of-payments crisis. It is important to note that both references were added during filming (they do not appear in the production script),[43] indicating Brocka and Reyes's desire to explain the ongoing economic crisis to their viewers.

In real life, the Central Bank of the Philippines restricted the outflow of dollars from the country after depleting its foreign exchange reserves. This policy made the importation of foreign goods unaffordable and even impossible for some firms. The scarcity of dollars was due not only to corruption but also to more than a decade's worth of flawed economic policies. As de Dios and Paul Hutchcroft point out, the Marcos government adopted a misguided strategy of "debt-driven growth."[44] The regime used money borrowed from abroad to foster economic development, but it financed too many projects that did not yield enough returns to service the debt, much less pay the principal. Equally important, the regime encouraged the growth of light manufacturing industries, many of which relied on technology and materials acquired with foreign currency.[45] The depletion of the country's dollar reserves crippled such businesses. As Broad relates, "The immediate effect of foreign exchange controls was to restrict effectively the flow of imported material inputs to many industries, causing numerous firms to cut back production, lay off or rotate workers, or simply close shop."[46] *Such Pain* attributes Melo's retrenchment and his employer's predicament to those very same issues.

Melo attempts to shore up his finances by placing his severance pay in an investment scheme recommended by a former coworker. His wife, Emma (Pilar Pilapil), tries to dissuade him but to no avail. "I'd listen to you if you were talking about kitchen matters," he tells her. "But this is about business, so you should shut up!" The chauvinistic and impulsive husband quickly loses the entire investment, as Emma had feared. He tells her, in between sobbing fits, that "the Chinaman" Mr. Tan had absconded with the funds. Melo's reference to the swindler's ethnicity is both an instance of mundane racism and another iteration of the motif of foreignness in Brocka's films about the economic crisis. The reference suggests that Melo was indeed to blame for his crushing loss but it is also the handiwork of foreign capitalists.

Melo's fortunes continue to slip as he fails to secure employment. His friend Charlie throws him a lifeline, offering him a stake in a profitable business wholesaling fish. Unwilling to let go of his white-collar identity, Melo refuses the kind offer. Without any income to draw on, he defaults on his loans and sees his assets forfeited. The family's sensible investment property, located in the picturesque hills of Antipolo, is first to go. Melo approaches his sister Susan (Tessie Tomas) about taking over the mortgage payments, already late by several months. When she declines, the longtime investment is sunk entirely. Around the same time, Melo admits that he could no longer afford to pay the mortgage on their roomy suburban family home. Susan is unable to help him save it as well but loans him money to rent a small apartment for his family.

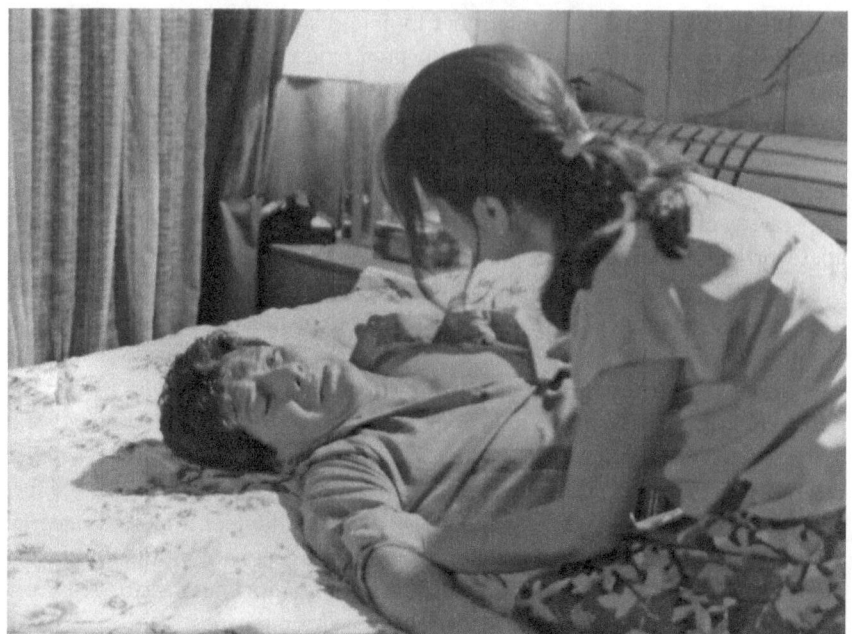

FIGURE 4.3. Emma (Pilar Pilapil) consoles Melo (Ronaldo Valdez) after he loses his life's savings to a fraudulent investment scheme in *Such Pain, Brother Eddie*. Courtesy of MOWELFUND.

From owning their dream house in the upper-middle-class Merville subdivision, Melo and his family end up renting a two-bedroom apartment in a grimy, working-class district (identified as Caloocan in the film's production script).[47] The foreclosure of the family home continues a pattern of devastating losses in the film's narrative. Their quickness and severity reflect the fate of the national economy.

One of the film's most wrenching scenes depicts Melo's family stoically watching truckers haul away their furniture. Emma tries to downplay the situation by remarking on the impracticality of holding on to oversized belongings, but the family's dispossession visibly rattles the teenage daughter Cynthia (Emily Loren). "For shame!" she mutters, betraying the feelings her mother tries to suppress. In another poignant episode, Emma discovers that her two teenagers have withdrawn quietly from their social circles after leaving private school. The fickleness of capitalism forms the context of their abrupt decline and deep sense of shame. Valorizing economic winners, capitalism also conditions the victims of greed and inequity to beat themselves up for financial woes that others cause. Marcos's "bureaucrat capitalist" state laid out the path to economic catastrophe by, among other things, cultivating the unsustainable export-oriented industry that employed Melo.[48] Ignoring the impact of flawed policies, the strongman's technocrats left ordinary people—like Melo's children—to bear its full weight.

Reminiscent of *Adultery*, the nuclear family in *Such Pain* becomes a prime casualty of the economic crisis. Melo and Emma's marriage sours as their finances worsen. He blocks Emma's efforts to lend him a hand in resolving their financial problems, disallowing her to work at a travel agency owned by her friend. He relents eventually but then belittles her job as one of wrangling "horny Japanese tourists."

After months of holding out for another supervisory position in Manila, Melo follows a growing national trend and takes a contract job in Saudi Arabia. Financial relief eludes him, however, when his Middle East employer only pays half the promised salary. For whatever reason, he fails to remit even a portion of that income to his family. Melo's disastrous financial mistakes greatly diminish his paternal authority. From Emma's perspective, he had become virtually useless. In a moment of deep resentment and anger, she tells him that he had become an abject failure as a provider, co-parent, and lover.

The theme of persons suddenly losing their value, like currency or stocks in an economic downturn, is not unique to Brocka's work. In her study of cinema during the financial catastrophe that swept Argentina in the new millennium, Joanna Page finds that the films contain themes of "unemployment, poverty, debt, and marginalization" similar to those in Brocka's work. Page also identifies visual tropes that correspond to those themes.[49] One of these visual motifs stages the interchangeability of human figures. Page gives as an example a series of identically composed mise-en-scènes or frames where one person is almost imperceptibly substituted for another between shots through the use of visual puns. Page interprets this motif of the "exchangeability of people" as a sign of their diminished status, as objects rather than human beings. Such human devaluation is the result of losing one's security of employment and other things that anchor a person's sense of self.[50] Brocka signals Melo's depreciation through more conventional methods, using dialogue and images of material dispossession to make statements similar to those found in Argentinian films.

Unlike the sexist narrative of Rimas's song, Brocka's film adaptation does not condemn Emma for exerting pressure on Melo to seek employment abroad or for being unfaithful to him. Reminiscent of *Adultery*, *Such Pain* depicts Emma's affair with a rich and older man named Willy (Charlie Davao) as a pragmatic choice instead of a morally reprehensible one. Their relationship is irreducible to gold digging or prostitution. While Emma benefits financially from their relationship, she also develops a strong affection for the older man and finds joy in his company. The film is likewise sympathetic to Cynthia, who also uses romance and sex to deal with her family's economic plight. She sleeps with her boyfriend Jimbo (Tani Cinco) to escape reality. When Jimbo grows tired of her, she takes up with a much older man who drives her around in a Mercedes Benz sedan. Cynthia ends her trysts with the latter after discovering she is pregnant with Jimbo's child. She makes a big leap into adulthood by continuing the pregnancy and moving into a place of her own despite her tender age.

The film builds empathy for Cynthia and Emma by showing how a conservative and sexist society denigrates hard-up women who engage in sexual relations with affluent men outside of marriage. While sympathetic to Cynthia and Emma's plight, *Such Pain* also uses their "compromised" virtues to signal the vulnerability of women and the erosion of middle-class values during times of financial crisis.

In Melo's family, it is Dino who proves most resilient to their economic setbacks. He stoically confronts their troubles even if he is hardly equipped to resolve them. He takes a job at a fast food joint where he runs into acquaintances who either mock or pity him. Among the latter is his almost-girlfriend Sandra (Janice de Belen). He initially pushes her away due to his masculine pride. But thanks to Sandra's persistence, and to his capacity for introspection, Dino opens his heart and begins to heal his wounds. In doing so, he becomes an emotionally wiser and stronger person than before. In the end, it is also this suddenly grown-up Dino who shows his father the wisdom of moving past his financial troubles and failed marriage. Dino's turning point occurs after he overhears his parents quarreling about his mother's infidelity. Full of self-righteous anger, Melo refuses to accept Emma's claim that he had been treating her for too long like a "servant . . . no, like a slave, because servants are paid while slaves are used, like property." Her words, which by coincidence recall Engels's characterization of housewives as victims of legitimized "domestic slavery," provoke Melo to raise his hand again at Emma, before finally backing away from her.[51] Following the confrontation and the couple's parting of ways, Melo assumes that Dino would readily choose to live with him instead of Emma. However, rather than picking one parent over another as Melo would have desired, Dino elects to live in a boarding house. Dino thus turns the situation into another teachable moment for his father. Through this gesture, Dino resists his father's machismo and selfishness. Dino also helps Melo take ownership of the damage he has inflicted on their family and forego his animosity toward Cynthia and especially Emma.

The son's decision to live on his own completes the separation of all his family members. It is an unusual conclusion for a family melodrama, which conventionally mitigates the fracturing of a nuclear family by offering a glimpse of its eventual repair.[52] As Christine Gledhill reminds us, melodramas typically engage in the nostalgic idealization of families, even dysfunctional ones.[53] Brocka's *Adultery* follows this particular tendency as well. Although *Adultery* dissolves the protagonists' romantic relationship, it ends by happily reinstating the mother-son dyad. *Such Pain* takes a different approach. The film concludes with Melo, Emma and their children taking their separate ways. By ending with a nuclear family still in ruins, the film opts for a more realistic conclusion and makes a subtle but powerful statement about the catastrophic impact of the economic downturn. Only a perfunctory note of happiness livens up the otherwise bleak finale. Dino and Sandra flash smiles as they walk side-by-side at the mall, bereft of parents but presumably heading into a brightening future.

Exporting Labor

The subplot of Melo's stint as an overseas contract worker is vital to the film's political critique. As mentioned earlier, *Such Pain* is one of the pioneering melodramas about Filipino migrant workers. It joined films such as Gil Portes's *Miss X* (1980) and *'Merika* (1984) in dramatizing the social costs of the Marcos regime's labor export program. Introduced in 1974, the government's scheme aimed to prop up a weak labor market and sagging dollar reserves.[54] It showed impressive results, bringing in millions of dollars in remittances. The program's success prompted the creation of state agencies and programs devoted to accelerating the out-migration of Filipino workers. Overseas labor deployment rose almost tenfold in a decade, from 36,035 workers in 1975 to 372,784 in 1985.[55] Their remittances grew from $111 million in 1976 to more than $1 billion in 1983."[56] For a short period, the Marcos regime even mandated overseas laborers to send back 50–80 percent of their income or lose the privilege of working abroad.[57] The government rescinded the policy after workers pushed back.[58] Despite such discontinued initiatives, however, the labor export program flourished, helping considerably to sustain the authoritarian state. The remittances of overseas workers substantially increased the government's supply of foreign currency and alleviated some of the socioeconomic problems that would have exacerbated political unrest.[59]

In Marcos's Philippines and elsewhere, the usual solution to capitalist crises entails what David Harvey calls a "spatial fix"[60] or "spatio-temporal fix."[61] Such remedies work by "imposing the devaluation of capital elsewhere."[62] Usurious loans that transnational banks routinely extend to third world countries (always with plenty of strings attached) exemplify this practice of shifting overages and losses from one place or country to another. The recruitment of cheap laborers from the third world is also a common form of spatial fix for developed economies,[63] a scheme often described in more flattering terms as the "new international division of labor."[64] From the perspective of the overseas worker, however, the pursuit of higher salaries abroad could also mitigate the inequity of the global north's self-serving spatial fixes. Labor migration can, as Gayatri Spivak puts it, serve as their path to "seeking justice under capitalism."[65] The trouble, of course, is that the migrant workers' displacement into foreign lands increases not just the amount of their wages but also the intensity of their alienation from their labor. *Such Pain* emphasizes these challenging predicaments.

FIGURE 4.4. Emma (Pilar Pilapil, second from right) and her children (Emily Loren and Aga Mulach, back) bid farewell to Melo (Ronaldo Valdez, foreground) before he leaves for the Middle East. *Such Pain, Brother Eddie*. Courtesy of MOWELFUND.

The film levels a critique of labor exportation in several ways. First, *Such Pain* partly attributes the family's disintegration to the prolonged separation of migrant workers and their families. Second, the film depicts the menace of illegal recruitment and the Philippine government's failure to ensure the welfare of its overseas workers. Melo's ordeal in the Middle East demonstrates that overseas contract jobs were unconscionably punishing and alienating and that the Philippine state is inept at protecting its exported workers. He describes working abroad as "enslaving oneself for dollars." In another scene, Emma expresses an unflattering opinion of the government's capacity to protect its overseas workers. When prodded by one of her friends to file a complaint against Melo's recruiter with the Ministry of Labor, Emma demurs, saying that it would not be worth the effort.[66]

Like Rimas's song, Brocka's film does not romanticize overseas work. Instead of money and presents, what Melo brings home in abundance are stories of his exploitation, loneliness, and Jedda's withering heat. "I'd rather go hungry here than die over there," he tells his family at his homecoming party. By characterizing Melo's stint abroad as a failure, *Such Pain* offers a counternarrative to the Marcos government's enthusiastic promotion of labor export.

The phrase "economic crisis" is never uttered in the film and is also glaringly absent in Reyes's production script. Such omission was likely an attempt to keep the Marcos censors and the authorities away from the film, which was produced by a scrappy independent outfit that the director wished to protect. In a 1984 speech, Brocka speculated that the failed economy was one of several sensitive issues for the regime. He said: "Anybody who tries to make truthful movies about the basic economic problems like poverty in our developing country, the prevalence of corruption, the structures of injustice in the past and in the present, will get into a lot of problems."[67] Both the production script and the assembled film of *Such Pain* seem to take account of the issue's touchy nature. Reyes's original script merely alludes to the economic crisis in a scene that was either left unfilmed or omitted from the assembled picture. In that scene, Emma tells her son that he must withdraw from private school because they can no longer afford his tuition. She blames the painful decision on the "unrelenting misfortunes" (*"sunud-sunod na kamalasan"*) that have befallen them.[68] In view of the nation's dismal finances, the phrase refers as much to the economic crisis as to the family's financial woes. The assembled film replaces this allusion with a couple of direct references to the economy's dismal state. In the first of these references, Melo's younger brother Ernie (Toby Alejar) predicts the nation's imminent collapse. He says: "You know, I give this country another three years, and that's it." Ernie makes a similar claim in another scene after he passes on the offer to take over Melo's real estate investment. "Only idiots," he says, "still buy property in the Philippines." Although the economic crisis was no longer a politically sensitive topic when the film finally reached cinemas in the post-Marcos era, those lines of dialogue were fighting words when they were spoken.

In his review of *Such Pain*, Raul Regalado mentions the film's thematization of the financial crisis. He describes Brocka's melodrama as an "examination of the disintegration of a family due to economic troubles."[69] He goes on to say that: "From the first shot of workers lined up outside a recruiting office to the detailed depiction of the family's compounded financial woes, the movie creates a scenario that is all too familiar to the middle-class moviegoer."[70] Regalado likely arrived at this interpretation on his own, but it is worth mentioning that publicists also highlighted the film's sociopolitical commentary in some of their earliest stories. In September 1985, six months before the film's release, one of those articles notes that: "The story is about a family torn apart by a severe economic crisis" (*"matinding krisis ng ekonomiya"*).[71] The article also quotes the screenwriter as saying that the film "is based on real life."

The publicity campaign's emphasis on social relevance probably aimed to attract other viewers besides fans of the film's stars. Brocka's independently produced movie was especially vulnerable at the tills because, as journalists noted, the previous films of its director and teenage stars (Mulach and De Belen) had failed miserably. Brocka hit a "losing streak" after the extraordinary success of *Adultery*, flopping at the box office with such films as *Miguelito* and *White Slavery*.[72] Similarly, the films of De Belen and Mulach lost money. I cannot find any references to how *Such Pain* fared at the box office, but because publicists typically reported successes, I take their silence to mean that *Such Pain* did not fare well. The box office results, unfortunately, seems to have mirrored the film's narrative of catastrophic loss.

CONCLUSION

I have attempted to illustrate how melodrama, a mode of entertainment replete with tales of lost fortunes and contested social mobility, registers the 1980s economic crisis.[73] Both of the melodramas discussed here evoke the financial disaster through stories of families experiencing sudden or worsening destitution.

I have identified narrative and visual tropes found in Brocka's tales of economic catastrophe. The first of these motifs is the devaluation of individuals. Many of the characters in Brocka's films find themselves diminished in their own eyes as well as those of their peers because of prolonged joblessness and economic want. The pain of being suddenly misprized or discarded wreaks havoc on the protagonists' intimate relationships. Another recurring trope is the sexual vulnerability of females. The figure of the sexually exploited woman appears in both of the films discussed here. In a chauvinistic society and during a time of economic want, this figure is impugned as a "whore" regardless of whether or not she engages in sex work. Such depictions seem noticeably fraught because mothers and sisters typically command reverence in family melodramas and Filipino movies. These aberrations in the portrayal of family women thus register the exceptional impact of the crisis. The third motif—the unraveling of the nuclear family—is generic to family melodramas, but in Brocka's films it also highlights the economic origins of the narrative conflicts. In those movies, the families disintegrate because of financial predicaments, and love alone is powerless to restore them. The suddenness or severity of the impoverishment of the families mimics the shocks that characterize economic downturns. Moreover, the pall cast by the nation's economic meltdown appears to be a lasting one for the characters.

Some of the tropes I have cited may also be present in the domestic melodramas of other countries that suffered economic crises in the 1980s or other decades. I have tried, when possible, to signal the broader significance of Brocka's work to the study of other films about financial cataclysms or that appeared during such periods. At the same time, I have attempted to discern the unique signatures of the 1980s economic crisis and Marcos's authoritarianism in two of his films. For instance, I pointed to a scene in *Such Pain* where a minor character references a shortage of foreign currency and blames it for the protagonist's joblessness. I also noted oblique references to the 1980s economic crisis as well as to the Marcos regime. Some of the more salient aspects of the economic crisis never surface in the works discussed here. Both narratives do not reference the Marcos regime's "crony capitalism," price controls, strike bans, and the painful "structural adjustment" reforms mandated by the IMF.[74] Self-censorship, comprehensibility and dramatic interest might explain the absence or omission of those elements.

In the Philippines and certain other nations, the economic upheavals of the 1980s weakened or toppled authoritarian regimes. As Barbara Geddes describes it, "populations plunging into poverty blamed their governments and gradually took the risk of demanding change."[75] The films I have discussed stay clear of these momentous developments. One must look to his other melodramas to trace the effects of the financial crisis upon the political realm. In those narratives, we find protagonists who confront the turmoil that came in the wake of a ruined economy and the concomitant weakening of tyrannical leadership. Those bold, politically urgent melodramas are the concerns of the next two chapters.

5

Men in Revolt

Two Experiments in Political Cinema

Popular sentiment began to turn sharply against Ferdinand Marcos and his autocratic regime in 1983. Two of his secret presidential decrees—products of his unchecked power to create laws instantly—leaked to the public early that year.[1] The first established the Presidential Commitment Order (later renamed as the Preventive Detention Action). It allowed the state to arrest and hold indefinitely without bail anyone the authorities considered a threat to national security.[2] The second decree turned subversion and even mere participation in public demonstrations into capital offenses.[3]

As discussed in the previous chapter, the country also ran out of funds to service its debts that same year. A substantial portion of the debt was believed to have been stolen by the strongman and his cronies.[4] The resulting economic crisis led to mass unemployment, the devaluation of the national currency by upwards of 120 percent, and hyperinflation.[5]

On top of his political and economic problems, the president was in poor health. He was rumored to have undergone yet another kidney transplant in the course of battling lupus erythematosus.[6] He denied it, but his morbid appearance betrayed him.

On August 21, 1983, former Senator Benigno "Ninoy" S. Aquino Jr. was assassinated on the steps of the tarmac at the Manila International Airport.[7] Aquino, the most popular of Marcos's political rivals, returned from exile in Boston to lead the opposition amid reports of the strongman's imminent death. He traveled against the express wishes of the Marcoses, reportedly turning down an unsolicited $10 million inducement from Imelda to stay put in the United States. He also risked imprisonment due to a life sentence for subversion and other false charges.

The military absurdly insisted that he was shot by a lone gunman, who somehow managed to skirt the numerous armed guards surrounding the plane in which he arrived. The Marcos regime denied any wrongdoing but was widely believed to have ordered the brazen killing.

Lino Brocka had thrown himself into political activism several months before Aquino's murder. He mobilized the film and arts community to protest the planned expansion of censorship laws. The draft of Executive Order 868 required actors to obtain licenses to work, subjected live shows (including theater) to censorship, and controlled foreign coproduction ventures, among others. Brocka cofounded the Free the Artist Movement, later renamed Concerned Artists of the Philippines (CAP), to fight the proposed law and lead the arts and media sector in tackling other sociopolitical issues.[8] They successfully lobbied to eliminate the most egregious features of the proposed decree.

Apart from organizing protests, the director made picking fights with Imelda Marcos a pervasive and daring component of his political activism. He withdrew his films from exhibition at the Manila International Film Festival, one of her pet projects. Along with fellow auteur Mike De Leon, he also criticized the festival's extravagant price tag.[9] More boldly, he tried to shame the first lady during his speech at the awards ceremony of the Film Academy of the Philippines, an entity she helped found.[10] A correspondent for *Variety* recounts that the filmmaker attended the event "garbed in black pants with a white shirt emblazoned with sparkling black letters that spelled 'free the artist' and 'ban the censors.'"[11] Brocka reportedly ad-libbed the following statement while presenting the best director award: "My [cue] card reads that this is a good year for the film industry. It will be a good year if the honorable lady [Imelda] will give us freedom from censorship."

Not content with his public tirades at Imelda, he and De Leon turned an invitation to an international film event into an opportunity to criticize the secret presidential decrees.[12] The directors previously agreed to grace a retrospective of Filipino films since 1979 at the Mostra Internazionale del Nuovo Cinema, a section of the film festival in Pesaro, Italy. They later rescinded their acceptance in protest of Marcos's edicts. In their statement to the international press, the directors claimed that the draconian laws aimed to quell political dissent and might well lead to "the total loss" of the "rights and freedoms" of Filipinos.[13] Brocka went a step further, joining legal challenges to the decrees, and on one occasion famously mouthing off about the issue to Supreme Court Chief Justice Enrique Fernando.

Brocka turned into a bolder political activist after Aquino's killing. He joined the executive committee of the Justice for Aquino, Justice for All movement, a burgeoning anti-Marcos organization. During an interview with an American journalist, Brocka recalled the profound impact of the assassination on him and other Filipinos. He said: "That was the turning point for a lot of people. It shocked the country. The moderates, the silent, the indifferent were so shocked; it brought us together."[14] As Serena Diokno notes, the assassination led to the "unprecedented galvanization of all anti-Marcos forces into a burgeoning united front."[15] Defying grave restrictions on public demonstrations, a coalition of activists, church groups, laborers, and citizens from various social classes held weekly mass actions. Brocka attended and helped organize many such rallies.

There were two early, notable efforts to bring the subject of the Aquino murder into Philippine film culture. *The Hollywood Reporter* related in March 1984 that a local film distributor was reissuing the French political thriller *I for Icarus* (Henri Verneuil, 1979) because "the film has a theme parallel to the assassination of Filipino opposition leader Benigno Aquino last year."[16] Loosely based on the murder of John F. Kennedy but set in a fictitious country, the film's representation of political conspiracy and a compromised investigative body resonated strongly with recent Philippine events. The news report went on to say that "The controversial film is having a series of premiere nights this month and in April and will have a one-week advance showing in the militant Makati area." For whatever reason, the regime tolerated this indirect but still legible criticism of the state.

Shortly after the screenings of *Icarus*, Regal Films, one of the country's leading producers of commercial movies, released a socially relevant drama that was supposed to end with "footage from actual Ninoy [Aquino] rallies and the [campaign to] boycott [the forthcoming election] movement."[17] The film, De Leon's *Sister Stella L.* (1984), centers on a nun who becomes a labor activist while ministering to factory workers. Footage of the political rallies and Aquino's burial procession were subsequently "edited out because the producers thought it would be the wisest thing to do." The deletion averted a second run-in with the censors, who previously rejected an earlier version of the film's story outline.[18] The film nevertheless retained an extraordinary amount of political content. Indeed, *Sister Stella L.* marked the rise of a new political cinema in the Philippines, along with the two Brocka films discussed in this chapter and another melodrama titled *Paper Boats on a Sea of Fire* (*Bangkang papel sa dagat ng apoy*, 1984). *Paper Boats* was written and directed by Edgardo M. Reyes, who also authored the novel that Brocka adapted into the film *Manila in the Claws of Light* (1975). A rejoinder to *Manila*, Reyes's film caught the ire of Marcos's much-feared National Intelligence and Security Agency for its depiction of labor unrest.[19]

POLITICAL CINEMA

The ferment of the times called for new ways of using cinema for political ends. The problem of how to create a political cinema—and for critics, how to appraise it—entailed considerations of content, form, and target audience, among others. In the next two years following Aquino's murder, Brocka made a couple of films that sought to reconcile his political activism with his long-term project of making commercial and prestige films. The French philosopher Gilles Deleuze acknowledges Brocka's work—although not specifically *My Own Country*—as one of the examples of an emergent "modern political cinema."[20] He distinguishes this "modern" version from the "classic" kind that preceded it on the bases of their programmatic objectives, stylistic features, and social impact. By Deleuze's account, the "classic political cinema" comprises agitprops, state propaganda, and even commercial films with nationalist themes. Such cinema seeks to advance a collective identity and ideology.[21] It aims, as Laura U. Marks suggests, to form and represent a "revolutionary proletariat."[22] D. N. Rodowick similarly notes that in classic political cinema "people are figured as a homogenous force waking to its collective power."[23] Modern political cinema, in contrast, seeks to engender radical social change by summoning forth new subjectivities and forms of community. Deleuze refers to these new beings and collectives as the "people who are missing," in contrast to the already existing social formations and identities that classic political cinema aimed to mobilize.[24] These emergent collectives will be heterogeneous and pluralistic, for their members will be brought together not by hardened ideologies but by nascent realizations, causes, and opportunities. He regards modern political cinema not simply as an object but a process: a "collective utterance" as well as the collaborative acts of producing and watching films in the service of remaking the world.[25] The task of such films includes depicting an intolerable state of affairs and, in doing so, inspiring the reinvention of the social order. As well, modern political films generate "new myths"—compelling new visions of the society to come.[26]

Deleuze's account of modern political cinema mainly valorizes stylistic features identified with European art cinema and with Third Cinema from Africa and Latin America. These features include multicharacter or prismatic narratives, disorienting alternations between omniscient and subjective narration, and the incorporation of documentary elements into predominantly fictional material (or vice-versa).[27] Because of Philippine cinema's wide commercial base, only a handful of films employ the atypical stylistic features and political engagement that Deleuze observes in modern political filmmaking. De Leon's *Sister Stella L.* meets some of those criteria. Although the film contains the basic components of the Hollywood formula (the vestiges of romance between a nun and her former boyfriend, a journalist), *Sister* incorporates techniques from modern cinema rarely seen in the Philippines.[28] These techniques include starkly naturalistic cinematography and dialogue, self-reflexive moments when characters directly address the moviegoers, and diegetic musical numbers inspired by political demonstrations and street theater. The film thematizes current political events, including the radicalization of the Filipino religious, the government's role in the suppression of unions, and the torture and summary execution of civilians by the authorities.

In spite of its stirring narrative and the casting of superstar Vilma Santos in the title role, De Leon's progressive and stylized film did not succeed at the box office. It also did not become the model for political films that followed. Filmmakers and viewers preferred a more familiar approach. For instance, Brocka in the mid-1980s devised two kinds of political films but made only a few stylistic changes to the pattern of social melodramas he had created in the previous decade. As I mentioned in chapter 1, those earlier pictures bore the influence of 1950s Hollywood melodramas, Philippine prestige films about the hardships of farmers and the country's troubles after World War II, the heightened realism of European new wave cinemas, and especially the sociopolitical critique of José Rizal. They employed largely conventional cinematic storytelling but incorporated barbed sociopolitical references and allegories. Spurred by his engagement in political activism during the early 1980s, Brocka revisited the approach of his 1970s films and strove to amplify their political discourse without sacrificing clarity and mainstream appeal.

With Brocka's films in mind, Deleuze recognized that creative appropriations of popular and Western cultural productions are exigent to some works of modern political cinema. Thinking about the value of transformative appropriations, the philosopher reflected on aesthetics in terms of "deterritorializations"[29] and "minorizations"[30] of influential cultural forms. He wrote: "The third world filmmaker finds himself before an illiterate public, swamped by American, Egyptian or Indian serials, and karate films, and he has to go through all this, it is this material that he has to work on, to extract from it the elements of a people who are still missing (Lino Brocka)."[31] Deleuze's choice to illustrate his concept of political cinema with Brocka's conventionally styled filmmaking affirms the capaciousness of the philosopher's notion of modern political cinema. Indeed, the fact that Brocka's films echo not just the style but also the social democratic political discourse of the "classic" political cinema demonstrates that these two modes of the political film are not wholly disparate.

My Own Country: Gripping the Knife's Edge (*Bayan ko: Kapit sa patalim*, 1984) represents the first type of political film Brocka made during his turn to activism. It is a proletarian tale and gritty social melodrama reminiscent of *Manila in the Claws of Light* (*Maynila: Sa mga kuko ng liwanag*, 1975). Modestly financed with foreign and local money, *My Own Country* was made both for the international film festival circuit and an unproven domestic audience for political cinema. Financed by entities from two countries, the picture was meant to function as a political instrument within a transnational arena. *Miguelito: The Rebellious Child* (*Miguelito: Batang rebelde*, 1985) epitomizes the second kind of political movie. This dramatic teen picture and social melodrama targeted a domestic mass audience, especially the fans of the actor playing the film's young protagonist. Although Brocka described *Miguelito* to the press as a commercial venture, critics wisely read it as a subversive tirade aimed at Marcos.

As with the other works discussed in this book, Brocka's political films feature gender-inflected narratives. Both *Miguelito* and *My Own Country* revolve around male protagonists caught up in dilemmas of a simultaneously personal and sociopolitical nature. Unlike in Brocka's earlier films, however, these two male protagonists summon the courage to buck the establishment or confront a Marcosian political figure. Moreover, Brocka pushes beyond a crucial limit point in his representation of politics. Specifically, *My Own Country* and *Miguelito* feature the director's most recognizable instantiations of two politically incendiary figures, namely: the insurgent young man and the authoritarian patriarch. As I mentioned in chapter 2, such figures were largely absent from the landmark films of the martial law era.

The balance of this section illuminates Brocka's efforts at making political cinema and his allegorical figuration of Marcos's authoritarian rule. I shall continue to use Deleuze's writings to elucidate Brocka's cinema politics. Such a treatment of the Brocka-Deleuze connection is especially significant, given that this subject remains largely unexamined more than two decades after the publication of the French philosopher's books on film.

MY OWN COUNTRY

My Own Country was cofinanced by the French company Stephan Films and a new local outfit called Malaya Films. These outfits were represented, respectively, by Vera Belmont, a producer involved in the prehistoric saga *Quest for Fire* (Jean-Jacques Annaud, 1981) and Jose Antonio Gonzalez, a wealthy businessman and anti-Marcos activist. The name Malaya Films—literally translated as "Freedom Films"—was used in place of another entity identified elsewhere as the film's actual production company: the Benigno S. Aquino Foundation.[32]

The screenplay was a revision of material that Jose F. Lacaba originally pitched to Brocka in 1976.[33] It was based on two journalistic pieces called "A Strike" by Lacaba and "Hostages or Hosts" by Jose Carreon, both published before martial law.[34] The script's title, *Kapit sa patalim* (alternately translated as *In Dire Straits* and *Gripping the Knife's Edge*), refers to an old saying that "a person in extreme need will clutch even at a sharp blade."[35] Brocka recalled declining the material when Lacaba first offered it to him because he did not think it would pass the Marcos regime's preproduction censorship standards.[36] In 1982, Mike De Leon and action star Rudy Fernandez took an interest in Lacaba's piece. The latter submitted a revised story outline, which the censors approved, but De Leon eventually abandoned the project. Lacaba offered the material again to Brocka when the latter asked for script ideas. Brocka or the producers added "*Bayan ko*" (*My Own Country*) to the film's existing title. The phrase is from an eponymous song long associated with nationalist causes, including the anti-colonial struggle against the United States in the 1930s and the anti-Marcos movements that began in the 1970s and blossomed anew after Aquino's murder.

The slim narrative follows the plight of Turing Manalastas (Phillip Salvador) a printing press worker who falls on hard times when his wife Luz (Gina Alajar) experiences complications in her pregnancy. She is forced to take leave from her job at the same press. Barely able to make ends meet when both of them were employed, the couple struggles all the more to cover Luz's medical expenses on one income. Turing (a nickname for "Arturo") turns to everyone in his small social circle for a loan but comes up short. The only person willing to front money is his employer, Jefferson Lim (Nomer Son). Following an ill-advised cliché in Brocka's films and Philippine cultural productions more generally, the malign capitalist is racially marked as Chinese Filipino. Lim offers Turing a salary advance on the condition that he sign a statement promising he would never join the union his fellow workers were forming. He takes the deal.

In keeping with the polarization of good and evil in melodramas, two contrasting solutions present themselves to the protagonist.[37] Turing's first option is to join the union and fight for a livable wage. Luz, a political activist in her college years, strongly favors this choice but it is incompatible with the document Turing had signed. The far more lucrative but also morally improper alternative lies in accepting the unusual proposal of his childhood friend Lando (Raoul Aragon) and the latter's associate, who goes by the obscene moniker of Boy the Shitter (Rez Cortez). They ask Turing to participate in an inside job of robbing his employers, but he demurs.

The strike begins. Turing crosses the picket line to honor his deal with Mr. Lim. As expected, the striking workers ostracize him and the other scabs. Lim sends armed goons to terrorize the picketers late one evening, causing the death of Ador (Venchito Galvez), an elderly worker and union leader. The proprietor then triggers a "lock-out," a provision of the capitalist-friendly labor laws that permits businesses to cease operations and bring in the government to help strong-arm workers. In the meantime, Luz prematurely delivers her child. With their newborn in an incubator, the couple racks up an enormous hospital bill. Turing picks up shifts driving a jeepney (a public transport vehicle), but the work is neither steady nor lucrative enough to sustain them.

The hospital denies Luz and their child a timely discharge, insisting that they first settle their bill in full. Turing appeals to hospital staff to put him on an installment plan so his family can come home and stop incurring further expenses. The hospital denies the request and assigns a security guard to deter mother and child from leaving the premises.

Following a tragic vein in melodramas about crime, the protagonist falls into a downward spiral.[38] He tracks down Lando and Boy the Shitter to proceed with the armed robbery scheme they proposed earlier. During the heist, Turing identifies valuable equipment to cart away and takes Lando and his crew to a safety vault in the owner's quarters above the press. At some point, Boy the Shitter raids the Lim's

FIGURE 5.1. Turing (Phillip Salvador, second from right) and his accomplices Lando (Raoul Aragon, left) and Boy the Shitter (Rez Cortez, far right) take his former employer's family hostage. *My Own Country.* Courtesy of Danilo Brocka/CCP Library.

refrigerator for a hearty snack before defecating on the kitchen floor. Apart from adding insult to injury, the flamboyant gesture embodies his proletarian antagonism toward the dwelling's bourgeois owners. The crew's noises rouse Mrs. Lim (Lorli Villanueva) from her sleep. She quietly phones the cops. Law enforcement arrives, and a hostage situation ensues.

Turing asks the authorities to bring in a popular radio correspondent (Joe Taruc, playing himself) to mediate their surrender. They comply, and Taruc conducts a live broadcast from the hostage site. Turing grabs the correspondent's microphone and demands that his wife and child be allowed to leave the hospital. In an abrupt departure from his usual self-centeredness, he appeals for justice for Ador. He also asks the state to provide jobs with living wages for the strikers and the country's unemployed. Lando vetoes Turing's requests, asking instead for a getaway vehicle. Luz and Turing's mother arrive at the scene to convince him to surrender. Soon after Luz enters the compound to reason with her husband, a SWAT team storms in. Turing surrenders, but Lando, Boy the Shitter, and Mrs.

Lim perish during the melee. As the police escort Turing out of the plant, Hugo (Paquito Diaz) the foreman at the press, gives him the middle finger. Turing, ever the hothead, grabs a policeman's gun and fires at the heckler. The cops swiftly mow down Turing, killing him instantly.

The Capitalist State

As with Brocka's *Manila*, *My Own Country* uses the story of an individual to depict larger social problems. One of the main differences between the two is that Brocka significantly raises the bar on political content, supercharging *My Own Country* with numerous overt political valences apart from covert ones.

Turing's predicaments shed light on adverse working and social conditions during the Marcos regime. Raymond Bonner notes that the president "had seen to it that Philippine labor was, by the end of the 1970s, among the cheapest in the world at 47 cents an hour, compared with 85 cents in Taiwan and 95 cents in Singapore."[39] Cheap labor attracted foreign investors and generated windfall profits for industries controlled by Marcos and his cronies. The depression of wages thinned the ranks of the middle-class and threatened the very survival of the proletariat.

Brocka's film illustrates the effects of the authoritarian state's collusion with rapacious capitalism in two emotionally galvanizing subplots. The first pertains to Luz and Turing's attempts to obtain medical care during her pregnancy. Early in the film, we see Turing struggling to pay for prenatal drugs at a small pharmacy. He only fills half of the prescribed order because the cost of medicines is out of reach for wage laborers like him. Much to his dismay, Turing discovers that similar conditions obtained at private hospitals. When he rushes Luz to deliver her child, the nurses insist they place a deposit before seeking medical attention. The exorbitant cost of hospitalization also makes it virtually inaccessible to the underclass. Turing agonizes over this fact, declaring early in his wife's pregnancy that a premature delivery would ruin their already shaky finances. His fears are confirmed when the hospital presents him with a bill he could not possibly afford to settle. In a moment that is especially painful to watch, Turing walks up and down the corridors begging hospital personnel to offer him a reprieve. The nurses refuse his appeals, at times speaking in English to intimidate him. They underestimate Turing's desperation. Moments later, Turing lashes out at one of the doctors, grabbing the latter's shoulder and getting in his face. What the film leaves unsaid but implies is the government's unwillingness, in the face of pressure from capitalists, to regulate vital social services such as medical care. Such apathy is especially grating when shown by an autocracy that tightly controls most other facets of civilian life.

The denial of affordable medical goods and services to Turing and his family stages the biopolitics of the Marcos regime. Biopolitics refers to the myriad ways in which the state nurtures and controls the lives of its citizens.[40] *My Own Country*

FIGURE 5.2. Hospital employees restrain Turing (Phillip Salvador, center) after refusing his plea to discharge his wife and child. *My Own Country*. Courtesy of Danilo Brocka/CCP Library.

shows that the authoritarian state's health policies leave working class persons vulnerable to public and private entities indifferent to their plight.

The second subplot dramatizes the conspiracy of state and private corporations in the suppression of organized labor. In reality, Marcos began a crackdown on that sector with a total ban on strikes following his declaration of martial law in 1972. The ban had a decisive impact on labor organizing, taking effect "just when Left-led labor unions were beginning to grow."[41] In 1975, five thousand workers at La Tondeña distillery went on strike, defying the ban. Marcos responded by enacting even harsher laws against labor actions, such as Presidential Decree No. 823, which declared strikes "illegal and subversive." The law penalized strikers as well as "people who supported strikes," which could mean anyone who displeased the authorities.[42] The suppression of unions and labor strikes served the dual purpose of keeping wages low and stamping out civil unrest. Brocka's film depicts Marcos's hostility toward organized labor most powerfully in the killing of blue-collar workers.

The first instance occurs soon after the beginning of the strike. Several armed men arrive in a vehicle and proceed to terrorize the picketers. The dispersal attempt is so violent that even the scabs, led by Turing, are compelled to aid the strikers. The goons flee after being overcome by the workers, but not before one of them impulsively shoots Ador, a friend to Turing. Ador expires clutching his chest wound, surrounded by his stunned coworkers. In this scene of violent repression, the thugs hired by the small-time capitalist function as proxies for the state. Due to censorship restrictions, the filmmakers would have been unable to blame the government for Ador's death, even if the state was at fault for normalizing the suppression of organized labor. Susan F. Quimpo recalls that in the 1980s "it became common [for business owners and the state] to use the police and military to break up picket lines to protect 'vital' industries defined as those that had a bearing on the national interest."[43] Apart from deploying its armed forces to break up strike actions, the state often turned a blind eye to the harassment of strikers by hired thugs. Moreover, by constantly labeling working-class union leaders as communists or fellow travelers, the state made them vulnerable to being harassed or killed with impunity. Ador perished in such a climate of antipathy toward labor activists.

The old man's killing foreshadows the ending, an even more violent scene picturing the demise of another underclass worker: namely, Turing. The police dispatch the hero in a hail of gunfire. The directions on Lacaba's script detail the aftermath of this violence: Luz "cradles his bloodied head. Turing convulses. His head goes limp."[44] Turing's death reads as an instance of state violence because he falls at the hands of the authorities. As I have suggested in the preceding chapters, the destruction of the flawed but sympathetic protagonist is a recurring feature of Brocka's films. Turing's shooting is one of the most piercing examples of what I call a "Marcosian moment," an instance of cinematic violence that plays to the viewers' emotions while also inviting an allegorical interpretation. The gunfire from military-grade weapons, the sight of Turing's bloodied corpse, and Luz's inconsolable howling in front of cameras—these details register the brute violence of the authoritarian state and evoke other aspects of the regime that can only be figured indirectly due to stringent censorship, among other reasons.

Some of the details of Turing's death—including the SWAT team's intervention and the pieta-like tableaux at the end—were already present in a story outline that Lacaba penned before the Aquino assassination, but the alterations made by the filmmakers were substantial and telling.[45] From the 1982 outline to the production script dated January 17, 1984, Lacaba called for Turing's killing to happen inside the printing press, where he would collapse, after being shot, near a cutting machine. He does not die in front of photographic and TV cameras.[46] As filmed, however, the protagonist's death becomes a public spectacle. It recalls facets of the political murder of Marcos's fiercest opponent. As with Turing's death, broadcast and print journalists heavily covered the Aquino assassination. One of the most famous images from the coverage showed broadcast camera operators and photojournalists jostling to capture Aquino's image as he nervously exited the plane before his death. News programs and documentaries often followed this moment with the sound of gunfire, and then a long shot of armed men circling Aquino's body on the tarmac before loading him into a van. Another notable element featured in the broadcast coverage was the bawling of a female eyewitness (a fellow passenger of the ex-senator named Rebecca Quijano) who came to be known as "the crying lady." Luz's prolonged sobbing is reminiscent of Quijano's outburst at the scene of the crime. Her wrenching cries stretch the film's emotional highpoint to an uncomfortable length. The omission of a reverse shot from Luz's perspective intensifies the pain of watching her ordeal, thus trapping the viewer in her agony. The lack of an answer shot also makes the object of Luz's gaze uncertain. She seems to be addressing the audience as fellow citizens mired in the same deplorable situation. At the same time, by gazing upward, she also appears to direct her appeal to the unseen powers that be, such as Marcos's elite supporters or even the global body politic, which had been showing concern over the plight of Filipinos under the dictatorship. Despite the static shot's seemingly interminable length, Luz's sobbing does not lose any of its power to move the viewer. The reprise of the protest anthem *Bayan ko* (*My Own Country*) increases the finale's emotional impact.

The wordlessness of the film's last minutes harkens back to a convention of stage and film melodrama in which dialogue and movements cease while the highly expressive mise-en-scène and sound continue the storytelling and tug at the heartstrings.[47] The suspension of dialogue and movement amplifies both Luz's distress and the ominous off-screen sounds of clicking cameras, the scrambling of reporters, and radio static.[48] Luz's intense gaze also suggests that she wants to say something in the presence of the mass media but cannot do so, because tragedy and fear have seized her.

The Strike

The strike at the printing press serves a dual purpose in Brocka's film. First, it references widespread unrest in the labor sector during the Marcos regime. Second, it functions as an allegory for anti-authoritarian resistance.

As mentioned earlier, Marcos engaged in a heavy-handed suppression of organized labor during martial law. The state rescinded the ban on labor strikes with the lifting of emergency rule in 1981 but continued to exclude workers engaged in "vital" industries. The much-touted liberalization was apparitional because "95 percent of industries were classified as 'vital.'"[49] The regime additionally set "limited strikeable issues" and "prescribed lengthy no strike and cooling off periods."[50] Despite these strictures, workers' mass actions increased during the 1980s, "the scale of which was unprecedented in number and the duration of strikes."[51] For instance, the strike at the Globe Steel mill went on for four years, setting a record as the longest in the nation's history. Less confrontational—but no less effective—were factory slowdowns, in which workers moved at a snail's pace to "drastically reduce production."[52]

FIGURE 5.3. Luz (Gina Alajar) cradles Turing (Phillip Salvador) in the film's closing tableau. *My Own Country.* Courtesy of Juan Martin Magsanoc and Archivo 1984 Gallery.

Because of solidarity among activists of all stripes, members of organized labor routinely joined political demonstrations. Labor activists viewed their sectoral battles as compatible with the broader national crusade against tyranny, in part because they could trace many of their problems to the doings of the authoritarian regime. Those problems include a ruined economy, far-reaching government interference in their lives, and pervasive state violence, among others.

The overlap between labor actions and political activism was apparent to the chroniclers of the Marcos regime. William Chapman noted that labor strikes "grew in size and intensity and became more politicized, more designed for generalized protest than for specific economic gains."[53] On rare occasions, workers of all stripes united in staging general strikes—called "welgang bayan" or "people's strike[s]"— throughout the country. The National Democratic Front envisioned an even more radical and expansive kind of general strike, "a day of insurrection when the government forces would be simply immobilized."⁵⁴ A coup directed by communists, the insurrectionary version of the people's strike never came to pass, but a similarly ambitious large-scale protest action deposed Marcos in the mid-1980s.

My Own Country charges its fictional images of union organizing and picketing with broader political significance by juxtaposing them with actual and restaged footage of political demonstrations against the Marcos regime. The film posits the printing press workers' strike as an allegory of anti-authoritarian resistance. The visual similarity of both kinds of collective protest actions underscores their allegorical correspondence. The singing of "Bayan ko" at the strike has a similar effect. The actual confluence of anti-Marcos rallies and labor-sector protests during the Marcos regime reinforces this notion as well.

Brocka's film weaves the footage of the political rallies and the fictional strike in both conspicuous and subtle ways. The narrative begins with a political rally that Turing encounters by chance during the "lock-out" at the printing press. The protesters flash banners and placards criticizing the de facto Marcos-US alliance, asking Marcos to resign, and seeking justice for Aquino. Turing, who watches from the sidelines, spots Willy (Ariosto Reyes), his former coworker at the press. They had a falling out after Willy criticized Turing for joining the strikebreakers. Willy comes up to Turing and apologizes for their row. He also mentions forgoing his longtime plan to work in Saudi Arabia, opting instead to move to Samar province. These details are significant. As I mentioned in the previous chapter, the Marcos regime pushed Filipinos to seek contract work abroad to shore up foreign currency reserves and compensate for a weak labor market. Willy's rejection of the Saudi option implicitly refuses the government's scheme of diverting its excess labor force overseas. Moreover, "going to Samar" was, as screenwriter Lacaba points out in an interview, code for joining the communist underground.⁵⁵

At the end of the conversation, the former coworkers say their goodbyes and Willy rejoins the rally. The scene anchors an extended flashback, during which much of the story of Turing and the strike unfolds. The narrative only returns to this moment almost two-thirds of the way into the film, shortly before Turing decides to rob his former employer. The fracturing of the narrative line reiterates the motif of the ethical crossroads at which the protagonist finds himself. Before him lies a choice between serving his interests (i.e., becoming a strikebreaker and robbing the Lims) and joining a larger cause whose benefits are deferred and uncertain (i.e., striking with his coworkers, participating in political rallies).

This scene of Turing and Willy's encounter invokes a similar moment in *Manila* when the hero Julio and his friend Pol happen upon a demonstration against fascism and US imperialism being held by youthful militants. In the 1975 film, the protagonist's friend jokingly dissuades him from joining the rally. The scene makes fun of the political apathy of some Filipinos. The corresponding moment in *My Own Country* takes on a somber tone, with Turing looking wistfully as his friend returns to the march. The protagonist's expression suggests a tinge of regret at turning his back on a worthy cause. The parallelism between these two scenes marks the transition from the covert politicking of Brocka's earlier social dramas to the frank political engagement of his current work. It also subtly casts *My Own Country* as another rejoinder to *Manila*.

The political rallies that Brocka filmed or recreated in *My Own Country* include the "Tarlac to Tarmac run," a demonstration that covered the distance between Ninoy Aquino's hometown in Central Luzon and the site of his assassination in Metro Manila. The film also shows footage of the "confetti revolution," referring to those spectacular occasions when employees at the commercial business district expressed their solidarity with anti-Marcos protesters by showering them with shredded yellow pages from telephone directories. The deluge of yellow confetti from tall buildings indexed the dramatic growth of anti-Marcos sentiment among the middle-class and elite.

A thirty-six-page treatment dated June 1982 and containing marginal notes in Lacaba's handwriting suggests that he and Brocka envisioned an even more radical treatment of the political demonstrations and labor strike than what the director filmed.[56] Near Lacaba's description of the scene where Luz delivers her child prematurely, he scribbles the words "news of Aquino's death." On another page, Lacaba describes a scene where the strikers try to block scabs from entering the press. He adds in scribbles: "Reading *Tempo* [a Philippine tabloid newspaper] headline of Aquino's death."[57] These notations indicate that he and Brocka toyed with the idea of explicitly synchronizing the fictional narrative of the strike to events surrounding the assassination.

Much of the remaining marginalia links the strike to protest actions inspired by the political killing. In one instance, Lacaba suggests that the "story about Ninoy's funeral" be folded into a "pep talk" given to the would-be strikers by Fely (Aida Carmona), Turing's former coworker and the vice president of the union. Another scene would have shown Willy, who had been fired by Hugo for talking back at him, either attending a political demonstration or selling "Ninoy pins."[58] Those pins were yellow buttons or strips of hard plastic embossed with pictures of Aquino or slogans such as "Ninoy, you are not alone" and "Marcos resign." Many Filipinos wore them to advertise their opposition to the dictatorship.

Brocka was so eager to sustain the interweaving of Turing's narrative with the story of anti-Marcos protests that he also tried to plant another song associated with civil unrest besides "Bayan ko"; namely, *Tie a Yellow Ribbon*. Filipino activists played or sang the 1970s ditty at rallies following Aquino's death. Its lyric tells the story of a returning soldier who waits for a sign that his lover is willing to take him back after his service. The lyric resonated with the real-life story of Aquino's heroic return from exile and the enduring loyalty of his admirers. Quite oddly, Lacaba's marginal notes propose the playing of the sappy tune during one of the scenes in the nightclub where Lando's new girlfriend, an exotic dancer, works the stage. Those particular scenes feature a semi-nude dance number—what, in nightclub parlance is called a "floor show"—with some female-on-female erotics. Brocka filmed the floor show but dropped the song. Most of the other suggestions in the marginal notes never made it into the finished picture, likely to preempt the censorship or the outright banning of the film.

The incorporation of fiction and history (represented by the references to contemporary events and the use of actuality footage) was not just a mercenary attempt to retrofit Lacaba's extant screenplay into a timely political film. The method also embodied Brocka's desire to integrate political activism and filmmaking as closely as possible. Brocka made the film not only between joining rallies and strikes but also *while* he was participating in such events. For instance, the first shooting day occurred on location at one of the rallies. In an interview with David Overbey for the film's publicity material, the director recalled, "At the time were making the film we were also attending meetings and rallies calling for a boycott of the elections and demanding the resignation of Marcos. But the filming was part of these other activities so that the energy we invested in the one thing benefitted the other."[59]

Making the film was part of Brocka's development as a political animal, and he offered up the finished product to help other Filipinos realize their emergence and growth as activists. Deleuze uses the concept of "double becoming" to describe a feature of modern political cinema. He writes: "the author takes a step towards his characters, but the characters take a step towards the author: double-becoming."[60] In directing *My Own Country*, Brocka took a step toward becoming a more committed and militant worker-activist, like some of his characters. At the same time, his creative efforts represented strikers and the restive proletariat as sympathetic if not heroic figures in popular culture.

As mentioned earlier, Deleuze also speaks of the power of modern political films to call into being a heterogeneous new community, a "people to come." In *Cinema 2: The Time-Image*, he writes: "In short, if there were a modern political cinema, it would be on this basis: the people no longer exist, or not yet ... *the people are missing*."[61] Deleuze characterizes this calling forth of a people who are "missing" or "not yet" as a fabulation. A fabulation is a creative and collaborative act of storytelling that brings people together (e.g., the artists, the characters' real-life counterparts, audiences), engenders transformative encounters among them, and prefigures a new collective.[62] In *My Own Country*, the images of the strike and political rallies serve to enable or—in Deleuze's terminology—"fabulate" the still-missing heterogeneous multitude that will soon rise against the autocratic state. The film's scenes of fictional strikes and actual political demonstrations represented or prefigured the monumental mass actions reshaping Filipino democracy at that time. The visual treatment of the political rally bookending much of the film generates a striking premonition of the "missing" people that Deleuze invokes.

FIGURE 5.4. Turing (Phillip Salvador, right) runs into his former coworker Willy (Ariosto Reyes, left) during an antigovernment rally. *My Own Country.* Courtesy of Danilo Brocka/CCP Library.

Turing traces the path taken by the endless line of demonstrators as they vanish into the horizon. The protesters—the force of change—lurch forward while Turing, who has yet to experience a political epiphany, remains in place. The gathering at the venue to which the convivial masses disappear evokes both a hopeful imminent future and the formation of a profoundly new collective. The "people power" revolution of 1986 that toppled Marcos arguably served as the culmination of the political becoming prefigured in Brocka's film.

Scholars of authoritarianism point out that mass uprisings rarely lead to the demise of authoritarian regimes.[63] Dictatorships often come to an end because of coup d'états, the death of autocrats, insurgencies, and invasions.[64] Although the 1986 revolution started with a coup, it owed its success to the concerted efforts of people from different sectors, social classes, and political backgrounds. True to Deleuze's conception of the "missing people" as a heterogeneous new community, "people power" brought together a multitude that did not previously exist before their world-changing appearance in Philippine politics.

Moreover, as Mark R. Thompson reminds us, "people power" had a "demonstration effect" on other nations, inspiring mass upheavals against repressive governments in China, South Korea, Taiwan, and Eastern Europe, among others.[65] The marchers in Brocka's film may well have prefigured the hitherto "missing people[s]" of the democratizing world who battled illiberal regimes and changed the course of history in the late 1980s and beyond.

Grandstanding in Europe

The film elements of *My Own Country* were brought to France after shooting and initial postproduction work in the Philippines. There, Brocka's mentor and friend Pierre Rissient supervised the film's completion, receiving credit as a sound supervisor. They submitted the film as planned to the Cannes International Film Festival. Since Brocka was, as Rissient puts it, already a "darling of the Left Bank" cinephiles, the festival placed the film in its prestigious main competition.[66] Agustin Sotto notes that Brocka's film was "reportedly disowned by the Philippine embassy in France," a rumor that that might explain why no country of origin appears in the "technical specifications" document provided to journalists by festival organizers.[67]

The publicity materials emphasized the political stakes behind the making of the film. The press kit mentions that the film draws upon real-life incidents "which happened a few years ago, but [that] the story itself is even more relevant today, for the Turings and the Luzs are currently themselves the hostages and victims of violence." Echoing the publicity campaign for *Jaguar*—Brocka's 1980 success at Cannes—in his essay for the press kit, the critic and film programmer David Overbey frames *My Own Country* as "a social melodrama which naturally develops into a film noir."[68] The characterization of *My Own Country* as a socially relevant crime film is apt because of the crucial robbery scene and the depictions of urban blight, civil unrest, and acts of violence against the proletariat. The reference to *Jaguar* is especially meaningful in light of our discussion in chapter 2, where I mentioned that an early draft of the narrative showed the desperate protagonist taking his employer's family hostage. *My Own Country* revolves around a similar incident, thus continuing a pattern of intertextuality and recurring scenarios in the director's work.

During the press conference at Cannes, Brocka dwelled on the same themes found in the publicity dossier. He remarked that his film was a "political tool" and that he brought it to an international audience because he understood "how sensitive the government was to criticism from abroad."[69] At the gala screening, Brocka wore a barong Tagalog (Filipino shirt) emblazoned with a map of his country and the word "justice" in bold red print. The stunt reprised his use of fashion to make a political statement a year earlier at the Film Academy of the Philippines awards ceremony. Agustin Sotto recalled that the Cannes audience received *My Own Country* with a standing ovation and "much weeping."[70]

Foreign critics were unanimous in their praise of Brocka's courage for making such a risky film, even as some expressed reservations about the finished product. Nigel Andrews considered the "simple but sulphurous little melodrama" one of the "ups" in the "ups and downs" of the Cannes offerings.[71] Other reviewers fittingly emphasized the film's combative tone, characterizing the film as a "brave and well-executed political drama,"[72] "an indictment of a whole political and economic system,"[73] and a work about "the proletariat under a dictatorial regime."[74] Collette-Marie Renard honed in on the filmmaker's skill in "weaving together the drama of a man and that of his homeland."[75] She also marvels at "the generosity of his gaze and the bewildered devotion he offers his compatriots." Michel Sineux explained how the narrative "gradually becomes exemplary," moving from Turing and Luz's story into a larger narrative, a leitmotif present in many of Brocka's films, "the common denominator being that of a hero who descends, irrevocably, into the hellish depths of a corrupt and murderous society, the Philippines today."[76] Jay Scott offered a unique take in his review for a Toronto broadsheet, suggesting that the film trenchantly delivers a political critique through an actors' performance. He pointed to the "devastatingly funny parody of Imelda Marcos in the character of Mrs. Lim (Lorli Villanueva), the wife of the owner of a printing plant threatened by unionization."[77]

Several critics favorably compared *My Own Country* to American film noirs and Italian neorealism.[78] James Leahy, in his review for *Monthly Film Bulletin*, likened Brocka's film to "classic Hollywood accounts of the doomed couple unable to go straight." He pointed out, however, that it "contains a range of explicit and specific political reference, precisely the kind of material seldom if ever to be found in the American films."[79] He also likened *My Own Country* to the politically radical and more formally innovative works of Third Cinema, specifically the Bolivian filmmaker Jorge Sanjines's *Blood of the Condor* (1969). He noted the illuminating depiction of labor issues, social conditions and state violence in both films.

Showdown in the Philippines

My Own Country was secretly brought back into the Philippines after the Cannes screening, bypassing the typical procedures for the importation of films into the country. Brocka showed it to a crowd of Filipino journalists and guests for the first time on July 12, 1984. They turned out in droves fearing that the censors would eventually "block the film due to its sensitive topic." The producers held a few more preview screenings, one of which was reportedly disallowed by the authorities.[80]

When the censors tried to block the theatrical release, Brocka and company pulled all the stops to show the film intact and reach as wide an audience as possible. Due to her animus toward Brocka (who previously led campaigns against her board), Chief censor Maria Kalaw-Katigbak made him fight an uphill battle, even when other members of the regime wanted her to compromise and put an end to the controversy.[81]

For three months—from August to October 1984—the censors refused to issue a decision on the film.[82] When it finally responded on October 23, the board rated the film "for adults only" and demanded additional cuts.[83] They asked for the deletion of the theme song and images of rallies and demonstrations, arguing that those "portions tend to undermine the faith and confidence of the people in their government and the duly constituted authorities."[84] The censors also withheld a permit for the film's exhibition. Katigbak later gave interviews to press in which she revealed even more requirements for the film's exhibition. These included removing "Bayan ko" from the film's title (because it "urges oppressed people to rise against the authorities") and surrendering the master negatives of the film. Additionally, she asked the producers to explain how the film was brought to Cannes without an export permit from her office.[85] The question was rhetorical, for she had already formulated a theory about what happened and related it to the press. She speculated that Brocka's "film was brought out of the country through the French diplomatic pouch."[86]

Around that time, Katigbak also insinuated that Brocka had lied about receiving a best picture award from the British Film Institute. His motive, she said, was to pressure her board into letting him off easy.[87] The director pushed back against the vicious claims. He and his fired-up artists' group CAP group protested outside Katigbak's house[88] and "staged a five-day street demonstration."[89] They threatened to sing "different versions" of *My Own Country* over and over again outside the censors' office "until their ears hurt."[90] Bowing to pressure, Katigbak offered to waive the requirement to surrender the master negatives. She also gave up on ordering the deletion of the entire song, saying that only a few lines needed pruning.[91] The verses in question, which were the same ones added by activists during the early 1970s, were the following: "The country that is suppressed / Tomorrow will rise in revolt / The East will turn red for sweet freedom"[92] ("*Bayang sinisiil bukas ay babangon din / Ang silanga'y pupula sa timyas ng paglaya*"). She described them as an inflammatory "bastardization" and "vulgarization" of the original lyric.[93] She was actually not incorrect about the verses' subversive implications: the references to the East turning red and the country's uprising suggest a socialist revolution, as was the intent of those who penned them.

In early January 1985, Brocka and writer Lacaba issued a lengthy press release about the censors' discriminatory handling of their film.[94] They also petitioned the Supreme Court to allow the film's exhibition without cuts and with a favorable General Patronage rating.[95] More broadly, they asked the court to nullify Executive Order 876-A (the law that created the prevailing board of censors) for exercising prior restraint and violating the filmmakers' right to free speech.[96] Their suit additionally questioned the censors' controlling standards for rating, censoring, and banning films.[97] Days after the publication of the press release and the filing of the court case, Marcos's Solicitor General Estelito Mendoza put pressure on the censors to ease up on Brocka and thus preempt additional public criticism of the board and the government.[98] By the middle of January, the censors approved the film without cuts, but still with a "For Adults Only" classification. To grant a more favorable rating, the censors demanded cuts to scenes "portraying female dancing of the lascivious type, some obscene nudities ... and excessive violence." The filmmakers did not withdraw their case from the high court despite the censors' concessions.

In the last days of January 1985, police arrested Brocka, fellow stage and film director Behn Cervantes, and thirty-nine other persons at a strike held by public transport vehicle drivers to demand a rollback of fuel prices.[99] The two directors had joined the rally in support of an organization whose members had previously attended their activist artist group's anti-censorship protests. A policeman falsely testified that Brocka gave a speech and screamed: "Join the bloody revolution!"[100] The filmmakers were charged with illegal assembly and inciting to sedition.[101] Additionally, the regime triggered a Preventive Detention Action (Presidential Decree 1834), which authorized the indefinite detention of the filmmakers[102] until Marcos himself orders their release.[103] It was the same decree Brocka and Cervantes had protested less than two years before their arrest. Leaders of the Film Academy of the Philippines, along with the "big names in local cinema," petitioned the regime for Brocka and Cervantes's freedom.[104] Through the efforts of Rissient and others, Brocka received support from Francis Ford Coppola, George Lucas, and other members of the Director's Guild of America.[105]

The Filipino directors' incarceration lasted eighteen days and took place in three detention facilities.[106] The state subsequently placed Brocka under house arrest, temporarily impounded his passport, and prevented him from leaving the country on at least one occasion. Brocka later voiced his suspicion that the government filed trumped-up charges in retaliation for his grandstanding at Cannes. During an interview for the BBC TV documentary series *Arena*, he said: "And I suspected Imelda had a lot to do with it because I think they were just waiting for the time when they can have a case against me, an actual case."[107]

On July 22, 1985, the Supreme Court affirmed the state's right to censor and ban films, but it stressed that both actions (especially the latter) were "allowable only under the clearest proof of a clear and present danger."[108] The court also opined that the censors had committed "an abuse of discretion" in rating the film. Brocka and his fellow plaintiffs thus secured a landmark ruling that would have a lasting impact on Philippine cinema.

Due to the litigation and the censors' obstructionism, *My Own Country* was not exhibited until November 1985, more than sixteen months after producers submitted it for review. By then, pirate copies on the popular Betamax home video format had eaten away at the film's audience. Unfortunately, the controversy did not translate into box office success.[109]

As with the film's foreign reviewers, Filipino critics praised Brocka for making another picture with a rare "socially relevant theme."[110] They also acknowledged the melodrama's tremendous emotional impact. "Phillip Salvador's Turing," wrote one reviewer, "is trapped in a situation so hopeless you leave the theater carrying his burden like a ton of bricks on your chest."[111]

Showing a keen grasp of the allegory linking Turing's narrative and the contemporary political situation, filmmaker and critic Emmanuel Reyes pointed out that the movie's center of gravity lies in dramatizing the stakes of political participation. He wrote: "The film addresses itself to a listless sector, that part of Philippine society that continues to hold onto neutral ground, who fear commitment to critical issues and who, perhaps, silently hold protest actions in contempt."[112] Reyes also observed that the film's treatment of politics contained gaps that viewers had to fill. He wrote that "Turing is a downcast creature who is aware of his oppression but remains unclear as to the bigger things that cause his misery."[113] The film leaves the identification of those "bigger things" to spectators, but not without providing them ample clues throughout the narrative. He went on to say that the film stops short of delivering a clear political agenda and that this was only appropriate. He averred: "Yet for all its intensity and commentary, *Bayan ko* remains very much an introspective piece. It does not attempt to settle an issue. Rather, it leaves it open to discussion and further thought."[114]

As Lacaba later admitted to Agustin Sotto, the bit of reticence in the otherwise provocative film was largely a function of self-censorship.[115] He said: "Maybe, at the time it was written, I was still thinking of what would pass the censors." At the same time, Lacaba acknowledged that he was likely aiming for subtlety. "Turing requires a more complex response from the audience," he added. "We are not telling our audience how to respond to these options. Because we tried to look at them from Turing's point of view . . . we did not clearly show how we as filmmakers felt about these options." Lacaba's comment about asking the audience to engage their intellect is consistent with modern political cinema's goal of fostering a critical spectatorship and subjectivity.[116]

Several Filipino critics disliked the film's depiction of politics, which they would have preferred to be more explicit. Luciano Soriano complained that the film was too ambiguous about the political convictions of the main characters. He argued that the script should have developed "the angle concerning the strike and Turing and Luz's private affairs."[117] He also called for a depiction of Willy's political awakening, and takes issue with the fact that "suddenly he appears marching in a pro-Aquino rally." Deedee Siytangco similarly complained that the film retreats from discussing Luz's political activism. She wrote: "References to her being a student activist should have been explored. This would explain why she was more politicized than her husband."[118]

The critics' response to *My Own Country* lent insight into their shared—but also often contradictory—expectations of political films. They desired a richer, more analytical political discourse; a fervent and yet subtler delivery of political statements; and an unambiguous dramatization of the characters' political stances. Brocka had to reckon with these clashing assumptions in his subsequent attempts at making political cinema.

MIGUELITO

Brocka had just been released from jail and was still fighting in court for the right to show *My Own Country* when he began filming *Miguelito: The Rebellious Child*.[119] The movie's financier Cheng Mulach hired Brocka to make a film "with a very commercial treatment" for his son Aga.[120] The young actor was best known for a string of teenybopper films, some of which were also produced by his father and uncle's independent production outfit.[121] *Miguelito* was to be his first lead role in a dramatic film.

The film's title echoes Nicholas Ray's *Rebel without a Cause* (1959), a film that Brocka admired.[122] For some of the film's viewers, including entertainment reporters, the word "rebel" invited a political reading.[123] They were right. Although *Miguelito* displayed the trappings of a teen movie, it was, in fact, a thinly veiled diatribe against Marcos.

Miguelito loosely remakes *Tinimbang ka ngunit kulang* (*Weighed but Found Wanting*, 1974), Brocka's social melodrama about a young man's disenchantment with his provincial town and his wayward father.[124] In *Weighed*, the son turns against his father after witnessing the latter's cruelty toward the most vulnerable persons in their community. I posited in chapter 1 that the detestable patriarch and the small-minded townsfolk of *Weighed* are nascent figurations, respectively, of Marcos the authoritarian patriarch and the docile citizens who supported his oppressive regime. *Miguelito* brings the political significance of those same narrative features into higher relief, most crucially by turning the patriarchal figure of *Weighed* into a corrupt and ruthless politician.

Miguelito opens with a deceptively blissful image of a political family in the country's rural north. On a sunny morning in the fictitious town of Rojas, Laguna, Mayor Venancio "Ven" Herrera (Eddie Garcia); his wife, Cristina Monfort (Gloria Romero); and their son, Mike/Miguelito (Aga Mulach), are eagerly greeting the crowd at the nuptials of an unnamed couple. Private affairs such as this—along with funerals and baptisms—are de facto political functions, as important to a mayor's career as building roads and stopping crime.

In the scenes that follow, Ven reveals himself as a corrupt politico, a womanizer, and an awful parent. As is too often the case in his country, the crooked mayor aspires to enter the national stage. Ven is currently running for a seat in the National Assembly but already has his eyes set on the presidential palace at Malacañang. Moreover, he plans to create a political dynasty, grooming his son to take his place one day.

The fifteen-year-old Miguelito is warm to the idea of a political career. Sadly, he is already beginning to take on some of his father's worst habits. For example, he can barely control his libido and keeps on pressuring his girlfriend to give up her virginity. He also thinks nothing of using his father's government position for personal gain. Mostly he uses the mayor's name to get himself out of trouble. Unfortunately for Miguelito, his mother is too emotionally fragile to rein him in or protect him from his father's influence. A sheltered heiress, she deals with most of life's challenges by obsessing over church activities and fixing herself a stiff drink.

The return of a long-absent character plunges the mayor's already dysfunctional family—and his political career—into crisis. Fittingly, she makes her entrance in a baldly allegorical moment. She alights from a motorcycle taxi and stands across from the town hall. To her right, a hearse and funeral party coincidentally pause on their journey to the cemetery. To her left passes a small Lenten procession similar to the Way of the Cross, with a man dressed as Jesus Christ dragging a life-sized cross and stopping intermittently at various stations. The mysterious woman is Auring Posadas (Nida Blanca). She is a former bar girl who became Ven's mistress and gave him a son—Miguelito. Ven, who was running for public office for the first time, tried to avert a scandal by getting rid of Auring and her then-unborn child. He does not succeed in killing them but contrives to put her in jail for fifteen years. Much to his dismay, Auring launches into a quest for justice on her first day of freedom. She seeks redress from each of the persons who conspired against her. She revisits a traumatic episode of her past at every stop in her journey, her itinerary reminiscent of the Via Crucis.

She calls first on a judge named Vic Gaerlan (Mario Montenegro). He served as her legal counsel after she killed in self-defense the man Ven had hired to eliminate her. Ven put the hit on her when she refused to abort their child and leave town. After the plot fell through, Ven connived with Vic to sabotage her defense and throw her in jail. Auring's long-awaited reunion with Vic following her release proves unsatisfying. He admits his wrongdoings but refuses to set things right. Speaking for the corrupt judicial system he represents, Vic tells Auring that no further remedies would be available to her. Coincidentally, it is at his office that she reencounters her long-lost son. Miguelito had tagged along with Vic's daughter Susan, who happens to be his girlfriend. Ironically, the significance of the reunion is lost on everyone in the room except for the corrupt judge.

Auring turns next to Peping Velez (Ric Rodrigo), the erstwhile bar owner who pimped her to customers such as Ven. Like Vic, he conspired with the aspiring mayor, testifying against her in court as a witness for the prosecution. Peping's reaction to Auring's return is similar to Vic's. He expresses his regrets and, reluctantly, offers her a menial job in his restaurant's kitchen. Seething with anger, Auring retorts: "I don't need a job. Or food. Only justice!"

The third person she visits is Felix Tantuico (Ronaldo Valdes), the physician who delivered her child. He had falsified the birth certificate at Ven's urging, reporting Cristina as the newborn's mother. Thanks to Ven's patronage in the years

FIGURE 5.5. Miguelito (Aga Mulach, back, right) encounters his estranged birth mother Auring (Nida Blanca, front, right) at the office of Judge Gaerlan (Mario Montenegro, front, left), the father of his girlfriend Susan (Gretchen Barretto, back, left). *Miguelito.* Courtesy of Mario and Cesar Hernando.

that followed, he was able to establish a small hospital of his own. Felix counsels Auring to move on after her release. "Don't cause trouble," he warns her. "The country is at peace. The people are tranquil." In the Filipino language as in English, the word for "country" (*bayan*) signifies both town and nation. This mundane double-entendre is part of the film's allegorical slant.

Only the fourth conspirator expresses genuine remorse for her doings. Luningning Sucaldito (Liza Lorena), one of Auring's fellow hostesses at the bar, apologizes for testifying against her in court, even if she only did so because Ven threatened to kill her. Auring implores her to recant her testimony. Luningning demurs, still fearful of Ven's influence. She instead offers Auring shelter and introduces her to a lawyer named Elmer Nuñez (Robert Arevalo), an upstanding man who plans to run against Ven in the coming elections. Elmer helps Auring build a new case against the mayor, one based on asserting her parental rights over Miguelito. Upon his prodding, Luningning finds the courage to testify as Auring's witness. As Luningning had feared, this upsets the mayor, and he orders her killing.

Almost everyone in town sees Auring's battle against the all-powerful politico as futile and reckless. They have an even harder time understanding why she would want to upend Miguelito's comfortable life. Her rationale for pursuing both of these seemingly lost causes is the same. "All I want is to seek the truth, however confusing and painful it might be," she tells Cristina after the latter implores her to consider Miguelito's welfare before dragging their family to court. Auring believes that bringing Ven to justice is a crusade she must undertake for herself and society. Her narrative illustrates Deleuze's point that in modern political cinema "the private affair merges with the social—or political—immediate."[125] The crimes committed against Auring and her path to finding justice at once implicate her personal life and the social order.

The allegorical significance of Auring's crusade against Ven is hard to miss. She is a stand-in for Ninoy Aquino, the political enemy whom Marcos imprisoned for many years. Similar to Aquino, Auring returns after a long absence with a mission to end the despot's political career. That said, the allegorical correspondence between her and Aquino is not always straightforward. Indeed, Auring—as channeled by Nida Blanca—bears an appreciable resemblance to Ninoy's wife Cory, in body type, hair style, and even in their preference for simple dresses. Moreover, like the Aquino couple, Auring took the great risk of standing up to a murderous tyrant. Finally, "Auring" is a nickname for Aurora, the name of Ninoy Aquino's mother.

Registering the indignation of many Filipinos against the Marcos dictatorship, Brocka's film never attempts to contain the righteous anger driving Auring's crusade. Her wrath spreads across town, testing the loyalty of the despot's closest associates. Not surprisingly, Auring's campaign impacts Miguelito's life. He instinctively takes to Auring and believes her claim that she is his biological mother. He also ignores his father's orders to stay clear of her. Miguelito's empathy for Auring does not mean, however, that he readily accepts her case against the mayor, whom he still loves and respects. Indeed, the agonistic process by which Miguelito comes to disavow his father occupies much of the film's second half, running parallel to Auring's fight against the same man. The film thus implicitly displaces the insurgent spirit invoked in its title from Miguelito onto Auring (and later to other characters), perhaps to avoid the provocative imagery of a youthful male dissident rising against a beleaguered political leader. That said, the protagonist's simmering internal rebellion is no less threatening to the mayor.

Miguelito's disidentification with his father indexes the torturous process by which many Filipinos became disenchanted with Marcos, the national patriarch they once greatly admired. The young man's tears and the images of Lenten mourning that suffuse the film illustrate the psychic burden of renouncing a charismatic figure whose tyranny has finally been exposed. Brocka's film shows this task as agonizing but urgent.

As a matter of melodramatic convention, the conflict between Miguelito and Ven develops an Oedipal cast.[126] The father and son engage in competition over the maternal figure, namely Auring. Their rivalry comes to a head when Ven orders her abduction and murder. As with some of the political killings attributed to the Marcos regime, Ven's recourse to violence is especially callous. He not only orders another attempt on the life of his son's birth mother but chooses Roy (Rey Abellana), Miguelito's best friend and the brother of Ven's paramour Janet (Beth Bautista), as the would-be gunman.

Wracked by guilt, Roy divulges the plot to Miguelito. The latter pleads with him to refuse the orders and break off from Ven, but Roy initially hesitates, citing his family's moral indebtedness to the mayor. Auring seizes the opportunity to plead their cause and make another political statement. Looking Roy straight in the eye, she says: "Why must you let him use you? Why must we allow him to continue using all of us? He will make slaves and beggars of us. And we will burn alongside him in the fires of hell. Defy him, not to spare my life but to save your soul." Her grandiloquent appeal is a thinly veiled message about the urgency of subverting the despotic patriarch. Moved by Auring's words and his affection for Miguelito, Roy takes a heroic stand and arranges their escape.

As in *My Own Country* and other Brocka films, *Miguelito* indirectly figures the menace of autocratic rule in a "Marcosian moment." This episode occurs in the film's climax. After smuggling Miguelito and Auring out of one of Ven's secluded properties, Roy takes them along to his sister Janet's place. He races there to warn her of reprisal by Ven's goons but finds the mayor himself already beating her up. Roy comes to Janet's aid, but Ven shoots him in the throat. Although the politico only fires one shot, the manner of Roy's demise makes for a chilling sight. The young man clutches his bleeding neck and makes gurgling sounds. Staring directly at the camera, he forces the movie's viewers to share his terror. The pathos of a young life cut short by political violence is, as I have pointed out in previous chapters, reminiscent of the authoritarian regime's brutal repression of student activists and other political dissidents.

The spectacular violence continues when Ven aims his gun at Auring. Miguelito rushes to place himself between his parents, inconsolably embracing and restraining his father. At this point, Janet, who has been crouching over Roy's body, picks up his gun and fires a bullet at Ven's chest. The shooting blindsides his henchmen. Seeing that their master has already fallen, they desist from retribution.

Miguelito rushes to his father's side, cradling him and weeping profusely. The pieta-like pose recalls a similar moment in *My Own Country*. Ven only musters enough strength to utter his son's name before expiring. Unable to express remorse, he dies unredeemed. This conclusion suggests that Ven's oppressive patriarchal and political authority will not be passed on between generations as he had hoped. Additionally, the ending poignantly reverses the historical outcome of the conflict between Ferdinand Marcos and Ninoy Aquino. In *Miguelito*, the despot falls while the formerly imprisoned dissident sees the coming of a new political era.

Figuring Autocracy

As in the case of *My Own Country*, *Miguelito* features a dense configuration of allegorical cues and political references. Luningning's murder rehearses the form of Marcosian state violence called "salvaging." The term refers to the brutal execution of political dissidents and personal enemies by those in power.[127] In this harrowing scene, three of the mayor's goons alight from a jeep and intimidate her. One of them then nonchalantly proceeds to stab her several times with a fan knife. The poor woman, who had just returned from a day of peddling *balut* (boiled duck eggs) and *chicharon* (pork crackling), instinctively holds on to her wares as she falls to the ground. Her murder, done casually by the roadside, would have been legible to some of the film's original viewers as a "salvaging" of someone who dared to stand up to a rotten politico.

Some of the political references in the film are, to be sure, more legible than others. For example, Cristina, the mayor's wife, is portrayed as an Imeldific figure. She wears her hair in a bouffant resembling the first lady's signature hairstyle. In a couple of scenes, she dons a sparkly dress with butterfly sleeves, precisely the sort of garb associated with Imelda. Her hysteria is consistent with parodies of Mrs. Marcos's emotional fits and highly affected mannerisms. Early in the film, as she weeps drunkenly at their living room bar, we see in the background a picture of Cristina's younger self, looking very much like Mrs. Marcos. The portrait invokes actress Gloria Romero's famous turn as Imelda in two biopics about the Marcoses: namely, *Written by Destiny* (*Iginuhit ng tadhana*), a 1965 film that helped Ferdinand win the presidency, and the 1969 follow-up *Bound by the Heavens* (*Pinagbuklod ng langit*).

The parallelisms between Ven and Ferdinand Marcos are alternately obvious and dissimulated. On many occasions throughout the film, pictures of Ferdinand appear in the settings of Ven's scenes. The physical resemblance between actor Eddie Garcia and the president—their build, hairstyle, dark complexion, eye shape—encourages such comparisons. One finds an example in the scene where Ven orders his henchmen to tail Auring. An official poster of the Marcoses figures prominently behind the mayor. The camera's focus is sharp enough to register the image of the president, looking unwell because of his health problems. The poster, which also functions as a calendar, denotes the current year—1985—thus locating the film's narrative in the current moment of political tumult.

In the scene where Ven confers with other political operators about rigging the forthcoming parliamentary elections, we see in the foreground a copy of *Newsweek* with a picture of Marcos on the cover. The poster of a more youthful Marcos hangs on a nearby wall. During the meeting, a corrupt official guarantees Ven 100 percent of the votes in his bailiwick while another one-ups that person by declaring that voting had already concluded in his territory even if elections were still a

FIGURE 5.6. Images of Ferdinand Marcos appear throughout the interior of Venancio's (Eddie Garcia) office. *Miguelito* (D'Wonder Films, 1985).

few weeks away! Such laughably barefaced electoral fraud was synonymous with the Marcos regime, which held plebiscites that returned over 90 percent of the vote in favor of the autocrat's policies or gave all but the most inconsequential seats to the ruling party.[128] Apart from what I have already stated above, the ubiquitous posters of the president and his wife mock the narcissism of the Marcoses and their idolization by corrupt small-town politicians.

Ven's characterization moves fluidly between a parody of Ferdinand Marcos and a broader critique of petty tyrants all over the country. The political scientist Barbara Geddes writes of a "personalist" type of authoritarian regime in which "one individual dominates both the military and state apparatus."[129] Such regimes comprise a leader and a clique "formed from the network of friends, relatives, and allies." Members of the clique help keep the dictator in power, and he returns the favor to this "predatory group" through "material inducements." Geddes notes that this form of autocracy was popular until the 1990s, coexisting with other forms of authoritarianism, such as military regimes and single-party regimes.[130] Milan Svolik prefers the term "personal autocracy" to describe the regime of an established authoritarian leader who has "effectively monopolized power" and successfully quelled rebellions in the past.[131] Apart from exercising control through brute force and paying-off both authoritarian elites and the masses, personal autocracies are often founded on and sustained by charismatic leadership.[132]

Geddes and Svolik's descriptions of personalist regimes apply both to Ven's regime and the Marcos dictatorship. Like Marcos, Ven is a charismatic politico with an exaggerated swagger and a well-cultivated superman mystique. The small-town mayor rules mainly to advance his interests. He uses his office to line his pockets. He bribes other public servants to do his bidding and maintain his hold on power. Heavy-handed in his use of intimidation and political violence, he quashes the opposition with impunity.

The film occasionally departs from its serious tone to poke fun at Ven's autocratic delusions. In one scene, Cristina pleads with her husband to finally come clean about Miguelito's parentage. The issue had been eating away at the young man. Ven warns Cristina not to interfere with their father-son relationship. He also reminds her that he enjoys a monopoly on far greater things than family matters. "I alone," he declares pompously, "have the right to determine the kind of truth to which he's entitled." Calculated to produce laughter, Ven's ostensible monopoly on truth parodies the megalomaniacal rhetoric of authoritarian leaders like Marcos.

The press coverage and critical reception of the film show that some of Brocka's audience successfully decoded its political allegories. Viewers were wise to such trenchant politicking because of Brocka's reputation as a maker of "socially conscious" films, his recent stint as a political prisoner, and the widely recognized politicization of popular culture during the years of the dictatorship.

The film's subversive politics did not catch anyone by surprise, except apparently its producer, who related in an interview that he explicitly asked Brocka to "stay clear of political undertones" and "make a simple but commercial film." The producer claimed (or pretended) to be puzzled when the censors found objectionable material in the picture.[133] Despite whatever assurance Brocka may have given his producer, he surely did not abstain from politicking, and the censors were eager to prove it.

The producer added that the censors initially assigned the film a dreaded "for adults only" rating and took issue with the subplot about "a politician impregnating a prostitute." Another journalist reported in passing that the melodrama "had rough sailing with the censors."[134] The producer went through a tedious appeal process—undoubtedly prolonged by the censors to harass Brocka—before obtaining a more favorable rating.

The dearth of censorship records prevents us from learning what else the censors may have found objectionable about *Miguelito* or how they interpreted the film's political message. The material trace of the film's reception lies instead in published notices by critics and entertainment reporters. In a review ostensibly about Nida Blanca's performance, Emmanuel Reyes discreetly slips in a couple of sentences to acknowledge the film's political statement. He writes: "*Miguelito*'s political angle and its critique on the abuse of power is well conveyed. Coming from a concerned artist like Brocka, such a work comes to us as no surprise."[135]

Another reviewer similarly points out that the film's political critique is especially legible. Ernie Pecho writes: "*Miguelito*'s real substance is not far beyond its worn-out, melodramatic plot. Lino Brocka's intentions (whether personal or sublime) in his latest film are so obvious that even the ordinary viewer can easily 'read between the lines.'"[136] He adds that "In every scene where his performers deliver well-crafted, meaningful lines, we can nearly see the placard-bearing

Brocka holding a screaming sign high enough for all to see." The clarity of the political statement is, for Pecho, an important measure of the film's success. He argues: "What the fighting director has been trying to achieve in joining all those rallies has been fulfilled in a more accessible mass medium—the cinema. Brocka effectively put across his convictions (political and otherwise) in *Miguelito Ang Batang Rebelde*, utilizing the major characters in the movie as mouthpieces." As with Reyes, Pecho sees Brocka's political engagement as something fully integrated into his work as a director. "At this point in his career, it's rather difficult to separate Brocka's politics from his art."

Other critics estimated, however, that the film's politics would only be legible to more discerning viewers. Ricardo Lo describes the film as one that "the perceptive [spectator] interpreted as Brocka's statement on the present political set-up."[137] Butch Francisco reinforces Lo's separation of "perceptive" and imperceptive viewers. He writes: "I would like to emphasize that the movie, while obviously a political metaphor, is honest-to-goodness soap opera, and that plain folk will enjoy it."[138] Francisco likely references "plain folk" to encourage his readers, particularly those not interested in politics, to see the film. Both he and Lo seem to bring up the issue of intelligent viewership because strong political content was not a customary feature of commercial films at that time.

Reflecting a variety of opinions on the place of politics in film, Mario Bautista, was less enthusiastic about *Miguelito*'s strident tone. His review spells out the film's political allegory and interprets the political significance of Ven's cabal. He writes: "The story is reminiscent of Duerrenmatt's [sic] *The Visit*, but there are those who would surely interpret the town as a symbol of contemporary Philippine society, what with the allusions to cronies who are Venancio's partners in crime."[139] Bautista makes fun, however, of the film's tendentiousness. He writes: "Auring's statement itself about how Roy allows himself to be used by Venancio reminds us of some political cohorts who allow themselves to be exploited by the powers that be. Somehow, *nakapagdaos din si* Lino (Lino was able to relieve his itch [for politicking])." The critic then offers faint praise, saying that "instead of making it just an Aga-movie, Brocka succeeded in giving us a fairly touching drama about injustice." He adds, however, that the film is "but a small gem compared to the real jewels Brocka did [sic] before." For Bautista, the "real jewels" were Brocka's prestige films, and presumably those that were not blatantly political.

Because *Miguelito* and *My Own Country* were released seven months apart, the two films—and the varieties of political cinema they represented—competed against each other. The government's Film Ratings Board awarded *Miguelito* the top-quality rating of "A," trumping *My Own Country*'s "B" rating.[140] *My Own Country* received the lion's share of honors during the awards derbies for that year, but *Miguelito* earned a similar number of nominations. Moreover, what Brocka described as the "commercial film not geared on romping away with awards" beat his prestige film in major categories, including Best Actor and Best Director.[141] Brocka was miffed when *Miguelito* won the best picture trophy in another contest, called the Star Awards (which are given by Philippine entertainment journalists). He told a reporter: "I cannot help it if I say I won for the wrong film when I won for *Miguelito* and not *Kapit [My Own Country]* . . . Because they missed the whole point of how I, as a director was trying to do *Kapit*."[142] Brocka's response indicates that, as with some of his critics, his cinema politics at that time still favored gritty independent pictures over more conventional genre movies.

CONCLUSION

Critics have not written of the prophetic aspect of the scenarios of Brocka's two ventures in political filmmaking. In starkly different ways, both films conjure the end of authoritarianism. *My Own Country* features images of mass actions that prefigured the February 1986 revolution. For its part, *Miguelito* portrays the death of a tyrant at the hands of those intimate to him. Both films overcome a conscious or unconscious aversion in Brocka's films (and those of others) to images of the youthful male revolutionary. As mentioned in chapter 2, in the director's earlier melodramas the provocative figure of the male insurgent achieved representation mainly by proxy, specifically through fiercely rebellious women confronting an autocratic matriarch.

Miguelito and *My Own Country* register a changed approach. In both films, a young man emerges as an unlikely dissident, either battling the system (as in *My Own Country*) or a malevolent patriarch (as in *Miguelito*). Through his depiction of the ruthless mayor in *Miguelito*, Brocka challenges the taboo on portraying autocratic politicos reminiscent of Marcos. Finally, both films depict extra-judicial killings, one of the most egregious forms of state violence practiced by the Marcos regime.

Critics largely recognized the value of Brocka's contributions to the fight against authoritarian repression. Some opined, however, that *My Own Country* and *Miguelito* ultimately did not pass muster. In his review of the former, Clodualdo del Mundo Jr., the screenwriter of Brocka's *Manila in the Claws of Light* (1976), cast doubt on the efficacy of Brocka's approach to political filmmaking: "I question what his melodramatic strategy has added to my understanding of the story of exploitation and oppression."[143] Similarly, Butch Francisco faulted *Miguelito* for gaps in the film's treatment of politics and the political implications of its ending. The reviewer rehearsed the familiar Marxist critique that "The story [of Brocka's film] does not trace the social and political evils to their roots, but it is a good enough portrayal of a social condition at a given time."[144]

Both films did not find a substantial audience in theaters and lost money. To be sure, a large audience and progressive content are reasonable indices of success for any theatrical film, political or otherwise. But these two measures cannot account for the impact of Brocka's political engagement with and through the art of melodrama. His mission to embarrass the Marcos regime on the world stage appears to have achieved success, as did his gesture of defying some of the government's restrictions on cinematic expression. He rammed progressive politics into film culture, battling courageously for his message movies and spurring debates about the role of cinema in politics. Equally important, he realized instructive failures and successes in placing the resources of cinema directly in the service of antiauthoritarian dissent, thus inspiring fellow filmmakers and moviegoers to keep faith in the mission and the medium.

A few months after the release of *My Own Country*, the censors acknowledged the emergence of a political cinema in the country. Speaking to the *Washington Post*, chief censor Katigbak noted: "Now, we have the problem with the movies that are the propaganda against the government. We have to be firm in interpreting what is subversive and what is not."[145] By suggesting a contestation over the decoding of "subversive" messages, Imelda Marcos's staunch ally and media gatekeeper implicitly recognized that dissidents were circumventing the regime's policies by recourse to coded messages and techniques. The regime's militancy against such acts of dissimulated subversion speaks not only to a paranoid attitude toward film and culture but also to the undeniable impact of certain experiments in political cinema.

6

A Dirty Affair

Political Melodramas of Democratization

Ferdinand Marcos was ousted from the presidency and exiled to Hawaii in late February 1986, during a four-day event called the "people power" revolution. The event was not, as the name might suggest, an armed uprising. It was, instead, a peaceful assembly of thousands of civilians who sought to protect the leaders of an aborted military coup from reprisal by the autocratic state. Many of those who gathered also sought to pressure Marcos into stepping down for stealing the presidential election held in December, not to mention other atrocities he had committed in the previous two decades.

Lino Brocka had every reason to be optimistic about the country's future after the dictatorship. The filmmaker campaigned for the newly installed leader, Corazon "Cory" Aquino, the widow of slain opposition leader Ninoy Aquino. Despite Brocka's reluctance to serve in government, President Aquino appointed him to the commission tasked with drafting a new constitution. Unfortunately, the experience left him disillusioned with realpolitik and the new government. He later recounted that his fellow delegates "really diluted" the policies relating to agrarian reform. He also spoke bitterly of colleagues "connected with multinationals" who backed provisions inimical to what he called "economic democracy."[1] Brocka quit the commission within four months. His most significant achievement was introducing the phrase "freedom of expression" into the constitution's bill of rights and thereby extending free speech protections to the arts.

Three years after the revolution and halfway into Mrs. Aquino's term, Brocka made an incendiary film about vigilante terrorism in the countryside. During a press conference for the Cannes screening of his film *Les insoumis* (also called *Oraprono-bis* and *Fight for Us*), the director criticized the post-dictatorship government. He said: "We are still facing the same problems today. There is poverty, hunger, corruption, repression and ongoing human rights violations, none of that has changed even though now we enjoy a democratic space."[2]

Brocka's reference to a "democratic space" gave Mrs. Aquino some credit for reforming government. As the political scientist Gretchen Casper points out, the president "successfully restored democracy to the Philippines" with the reestablishment of civil liberties, the return of democratic elections, and the ratification of a new constitution. That said, the filmmaker was right about the chief executive's shortcomings. Casper reports that the persistence of social inequality led to "a rising sense of dissatisfaction in the country" during Aquino's six-year tenure.[3] Moreover, problems from the Marcos era such as human rights violations and graft and corruption remained intractable under her watch. Much to the president's dismay, landowners (including members of her own family) used their influence to undermine the land reform program that served as the centerpiece of her campaign.[4] Its failure bolstered the communist insurgency that had flourished in the latter years of Marcos's rule. To make things even worse, Aquino reneged on a pledge to broker peace with the communists, declaring a "total war" against them after her first year in office.[5]

The Philippines' rocky path to democratization—the transition from authoritarianism to a liberal democracy—was by no means exceptional.[6] Indeed, political conflicts, weak institutions, and bad economies have plagued the successors of deposed autocracies all over the world. Moreover, the slow process of change within new democracies has frustrated persons and institutions habituated to the swiftness of autocratic measures. In many cases, the temptation to return to old ways has thus proven too strong to resist. Casper coined the phrase "fragile democracy" to describe the nation's state during Aquino's presidency, marred as it was by throwbacks to illiberal practices as well as political instability.[7]

Brocka did his part to hold the country's fragile democracy together by returning to filmmaking after his stint in the constitutional commission. He began reworking the political cinema he developed during the Marcos regime while making commercially appealing films to reach a wider audience and pay his debts from producing films in the 1970s. Several critics used the term "political melodrama" to describe his recent militant films, especially *My Own Country: Gripping the Knife's Edge* (*Bayan ko: Kapit sa patalim*, 1984).[8] The term was even more appropriate to the socially relevant pictures he made after the 1986 uprising. "Political melodrama" invokes three aspects of his post-dictatorship oeuvre. First, those films are explicitly about politics. They follow Brocka's durable strategy of using local politics as a microcosm for national affairs, seen most notably in *Miguelito: The Rebellious Child* (*Miguelito: Batang rebelde*, 1985). Second, the films draw on conventions associated with melodrama in treating political matters. Their approach is sensational, moralistic, and charged with primal emotions. Third, the films use melodrama as a political tool. To realize cinema's democratic potential as a mass medium, the films treat political material in a manner that is both comprehensible and appealing to a broad audience. The works harness cinema's utility for political pedagogy.

For some scholars, the notion of using melodrama for political ends is largely problematic. Their arguments are well-known and intuitive, and I have already rehearsed some of them in earlier sections of this book. For instance, certain scholars believe that melodrama is ill-suited to presenting sound political thinking.[9] Melodrama, they suggest, is often unable to render the complexities and contradictions of sociopolitical realities. Other scholars observe that the tendency of some melodramas to rehearse Oedipal scenarios does not enhance one's understanding of politics. Such films, they claim, tend "to personalize public and political conflicts"[10] or merely revisit time-worn scripts for apprehending politics instead of devising new scenarios that might be more responsive to contemporary reality.[11] Finally, scholars also regard melodrama's traffic in powerful emotions as troublesome for political discourse.[12] They argue that feelings usually escalate in melodrama well before the narratives thoroughly explain the issues at hand, before they work out the consequences of acting versus not acting, and before they chart alternative courses of action. Other scholars point to cases in which intense emotions cloud reason, taking the form of perplexed rage or melancholic inaction from the film's viewers.[13]

My discussion of Brocka's political melodramas will take up the issues I have identified above. I am concerned with his exploration of a post-authoritarian cinema politics, including his attempts at performing the vital task of memorializing the nation's authoritarian past and depicting the stakes of political involvement during the transition to democracy. The films in question here are *Orapronobis/Les insoumis/Fight for Us* (1989), *A Dirty Affair* (*Gumapang ka sa lusak*, 1990), and *Above Everything Else* (*Sa kabila ng lahat*, 1991). I shall discuss their stylistics, political rhetoric, and reception in light of historical events, Brocka's career, and developments in Philippine film culture.

ORAPRONOBIS

Early in his stint as a delegate to the constitutional commission, Brocka witnessed an incident that served as the germ of his next political film. He recalled: "I went to Misamis Oriental with [screenwriter Jose F. a.k.a.] Pete Lacaba, and we happened to pass by a town where a massacre of eighteen men, women and children had just occurred."[14] The dead were members of a pro-Marcos religious cult known as the Tadtad, whose name meant "to cut into little pieces." Brocka and Lacaba learned that some of the cultists also participated in anti-insurgent vigilante groups. They were known to summarily execute, mutilate, and even cannibalize persons they suspected of being communists. Lacaba and Brocka developed a project out of this material, with some encouragement from a major Philippine movie studio called Viva Films. The director related: "At the time, I was really thinking in terms of an action movie for [famous leading man] Phillip Salvador because that's what Viva wanted me to do."[15] The project fell through for unknown reasons.[16]

In October 1987, Brocka once again witnessed the seriousness of the vigilante problem.[17] More than two hundred people from Leyte province sought refuge in Manila from a paramilitary group that vowed to kill them for giving "water and food to rebels who knocked on their doors."[18] When a state university president agreed to house the refugees at his campus, the vigilantes and their military connections in the capital tried to assassinate him. Brocka offered his utility vehicle to move the refugees "to different convents and houses to hide them."[19] He also hosted two dozen refugees at his mother Pilar's home, smuggling them in "in groups of five, at night."[20] Brocka also attended their court hearings to express his support. On one occasion, as he stood outside a courthouse with a refugee named Pacita Dellosa, police officers arrived to seize her. Brocka held on to her arm and engaged "in a tug-of-war with the police."[21] The director recalled feeling "very manly" and launching into a "flying kick" to fend off the abductors.[22] The incident—minus the filmmaker and his daring stunt—would later be reenacted in his movie.

Brocka eventually found the opportunity to make his film about vigilantes in 1988 when, as he recalled, "Bernadette Films signed me to make a film for $300,000 on anything, as long as it was a 'Lino Brocka' film."[23] He volunteered that the producers turned to him because they "wanted a movie they could get into Cannes cheaply."[24] The outfit was a "Paris-based production company and a French affiliate of the Hollywood-based Cannon Group,"[25] the latter known for churning out low-budget films. From September 1988 to January 1989, Lacaba reworked his proposal for a commercial action film into a political thriller aimed at a global audience.[26] Brocka completed principal photography in just twenty-two days, filming in Manila and nearby Boso-Boso, Rizal Province, and Lubao, Pampanga. For safety reasons and to save money, the film is set near the Philippine capital instead of in the south, where vigilante bailiwicks were located.[27] As in the case of Brocka's fiery Marcos-era political film *My Own Country*, the motion picture elements of *Orapronobis* were sent to France for completion after preliminary editing in Manila.[28] The film premiered as *Les insoumis* at Cannes on May 22 and, by the screenwriter's account, "opened in eight Paris theaters on May 24."[29] The number of screens in the film's engagement is telling of the director's considerable popularity among French moviegoers.

Orapronobis begins with a title card stating that the picture was "filmed clandestinely" and that "all that you will see in this film is authentic." These claims—half-true at best—follow a tactic in exploitation filmmaking of hawking a sensational picture as forbidden fruit. Brocka claims he requested the European producers to delete the misleading title card, but they ignored him.

FIGURE 6.1. Commander Kontra's (Bembol Roco) militia, called Orapronobis, is a composite of vigilante groups from both the Marcos and Aquino regimes. *Orapronobis/Fight for Us.* Courtesy of Danilo Brocka/CCP Library.

The narrative continues with a prologue set in the Marcos era. It is October 1985, and militia members sporting fatigues and red bandanas flag a Caucasian priest traveling on a motorcycle. Among them is Commander Kontra (Bembol Roco), their leader. They allow the traveler, Father Jeff (Gerard Bernschein), to pass through but remind him that he is venturing into unsafe territory. Checkpoints such as this one proliferated during the Marcos regime as part of its militarization of the countryside. Petty authoritarians like Kontra operated them, terrorizing denizens and travelers.

The prologue continues as the priest reaches the fictitious and allegorically named town of Dolores, where he ministers at the wake of a man hacked to death by vigilantes. Kontra interrupts the ceremony and berates the priest for tending to the corpse of a communist and "demon." He then sets the priest's motorcycle on fire before shooting him point-blank in the head. In the French theatrical version of the film, the scene continues with shots of Kontra scooping out the priest's brain matter with his hand and preparing to feed on it. The tamer and more widely distributed US version ends the scene with Kontra's bullet hitting the priest.

The cold-blooded killing and the horrified expressions of the victim and onlookers comprise what I have been calling in this book a "Marcosian moment." As with many of Brocka's martial law melodramas, the Philippine experience of authoritarianism registers in such passages of explosive violence and extra-judicial killings. Father Jeff's murder slightly fictionalizes the horrific fate of the Italian missionary Tullio Favali in the hands of vigilantes led by Norberto Manero Jr. Like Kontra, they reportedly fed on the priest's brains for superstitious reasons.[30]

In both versions of the film, the scene of the priest's murder cuts to black, followed by the whirring of helicopters, and then a title sequence comprised of re-photographed television footage of the 1986 revolution. The uninterrupted flow of sound between the prologue and the title sequence provides an elegant overture to the film's argument. It links the authoritarian and the postrevolutionary eras, subtextually prefiguring the changelessness of the national situation even after the autocrat's ouster.

The scene following the title credits introduces the protagonist, Jimmy Cordero (Phillip Salvador), an ex-priest, former eight-year member of the communist underground, and political detainee. Jimmy and his cellmates have just received news that they will be among the more than five hundred political prisoners to be released by President Aquino at the beginning of her term.[31] Both Jimmy's character and the amnesty program for political prisoners derive inspiration from real life. Jimmy brings to mind several priests who became guerrillas, including Conrado Balweg.[32] Following his release, Jimmy rejoins the political mainstream by signing up with a nongovernmental organization (NGO) called the Alliance for Human Rights. In the interest of narrative and thematic clarity, Lacaba makes the other characters in Jimmy's story share his interest in human rights advocacy. Jimmy's wife, Trixie (Dina Bonnevie), works as a media liaison for the same NGO. Her brother Rolan (William Lorenzo), a student activist, volunteers there as well. The allegorically named Sister Marie Dipasupil (Ginnie Sobrino) heads the organization. Dipasupil, whose name means "unconquerable," is a fictionalized version of Sister Mariani Dimaranan, an activist-nun and head of the Task Force Detainees of the Philippines, a human rights organization connected with the Catholic Church.[33]

Alongside developing Jimmy's story, the narrative follows the ordeal of internal refugees from Santa Filomena, a town adjacent to Dolores and the place where Jimmy was assigned as a guerilla. The refugees include family members of persons murdered by Kontra and his men. In a coincidence typical of melodramas, one of the refugees happens to be Esper (Gina Alajar), who was once Jimmy's former comrade and longtime flame. Esper ended up marrying Jimmy's fellow guerila and friend Roque. Kontra slew the latter in a massacre that Esper's father (Ray Ventura), with whom he was traveling, narrowly survived. Jimmy returns to Santa Filomena with Rolan and their colleagues to investigate the massacre and see if they could do anything for Esper and the villagers. To Jimmy's surprise, one of Esper's three children, a boy named Camilo (R. R. Herrera), bears his old nom de guerre. (The daughter is named after the leftist revolutionary heroine Lorena Barros.) Esper later states the obvious: the boy is Jimmy's son, but the child does not know it yet. Jimmy's discovery of his paternal ties to Santa Filomena only toughens his resolve to aid its people.

Meanwhile, the investigation at Santa Filomena exposes the Manila contingent to the vigilantes' reign of terror. Jimmy's group meets the highest-ranking military official in the area, an eccentric who uses a human skull as decoration on his office desk. Colonel Ricardo Mateo (Joel Lamangan) dismisses their concerns about human rights abuses while absently caressing the skull. Mateo also insists that the killing of Esper's husband and the others was justified because they were either communist insurgents or sympathizers. He zealously defends the vigilantes, parroting the Aquino government's claim that the fight against communism requires "the help of all our citizens," and not just the authorities. The staging of the scene at Mateo's office emulates key moments in *Miguelito*, Brocka's last political work of the Marcos era. In both films, a poster of the Philippine president appears conspicuously near or behind one of the villainous characters, thus linking the two figures together. In *Orapronobis*, two pictures of President Aquino are seen in the background as Mateo spouts his defense of vigilantism. A poster of Sylvester Stallone portraying a rogue cop in *Cobra* (George P. Cosmatos, 1986) also hangs near one of the president's pictures, adding a satirical note to the scene and implicating the United States in the rise of Philippines vigilantes. The *Cobra* poster and Mateo's crazed demeanor both poke fun at a real-life figure named Lt. Col. Franco Calida, the top cop in a southern province who was a fierce supporter of the notorious vigilante group Alsa Masa (Rising Masses) and a fan of Stallone's film. Calida, who trained with US Special Forces, was known to make such bombastic quips as "We will cook them [communists] in their own oil."[34]

Jimmy and his party proceed to Esper's home after their meeting with Mateo. They find Kontra waiting for them across the street, armed with heavy weapons. They learn to their horror that the vigilante chief has just sprayed bullets at the shack, terrorizing the children inside it. Kontra threatens to kill Esper and others who speak against or resist the militia. The incident prompts a mass exodus to another town.

The evacuees turn for protection to their archbishop, who is named Romero after the martyred clergy from El Salvador but whose story draws inspiration from the experiences of the Filipino Cardinal Ricardo Vidal. Kontra follows the refugees to his church and holds a big rally outside. The scene is one of the film's satirical highlights. It shows demonstrators carrying a human skeleton (supposedly a victim of the communists) and placards that read "Priests and nuns deserve to be barbecued" and "Communism = Satanism." The scene is more provocative than it appears because Kontra's fanatical supporters include police officers and other members of the Philippine armed forces. The direct criticism of the military in this and other scenes in *Orapronobis* was unprecedented in Brocka's films.

On the evening after the rally, two men in a jeep lob a grenade at the cardinal's residence, missing him and Jimmy by a few meters. The incident sends the refugees fleeing all the way to the nation's capital. Like many others in the film, the scene drew inspiration from recent history.

In the meantime, the country's militia problem and the domestic issues from Jimmy's past creep into Trixie's life in Manila. First, her coworker Jun disappears after getting nabbed by armed men—likely also killed or "salvaged" (in the Marcos-era parlance). The coworker had been investigating a vigilante killing spree in another town when armed men abducted him. Trixie accompanies her coworker's wife to a TV show as the latter appeals for President Aquino's help. In a jab at the chief executive, the wife tells Aquino (whose husband was detained by Marcos for over seven years) that she must know what it was like to have a loved one disappeared by armed men. Secondly, Trixie's brother Rolan and Jimmy are ambushed by goons after criticizing the government's support of vigilantes in a TV talk show. Jimmy is wounded while Rolan is gunned down in another of the film's Marcosian moments. Thirdly, Trixie gives birth to her and Jimmy's child, only to find that she must compete with Esper and her children for Jimmy's attention.

The refugees discover that Manila cannot offer respite from their troubles. Members of the military seize Esper's father and other refugees seemingly picked at random by a hooded informant in a midnight raid at another university campus sheltering the displaced provincials. Shortly after the court hearing on their disappearance, armed men kidnap Esper and Camilo. Her abduction recalls the incident (described earlier) that Brocka witnessed in 1986. Esper is separated from her son and taken to a house in a secluded area. While her abductors are careful not to reveal themselves as military, their interrogation techniques and access to a safe house say as much. Reminiscent of torture practices during the Marcos-era, the abductors take turns abusing her. (The scene is truncated in the widely available version of the film.) They then take her back to Santa Filomena and hand her over to the vigilantes. At Kontra's hideout, she is reunited with her son, father-in-law, and other refugees.

Kontra's dimly lit shack recalls a serial killer's den in American horror movies. As in the rest of *Orapronobis* and many of Brocka's other films, the mise-en-scène speaks politics. A poster of Ferdinand Marcos hangs alongside one of Sylvester Stallone playing the mercenary Rambo. The posters invite comparison with the pictures of Stallone and President Aquino in Colonel Mateo's office. They also snidely imply that the military officer and Kontra are virtually interchangeable. Elsewhere in the hut, a large American flag is pitched beside an altar, hanging over Christ images and human skulls. A tiny Philippine flag is stitched into the middle of the oversized banner's red and white stripes. The nested flags once again implicate the Americans in the Filipino vigilantes' atrocities. As with many in the Philippine Left, Brocka was openly critical of US interventionism.[35] He believed that the US was exerting undue influence on Aquino to retain its military bases in the archipelago. American meddling directly exacerbated the vigilante problem as well. David Wurfel notes that in October 1986, a CIA veteran and chair of the World Anticommunist League may have assisted the Philippine military in "developing an anti-communist vigilante movement in the countryside."[36] He goes on to say that "the CIA had allocated $10 million to finance counterinsurgency efforts in the Philippines" in what was the United States' "most massive intervention in Philippine affairs since the Magsaysay era [in the 1950s]."

Kontra preaches incoherently to Esper about the necessity of saving her soul and learning secret chants that would make her invincible to bullets. He then rapes her within earshot of the other refugees and in front of her son, before passing her on to his comrade Jango (Abbo Dela Cruz). Camilo, understandably outraged after his mother's rape, attacks Kontra with a toy sword. Kontra shoots him dead. Esper grabs Jango's gun and fires at Kontra (and, on Brocka's instructions, actress Gina Alajar also imagines killing Marcos whose ubiquitous portrait had established in Philippine cinema a synecdoche between all bosses and the dictator).[37]

Kontra responds with his high-powered—and American-made—M-16 rifle, killing her and then mowing down the rest of the captives. Jango notices Kontra's wound, berates him for falsely claiming he was invincible to bullets, and fatally stabs him. In the French version of the movie, Jango uses his knife to cut Kontra's chest and carve out a piece of his heart. He singes the organ meat and feeds it to a comrade.

In the meantime, Jimmy and Trixie make frantic attempts to rescue mother and child by using connections to society's powerbrokers and elites. Their quest unravels the web of complicity that has kept the vigilantes in power. They begin their search by approaching two military officers. One denies commanding his men to abduct Esper and Camilo while the other disavows any knowledge of their whereabouts. Finally, the couple pleads with the highly influential archbishop of Manila, a man Jimmy knew well from his days as a priest. The former refuses even to see him, sending a monsignor in his stead. The latter rehearses the cardinal's line that vigilantes were unarmed, God-fearing citizens who were doing the church a service by opposing "those who spread atheism." The archbishop's response reflects the position of his real-life counterpart, Jaime Cardinal Sin, who endorsed the militia.[38] Sin was an immensely popular figure, but that did not deter the makers of *Orapronobis* from criticizing him.

In the film's extended denouement, the spectacle of grisly violence is placed once more in the service of political agitation. Outside the ruins of the church at Santa Filomena, the narrative slows down to examine the aftermath of the militia's

FIGURE 6.2. Jimmy (Phillip Salvador, center) carries the remains of his son Camilo (R. R. Herrera). *Orapronobis/Fight for Us*. Courtesy of Danilo Brocka/CCP Library.

latest carnage. With almost pornographic attention, the camera studies the remains of Esper and the other victims. Shots linger on their pale and mangled bodies, and on faces made almost unrecognizable by caked blood and dirt. As the bereaved wail in the background, Colonel Mateo mugs for the TV and photojournalists' cameras and makes the outrageous claim that the fallen were all communist guerillas. Jimmy quietly tends to Esper's corpse, not quite knowing what to do. Suddenly, the camera assumes his point of view and spots Camilo's body in the same trailer that brought in her remains. Time dilates and everything—save for birds chirping in the distance—falls silent as Jimmy scoops up his child and carries him into the partially burned church.

The film ends with Jimmy making an unexpected political move. Back in Manila, he takes a final look at his sleeping wife and their newborn before delivering a cryptic message on the phone to an unknown party. The call indicates Jimmy's decision to return to the underground movement.

Brocka called *Orapronobis* his "most political film" in an interview he gave to the French periodical *Revue du Cinéma*. "This time," Brocka said, "the [political] events do not just serve as a backdrop but are front and center."[39] He added: "They take precedence over the personal drama. They affect everything." *Orapronobis* was indeed his most overt and sustained representation of political issues. It was also his most confrontational statement about a sitting president and the military. A critic from *Variety* correctly surmised that the film is "perhaps even more violent and angrier than the films he [Brocka] made under the Marcos dictatorship."[40]

The philosopher Alain Badiou cautions that transparent and spirited depictions of politics—such as those featured in *Orapronobis*—can be problematic. It is often more difficult to appraise a film's politics, he says, "the closer the film in question was to the political subject matter [it treated]."[41] He goes on to say that "The more contemporary the politics, the more important the [film's] nuances."[42] Equally pertinent, filmmakers, critics, and viewers have different assumptions—some contradictory and unexamined—about the proper form of political cinema. It thus behooves scholars and viewers to embrace a capacious notion of progressive filmmaking.

Documentary Material

Taking a page from the politically charged melodramas he made in the Marcos years, *Orapronobis* weaves documentary material and depictions of contemporary political events into a stirring fictional narrative. The film utilizes real-life incidents more extensively, however, than in his earlier political works, and Brocka was proud of it. While promoting the film, he emphasized that Lacaba's screenplay drew extensively from published accounts of vigilante atrocities. And when some of the film's critics charged that the film was replete with historical fabrications and distortions, Lacaba joined the director in defending the truthfulness of their work, enumerating the film's documentary sources, such as pieces of investigative journalism and reports from Amnesty International, the US government, and the Philippine Senate."[43]

The film's incorporation of nonfiction material found reinforcement in the visuals, which emulated the stark and gritty style of documentary and news footage. Rody Lacap's flat and often unvarnished cinematography markedly deviated from the moody and lushly composed images of Brocka's longtime director of photography Conrado Baltazar. The banal appearance of Lacap's TV news–like images suited the film's proposition that the outrageous horrors of vigilantism reflected an actual state of affairs that Filipinos could no longer afford to ignore.

Brocka's investment in nonfiction material also served to affirm his commitment to depicting sociopolitical conditions as truthfully as possible. Such vocation was just as important in an era marked by complacency in political matters as it was at the height of autocratic rule and its regime of falsehoods. The director's new, post-Marcos iteration of political cinema thus attempted to take full advantage of the relative unfettering of the media to castigate the failures of democratization and the weaknesses of Aquino's liberal-democratic regime.

Critics lauded the realism and documentary-like quality of Brocka's first big post-Marcos salvo. The reviewer for *Variety* commended the film's "wrenching documentary immediacy, enforced by the unflamboyant, committed acting."[44] Joel David referred to the film's true-to-life depictions as "documentary events onscreen" and to the "narrative [as one] which has drawn voraciously from known facts."[45] Sociology professor Randy David (no relation) praised the movie's fidelity to the truth. He wrote: "*Orapronobis* is an objective report about the violence and continued harassment inflicted upon the masses. It contains no slogans. It makes no ham-fisted cries of revolt."[46] A host of public affairs programs, David characterized the film as an "equivalent to one million commentaries on newspapers and radio, and perhaps a whole year of television talk shows."

The critics' enthusiasm for a political cinema with the characteristics of documentary requires little explanation. The use of images resembling those of nonfiction movies signals the filmmaker's desire to address real-life issues and convey their urgency to viewers. Additionally, political movies often benefit from adopting the episodic structure of documentaries, which allows for the representation of complex phenomena without the strictures of conventional dramatic development (such as having to use a limited set of characters and link scenes in a tight, cause-and-effect structure.) The narrative of *Orapronobis* constantly breaks free of tracking Jimmy's story to follow other characters and engage in documentary-like explorations of the scourge of counterrevolutionary vigilantism. Implicitly framed as reportage or exposé, these digressions from the protagonist's story depict numerous fact-based episodes and treat the sociopolitical factors behind the rise of paramilitary groups. That said, this advantage is neither unique to documentary-like narration nor entirely new to Brocka's filmmaking. In some respects, the sprawling narrative of *Orapronobis* harkens back to the picaresque structure and multicharacter plots that Brocka utilized to draw panoramic social portraits in films like *Manila in the Claws of Light*.

A Political Slasher Film

As mentioned earlier, one of the most unusual features of Brocka's political melodrama is its unforgiving depiction of state-sanctioned violence. The American critic Richard Corliss excoriated this aspect of *Orapronobis*, characterizing Brocka's work a "political slasher film" and a piece of "wily exploitation."[47] His criticism suggests an underlying belief that sensationalism, a hallmark of genre films and melodrama, is inappropriate to sociopolitical discourse.

It must be said, however, that many of the European critics familiar with the Filipino director's work approved of his film's use of graphic violence. Writing for *Revue du Cinéma*, Raphäel Bassan observed that the gory film "is effective in its key goal: to make the viewer aware of the horror of the situation."[48] Similarly, the Dutch critic Anselm Jungeblodt remarked that the picture's "spiral of violence" is "applied to cathartic effect."[49] Most liberal Filipino journalists and critics reacted like the Europeans. Sheila Coronel, who authored pioneering investigative reports on the vigilante groups, averred: "The problem lies in the critics' refusal to accept that there exists in this seemingly gentle country a dark and brutal underside that manifests itself in the conduct of counterinsurgency warfare in hinterland villages.

Brocka's film simply focused the klieg lights on this underside, and that is what makes '*Les insoumis*' so shocking and so unpalatable."[50]

It is worth unpacking Corliss's apparent bias against political films that are replete with violence or packaged in sensational genres. Neither Brocka nor Lacaba mentioned having seen the films of Constantin Costa-Gavras, but *Orapronobis* resembles the kind of filmmaking popularized in the previous decade by the Greek-born director. Alternately described as "political thrillers," "political fiction," and "political melodrama," the best of Costa-Gavras's oeuvre explored the workings of politics through narratives supercharged with action sequences and primal emotions.[51] Such Costa-Gavras films as *Z* (1969) and *State of Siege* (1972) wove fictionalized but realistic narratives out of a series of unrelated political events. *Orapronobis* treated its true-to-life material similarly, using dramatic license to connect events relating to counterrevolutionary vigilantism that occurred across the nation for over a decade. In its portrayal of human rights abuses, *Orapronobis* especially resonates with Costa-Gavras's *Missing* (1982), a melodramatic political thriller that harrowingly details the search for a US photojournalist who disappeared in an unnamed Latin American country.

By the time *Orapronobis* was released, however, Costa-Gavras's films—as well as the subgenre of the political thriller—had already fallen into disfavor. Among other things, critics had grown tired of his ostensibly heavy-handed approach, exemplified they say by his "manipulative use of staccato montages" to punch up scenes of political conflict and violence.[52] Alain Badiou opined that Costa-Gavras's films were "reactionary" and thus undeserving of their reputation for espousing progressive politics.[53] Another reason for the backlash against political thrillers is the notion, which Corliss raises in his review of *Orapronobis*, that their depiction of violence could be gratuitous and mindless.

To be sure, violence had long been a staple of sociopolitical films and world cinema more generally when Brocka made his film. Karl Schoonover points out, for example, that Italian "neorealist classics pivot on scenarios of the violenced body."[54] They use what he calls "corporealism"—a visual idiom of bodily display—as a transcultural strategy for making statements about sociopolitical conditions in a manner that appeals both to the emotions and the voyeuristic desires of moviegoers.[55] Schoonover's work reconsiders the cross-cultural politics of using images of "the suffering body to convene a global audience of moral onlookers."[56] This practice, he suggests, "authorizes the foreign gaze to adjudicate local politics."[57] The cross-cultural dynamics involved in this spectatorial position is quite tricky, however, as Schoonover acknowledges. For one, the foreign viewers of these films, some of whom were ill-equipped to weigh in on sociopolitical issues, might end up supporting interventionist policies detrimental to the real-life counterparts of the characters or the citizens of foreign countries depicted in a movie. The foreign spectators might alternatively end up doing nothing instead of trying to help fight for worthy causes, satisfied that they had already done their part by vicariously bearing witness to the suffering of others, even if they only did so from the comfort of a movie theater. The term "proxied engagement"—merely "looking as a form of political engagement"—describes the latter scenario.[58]

Orapronobis utilized a less culturally prestigious version of "corporealism" than what Schoonover describes, but it shared the humanitarian and geopolitical purpose of summoning "a global audience of moral onlookers."[59] By setting up *Orapronobis* as a transcultural cinematic project, Brocka asserted the continuing value of foreign viewership to his practice of cinema politics. Following his Marcos-era strategy, Brocka aired his country's dirty linen abroad to shame the Philippine government into changing its repressive policies. He raised the stakes in *Orapronobis* by staging an exponentially greater number of scenes of extrajudicial killing and torture (all of them Marcosian moments) than he did previously, using shock tactics to provoke outrage among domestic and international viewers who may have grown complacent about the fate of Philippine democracy after the fall of Marcos. Brocka counterintuitively posited the film's over-the-top images of unhinged despots, bloody massacres, gang rape, and cannibalism as honest depictions of the current state of affairs in the country.

The recourse to extreme cinematic violence created problems for Brocka's new political melodrama, but for reasons he did not anticipate. His goriest depictions fell victim to censorship at home and abroad. Lacaba relates that French producers demanded the shortening of the second cannibalism scene while the film was still in postproduction. The excised portion was an insert shot of the vigilante named Jango (Abbo De La Cruz) handling Kontra's still-beating heart.[60] Following the screening at Cannes and the theatrical run in France, the distributor made cuts to the film's three most violent scenes, in addition to other less significant alterations. The Motion Picture Association of America reportedly asked for the excisions in return for issuing an "R" rating for the film.[61] The deleted portions included shots of the the Caucasian priest's mangled head; Kontra scooping out brain matter and preparing to consume it; a scene of the vigilantes exhibiting the decapitated head of one of their victims to horrified onlookers; Jango cutting into Kontra's chest; Jango looking at the chunk of Kontra's heart on the tip of his knife; and Jango saying a prayer before offering the piece of human offal to another cult-member.

Despite their gory content, the deleted shots did not seem as though they belonged, as Corliss puts it, in the oft-maligned slasher film subgenre. The images had a realistic appearance, thanks to well-made prosthetics and clever editing. Unfortunately, the frankness of those depictions made them almost permanently inaccessible to viewers in the Philippines and other countries besides France. The print of the film that circulated in a handful of private screenings in the Philippines was of the bowdlerized MPAA version. The censored portions were never restored, not even when the film was released on home video in the United States

FIGURE 6.3. This composite features images from the two censored depictions of cannibalism in the film. The top images show Commander Kontra (Bembol Roco) blasting the priest's skull and preparing to eat his brain matter. The bottom images show Django (Abbo De la Cruz) ripping open Kontra's chest and preparing to eat a piece of his heart. *Orapronobis/Fight for Us.* Courtesy of Cinémathèque Royale de Belgique.

and Italy. To my knowledge, only the French subtitled prints—held at archives in Paris and Brussels—contain all the material taken out of the MPAA cut.

Brocka's detractors capitalized on the inaccessibility of the censored scenes in mounting a smear campaign against *Orapronobis* and its makers. They offered hysterical secondhand descriptions of the excised sections and their effects on viewers. Newspaper columnist Belinda Olivares-Cunanan blasted the film's depiction of cannibalism and accused the filmmaker of casting "a slur on the entire Filipino race." She went on to falsely report that "Filipinos who saw the film in the French capital came out crying and covering their face in shame."[62] To give credulity to her account, she added that television preacher Fr. Sonny Ramirez—one of the few Filipinos who saw the film's integral version in France—told her "a foreign woman sitting beside him vomited at the film's end." In the most outrageously spurious of her hit pieces, the columnist blamed Brocka for getting Filipina nannies sacked from their jobs in Paris, implying that employers feared they might be cannibals like the characters in his film.[63]

Other figures identified with Mrs. Aquino and her government joined the columnist in mudslinging. TV director Nick Lizaso suggested that the film's engagement in France was "part of a leftist black propaganda [campaign] to downgrade [sic] President Aquino's scheduled visit to Europe in July."[64] He subsequently floated the laughable theory that the film was secretly funded by the Marcoses (specifically former presidential daughter Imee) to get back at Aquino.[65] Behaving much like—but also far worse—than Marcos's cordon sanitaire Maria Kalaw Katigbak, Aquino's chief censor Manuel Morato Jr. repeated Lizaso's baseless claims. Additionally, Morato hurled more accusations against Brocka in his newspaper columns and interviews with the media. He even tried to make an issue of the director's sexuality, boasting that he had salacious information about the director's "nocturnal activities."[66] Worst of all, the chief censor sought to get the director and the scriptwriter in hot water by testifying to Congress about the alleged proliferation of communists in the film industry, obviously alluding to them.[67] Brocka responded defiantly to the red-baiting, declaring that "If someone who fights for human rights is a communist, then I can be called a communist."[68]

Apart from his demolition job against the filmmakers, Morato suppressed *Orapronobis* by leveraging the power of his office. After hearing of the film's acceptance at Cannes, Morato sent a letter to festival director Gilles Jacob, accusing Brocka of falsely picturing himself "as a victim of censorship . . . [in a] publicity gimmick to generate sympathy and call attention to himself."[69]

Viva, the Philippine distributor of films made by the Cannon Group, begged off from representing *Orapronobis*, likely out of fear of offending the censors and the government. Brocka was only able to obtain a print of the film by cutting a deal with Pathé, its international distributor. After a few private screenings, he submitted the print to the censors for review, hoping it would eventually find a local distributor. The censors slapped the film with an R-21 rating, limiting admission to persons aged twenty-one and over. The rating technically did not even exist. Morato initially assigned the same rating to Brocka's gay-themed film *Macho Dancer*. The censors adjusted the latter's rating to another previously nonexistent designation called "R-18" on appeal but then, according to Brocka, pressured the distributor (also Viva) to pull out of theaters after just "four days."[70]

Emulating his Marcos-era predecessors, Morato likewise withheld the permit for the film's commercial exhibition, citing deficient paperwork and accusing the director of bypassing export-import requirements.[71] Morato's rancor scared off distributors and, much to Brocka's dismay, the film never enjoyed a commercial run in Philippine theaters. Ironically, the fate of *Orapronobis* in Aquino's "democratic space" was worse than what *My Own Country* suffered under the Marcos dictatorship. The new constitution's guarantee of free expression, which Brocka wrote into the document, did not save his film from the tyranny of Mrs. Aquino's censors and her attack dogs in the press. She reportedly even joined the public bashing of the film. Referencing the cannibalism in *Orapronobis*, Mrs. Aquino was said to have quipped in a speech that the Philippines was "not a nation of brain-eaters."[72]

Despite the problems it caused in 1989, the gruesome violence of *Orapronobis* truly set it apart as a daring and unorthodox work of political filmmaking. Although screenwriter Lacaba felt pressure to downplay the film's graphic content at the height of the smear campaign, the integral cut of *Orapronobis* was true to his and Brocka's vision of using violence *in extremis* as a fiercely political cinematic statement. The boldness of this vision was already present in an early outline of the narrative, which was included by mistake in the film's press kit. The document laid out a climax of unbearable harshness, which reads: "In an abandoned house, an orgy of hideous cruelty occurs when Kontra rapes Esper and kills her son, eating his brains in front of her eyes."[73] Regrettably, the turn to "corporealism" that animated Brocka's political melodrama has found new relevance more than a quarter century later as a vital strategy of human rights advocacy and antiauthoritarian critique. Widespread vigilante killings returned with a vengeance in 2016 with the election of Rodrigo Duterte to the presidency. In keeping with his campaign promise to launch a ruthless "war against drugs," Duterte encouraged the authorities to kill thousands of alleged drug users and traffickers. The chief executive's incitement to murder came with half-joking guarantees of impunity for the armed forces and even civilians heeding his call to action. Not surprisingly, the Philippines's new strongman had also been a part of the checkered history of counterrevolutionary vigilantism and political violence in the late 1980s. The young Duterte, a former appointee of President Aquino and the newly elected mayor of Davao, figured in a piece of investigative journalism that Lacaba cited as one of the inspirations for *Orapronobis*. The article quotes Duterte as claiming that the widely reported human rights violations by vigilantes were just "isolated incidents." Pointing to famously unreliable public records as proof, he challenged the reporter "to check the police station blotters to see if reports of criminal acts by vigilantes are true."[74]

In the Duterte era, outraged citizens have railed against state-sanctioned killings by circulating high-definition pictures of victims' corpses on social media. As in Brocka's film, the mangled remains of the purported drug users and sellers function as shocking testaments to the malevolence of the new strongman regime. Although even the ghastliest pictures are incommensurable to the traumatic reality they index, the stomach-turning obscenity makes for powerful weapons of antiauthoritarian politics. When viewed anew amid the spectacular carnage of Duterte's rule, *Orapronobis* registers as a vivid and chilling history of the present written almost three decades previously. In the 1989 film's uncannily prophetic account of the late 2010s, the unhinged Kontra is both Duterte's precursor and equally fearsome stand-in.

A Trenchant "Communist" Melodrama

If some foreign and domestic critics had misgivings about the sensationalism and violence in *Orapronobis*, others—as I have mentioned—took issue instead with the melodramatic character of Brocka's political film. These reservations about the film's form are not surprising, however, since critics routinely denigrated melodramas and thrillers. Coco Fusco's described the film in *The Village Voice* as an unsuccessful outing that "combines soap opera romance with social consciousness."[75] Vincent Canby gave a backhanded compliment that similarly took aim at melodrama, citing the film's more restrained aspects and moments as its redeeming qualities. "The story," he argued, "is simply and effectively told without undue melodrama." Luis Francia, a Filipino American critic, echoed Canby's sentiments. He stated: "Though very much a melodrama, *Fight for Us* keeps theatricality to a minimum."

Critics who disparaged the film's use of melodrama while admiring its progressive politics misapprehended the former's importance to the latter. Alongside its bombastic treatise on human rights, *Orapronobis* is also deeply melodramatic in its nostalgia-laced celebration of the idealistic middle-class intellectuals who spent their youth fighting the Marcos regime and campaigning for social justice. The fictional Jimmy Cordero belonged to a generation of radicalized youth who read Marx and Mao and left the comfort of their urban middle-class homes to live and fight among the peasants. The battle of their lives was not the hasty uprising that toppled Marcos but rather the protracted "national-democratic revolution" that was reignited in the early 1970s and remained unfinished at the close of the following decade.[76]

A fuller picture of Jimmy's former life as a revolutionary reemerges at the start of *Orapronobis*, prompting him (and the film's viewers) to reassess the validity of socialism as a political project. Initially, he opts to bury the past as he hastens to begin a new family after his release from prison. His approach espouses the rhetoric of a new beginning that came with President Aquino's amnesty program for political prisoners and leftist revolutionaries. As the narrative progresses, the returning past collides with Jimmy's forward push into the future. This collision generates one of the film's emotional highlights. Revisiting Santa Filomena after many years, Jimmy sits outside his former lover's hut and reminisces with her about their experiences as underground fighters. The nostalgic journey is interrupted by the revelation of young Camilo's true paternity. Believing up to this point that fatherhood was the beginning of his new life in mainstream society, Jimmy realizes that it had also been a buried facet of his past. Although Esper begs Jimmy to withhold the information from Camilo just yet, the news of Jimmy's newly discovered paternity visibly thrills him. Similarly, the traces of his former life in the underground—the decaying former homes, the well-remembered songs of protest, the fading but primal connections with ex-comrades—fill him with joy once again. The melodrama of Jimmy's paternity thus becomes an objective-correlative for his abandoned youthful dream of socialist revolution.

One of the most heartfelt but understated episodes of Jimmy's paternal melodrama stages yet another collision of past and future. Sometime after Esper and her children seek refuge in Manila, Jimmy and a pregnant Trixie take them out shopping. The episode is rendered in montage, heightening the already strong emotions within the scene by replacing dialogue with the melodramatic spell of mute gesture and swelling music. Underneath the dramatically suspended escalators of Vira Mall—an upscale shopping center—Jimmy and Trixie ply Esper and her children with clothing and gifts. The montage sequence is quite moving. To make up for lost time, Jimmy buys Camilo a toy: a plastic sword, the same one the child would brandish before Kontra guns him down near the film's end. Trixie matches his generosity and tries to get over her jealousy toward Esper by buying her a dress. Jimmy looks on with pride at his wife's charity. The crisscrossing pattern of the escalators at the mall evokes the Janus-faced vision of Jimmy's past and future lives with his two families. This bittersweet episode passes all too quickly, however, as if to show the untenable coexistence of his two domestic lives and the political ideologies he had alternately embraced. Shortly after the idyll of the family outing, Jimmy and Trixie return Esper and children to the refugee center where the violence of the present catches up with them. Esper and Camilo are abducted and killed in the span of just a few scenes.

The matter of Jimmy's conflicting paternal obligations—and the related pattern of clashing elements within the film's narrative and mise-en-scène—is resolved in the final sequence. The film's fast-paced editing dramatically slows down in the scene when Jimmy recovers Esper and Camilo's bodies. Following the conventions of male melodramas, the film reaches an emotional flashpoint when Jimmy tries—and largely fails—to fulfill his paternal duties.[77] Filled with remorse for not saving his child and missing the chance to disclose his paternity, Jimmy breaks down while cradling the child's body. Jimmy later realizes that he can still help create a better world for his new wife and their child, but to do so he must leave them and everything else behind, as he had already done in the past to Esper and Camilo. In another instance of melodramatic contrasts, Jimmy goes from living with two families to virtually losing both.

In the meantime, Jimmy's reversion to the underground grated at the centrists among the film's viewers, including those in academia. Randy David, a sociologist, admired the film but remarked that he "would have liked it more if [Jimmy] Phillip Salvador's decision to take up arms once more were left open rather than considered as a sure and inevitable course of action."[78] David's response is understandable because the film's ending is bracingly abrupt and provocative. Jimmy's rapprochement with socialism militated against the rightward drift in President Aquino's politics. She had famously abandoned the leftist members of the diverse coalition that brought her to power after realizing that her political survival depended on embracing rightist military allies as well as the neoliberal economic policies of her country's transnational financiers and investors.

The film's attempt to portray socialism as the answer to Jimmy's quest was especially brave because the communists, who served as the main exponents of socialism in the country, were especially unpopular at the time of the film's release. They had lost their footing in opposition circles by sitting out the "people power" uprising.[79] Their public image also took an enormous hit due to their much-publicized spate of political killings in urban areas as well as for murdering hundreds of their members in an internal purge.[80] *Orapronobis* illustrates the former in one scene. The episode shows how the party's urban guerilla force (also called a "sparrow unit") guns down a cop in broad daylight, with a brazenness reminiscent of the rightist vigilantes, one of their mortal enemies.[81] The assassin is Jimmy's friend, ex-comrade, and former prison cellmate Rene (Pen Medina), whom the film unflatteringly portrays as a hardened ideologue.

In *Orapronobis*, the characters use the term *kilusan* (movement) to refer to what in real life would have been the Communist Party of the Philippines (CPP), the organization to which Lacaba once belonged and also the political entity that Brocka thought "should be legalized" in the Philippines if the country were to be a true democracy.[82] The tarnished reputation of the Maoist CPP may well have been one of the reasons for the slight "ambiguity" behind the film's references to the "movement." At the same time, the "movement" is also a placeholder for the dream of society's radical transformation, far beyond the reforms that the 1986 revolution yielded. An aspect of the Philippine experience dating back to the Spanish colonial times, taking to the hills or joining the "movement"—or, in the 1970s, the "revolution" and the "underground"—has never been coterminous with just one ideological position.[83] In having Jimmy return to the movement, Lacaba affirms that for all their missteps, the work that he and his generation of revolutionaries did in their youth was ultimately not for naught. Rather than simply depicting the protagonist's rapprochement with the CPP, *Orapronobis* closes with the notion that socialism continues to offer inspiration to those who wish to realize the unfulfilled promise of the "people power" revolution or the profound social transformation that should have followed the triumphant struggle against authoritarian rule.

A DIRTY AFFAIR

Before making *Orapronobis*, Brocka told the American journalist Todd McCarthy of his plans "to make a B movie called 'Cryselda R.,'" a political satire based on the life of Imelda Marcos. Sounding delighted, he described the project further: "It's going to be more than sleazy. It's going to be tacky. It will have George Hamilton and his mother arriving dressed just like they were coming out of a Universal movie. It will have Van Cliburn playing the piano on the lawn."[84] Sadly, "Cryselda R." was not meant to be, but Brocka realized his desire to poke fun at his old enemy and recall the sordid history of her reign in the next iteration of his political melodramas.

Brocka delivered a string of box office hits in the late 1980s, and this encouraged Viva Films to give him considerable leeway in developing a new and substantial project.[85] The completed work, *A Dirty Affair* (*Gumapang ka sa lusak*), utilized the elements of Brocka's previous commercial successes. These include employing the adult melodrama subgenre, weaving a convoluted plot reminiscent of *komiks* or serialized graphic novels, casting stars in lead roles, and maintaining high production values. Brocka used these elements to deliver a narrative about Philippine political culture during and beyond the Marcos regime.

Without detracting from its achievements, I should mention at the outset that the film's treatment of politics is not without compromise. The hellish backlash that Brocka endured after criticizing President Aquino's policies in *Orapronobis* appeared to have set a limit-point for the political discourse of *Dirty Affair*. Unlike *Orapronobis*, *Dirty Affair* makes no explicit references to Mrs. Aquino's government. Instead, the narrative anachronistically re-creates episodes from the Marcos era in a largely fictive present-day setting. This mixing of temporal perspectives works on multiple levels. It creates an engrossing narrative and history lesson by alternately invoking and dissimulating the familiar story of the Marcos regime. It also formulates a novel approach to political critique in Brocka's cinema: namely, the coupling of a critical recollection of the failures of authoritarianism with a reflection on the enduring problems of Philippine democracy.

The film begins with a prologue that exemplifies the anachronism and temporal shifts that occur throughout the narrative. In the Japanese-occupied Philippines during World War II, a gang of soldiers from the Imperial Army corners a distressed young Filipina (Maureen Mauricio). They rip the back off her dress and are about to pounce on her when a disembodied voice suddenly yells "cut!" and a man who turns out to be the young woman's boyfriend chastises her for agreeing to film yet another tacky nude scene. As it turns out, the prologue is a self-reflexive depiction of using historical trauma to make an exploitation film. This pre-title sequence sets up a critical attitude toward historical narratives and how the media constructs them. It also plants the seeds for what will turn out to be an unflattering statement about the country's political culture.

The scenes following the title sequence identify the film's principal characters. Jonathan (Allan Paule), a pal of the angry boyfriend in the prologue, encounters an older movie sexpot named Rachel Suarez (Dina Bonnevie) at a disco. He makes small talk with her, but she eventually walks away from him. Jonathan later finds out that Rachel is the mistress of Eduardo Guatlo (Eddie Garcia), a corrupt mayor in one of Metro Manila's cities. Guatlo's physical appearance, mannerisms, and life story are uncannily reminiscent of Ferdinand Marcos. Also not coincidentally, his relationship to Rachel brings to mind the scandalous affair between Marcos and American starlet Dovie Beams. Beams starred in *Maharlika* (1970) a film based loosely on Marcos's false claims of leading a guerilla outfit during World War II. Marcos's supporters raised money for the film to help with his reelection campaign. After learning of his sexual interest in the actress, they also set up a love nest for the couple in the posh Greenhills neighborhood. Beams was already thirty-six at the start of the affair but claimed to be twenty-four.[86] Like Beams, Rachel made her career in sleazy movies and was already past a starlet's prime when she took up with a politico.

As was the case with Marcos, Guatlo's oppressive treatment of women such as Rachel reflects his authoritarian character. He keeps her on a tight leash, having her tailed almost incessantly by his henchman, the allegorically named Falcon (Bembol Roco). Guatlo disallows her from making new movies, worried that her fame will fuel gossip about their affair. Rachel asserts her independence, however, by frequenting night spots and flirting with other men. In the course of several encounters, she develops a relationship—albeit a platonic one—with Jonathan, a man whose naivete she finds charming.

Election season rolls along and, in a subplot borrowed from Brocka's Marcos-era film *Miguelito*, Guatlo sets his sights on the higher office of congressional representative. His wife Rowena (Charo Santos)—who looks and acts unmistakably like Imelda Marcos—reminds him that he must get rid of his mistress at once. When he hesitates, Rowena confronts Rachel, offering her a settlement to stay away from Guatlo and threatening to have her raped and doused with acid if she made trouble. The latter references the threat that Imelda Marcos allegedly made to Beams at the time of the dalliance.[87]

Guatlo meets with Rachel separately and offers to continue her allowance and fulfill an earlier promise to pull strings for the release of her ex-boyfriend Levi (Christopher De Leon). Unknown to her, Guatlo has an ulterior motive for freeing the inmate. He intends to use Levi as a triggerman for the assassination of his political rival, a lawyer and gentleman farmer named Ricardo Tuazon (Ray Ventura). This subplot's correspondence to recent history may have been obvious to viewers at that time: Tuazon functions as the stand-in for Aquino while Levi is the fictive counterpart of Rolando Galman, the "lone assassin" who supposedly killed Aquino before being gunned down by aviation security.

Unaware of Guatlo's intentions, Rachel asks for Levi's release and is also first to visit him. When she finally learns of the plan to use Levi as a hit man for his opponent, Rachel tries to dissuade the politician and, failing that, attempts to derail his plans.

The scheme to assassinate Tuazon exemplifies the film's use of historical references to comment on both past and present political realities. Guatlo personally

FIGURE 6.4. Mayor Guatlo (Eddie Garcia, left) and wife Rowena (Charo Santos) mimic the appearance and mannerisms of Ferdinand and Imelda Marcos in *A Dirty Affair*. Courtesy of MOWELFUND.

briefs Levi on his mission but the overbearing Rowena listens in and constantly interrupts them. The scene is essentially a retelling of the plot to kill Aquino. It suggests the Marcos couple's direct involvement in the assassination, something they denied but which the public nevertheless believed was true. In the days preceding the murder, Rowena and Guatlo separately accuse Tuazon of being a communist and, because of his lack of political experience, of being ignorant as well. The malicious and elitist accusations are not throwaway details but rather political jabs directed at both the Marcos and Aquino regimes. In the 1970s Marcos accused Ninoy Aquino of conspiring with communists to subvert his presidency. Marcos later tried to pin Ninoy's assassination on the left, particularly Communist Party of the Philippines Chairman Rodolfo Salas. During the snap elections he called in the mid-1980s to legitimize his presidency, Marcos tried to discredit Cory Aquino by accusing her of having communist backers. Sadly, when Mrs. Aquino became president, her regime embraced the autocrat's tactic of branding dissident labor organizers, activist farmworkers, and political opponents as communists. As Walden Bello and John Gershman note, the country's civilian and military elite defined "all those advocating programs that seek substantial social and economic reform of the current social order as being outside the democratic pale, as being 'communists.'"[88]

The "anti-elite candidates with radical political programs" were thus "driven from the electoral arena by the threat of force," becoming "fair game for death squads and right-wing vigilantes." Tuazon suffers a similar fate. The film emphasizes the injustice of red-baiting in a scene where Guatlo privately acknowledges that the character of the man he defamed and whose murder he ordered "was spotless."

The parallelism to Aquino's killing and the reference to contemporary politics continues in the sequence dramatizing Guatlo's use of state-sponsored violence to silence Levi after his mission. The mayor orders his heavies to hunt him down. Rachel and Jonathan come to Levi's aid, but the latter ends up saving them instead by drawing the goons to himself. The film stages the summary execution of Levi as a Marcosian moment, with the thugs encircling him and firing at close range. Rachel screams in silence as she watches the incident from a dark corner. Looking almost directly at the camera, she implicates the film's spectator as a witness to her terrifying ordeal. When she and Jonathan later flee the murder scene, the film makes another intertextual reference to Brocka's earlier crime melodramas, specifically *Jaguar* (1979) and *Angela, the Marked One* (*Angela markado*, 1980). The ensuing nighttime chase, which leads Rachel, Jonathan and Guatlo's heavies through the slums and into a junkyard littered with gigantic concrete piping, invokes the climactic moments of the director's earlier films. As in the case of *Orapronobis*, the director's recycling of some of the set pieces of his Marcos-era work is itself a cinematic statement. This intertextuality suggests, among other things, that the scenarios of political violence remained virtually unchanged since the reign of authoritarianism. Guatlo's politically motivated killing spree then continues as his goons pursue Rachel and Jonathan. In a series of additional Marcosian summary executions, Falcon and his fellow goons brutally dispatch Rachel's parents and Jonathan's friend RJ (Francis Magalona).

As the Guatlos' henchmen continue the hunt for Rachel and Jonathan, the mayor and his wife begin to suffer the fallout from Tuazon's assassination and other murders. At one of Rowena's public appearances, a middle-aged woman attacks her with a machete-like bolo knife. Bodyguards promptly subdue and kill the assailant, who turns out to be Levi's mother. The scene pokes fun at the attempted assassination of Imelda Marcos by an engineer named Carlito Dimaali. The attack occurred during a televised awards ceremony in December 1972, less than three months after the imposition of martial law.[89] Imelda's wounds required seventy-five stitches but, as biographer Katherine Ellison recalls, just the next day "she was preening for television cameras in a silky, frilly gown unlike any her attending doctors have ever seen."[90] Like Imelda in 1972, Rowena capitalizes on the incident to generate public sympathy. The mayor's wife hams it up in an interview with the press, tearfully recounting her pleas to God following her attack. Guatlo interrupts Rowena and declares, "Everything is getting out of hand. Chaos and anarchy have set in!" The mayor's alarmist discourse makes fun of Marcos's rhetoric for justifying the imposition of martial law. Marcos falsely claimed that a conspiracy of radical leftists and nefarious oligarchs was using violent "dissident agitation and activity"[91] to set the stage for a "bloody social revolution."[92] No such conspiracy existed and, as many had suspected, the president's allies staged many of the violent disturbances they attributed to the opposition.

The film's unlikely combination of history lesson, soap opera, and contemporary political satire continues in the grand finale. Rachel crashes Guatlo's biggest political sortie, telling the audience of their adulterous liaison and the politically motivated killings he masterminded. With the help of Jonathan and his friends—who have taken over the audio control booth and hogtied the technicians there—Rachel plays a taped conversation between her and the mayor. The recording incriminates Guatlo for the abduction and killing of her parents.

Rachel's political bombshell is a historical reference to Beams's secret tape recordings of her sexual encounters with Marcos. Student activists aired the tapes on campus radio to humiliate the dictator. The American starlet played additional excerpts to a crowd of journalists before finally departing the Philippines.[93] Marcos reportedly tried to have Beams killed during her stopover in Hong Kong, even putting the would-be assassin on the same plane as the starlet.[94] When the murder plot failed, the president allegedly leaked nude photos he took of Beams to the press. She fired back by releasing more tapes of the raunchy pillow talk.[95]

The film alters the outcome of the Beams affair as well as the means by which the tyrannical Guatlo is ousted from politics. The deviation from history is alternately more tragic and hopeful than real events. Rachel's incriminating tape agitates the crowd at the campaign event. Falcon retaliates by shooting at Rachel. Jonathan cradles his mortally wounded idol, who thanks him for assisting her in their mission. Before she breathes her last, and through her tears, Rachel flashes what film scholar Joel David aptly describes as "the most blissful smile ever seen in local cinema."[96] The heroine's beautiful death,[97] a classic trope of sentimental literature and melodrama, is made more poignant by the triumph of justice. The tape continues to play after Rachel expires, giving details of her relationship with Guatlo. "He was spending the people's money to keep me," she relates, before rattling off the mayor's other crimes. The tape concludes with a plea, addressed to the people, "to end his [Guatlo's] evil doings" once and for all.[98] The tape, and indeed the entire incident, play over live radio and TV broadcasts. The Guatlos—realizing that their careers are finished—dejectedly leave the stage.

The Politics of Time and Intertextuality

Temporal shifts and intertextuality play crucial roles in the cinema politics of *Dirty Affair*. As mentioned earlier, the film engages in an anachronistic retelling of the history of Marcosian rule. Although set in the present, the narrative comprises historical episodes from the Marcos dictatorship, some of them already

FIGURE 6.5. Rachel (Dina Bonnevie) drops a bombshell during Mayor Guatlo's campaign sortie in *A Dirty Affair*. Courtesy of MOWELFUND.

over a decade old when the film reached theaters. By unhinging recognizable events and figures from their proper historical moment, the film creates an altered picture not only of the past but the present as well. This anachronism engages the viewers' historical memory and tests their knowledge of contemporary issues. More specifically, the aberrant temporality allows for a postmortem on the authoritarian state and, more subtly, a critique of stumbling democratization in the present.

Dirty Affair's postmortem on the dictatorship recounts the features of Marcosian authoritarianism in sensational and often humorous episodes. Apart from what I have cited earlier, the film depicts the authoritarian leader's cabal (through his wife and cronies), his exercise of state violence (through Falcon's surveillance and salvaging operations), and his regime's pay-offs to the masses (Rowena's reference to BLISS, Imelda's low-income housing program). The film also invokes Marcos's overpriced infrastructure projects (the Light Rail Transit or LRT trains that appear in the background of some of Levi's scenes) and his blatant rigging of elections. The function of the film's postmortem of the Marcos regime is educational and cathartic. Satire both thrives on and inspires a sense of mastery. To denounce and laugh off the follies of authoritarian rule, the viewer must first become wise to them. The film's easily recognizable historical references facilitate insightful remembrance and scathing criticism.

The pleasurable recollection and catharsis that the serio-comic reenactment of history prompted may have been helpful in not only in providing civic education but also in renewing public support for democratic reform. One of the film's reviewers notes that audiences burst into applause during screenings. He said: "It was not possible to make films like this during the previous regime." ("Talaga namang hindi puwedeng gawin ang ganitong pelikula noong nakaraang rehimen.") The French philosopher Alain Badiou has written about the progressive potential of humorous movies with a political slant. "Farce and comedy," he says are "potent political, social, and esthetic weapon[s]."[99] The cathartic laughter generated by *Dirty Affair* points to a collective desire to banish the traumatic vestiges of authoritarianism and prevent its recurrence.

There is a second, decidedly more obscure level of intertextuality and temporal shift in *Dirty Affair* that is particularly legible to audiences familiar with Brocka's 1979 film *Jaguar*. *Dirty Affair* revisits the main protagonists, basic narrative features, and some highlights of that film. The critic Mario Bautista correctly pointed out that *Dirty Affair* is "basically a continuation of '*Jaguar*' and shows what happens to these two characters eleven years later." His use of the word "basically" is an apt qualification because *Dirty Affair* renames *Jaguar*'s protagonists and makes other substantial changes.

Those familiar with the 1979 film might recognize Levi as a renamed version of its hero Poldo. The latter is a security guard who accidentally kills his boss's romantic rival. The boss abandons him, and he languishes in prison. Poldo's only champion is a former go-go dancer and rising movie starlet named Cristy, who was also a former girlfriend of his boss. Cristy is the counterpart of *Dirty Affair*'s Rachel. At the end of *Jaguar*, Cristy distances herself from Poldo, fearing his notoriety would hurt her career. In *Dirty Affair*'s updating of the *Jaguar* narrative, the hero's incarceration only lasts seven years, and the heroine never abandons him. Although the passing of time demonstrates the lovers' fidelity, it hardly engenders progress in their personal lives and the larger sociopolitical realm. Indeed, Rachel/Cristy and Levi/Poldo find themselves stuck in a temporal limbo in the same way that Philippine society and politics remained mired in some of the problems that existed under authoritarian rule.

Before Guatlo's intervention, Levi/Poldo languished in prison, obsessed with the fear that his jailing will "drain away my humanity." He was in such deep despair that he was "willing to do anything" in exchange for freedom. He seemed to be aware that the temporary freedom Guatlo was offering would cost him his life. As for Rachel/Cristy, her economic situation may have improved over the years, but the decline in her reputation and professional career had canceled out her gains. Already washed up in her thirties and tainted by her affair with Guatlo, the only

FIGURE 6.6. In *A Dirty Affair*, Rachel (Dina Bonnevie, right) and Levi (Christopher De Leon) appear as reimagined versions of Cristy and Poldo from Brocka's 1979 film *Jaguar*. Courtesy of MOWELFUND.

roles offered to her are in "semi-bold dramas," the tamer but still disreputable versions of the sexploitation films that once catapulted her from the slums to the silver screen. She cannot even take those parts, however, due to the mayor's insistence that she "perform" only in his bedroom.

As in the past, Levi/Poldo and Rachel/Cristy continue to be pawns of the rich, although now it is the political and not just the economic elite that controls them. Their plight is symptomatic of the fundamental stagnation lying beneath the surface of the ostensibly radical political transformations of 1986. The uprising that toppled the Marcos regime may have restored the trappings of democracy, but it was failing to serve the precariat to which Levi and Rachel belonged. Walden Bello characterized the aftermath of the "people power" revolution as a "narrow process of democratization" in which free elections were restored "but social and economic structures remain[ed] as frozen as ever." He argued that what the Philippines actually regained in 1986 was an elite democracy that "generates the illusion of democracy at the formal political level to defuse the reality of social and economic inequality." The Filipino masses' obsession with free elections (and their use of it as a fetish for a participatory, mass-based democracy) was evident in the staggering 90 percent turnout during the congressional and senatorial elections of

1987.[100] Ironically, roughly the same percentage of newly elected congressional representatives were members of the landed elites, who proceeded to legislate according to their ruling-class interests.[101]

Bello's notion of an elite democracy is useful in reading *Dirty Affair*'s transposition of Poldo/Levi and Rachel/Cristy's standstill lives into a post-authoritarian Philippines gripped by election fever. If the protagonists' fates suggest the consequences of an elite democracy for the lower classes, then the film makes a statement about Philippine political culture that is at turns deeply cynical and hopeful. *Jaguar*'s Poldo killed a man because of his misplaced loyalty to his boss, the womanizing and trouble-making son of a millionaire. *Dirty Affair*'s Levi rehearses Poldo's fate: he kills Tuazon for Guatlo's benefit. His loyalty to the corrupt politico costs him his life. Rachel fares a little better than Levi, redeeming herself in a heroic act before her demise. But compared to her alter ego in *Jaguar*, Rachel is obviously far worse off at the conclusion of *Dirty Affair*. Whereas Cristy managed to buck the patriarchy and the class system by doggedly pursuing stardom, her contemporary incarnation perishes in a quicksand of political corruption and violence.

The demise of *Jaguar*'s two protagonists, both of whom implicitly survived the tumult of the Marcos dictatorship, paints an unfavorable picture of the present under Mrs. Aquino's leadership. Similar to the deplorable state of affairs in *Orapronobis*, the elite democracy of *Dirty Affair* testifies to the failures of democratization after 1986. But, as I intimated earlier, a flicker of hope separates *Dirty Affair* from *Orapronobis*. *Jaguar*'s Poldo splits off into the two male protagonists of *Dirty Affair*: namely, Levi, the broken-down prison inmate, and Jonathan, the doe-eyed lad from the slums who clings to the dream of social mobility and a better world. Jonathan is the counterpart to Poldo's innocent and optimistic self at the beginning of *Jaguar* while Levi represents the cynical Poldo.

Something of a relay between Poldo and Jonathan occurs during *Dirty Affair*'s reprise of a memorable scene from *Jaguar*. In the epilogue to *Dirty Affair*, we see Jonathan reminiscing at the breakwater of Manila Bay, where he and Rachel talked a couple of times. A sound flashback replays the advice Rachel gave him early in their friendship: "Your life is just beginning. Start it right. Start it clean." The scene recalls a similar conversation in *Jaguar*. Set in the same location, the scene shows Cristy speaking ruefully about her sordid path to a career in cheap movies. She offers her story to encourage Poldo to be more critical of her ex-lover, the boss whom he idolizes. Poldo unwisely ignores the advice Cristy gives him in *Jaguar*, but his counterpart Jonathan gets it right in *Dirty Affair*. Heeding Rachel's counsel, he comes out unscathed in the end. The sound flashback of Rachel admonishing the young man to "start right" and "start clean" doubles as a plea to the film's viewers to reaffirm their promise to better society—to fulfill the promise of democratization—against all odds.

For a majority of the Filipino entertainment journalists and critics, *Dirty Affair* represented a breakthrough in Brocka's political filmmaking. Many of them pointed to the mass patronage of the film as a rare achievement. The film reportedly grossed 2 million pesos—the entire budget of an exploitation film at that time—on just its first day.[102] "We had a difficult time entering and leaving the theater because of the thick crowds," remarked film reviewer Mario Bautista. Entertainment reporter Bibsy Carballo noted that "after two weeks" the film was "still bringing in the crowds."[103] Nestor Torre declared that the film's "popularity refutes the hoary notion that local moviegoers will reject any production that asks them to think."[104]

Apart from marveling at the film's strong following, the critics noted the viewers' hearty response. Bautista reported that during the film's climax, "the audience in the theater where we saw it applauded several times." Torre's *Inquirer* review cited the same episode for having "a stunning and pure effect on the viewer." Along similar lines, Joel David lauded the film's "careful working out of viewership psychology, particularly when placed in the context of its director's body of work." David found that Brocka was able to establish a rare compact with his wide audience, one in which the film's political statements were transmitted between them but remained opaque to the subjects of the film's critique. He said: "It is an indication of the gap between our officials and the masses they aim to represent when no one among the former thus far has raised a peep about the wholesale (and well-deserved) defamation being visited upon them by our moviemakers . . . and something must also urgently be said about the way the mass audience laps it all up."[105] *Dirty Affair's* success demonstrated the potential of film melodrama—a plebian art form—for invigorating democracy.

The warm response of some critics suggested that the success of *Dirty Affair* may have raised melodrama's standing as a vehicle for political discourse. Luis H. Francia, who once criticized the melodramatic underpinnings of Brocka's *Weighed but Found Wanting* (1974), found the "noirish melodrama" of *Dirty Affair* useful in staging a "chilling allegory of the terror that gushed through the open sewer of the Marcos regime."[106] David found the melodramatic base perfectly suitable to a movie about Philippine political culture. He opined that the director "advanced a proposition audacious even for himself: Philippine politics, per Brocka's latest, is more than just a matter of intrigues and chases and shoot-outs; it is actually one big noisy and unending melodrama." David's take on the correspondence between form and content was right on the mark. Indeed, from the "film-within-a-film" opening to the series of histrionic episodes that depict Rachel's political misadventures, *Dirty Affair* self-consciously exposes that country's politics as a cynical spectacle of violence and histrionic playacting—a shrill and pointless melodrama—that is inimical to the people's interests.

As in the case of *Orapronobis*, the success of *Dirty Affair* did not impress some critics, who declared the film's melodramatic form—or rather their idea of what the term meant—to be incompatible with political critique. For example, Torre, an influential critic, noted in his largely sanguine piece that *Dirty Affair's* "melodramatic devices deflect the production's more purposive intentions."[107] Melodrama, in other words, was the very aspect that prevented *Dirty Affair* from realizing its full potential as a political film. Isah Red expressed a similar idea in his scathing assessment, tellingly headlined as "Sudsy Politics." Red complained that the director merely uses "politics as the jumping board for an obvious [sic] soap operatic movie."[108]

ABOVE EVERYTHING ELSE

The box office triumph and warm critical reception of *A Dirty Affair* earned Brocka the opportunity to make another political melodrama for the same movie studio. *Above Everything Else* (*Sa kabila ng lahat*, 1991) retained characters, plot devices and other elements from the previous film. The familiar characters include a Marcosian couple, a mistress who works in the entertainment industry (another faint echo of Dovie Beams), and a small crew of political henchmen. As in *Dirty Affair*, *Above Everything's* narrative is set during election season. These similarities notwithstanding, the film is not a remake of *Dirty Affair*, and its political critique is markedly different. Apart from the Marcosian couple and the mistress, the characters of *Above Everything* seldom reference specific historical figures. Similarly, instead of *Dirty Affair's* liberal restaging of events from the Marcos era, the narrative of *Above Everything* centers on fictional situations.

In a novel turn for Brocka's political melodramas, *Above Everything* largely dispenses with a critique of authoritarianism. Instead, the film's assessment of both Philippine political culture and political economy treats other, less conspicuous issues that might account for the country's weak recovery from autocratic rule. More specifically, *Above Everything* generates an expansive vision of the Philippines as a predatory state. Political scientist John T. Sidel characterizes the latter as a government that exploits "the archipelago's human, natural and monetary resources" to enrich the "main predators . . . elected government officials and their allies."[109] Within predatory states, politicians behave as gangsters and criminal bosses rather than as public servants. This feature of Philippine politics as a ruthless enterprise of dispossessing people and plundering the nation for personal gain preceded, accompanied, and outlived the Marcos dictatorship. Sidel writes: "The Philippine state, even under the authoritarian Marcos regime, remained essentially a multitiered racket. Though never wholly nor solely a racket, the Philippine state's racket-like dimensions decisively shaped electoral competition, capital accumulation, and social relations in the archipelago over the course of the twentieth century."[110] Unfortunately, this feature of Philippine political culture persisted during the Aquino regime. In spite of her benevolence and sincerity, Aquino

FIGURE 6.7. Mayor Velasco (Ronaldo Valdez, center) and his wife Cresencia (Celeste Legaspi, left) console the bereaved family of a victim of their misdeeds. *Above Everything Else*. Courtesy of Juan Martin Magsanoc and Archivo 1984 Gallery.

unwittingly engaged in political bossism due to what Walden Bello and John Gershman describe as the "tolerance of corruption in her family and the upper rungs of government."[111]

As in the case of *A Dirty Affair*, one of the pivotal characters of *Above Everything* is the mayor of a city in Metro Manila. Ventura Velasco (Ronaldo Valdez) is a former movie actor who owes his political career to the affluent family of his wife, Cresencia (Celeste Legaspi). His in-laws have bankrolled his career in exchange for political influence and kickbacks from government contracts. Actor-politicians became a fixture of Philippine politics after the Marcos regime, helped considerably by their participation in Marcos's reelection campaign and "people power."

Above Everything details Velasco's methods of accumulating wealth by leveraging the power of his elected office.[112] As with the gangster-politicians described by Sidel, Velasco takes bribes and illegally parcels city contracts and franchises. He also sanctions all manner of illegal activities, such as gun running, foreign currency trading, and drug trafficking. The mayor works closely with two rival gangster figures. One is a government employee who simultaneously acts as his enforcer. Boy Boga (Mark Gil) runs a "death squad" to support the mayor's illegal activities and pursue schemes of his own. The other gangster, named Daniel Fu (William Lorenzo), is a Chinese Filipino who runs drug trafficking and protection rackets. Fu is both a racialized stereotype and an allegorical figure of transnational capital. As Sidel notes, "many of the entrenched politicians and magnates in the country derive[d] their power and wealth ... from state resources and foreign (mostly overseas Chinese) commercial capital."[113]

The film's depiction of the pervasive threat that greed and corruption posed to a struggling democracy was especially relevant to the post-1986 situation. While public discourse on crony capitalism ebbed with the ouster of Marcos, opportunists in the underworld, politics, and the business sector were as ruthless as ever in fleecing the nation. Additionally, Brocka's habit of using local politics as a microcosm of national politics took on greater significance during the Aquino presidency. Early in her term, President Aquino rechanneled development efforts to the countryside, creating jobs and stimulating local economies in the hope of weakening the communist movement.[114] These programs, as well as development projects from the private sector, greatly benefitted local leaders, including gangster-politicians. In a bid to undo Marcos's concentration of power in the central government and to foster a more inclusive democracy, Aquino pushed to toughen the hand of local governments even further. Her pursuit of decentralization culminated in the Local Government Code of 1991, which devolved certain functions of the national government to local government units. It became law less than half a year after *Above Everything* screened in theaters. Regrettably, even as the law promoted greater participation in governance, it also expanded the influence of gangster-politicians and increased the spoils available to them.[115]

Democracy, Documentary, and the Fourth Estate

Alongside its depiction of gangster-politicians, *Above Everything* self-reflexively thematizes the media's role in enabling and resisting the enemies of democratization. The film's protagonist Maia Robles (also played by Dina Bonnevie) is Mayor Velasco's mistress and a broadcast journalist. Thoroughly corrupt, Maia uses her shows to improve her lover's public image and to disparage his enemies. She grants sexual favors with the expectation of landing government contracts, often sealing deals while engaging in pillow talk with the mayor.

Mike (Tonton Gutierrez), an idealistic junior producer and colleague of Maia's, embodies the media's conscience. They collaborate in producing documentary segments for public affairs programs. Their pieces on corruption, social problems, and political issues are hard-hitting, much like the print and broadcast journalism during the Aquino era. Maia underhandedly waters down or blocks Mike's legitimate exposés, however, reserving for herself the privilege of dropping political bombshells on her lover's enemies. Her unmatched bluntness cultivates the illusion of probity, which she then uses to cover up her unethical and illegal doings. Her career ends abruptly after the mayor suffers a heart attack during one of their trysts. (The incident is inspired by a rumor about the bout of lovemaking between a movie actress and a Manila mayor that killed the latter in the early 1960s.) The network dismisses her to distance itself from the scandal. Even worse, the mayor's wife orders their henchmen to kill her. Maia decides to use the mass media one last time, to tell a lie that might save her life while also taking down some of the city's most notorious criminals. She convinces Mike to broadcast fake news stories aimed at turning the mayor's criminal associates and henchmen against each other. The plan works, but the feuding criminals kill Mike for exposing them.

Echoing Marcos's death in Hawaii in 1989, Velasco perishes while seeking medical treatment in the United States. Moreover, the authorities arrest the mayor's wife on corruption charges, calling to mind the trial of Imelda Marcos, which had recently occurred in the United States. The film ends with Maia accepting a posthumous award on behalf of Mike. While praising fearless journalists like him, she also chastises those (such as herself, although she does not say so) who fail their noble profession.

Reusing a device from Brocka's landmark political film *My Own Country: Gripping the Knife's Edge (Bayan ko: Kapit sa patalim,* 1984), *Above Everything* incorporates various types of documentary material into its narrative. The film contains footage of real political demonstrations as well as documentary-like passages that combine footage of real events with audio from simulated radio broadcasts. Additionally, the film features snippets of the TV programs created by Maia and Mike. These documentary elements comprise an almanac of sociopolitical issues during the penultimate year of Aquino's tenure. They traffic in stories of pollution, homelessness, unemployment, drug addiction, crime, runaway inflation, and skyrocketing gas prices, among others. Through these actual and simulated documentaries, the film acknowledges the important muckraking role that the fourth estate performed during the Aquino presidency. That said, the film uses Maia's underhanded practices and the excerpts from her programs to illustrate how popular forms of documentary can be used to distort reality and betray the public trust. The film warns that the free press—whose return after the dictatorship Filipinos roundly celebrated—continued to be fettered by the influence of rotten politicians and the threat of violence from other powerbrokers. More subtly, the grandiloquence of Maia's voiceover commentary brings into relief her tendentious rhetoric. Her habit of representing social ills with already hackneyed images of teeming slums and half-naked street urchins emphasizes the lazy reporting of some broadcast journalists. The film thus occasionally undermines the viewer's faith in nonfiction programs to foster a critical attitude toward the mass media and its relationship to democracy.

Above Everything premiered on May 15, 1991. Six days later, Brocka died in a car accident, on the eve of starting a new picture. Actor William Lorenzo, reportedly inebriated, was at the wheel. The Good Samaritan who came to their aid had recently seen *Above Everything* and recognized Lorenzo after pulling him and the director out of the wreckage.[116] Hernando noted that while *Above Everything* opened successfully, Brocka's death "boosted the box-office success of the movie."[117]

Reviewers warmly received Brocka's final political melodrama. Mario Hernando characterized *Above Everything* as "a bleak and disturbing mirror of a vital segment of Philippine society—those in media, local government and the underworld."[118] Along similar lines, the Young Critics Circle described the work as a "filmic treatise on the conjugal dictatorship," one that coherently represents "Philippine democracy's state of disrepair in such a darkly pessimistic style and from a thoroughly cynical point of view." The group named it the best film of 1991 for "realizing Brocka's negative vision of elite power and its destruction."[119]

Grace Alfonso praised "Brocka's consistency in managing to comment on existing conditions" but still had trouble with the film's adherence to "traditional film norms."[120] Her definition of a traditional film—one with "untiring twists and turns in the storyline; a convoluted plot; two-dimensional characters; unidentifiable timeframes; a ray of hope in the end"—recalls belittling characterizations of melodrama. Presumably a fan of social realism and oblivious to the film's self-reflexivity, the critic faulted *Above Everything* for its "lack of radical questioning on [sic] the medium's form."[121] As I have pointed out in responses to Brocka's other political melodramas, implicit in this line of critique is an unexamined notion of a proper, ostensibly uncompromising form of political filmmaking. If we were to believe most of the critics and commentators that appraised *Above Everything Else, A Dirty Affair*, and *Orapronobis*, the ideal kind of political film—in whatever way they did or did not happen to have defined it—eluded Brocka despite his worthwhile efforts and demonstrable successes.

CONCLUSION

After the fall of Marcos, the "socially relevant" filmmaking for which Brocka was acclaimed noticeably gravitated toward more topical and expansive analyses of politics than seen in his earlier work. The achievement of the director's latter political melodramas rests on several factors. First, the films contributed to the process of democratization by offering a robust critique of systemic and particular sociopolitical issues. They explored what Rancière might describe as "a politico-cinematic approach now turned less towards the exposure of mechanisms of domination than the study of the aporiae of emancipation."[122] Specifically, they traced the residual but still powerful influence of authoritarianism and called out the failings of Aquino's liberal democracy. They also shifted from focusing on antiauthoritarian politics to offering a broader view of political culture, especially in the Philippines. Secondly, Brocka and his collaborators continued to devise new ways to widen the popular appeal of his films, mainly by more aggressively appropriating genre structures and other elements from commercial cinema. More successfully than in the past, his final two political works drew a large audience and boosted his commercial prospects as a filmmaker. His successful bid to engage a wider viewership arguably did not force him to turn his back on intelligent political discourse. Indeed, the filmmaker used his considerable influence to continue hiring progressive artists with whom he had made prestige films. They include writers Jose F. Lacaba and Ricardo Lee, both political activists who had internalized the intellectual rigor and plebian loyalties of socialist politics during their time in the revolutionary underground.

I have also attempted to show in my discussion that the director and his collaborators renewed their attempts to explore the affordances of both melodrama and documentary forms in crafting engaging political films. As in the past, most critics favored Brocka's emulation of nonfiction imagery and narratives over his continued exploration of melodrama's discursive and aesthetic possibilities. Many of those critics were beholden to unexamined notions of Marxist cultural critique and Third Cinema aesthetics. They sneered at Brocka's twinning of politics and populism[123] and faulted his narratives for not delivering the kind of comprehensive structural analyses of sociopolitical conditions they expected.[124] That said, Brocka's newfound success prompted other critics to reconsider their views about the proper form of political movies. To cite an example, the captivating political diatribe of *Orapronobis* revived interest in the ostensibly moribund subgenre of the political thriller. The film also demonstrated the value of appropriating for political discourse such unlikely cinematic forms as exploitation cinema. To be sure, even the disagreements among critics and viewers were productive in sustaining the progressive film culture that emerged during the post-dictatorship campaigns to fortify democracy in the Philippines.

The glowing reviews and box office performance of *A Dirty Affair* and *Above Everything Else* showed that the glossy aesthetic of high-end melodramas was not incompatible with political discourse or with the elements of documentary and nonfiction. Moreover, in both of those works, Brocka and his collaborators successfully wagered that comedy would not be out of place in political filmmaking nor trivialize its purpose. As Mike Wayne points out, the cause of political cinema is best served by a "non-prescriptive openness as to the forms, strategies and subgenres" that filmmakers might use to fight the battles of their era.[125] To his mind, "a cinema of social and cultural emancipation"[126] would benefit from drawing on dominant commercial cinemas "as a potential resource" to reach a substantial audience.[127] Brocka's post-Marcos political melodramas demonstrated the potential rewards of such aesthetic openness and argued for the necessity of expanding the resources of political filmmaking.

Reflecting on Brocka's post-Marcos work, Joel David characterized the relation between the filmmaker's political commitments and his artistry as follows: "When Lino Brocka walked out on the 1986 Constitutional Commission, it seemed like an act of futility, a typical if oversized artist's tantrum.... What we mostly failed to realize then was that Brocka intended to continue conducting his side of the political debate in the venue where his expertise lay—the mass medium of film—and more alarmingly, that his decision to do so would be accompanied by a quantum leap in his creative faculties."[128] As David saw it, the pursuit of relevant political filmmaking did service to the director's craft, and vice-versa. Indeed, by constantly renewing his sociopolitical vision and recalibrating the style and rhetoric of his melodramas, Brocka won new followers and further strengthened popular cinema's power to articulate and illumine politics.

7

Picturing "A Faggot's Dilemma"

Sexuality, Politics, and a Commerce in Queer Movies

In the early 1980s, the French critic and screenwriter Jacques Fieschi wrote of a pervasive but highly coded subtextual homosexuality (*homosexualité occulte*) in Lino Brocka's films.[1] The critic detected such a pattern after seeing a handful of the director's works, which were streaming into Europe after the breakthrough success of *Insiang* at the 1978 Cannes International Film Festival. As mentioned in the preface, Fieschi illustrated his point with a scene from *Bona* (1980), a melodrama about a female movie fan's obsession with a dashing bit player. He stated that the pair's lone sexual encounter is suggestive of a male homosexual forcing himself on another man. Fieschi's provocative over-reading of the scene—and, by extension, of the film's heterosexual romance as subliminally gay—represented an early attempt to apply a queer hermeneutic to films from the Global South. The critic added that the gay undercurrent in *Bona* coexists with overt and stereotypical representations of homosexuality in Brocka's other work. Those "effeminately figured"[2] characters include patrons of a gay brothel in *Manila in the Claws of Light* (*Maynila: Sa mga kuko ng liwanag*, 1975) and the high school teacher who fawns over his male students in *Weighed but Found Wanting* (*Tinimbang ka ngunit kulang*, 1974).

Although probably unfamiliar with censorship laws in the Philippines, Fieschi had correctly assumed that they proscribed cinematic representations of gayness. The Marcos censors' 1975 guidelines declared that the state "disfavors or disapproves" of using "perverted or abnormal personalities" such as "homosexuals, prostitutes and the like as central figures in films."[3] Previous guidelines did not expressly target homosexuality, thus giving the censors more leeway to approve films with such content. Not surprisingly, a handful of movies depicting gay male eroticism—including two of Brocka's—opened in theaters when those regulations were still in effect. By and large, however, the censors used their discretion to restrict portrayals of gayness. Describing censorship practice before 1975, the chief censor whom Marcos appointed before the end of his first term in 1969 wrote that "the Board [of Censors] may accept intimations of homosexuality, provided modes of actual sexual practices are not pictured, even if only implicitly."[4]

In chapter 1, I followed Fieschi's lead by briefly touching on the gay characters and male same-sex encounters in Brocka's social melodramas. I shall expound on that topic in this section. I shall examine three of the director's films that, to use Karl Schoonover and Rosalind Galt's phrase, "depict queer people diegetically" (apart, that is, from the subtextual representations Fieschi describes).[5] Contemporary academic usage of the term *queer*, especially in the Anglo-American world, denotes a capacious terrain of "identity-forming" and "identity-fracturing" modes of sexuality, gender formation, and social positioning that mainly relate to gay or same-sex desire.[6] For want of a better term, I shall refer to the films discussed here as queer melodramas. Aside from their preoccupation with the subject of nonnormative sexuality and eroticism, these movies might also be regarded as queer because of their authorship (not just their director but also writers, actors, designers, etc.) and their cultural work of exposing spectators to perverse sexualities and visual pleasures.

I label Brocka's work as "queer" even as I am mindful of the fact that the director's contemporaries used the term "gay-themed film."[7] I also understand that the form and sexual politics of Brocka's films do not always conform to some conceptions of queerness and queer cinema. For instance, Joel David rightly points out that gay males comprise the bulk of non-straight characters in Philippine movies, including Brocka's.[8] He adds that certain aspects of the director's work—such as the famous sequence involving male hustlers and their clients in *Manila*—may even represent an "anti-queer" gender politics.[9] I favor a more inclusive notion of queer cinema than what other scholars might espouse, although I share their concern in reckoning with the internalized homophobia and other problematic aspects of films by or about queer persons.

John Champagne characterizes queer melodramas in movies, music, and popular culture as emotionally fraught narratives centered on nonnormative sexuality and erotic relations. He observes that a shared predilection for melancholy makes melodrama especially suited to narratives of queerness.[10] Like many protagonists in melodrama, queer figures are consumed by the predicaments of harboring illicit desires and battling society's oppressive norms.[11] The pathos of unjust suffering, alienation, and nagging unhappiness sharpens melodrama's rendition of the experiences of queer characters. Predictably enough, the relationship between queerness and melodrama can be fraught. The messiness of queer people's desires and the rebellious visions of queer directors carry the potential of upending conventions associated with melodrama. Such conventions include Manichean binaries of villainy and victimhood or an abiding sense of moral certainty about the protagonists and the world in which we live.[12] Brocka's queer melodramas do not always undermine these and other features of popular filmmaking nor openly challenge conventional morality at every turn. None of them feature radical stylistic innovations. Additionally, their gender politics, including their notions of gender fluidity, may not measure up to the expectations of today's critics. But as I hope to show in this discussion, the value of their cultural work cannot be ignored.

Brocka made five queer films in the course of his three-decade-long career. Four of those reached theaters during the Marcos regime, namely: *Gold Plated* (*Tubog sa ginto*, 1971), *Stardoom* (1971), *My Father, My Mother* (*Ang tatay kong nanay*, 1978), and *Always Changing, Always Moving* (*Palipat-lipat, papalit-palit*, 1982). His fifth and last one, *Macho Dancer* (1988) appeared two years into Corazon Aquino's presidency. I shall cover three of his Marcos-era films in this chapter, reserving his final one for the book's coda. I shall leave *Stardoom* out of this study, mainly because the campy teen musical and self-reflexive showbiz morality tale deserves its own essay, if not also a trial run as a midnight movie. I should also note that this chapter excludes the unknown number of television programs with queer protagonists that Brocka made, although it is unlikely that any of them have survived. One of those programs, the tale of "a homosexual [played by 1940s matinee idol Jaime de la Rosa] involved with his daughter's boyfriend,"[13] never even aired. A journalist reported that the tapes of *You're No Longer a Child, Sally* (*Hindi ka na bata, Sally,* 1979), which Brocka also produced, were "accidentally and incredibly, erased a few days before the telecast date."[14]

As with most accounts of queer cinema, my analysis of Brocka's work pursues several objectives. I shall critique the figurations of nonnormative sexualities in his films, examining their narration of perverse desires, assessing their sexual politics, and describing their relation to the history of Marcosian rule. My attempt to illumine Brocka's project of queer figuration admittedly risks disturbing the coherence of this book, which has unfolded up to this point as a study of antiauthoritarian cinema politics. In the spirit of a queer critique, however, I venture that such disruptions in the creation of knowledge about minoritized cultural objects are only appropriate.[15]

GOLD PLATED

In the politically tumultuous year before the imposition of martial law, Brocka signed with the independent film outfit LEA Productions to write and direct a film adaptation of *Tubog sa ginto* (*Gold Plated*), a *komiks* or serialized graphic novella by the famous author Mars Ravelo. Ravelo, who also wrote the *komiks* that Brocka adapted into his debut film *Wanted: Perfect Mother* (1970), often loosely based his writings upon films and literary materials from the West. For instance, the plot of *Wanted*—about an attractive female tutor filling in for an upper-middle-class family's deceased mother—closely resembles that of *The Sound of Music* (Robert Wise, 1965). It thus seems possible that *Gold Plated* also drew inspiration from a Western text, particularly British filmmaker Basil Dearden's *Victim* (1961), a melodrama about the downfall of a prominent lawyer in the aftermath of a homosexual liaison and related extortion plot.

Gold Plated begins with the sixteenth birthday party of Santi (Jay Ilagan), the only child of Benito (Eddie Garcia) and his wife Emma (Lolita Rodriguez). Many of the young guests, including Santi's girlfriend Jonee (Hilda Koronel), either frolic at the pool or dance alongside their parents to the tunes of a small "combo" band. Before the festive scene ends, a brief sequence of shots foreshadows the crisis that will disrupt both the family and the son's coming of age. At the buffet table, the man of the house is unable to take his eyes off the teenage boys still dressed in swimming trunks while loading their plates with food. The nearby tray of roast pork gives Benito an excuse to ogle their crotches.

Within the next few days, the film methodically reveals the various sexual troubles haunting his family. We learn that Benito has failed in his marital duties for over a year, and his wife can no longer resist complaining about it. She accuses him of having an affair, but he counters that he is simply afflicted with "curable" problems "down there" in his "pituitary glands." Although distressed by her unmet needs, Emma laps up his absurd excuse.

As it turns out, Benito is only impotent in the presence of his wife and other women, for he has been frequenting the haunts of gay men to satisfy his sexual cravings. He usually picks up his conquests at an upscale bar and romances them at the parking lot or a posh hotel. Benito's guilt about his gayness feeds his paranoia about Santi's masculinity. Secretly fearing that his son would also turn into a homosexual, he hires a call girl to take Santi's virginity, but the young man finds her too aggressive and flees her bed. The father books another woman, and this time the son comes through. In a desperate bid to feel manly, Benito hires a sex worker for himself as well but fails to perform as usual. He then retains the woman, whose name is Gracita (Marissa Delgado), as his "social secretary" and public escort. To his delight, she succeeds in helping him project the image of a macho womanizer, impressing Santi and making Emma jealous.

The ruse is short-lived, however, as Benito's indiscretions catch up with him. One night, Diego (Mario O'Hara), a grifter and fellow bar patron hatches an extortion scheme. Pretending to be a country bumpkin lost in the city, Diego waits to catch Benito's attention at a street corner near the drinking spot. The latter instantly falls for the trap. With a sob story about an ailing father to support back in the province, Diego lures Benito into taking him in. Benito dismisses his chauffeur and offers Diego the job and quarters in the family home. More often than not, they conduct their amorous encounters at the hotel where Benito takes his other lovers, but they also get intimate in public spaces and at the family home. One fateful afternoon, the two have sex in Diego's bedroom near the garage. Emma, overhearing their noises, peers through the glass window and gets an eyeful of the two men. She does not interrupt the lovers, however, and even plays dumb while watching Benito rinse his mouth in the master bathroom after the tryst. She retaliates—and tries to put an end to the affair—by asking Benito to terminate Diego, accusing the driver of making eyes at her. Benito and Diego's relationship continues after his firing. With extra time on his hands, Diego pursues his extortion scheme. He hires someone to photograph one of his bedroom encounters with Benito secretly. The incriminating pictures cost Benito hundreds of thousands of pesos in hush money. Diego uses the funds to live extravagantly and feed his gambling habit.

Like Emma, Santi discovers the truth about Benito's sexuality by accident. In an ill-fated coincidence typical of melodramas, Santi and Jonee drive past Benito's car on the road somewhere. Noticing that Benito and Diego are quarreling, the teenage lovers follow them to a well-appointed home. Santi leaves his girlfriend in the vehicle and snoops around. He peeks through a window and observes Benito groping Diego and then kneeling in front of him. Visibly shaken, the young man dashes back to the car and drives away with Jonee. Recovering from shock at a nearby park, he gives her a willfully sanitized account of what he had just witnessed, saying "I saw Papa and Diego embracing!"

Santi does not mince his words, however, when his parents confront him some days later about his bouts of depression and frequent consumption of alcohol and marijuana. He pins the blame on his father's gayness, declaring that he loathes Benito. He then screams repeatedly, "*Bakla! Bakla! Bakla!*" Benito's nomination as a "faggot"—especially by his son—devastates him. As Neil Garcia points out, "*bakla*" is "painful sounding," in spite of being the most prevalent word for male homosexual in the Filipino language.[16]

With the encouragement of his parents, Santi turns to their family doctor Celso (Luis Gonzalez) for help. Celso implores the boy to pity rather than lash out at his father. He tries to destigmatize gayness by comparing "the homosexual" to one "who is mute, crippled, disfigured or blind." Santi finds some comfort in the doctor's counsel, especially when reminded that his father "loves [him] more than life itself." Sadly, as is often the case in melodramas, the rebellious son reciprocates his father's love but does so too late.

Diego sets the film's climax in motion. After squandering his remaining hush money in a round of poker, he charges into Benito's house to demand more. Not finding Benito there, Diego harasses Emma instead. "I pity you," he taunts her. "You're a beautiful woman, but you ended up with a *bakla*!" He then forces himself on Emma, but Benito arrives and defends her, impulsively shooting Diego to death. Santi and Jonee barge into the master bedroom and witness the confrontation. An ellipsis in the narrative—likely caused in certain versions of the film by more than one round of censorship—omits a crucial event. The final moments of the film show Santi cradling Benito, now also bloodied and inert. A traveling shot moves the camera away from the tableau vivant, out the window and almost up to the sky, as if to trace the departure of Benito's soul.

A film critic describes what has happened to Benito during the ellipsis: "A faggot's dilemma, according to Mars Ravelo, and as executed by Lino Brocka, would consist of an almost incurable mania toward self-extinction."[17] Benito's demise rehearses "the obligatory suicide" that Vito Russo finds disturbingly common in popular narratives and films about homosexuals.[18] To its credit, however, *Gold Plated* ends without depicting the reconstitution of the nuclear family or the salvaging of heterosexual romance from the damage ostensibly wrought by the husband's perversity. There is no epilogue showing how Benito's death might free Emma to be with another man and relieve Santi of the psychic burden and social stigma of having a gay father (something that, in a homophobic society, would make him unworthy of being with a respectable woman such as Jonee).

Staging Gay Male Eroticism

The candid depiction of same-sex desire in the face of what Niall Richardson calls "heterocentrist squeamishness" is a vital aspect of queer cinema's cultural work.[19] Brocka tested the limits of such intolerance by plying viewers with frank depictions of male-male sex. By necessity—and also by design—these provocations often worked against the film's moralizing about Benito's infidelity and gayness. The director understood that he needed to pay lip service to conventional morality if he wanted to avoid turning off straight-identified viewers and discourage the censors from obliterating his film. He did not allow such constraints, however, to prevent him from making advances in the representation of gay sexuality. He created daring portrayals that enhanced queer visibility while protecting the film's commercial prospects.

One of the reviewers of *Gold Plated* noted that other sexploitation films such as *Hayok* (*Horny*, Ruben Abalos, 1970) had already touched on the "verboten passion" of "homosexual love" earlier, but only "to a very limited extent."[20] *Gold Plated* eases into the first of many depictions of gay encounters just twenty-five minutes into its two-hour running time. The episode commences with an act of solicitation involving Benito and a hustler named Vic, whom he has previously hired. Vic strikes up a conversation with a crass double-entendre. "Hi, Benny," he begins. "Long time no-see, you want to play *poker*?" He then grabs Benito's thigh before whispering that he is "really in the mood right now." The gigolo, leaning in, adds: "And you know that I can go all night when I'm in the mood." The encounter continues into Benny's hotel room, where the script calls for a scene of "Benito and Vic

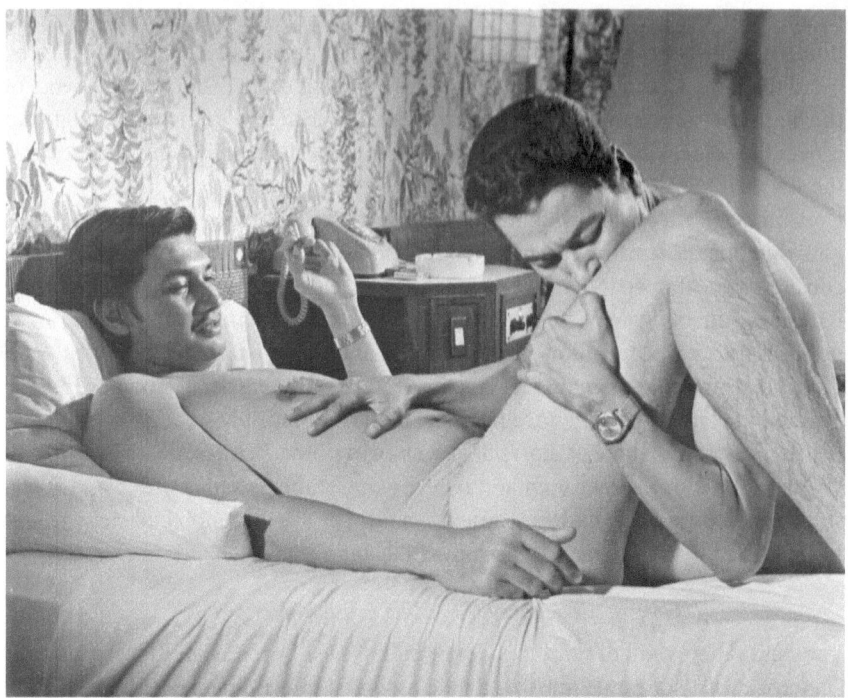

FIGURE 7.1. Benito (Eddie Garcia) romances a hustler who interrupts him to negotiate a higher fee. *Gold Plated*. Courtesy of Danilo Brocka/CCP Library.

making love."[21] As filmed, the scene pictures the sex worker in his flesh-colored underwear, reclining in bed while waiting for Benny to service him. For some of the film's gay viewers, the real-life identity of the actor playing Vic may have reinforced the verisimilitude of the sex scene. Brocka recalls in Christian Blackwood's documentary *Signed, Lino Brocka* (1987) that he had cast an actual "hustler"—a "half-American" whose name he had forgotten—in that role.

The film steadily raises the bar on gay content in subsequent episodes. The scene of Benito's parking lot encounter with another bar patron flashes a shot of groping. Brocka's screenplay proposes an even more risqué depiction than what occurs in the assembled film. His directions read as follows: "Benito puts his hands on the lap of the man and starts to feel him out. Reaction shot of man and of Benito—passion building up." The phrase "passion building up" suggests the erotic act's progression. As for the scene in which Santi witnesses Benito and Diego's tryst, the script likewise calls for groping but raises the stakes with a more explicit depiction. The directions call for Diego to shove Benito's hand in his crotch. Diego then "starts an erotic circular motion of his hips ... pressing closer and closer to Benito." Benito then "begins to perspire and gasps for breath as he feels the growing excitement in him." In the finished movie, the camera frames the bulge in Diego's pants, albeit without actually depicting the "growing excitement" of genitals. The extended crotch-grabbing recalls the lead-up to the gay lovers' first sexual encounter, during which Benito rubs Diego's crotch through his pants to arouse him.

As with depictions of gay sex, male nudity has historically functioned as a rare, transgressive element in mainstream cinema, whether in the Philippines or elsewhere. The homosexual content of Brocka's film was both plentiful and explicit for a mainstream film, especially when compared to Hollywood releases of the period. It is worth noting that even in the 1980s both graphic nudity and same-sex love scenes were absent in pioneering American gay melodramas such as *Making Love* (Arthur Hiller, 1982).[22] Films containing both elements had been in existence, however, in Euro-American pornography and underground and avant-garde cinema since the 1950s.[23]

Brocka tried to manage the risk of censorship by playing up the appearance of restraint and artfulness in his use of male nudity. Despite the short-lived relaxation of censorship strictures in the late 1960s and early 1970s, the exposure of "human anatomy" was still considered "highly censorable"[24] by the Philippine state, especially when sex was involved. The stricture reads as follows: "Partial or complete nudity [is prohibited] if coupled with an independent aspect of indecency."[25] The closest the film gets to showing both full nudity and erotic activity is when Benito romances Diego for the first time. A long shot frames the full length of Garcia's body atop O'Hara's, exposing the former's bare buttocks. The camera's focus on the lovers is deliberately soft, however, and the shot captures only the reflection of their bodies in a floor-length mirror. In another scene, Brocka offers even more revealing images of the two lead actors—including tufts of their pubic hair—albeit only in the form of black-and-white photographs that Diego presents as blackmail material to a horrified Benito. Also in keeping with censorship guidelines, the most graphic images of male nudity occur in non-sexual situations. The first of these scenes shows Emma spying on Diego as the latter prepares to take a dip in the pool. Aware that the boss's wife is watching, Diego teases her by shedding his trunks before taking the plunge. Although filmed from a long distance to simulate the view from Emma's bedroom, the shot framing is tight enough to clearly show Diego's bare buttocks. The other instance of graphic nudity—the lone scene of male full-frontal exposure—occurs in a dream sequence that illustrates Emma's sexual yearnings and her precognition of Benito's homosexuality. The shots feature solarized images of tree branches and trunks superimposed over the naked torsos of three young men. The buttocks and penises are visible, although party obscured by solarization and the superimposed, obviously phallic images of trees. The nude men gesture at an unseen person (presumably Emma, the person whose dream we are seeing) to come to them.

Brocka's script originally called for two dream sequences. His description of the scenes once again indicates a contradictory attempt to push the envelope on male nudity and gay eroticism while incorporating "artistic" touches and similar alibis to fend off the censors. The script suggests the creation of a "surrealistic atmosphere" in the staging of the first dream, which is supposed to depict "Emma trapped in a sea of bodies."[26] As filmed, the episode—rendered in montage—does not place Emma in the same space as the men, thus eliminating any suggestion of sexual contact. The other dream sequence, which also precedes Emma's discovery of her husband's gay affair, calls for "hazy artistic shots of Diego and Benito in different stages of lovemaking."[27] The phrases "surrealistic atmosphere" and "hazy artistic shots" point to Brocka's strategy of packaging the risqué material as tastefully rendered erotica. This second dream sequence was either omitted in the assembled film or added to the shots of the gay lovers' initial tryst at the hotel.

The film also risked upsetting the censors and straight-identified, morally conservative viewers with its sympathetic portrayals of same-sex affection. Prevailing censorship guidelines in 1970 did not specifically prohibit depictions of homosexuality but achieved the same effect by restricting "indecency, immorality, unmarried sexual relations, bedroom scenes, and nudity, among others."[28] Brocka not only challenged these strictures but also portrayed the dignity of queer love in the face of homophobia. His screenplay calls for not one but three passionate kissing scenes for Benito and Diego at a time when romantic kissing between men was rarely shown on film. To cite an example, in the scene where Benito dismisses Diego as his chauffeur (to placate Emma) but then offers to make him a kept man, the script specifies that "Benito . . . kisses Diego full on the lips" and the latter "as an answer, tenderly kisses Benito on the lips, who is completely carried away by his emotions."[29] Diego's plot to blackmail his boss-lover taints the romance in this scene but, as I shall explain later, there is more to their relationship than viewers are initially led to believe. Depicting passionate kissing between men was a gutsy move on Brocka's part. Although the censors had already lifted restrictions on "lustful kissing" and "lips-to-lips kissing" as early as the 1960s, they did not automatically leave such depictions untouched in the ensuing years. Indeed, they reinstated those strictures, albeit inconsistently enforcing them, after the declaration of martial law in 1972.[30]

In addition to a calculated restraint and artfulness, Brocka employs a third strategy in presenting male nudity and gay romance. Anticipating the homophobia of some moviegoers and censors, *Gold Plated* uses two leitmotivs to rationalize the viewers' witnessing of male-male erotics. The first motif is surveillance, and it figures in several instances of distant observation, including scenes of Diego stalking Benito, Emma and Santi spying on the gay lovers, and the patrons of a beauty parlor gossiping about Benito's homosexual liaisons. This motif of multiple prying gazes aligns the visibility of male-male eroticism in the film with society's moralistic policing of deviant sexuality. Apart from serving the gay-averse viewer's prurient fascination, this framing of male erotic imagery reassuringly evokes society's efforts to root out gay perversity. A related motif—reminiscent of Douglas Sirk's melodramas—either shows the characters framed by mirrors or looking at their own mirrored reflections. For instance, mirrors frame shots in which moral transgressions related to Benito's homosexuality are committed or discussed. Those scenes include Benito's trysts with Vic and Diego at the hotel, the erotic encounters with prostitutes that Benito sets up for himself and Santi, and Emma's bedroom conversations with Benito about his sexual dysfunction and infidelity. The mediation of images through mirrored reflections suggest the characters' self-consciousness of their perverse desires (or those of their loved ones) and their status as objects of society's judgmental gaze.

The mix of praise and criticism for Brocka's film indicates that his efforts to manage the viewers' homophobia only went so far because the prejudice against gayness was simply overwhelming. The nudity and sex scenes in *Gold Plated* were considerably tamer than most sexploitation films of the time, which were popularly called *bomba* (bombs) and catered primarily to straight-identified viewers. The "bombs" referred to shots of graphic nudity and simulated or actual sexual contact that the exhibitors spliced back into the films after deletion by the censors. Marcos allowed the screening of soft- and hard-core pornography during a time of heightened political unrest but reversed course after facing strong pushback from the Catholic Church. As one of the reviewers of *Gold Plated* noted, the government liberalized its stance on such content for less than a year. "From September 1970 to June 1971," the critic wrote, "the Bomba (sex) movie ruled the roost." He added: "Then the Board of Censors laid down the law and that was the end of that."[31] *Gold Plated* was released, after some delay, in January 1971, before the state officially closed the window on *bomba* movies. One of the producers claimed in an interview that the film "slipped past the censors without cuts," but a journalist reported elsewhere that *Gold Plated* missed its previously announced Christmas opening.[32] The reason was purportedly because "Brocka had to defend to the censors his right to keep several 'bold scenes' [depictions of nudity and sex] he considered integral to the plot."[33]

Like the censors, moviegoers and critics also regarded *Gold Plated* as a *bomba* film,[34] and yet its depiction of male-male sex still provoked strong reactions. Commentators such as Julie Yap Daza, who otherwise called the film a work of "art" and lauded its "verisimilitude," described "the homo 'love' scenes" as "revolting."[35] Her article makes the following claim, stunning in its anti-gay prejudice: "Yet no matter how you look at it, unless you are born homo love between one man and another is a sickening thing to watch." Incorrectly assuming that Brocka was straight (because he was not yet openly gay at that time), she offered the theory that the "sickening" depictions reflected Brocka's actual stance on same-sex relations. She wrote: "If the scenes were lacking in subtle, seductive sexuality, it could well be the personal expression of the director's blunt abhorrence for the subject." The writer added: "His subjective views and feelings about homosexuality may have intruded into the handling of the camera and the actors." A male reviewer, who praised Garcia's performance and called the film's treatment of male-male romance "pretty serious stuff," also warned his readers that the film's scenes of "sexual heat" did not offer "a lot of titillation" and that the gay romance, in particular, was "guaranteed to give you the creeps."[36]

Clodualdo del Mundo Jr.—who went on to work with Brocka five years later as scriptwriter for *Manila*—complained in his review that Brocka was so "carried away" in his "treatment of the homosexual problem" that he saw it fit to show "in profile that bulging thing on Diego's hips, which Don Benito holds and caresses."[37] Despite his misgivings, however, del Mundo adopted a more measured tone than other reviewers. He at least acknowledged the possibility that Brocka was trying to make a statement with his extensive portrayals of male-male sex. He ended, however, by saying that the scenes were neither "courageous" nor "artistic" but simply excessive.[38] The obvious "heterocentrist squeamishness" in these critics' words was—and still is—not an uncommon response to queer cultural productions. As Lee Edelman points out, heteronormative societies scoff at the "grossness of the sodomitical vision,"[39] at times even characterizing representations of homosexual erotics as "infectious" to straight-identified viewers.[40]

THE BELEAGUERED PATRIARCH

Gold Plated was completed in December 1970, less than a year after Ferdinand Marcos handily won reelection to the presidency. Much to the chief executive's surprise, however, violent protests occurred during the first State of the Nation address of his second term in office.[41] The demonstrators—mostly student activists and both middle- and working-class leftists—found much to criticize in the deteriorating socioeconomic conditions as well as the government's coziness with Washington. Brocka's film does not tackle politics directly but makes several passing (yet barbed) references to the national situation.

During Benito's session with the male sex worker, the latter alludes to the state of the economy by using a term that was especially relevant during the 1970s. As Benito kisses his way from Vic's legs to his nether regions, the latter attempts to negotiate a higher fee, citing the "floating rate" of the Philippine currency as justification. This talk of a "floating rate" invokes the devaluation of the Philippine peso by more than half its previous worth in February 1970.[42] The devaluation was to compensate for Marcos's raiding of the nation's coffers to fund his 1969 reelection campaign.[43] One of the autocrat's biographers—a man who once acted as his censor for the press and whose killing the regime allegedly ordered some years later—

estimated the amount of election spending at 900 million pesos.[44] Filipinos were especially bitter about the latest hit on their currency because it went against a campaign promise of the president.[45] Vic's demand for a price hike is meant to be humorous but it also implicitly links the political economy of the Marcos regime to the sexual perversity of the film's patriarchal figure. The transgressions of flawed paternal figures in Brocka's melodramas would take on a markedly political cast after the declaration of martial law two years later. The characterization of Benito anticipates the director's usage of malign patriarchs and sexual perversity as figures and symptoms of authoritarianism in his later work, such as *Weighed* and *Miguelito: The Rebellious Child* (*Miguelito: Batang rebelde*, 1985).

To be sure, there are no explicit cues in the narrative, dialogue, or mise-en-scène of *Gold Plated* that present Benito as a proxy for Marcos. One of the things that would have established such a link was the retention of a seemingly trivial piece of dialogue in Brocka's screenplay. The line—actually a single word—would have been delivered in the scene of Emma charging into Benito's office to confront him about his rumored affair with Gracita. The irate housewife finds Benito casually speaking with his "social secretary." Benito calmly introduces the women to each other. In Brocka's script, he is supposed to say: "Emma, this is Miss Gonzales—my new social secretary. Miss Romualdez—this is Mrs. Lizares."[46] In the finished movie, the inconsistency in Gracita's surname is resolved by settling on "Gonzales." "Romualdez" happens to be the maiden surname of First Lady Imelda Marcos and the family name of her also influential politician relatives. Brocka's naming of a prostitute after a famous political family may have been made unconsciously—something of a Freudian slip—but the decision not to use the name during filming would have been deliberate, even if it was done simply to correct an error. Because of Gracita's illicit occupation and close association with the deviant protagonist, her naming as a "Romualdez" probably would not have escaped the censors' attention. The latter would have likely flagged it as a political jab.

Proscribed Sexualities

Up until this point, I have kept separate my discussion of the film's political critique and its politics of gay representation. I have purposely done so to emphasize the latter, which I believe is more central to the film's concerns and the larger project of Brocka's queer oeuvre. I must end this discussion, however, by bringing these concerns together. Treating the alteration of two important episodes in the film presents us with the opportunity to do just that. My discussion supplements Karl Schoonover's and Rosalind Galt's account of the film's censorship.[47] In addition to the abridged television version of *Gold Plated* that those scholars accessed on YouTube,[48] my analysis will refer to the film's script and a more integral cut released on home video.[49]

The first of the altered episodes includes a montage and a short scene portraying one of Emma's extramarital affairs. Brocka originally wrote both episodes without dialogue. The montage depicts her one-night stand. It begins with Emma getting "picked up by a young man" at a soiree.[50] The script indicates her conflicted feelings toward the man's proposition by drawing a contrast between the "party sounds and continuous talking, and laughter and band music all throughout the scene" and the camera's "focus on Emma's reactions." This episode registers as little more than a blip in the television version and runs just a couple of seconds longer in the home video release. Both versions include an establishing shot of the gathering, followed by a different angle showing Emma descending the first few steps of a long staircase. The conversation between her and the young man does not appear in either version, even if an extant still photograph suggests that the scene had been set up for filming. The script describes the next portion of the montage as follows: "Man makes love to Emma." If Brocka filmed this depiction, it too was deleted from the extant versions. Both versions do include a shot of Emma in bed with a hirsute man. She sits up, apparently wracked by guilt, while he lies sleeping. Another depiction of her remorse follows this shot. She takes a pensive stroll at daybreak, along a desolate commercial mall and then on neighborhood streets. In contrast to the fleeting shots of the affair, this portion runs over ninety seconds. The needlessly prolonged action registers the adulterous wife's attempt at purging her guilt. The other scene of Emma's infidelity does not even suggest any sexual activity. In a series of wordless shots, she exits a movie theater with a well-dressed man and stumbles upon Santi and his girlfriend. Emma is mortified and, as the succeeding shots indicate, so are the teenagers.

Brocka seems to have opted for a passing depiction of Emma's flings to preserve her moral superiority over the promiscuous husband. But this already scant treatment appears to have been reduced even further in the assembled film, either at the direction of the censors or by the persons who prepared the broadcast and home video versions. (It is also possible that print damage accounts for the omissions.) Whether due to Brocka's desire to maintain Emma's righteousness or concerns about censorship, the film's stinginess in depicting the mother's romances points to a sexist double standard. Because it is unlikely that those scenes would have been more explicit than Benito and Santi's trysts with female prostitutes—who bare their breasts and buttocks in lingering shots—it would appear that the grounds for censorship and self-censorship rested on the perceived grievousness of the mother's extra-marital liaisons. The handling of the episode reflected the view that that married women, especially mothers, carried a greater moral burden than men. It also implied that the erotic doings of married women should be more stringently policed than those of men, even gay ones.

The second censored or altered episode of note occurs in what I described earlier as the ellipsis between Benito's shooting of Diego and the circumstances lead-

FIGURE 7.2. A shot apparently excised from the film depicts the sexually deprived housewife Emma (Lolita Rodriguez) getting "picked up" at a party. *Gold Plated*. Courtesy of Danilo Brocka/CCP Library.

ing to his death. After Benito guns down his lover, the script describes the latter "reaching out for him." Benito then "cradles the dead body like it was a child" and while looking "at the bloody face of Diego . . . very tenderly, he kisses him full on the lips." Benito screams: "I love you! Forgive me! I love you!" The final kiss and the professions of love and remorse that preceded it are missing from the home video version. Most of what remained of the filmed moments before Benito's suicide flashes onscreen in Blackwood's documentary. Those shots depict an inconsolable Benito embracing Diego's lifeless body before putting a gun to his head. Emma, Santi and Jonee watch in horror as Benito pulls the trigger. It seems quite possible that the censors or other parties excised the now-missing elements for depicting homicide and suicide, the latter specifically proscribed by censorship guidelines in addition to being taboo in the Catholic-dominated Philippines.

Also excluded from *Gold Plated*'s journey from Brocka's script to the film's home video version was a series of gestures that might have suggested Diego's desire to redeem himself. It is possible to read Brocka's description of Diego's attempt at "reaching out" to Benito as the blackmailer's expression of a final yearning for his lover's touch or even an apology for the wrongs he had done. In gay-themed films, the presence of the stock character Parker Tyler calls the "scheming hustler" usually reinforces the stereotype of sex between men from different social classes as transactional, especially for the less affluent person.[51] *Gold Plated* appears to challenge this idea through Diego's last-ditch attempt at redemption. As for Benito's final kiss—the third iteration of a motif of "full on the lips" kissing in Brocka's screenplay—it affirms his profound affection for Diego, regardless of the latter's sincerity.

The implications of Benito's suicide are more difficult to interpret, however. The suicide may have been an expression of unbearable shame for his perversion and his guilt at dishonoring his family and killing his lover. But it could also be read against the grain as a willful choice to join Diego in the afterlife, because he could not bear the thought of being parted from him. In Blackwood's documentary, Brocka cringes and screams in embarrassment while revisiting the scene of the gay lovers' deaths, blaming his youthful inexperience for its defects. The scene is actually not as clumsily done as the director's reaction would lead one to expect. The motivations behind Benito's actions and the histrionics of the actor portraying him are well justified both in the scripting and staging of the scene. That said, Brocka's reaction, whether prompted by Benito's suicide or the actor's performance, is understandable. Like other cultural productions, the queer texts of yesteryears contain stylistic elements and politics that have not aged well, and Brocka's work—as he acknowledged while discussing *Gold Plated* in Blackwood's documentary—is no exception.

The apparent censorship of the sequences mentioned above of the mother's transgression and the disgraced father's suicide hints at the depths of the nation-state's attachment to the patriarchy and the nuclear family. As discussed in chapter 2, challenges to the traditional order of familial and sexual mores troubled the state beginning in the late 1960s. The influence of the West's sexual revolution on Philippine society was eroding its moral conservatism. Around the same time, youthful activists boldly rebelled against the patriarchal state and the society their parents helped create. The state worried over the stability of the patriarchal and hierarchical structures upon which it traditionally depended—structures that, not surprisingly, authoritarianism would later exploit. The shortening or removal of the scenes of the mother's infidelity and the final affirmation of Benito and Diego's queer love implicitly politicized the characters' perverse desires. At the very least, the censorship of those episodes suggested that the intimate realms of family and sexuality were not entirely separable from the nation-state's concerns about its moral influence on citizens. Brocka's pioneering queer melodrama showed that Filipino citizens were capable of forming other kinds of moral economies and affective bonds apart from society and the state's traditional modes of regulation.

FIGURE 7.3. In another shot excised from extant copies of the film, Benito (Eddie Garcia) kisses Diego (Mario O'Hara) "full on the lips" before turning the gun on himself. *Gold Plated*. Courtesy of Danilo Brocka/CCP Library.

Fortunately, censorship did not prevent the film from achieving considerable success at the box office.⁵² Still, some months after the film's release, Ravelo used fighting words to describe Marcos's censors, calling them "skunks, [and] hypocrites." In the same article, he praised Brocka's adaptations of his work and expressed support for social "activism" in the country, even as he confessed that his own political views were incoherent.⁵³

For reasons that may or may not have something to do with the film's "activism" in matters of gender politics, the association of Filipino film critics awarded Brocka the plum for Best Director, further legitimizing his transgressive but warmly received picture about a "faggot's dilemma."⁵⁴ Writing a half-decade after the film's premiere, film critic Gino Dormiendo affirmed its achievement as "a bold pioneering attempt to treat the subject [of homosexuality] with honesty and compassion."⁵⁵ Indeed, *Gold Plated* established the "gay-themed" film as a viable form of mass entertainment by accommodating the often contradictory goals of attracting a mainstream audience, destigmatizing sexual deviants, and advancing a provocative—if also tactically calibrated—politics of visibility. As mentioned earlier, five years after the premiere of Brocka's film, the censorship board declared that it expressly "disfavors or disapproves" of using "perverted or abnormal personalities" such as "homosexuals ... as central figures in films."[56] Even if the censors enforced the rule arbitrarily, the formalized interdiction of gayness on film impacted subsequent figurations of same-sex relations. The edict also acknowledged the government's fear that queer sexuality posed a threat to the culture of Marcos's authoritarian regime.

MY FATHER, MY MOTHER

My Father, My Mother (1978) is a tale of gay parenthood set in one of Manila's lower-class districts. An entertainment journalist reports that the film was based upon "a magazine account of a true-to-life legal [case]," but she does not identify the source material.[57]

The film offers a markedly different representation of queerness and family life than *Gold Plated*. Unlike the closeted homosexual in that film, the protagonist of *My Father* is an avowed *bakla* or effeminate gay man. Dioscoro Derecho or Coring (played by the top comedian Dolphy) is a beautician and wigmaker who occasionally competes in drag queen beauty pageants. Consistent with what Richard Dyer describes as a politics of affirmation in gay cinema, *My Father* features not only an "out and proud" lead, but also several minor queer characters and extras with varied social backgrounds and sexual identifications.[58] They include Rodrigo (Larry Leviste), a couturier who dreams of having sex reassignment surgery and Salvador or Bading (Soxy Topacio), a vivacious queen who makes his living peddling imported dry goods. Another featured character, Crispino Villa (Orlando Nadres, also the film's screenwriter), is a literature professor with a wife and children. He is closeted to some people but associates in public with his gay friends. Nadres confirmed the film's interest in projecting such diversity, noting in an interview that "Lino and I want[ed] to show the different kinds of *mujers* [gays]."[59]

The narrative begins a year after the departure of Dionisio "Dennis" Hammond (Phillip Salvador), the much younger half-American lad whom Coring took in as a teen and put through school for five years. Dennis up and left for no apparent reason, and did not even bother to inform Coring of his whereabouts. Throughout their relationship, Dennis addressed Coring as "uncle," and the latter still plays coy when his gay pals tease him about the furtive romance. One day, Dennis shows up out of the blue at Coring's apartment, bearing an infant in his arms. The child is the fruit of a brief affair with a prostitute named Mariana (Marissa Delgado, also the call girl in *Gold Plated*). She does not wish to raise the child, and neither does Dennis. The young father cites his plan to enlist in the US Navy as an excuse for offering the infant to Coring.

Because the film is also structured as a maternal melodrama and not just a tale of gay affirmation, the narrative binds Coring to the child. The decision to carry the burden of irresponsible heterosexuals does not come easy, however, for Coring and most of his queer friends. Bading, whose nickname is also slang for "faggot," advises Coring to follow his intuition and refuse the child. Bading reminds Coring that the cost of having a ward—whether a baby like Dennis's son or a fifteen-year-old like Bading's current boyfriend—is prohibitive. When Coring expresses worry that taking in a child might also ruin his "nocturnal cruising" sprees, Bading warns him that those fears would likely come true. Rodrigo the fashion designer chimes in with his opposition to gay fatherhood, telling Coring that he would "no longer be able to wear long gowns" should he decide to adopt the infant. Not surprisingly, Crispino disagrees with them and extols the joys of raising children. The film resolves Coring's tricky dilemma by taking the decision out of his hands. Coming home from work that same evening, he finds that Dennis has already fled yet again, leaving behind the crying baby and a note begging forgiveness for putting "a son I am unable to care for" in his charge.

Apparitional Masculinity and Heteronormative Parenting

The film argues for the social acceptance of gays and gay parenting by associating them with the formation of strong nuclear families. Such rhetoric, as Richard Dyer points out, is a long-lived if problematic trope in gay identity politics.[60]

Coring and his friends do their utmost to fulfill the roles of parent and "fairy godmothers," respectively, to Dennis's son. At the infant's christening, Coring names the child Marlon Brando Derecho, lending his surname while drawing the given name from his hypermasculine movie idol. He gives him the nickname Nonoy. Coring's full name is just as odd-sounding and meaningful as the child's baptismal name. "Dioscoro" roughly translates into "God's succor" while "Derecho" corresponds to the English word "straight."

The gay protagonist's allegorical name suggests his need for a miracle to function as a model of conventional masculinity for his new ward. This struggle becomes the focus of the film's narrative, which jumps forward by six years early on in the film. Coring's vigilance in regulating the child's gender identification comes across as alternately comic and melodramatic. The humor is fueled in part by a long tradition of what Parker Tyler calls "fag gags"—jokes and slapstick humor that mock gays.[61] *My Father* is replete with "fag gags" that emphasize Coring's incompetence at feigning conventional masculinity and instilling it in his son. Such jokes generate laughter by appealing to latent homophobia and what some critics call "effeminophobia."[62] One comical scene shows Coring ineptly teaching Nonoy (played by child wonder Niño Mulach) how to box after the neighborhood kids bully him for having a gay parent. Other moments of gender policing are especially painful. For instance, Coring upbraids and spanks Nonoy after catching

FIGURE 7.4. Coring (Dolphy, right) tells a white lie about his cross-dressing to his foster child Nonoy (Niño Mulach) in *My Father, My Mother*. Courtesy of Mario and Cesar Hernando.

him smearing lipstick all over his face. What Coring mistakes for an unmasculine interest in cosmetics turns out to be the child's attempt to paint his face like the American Indian warrior pictured in his coloring book. Coring apologizes, but not after traumatizing the child and making a fool of himself.

The film likewise generates much pathos out of Coring's sacrifices to meet society's rigid standards of proper fatherhood. He dresses more conservatively than before, battles his tendency to lisp, and tries to prevent his wrists from limping. As Rodrigo had predicted, Coring quits attending drag balls with his friends. In a poignant scene, Coring takes a break from manhood by joining a gay fashion show. The event is held at a basketball court near his house. Coring tells his aunt to send the child to bed, but Nonoy sneaks out and goes to the pageant. A fight breaks out in the middle of the event, sending the drag queens and viewers into a stampede. Coring and Bading duck under the stage, where Nonoy coincidentally discovers them. On the way home, the child inquires about Coring's cross-dressing and effeminacy at the event. Coring quickly makes up an excuse. He tells the child that he only appeared in drag to impress the public with his cosmetology skills, as a way of promoting his beauty parlor. Nonoy accepts the explanation and even marvels at Coring's industry, exclaiming: "Oh, how difficult your job must be!"

Coring's melancholia for his repressed gayness lends emotional force to the idea that queer people should not shy away from disclosing their non-normative sexual orientation or gender identity. The valorization of "coming out" in gay movies reflects both the influence of Western identity politics and Nadres's personal stance.[63] As one journalist points out, *My Father* seems to be of a piece with Nadres's landmark stage play *That's All for Now and Many Thanks* (*Hanggang dito na lamang at maraming salamat,* 1974). Similar to Coring and Dennis in *My Father,* Nadres's drama features an older effeminate homosexual who desires and financially supports a younger, ostensibly straight man. Brocka portrayed the gay protagonist in the play's acclaimed premiere. Neil Garcia describes *That's All for Now* as "an unequivocal and powerful indictment of 'closetedness'—against which Nadres inveighs—because to hide one's real identity is to be a hypocrite."[64] *My Father* adapts the play's basic narrative but replaces certain aspects of the original material's gender politics with more progressive ideas. For example, the play frames the relationship between the older man and his young ward as strictly nonsexual while the film casts doubt on a similar claim made by Coring and Dennis.

If melodramas, as Linda Williams notes, are fueled by the spectacle of virtuous suffering, then the queer melodrama of *My Father* embraces the torment of a homosexual who heroically but misguidedly takes on a role for which a prejudiced society deems him unfit.[65] While the film points out the irony of Coring's situation, it does not stringently question his investment in what Sara Ahmed calls "compulsory heterosexuality."[66] The film addresses this matter only indirectly when Coring tells his aunt that he wants to spare Nonoy from experiencing the homophobic prejudice and violence he had suffered as a child. This revelation suggests that Coring's defense of gender conformity comes not only from an internalized self-hatred but from firsthand knowledge of homophobia's pervasive influence.

Alongside *My Father's* contradictory politics of gay self-affirmation and masculine conformity lies an ambivalent critique of heteronormative conceptions of family. Rather than idealizing the heterosexual nuclear family, the film depicts Nonoy's birth parents as hopelessly dysfunctional. While Dennis is naturally tender toward his son, the film emphasizes that he abandons the child and reneges on his promise to pay child support, even after landing a well-paying job in the US Navy. When Dennis returns yet again to Coring's house—this time after more than half a decade's absence—he takes the child to the carnival without bothering to inform Nonoy's guardians, needlessly panicking Coring and his posse. The most Dennis ever does for his child is to slip a few large bills into Coring's hand moments before taking off again—this time for good, as the screenplay notes.[67] Worst of all, Dennis's paternal incompetence lands Coring in serious trouble. When Nonoy's birth mother, Mariana—now a rich widow—presses him for their son's whereabouts, Dennis provides the information without giving a second thought to its consequences. His carelessness prompts a tug of war for Nonoy. Mariana threatens to sue Coring for custody of the child. Coring initially vows to fight her but relents after considering the long odds of winning. His aunt exacerbates his insecurity about his paternal competence by insisting that children like Nonoy need to be with their mothers and that his advancing age leaves the child with an uncertain future.

Coring reluctantly surrenders Nonoy to Mariana, but not before deliberately turning the child against him. Tom Lutz notes that male melodramas often reach their "emotional flashpoints" when estranged or distant fathers finally seize the opportunity to satisfy their parental obligations.[68] For Lutz, the fulfillment of a belated—and almost irretrievably lost—opportunity for paternal redemption dramatically affirms the innate competence of the biological parents in caring for their children. Brocka's film suggests that adoptive parents, including gay ones, possess the same natural ability. The emotional flashpoints in *My Father* occur in scenes that depict Coring purposely souring on Nonoy to make their separation more bearable for the child. The melancholy pathos of the situation comes from the greatness of Coring's love and the fact that he is unwittingly harming both the child and himself through his wrongheaded actions.

Predictably enough, Mariana proves in short order that she is an unfit parent like Dennis. Although she adequately provides for the child, she rarely spends time with him and is often short with him as well. Fed up, Nonoy runs away and makes his way back to Coring's house. In a heartrending moment, he tells Coring that he never wants to return to Mariana, no matter how many times she tries to claim him. At first glance, the film's gender politics appear to be at their most progressive when valuing Coring's queer adoptive relations over his biological parents. But even this aspect of the film is also not without contradictions. On the one hand, the portrayal of Coring's functional queer family permits, as Ahmed puts it, the "exposure of the failure of the ideal [nuclear family]."[69] On the other hand, the film's attempt to validate queer kinship by likening it to a functional nuclear family reinforces the latter's status as the ideal form of relationality. As Robin Wood points out, the nuclear family is an especially insidious part of the "dominant ideological norms of the society within which we live."[70] He cautions gays devoted to forming nuclear families that they might be "aping" a form of social relations built on heteronormative foundations rather than exploring non-conforming alternatives.

It might be said that the plot of an aging "faggot" sacrificing almost everything to raise a masculine boy betrays an unexamined investment in the promise of reproducing a heteronormative society. As Lee Edelman points out, the social order is "condensed in the image of the child."[71] Indeed, one might venture that *My Father* anticipates a joyous future for Nonoy, thanks in part to Coring's efforts to block the transmission of queerness from the child's adoptive family to his impressionable young soul. As I shall demonstrate later, however, the film's progressive elements discourage such a severe interpretation.

In Defense of Queerness

Although packaged as family entertainment, *My Father* also addresses itself to gay audiences as a revisionist portrait of a Filipino family and a celebration of queer subculture. The film challenges the tendency in maternal melodrama to deny the mother's erotic desires as a condition of proper parenting.[72] *My Father* makes sly references to "mother" Coring's desire for men and depicts his and his friends' vibrant nightlife.

The film opens at a dance party where cross-dressed men and trans women can pay other men to dance with them. The event is held out in the streets, fully visible to adults and children in the neighborhood. The scene, as described in Nadres's script and filmed by Brocka, is inspired by real-life dances in the working-class districts of Tondo and Marikina. Two additional scenes take place at a gay fashion show and gay beauty pageant, both of which are also free and open to everyone. Coring's cross-dressing at these events is a form of public eroticism and an opportunity to flaunt his association with the sexually available men in the community.

In a nod to the newfound legitimacy of gay liberation discourse in the Philippines, entertainment journalists highlighted the film's efforts to make queer subcultures visible to a mainstream audience. An article publicizing the film reported that the scenes of urban festivities feature "real gays garbed in the most elaborate of gowns."[73] Another described the queens as "select members of the gay community (who, these days, are no longer considered 'minorities')."[74] A third article stated that Brocka cast "real-life participants in such events."[75] In *My Father*, the heterogeneous community gathered at those festivities appears to enjoy sharing the nocturnal space and time with queers. Moreover, the crowd seems wise to the homoeroticism occurring in their midst. The conviviality between gay and straight-identified persons thus offers a vision of tolerance for queer people to viewers whose conservative values may include prejudice against homosexuals, transgender persons, and cross-dressers.

One of the film's most candid references to gay eroticism occurs, significantly enough, in a moment of cinematic self-reflexivity. The scene depicts Coring and Nonoy running into some of the latter's old acquaintances at the lobby of a movie theater. Loud and uncouth, several effeminate men scream Coring's name upon spotting him. Coring panics and pretends not to notice them. After realizing, however, that they were coming toward him, Coring affects a hypermasculine demeanor to distance himself from their behavior. The flamboyant ones scoff at Coring's masculine affectations. Worse, one of them half-seriously chastises Coring for taking a male child that is obviously not his son to a movie, telling him it is "imprudent" to be with such a tender "chick" (*sisiw*). Coring launches into an angry tirade after hearing their insinuations. His explosive response betrays his anxiety about the inappropriate relations he may have had with Nonoy's father.[76] As mentioned above, he and

Dennis characterized their relationship as avuncular, but it is obvious that Coring was deeply infatuated with his ward and, as implied by the merciless teasing of Coring's friends, quite possible the two had a long-term affair. This history of fostering an improper fictive kinship threatens to shatter Coring's image of himself as an altruistic foster parent. The movie theater is an apt setting for this episode because it is a place associated with illicit homosexual encounters as well as a repository of idyllic fantasies of self and other that perish in the harsh light of day. Coring's hysterics also surface his internalized effeminophobia, but the scene underscores the oppressive force of heteronormativity rather than harshly faulting his character.

The film returns to the question of queer parenting in its final scene. Through an understated ending, *My Father* tries to reconcile its progressive politics of gay liberation with the conservative notions of proper, heteronormative family structures often found in melodramas. In the movie's finale, Nonoy turns up at night on Coring's doorstep. He carries his most precious possession: a birdcage, with lovebirds inside, gifted by Mariana in happier times. The animals are the paltry remainders of the child's forfeited claim to a traditional nuclear family. The scene lingers for several minutes more on Nonoy's melancholia before Coring arrives, soaked and disheveled from the rainy stampede that disrupted his beauty pageant. The child, studying his adoptive parent's garish dress and smeared make-up, inquires: "Father, what happened to you?" Coring, instinctively shifting to a deeper voice and masculine affectations, returns a rhetorical question to the child: "Why are you here?!" The child asks Coring if he would take him back. He then shifts from addressing his cross-dressing parent as "Pa" to calling him "Ma." The child, seeing Coring in tears, gently raises his parent's chin. Moved by the child's recognition of his superior parenting and the nuance of his gender nonconformity, Coring lets out a hearty and knowing laugh.

This moment confirms that the resolution to Nonoy's parental dilemma hinges on his tacit acknowledgment of Coring's gayness or, more precisely, his liminal status between paternal and maternal registers. By telling Coring to keep his chin up, Nonoy encourages him to end his self-abjection, so that he can raise a son without suppressing his queer subjectivity in the process. At the same time, the ending affirms the necessity of sustaining a lie. The ending shows that the child grasps the importance of shifting between "Ma" and "Pa" in addressing Coring, depending upon the situation and the people around them. One can surmise that father and son will continue to tell some harmless lies about themselves to others and each other because that is what it takes to survive as a nonnormative family in a country still plagued by homophobia.

Political Erasures

The screenplay of *My Father* makes passing references to the nation's historical and political situation. Although hardly controversial, the references were excised during the process of filming, for reasons that have been lost to history.

FIGURE 7.5. Coring (Dolphy, left) tends affectionately to Nonoy (Niño Mulach). Behind them are pictures of Dennis (Phillip Salvador), Coring's former ward and Nonoy's birth father. *My Father, My Mother.* Courtesy of Mario and Cesar Hernando.

The film's production script indicates that the narrative begins in the first year of martial law. The camera is supposed to reveal this detail during a montage showing Coring removing his female habit and decompressing after the dance party that opens the film. The script calls for the camera to show "a 1972 calendar on the wall, and it is the month of November, with almost half of the dates pencil-crossed."[77] The time frame is barely two months after the declaration of martial law (on September 21). The script never explains the significance of the year, but the shot of the calendar signals nonetheless that the entire narrative unfolds during a historic period.

The film also drops a scene from the script that makes a passing reference to the politically motivated bombings that rocked Manila during Marcos's tenure. The omitted scene depicts Coring visiting Nonoy at Mariana's house after surrendering the child. Mariana's housemaid declines to admit Coring and refuses the present he brought for Nonoy. She tells him that her employer warned her against "letting gays inside the house" or accepting parcels from them, which might contain a "time bomb."[78] Both the Marcos regime and political dissidents used such explosives before and during martial law. For instance, the president's men planted bombs that they falsely attributed to rebels to justify the imposition of martial law.[79] Much later, activists bombed government structures to challenge the autocrat's monopoly on violence. The housemaid's paranoia about time bombs humorously references the country's tense political situation. At the same time, her implicit association of gays with perpetrators of political violence jokingly hints at the antipathy toward queer people among the bourgeois and their surrogates.

In the assembled film, one might also discern the symptoms of authoritarian rule during several moments that depict the vulnerability of homosexual characters. For instance, while rain and petty squabbles lead to the disruption of gay festivities, the ensuing chaos indexes the manner in which such events ended in real life. As Ferdinand Lopez relates in his study of drag queen beauty pageants and dances in Manila, the curfew instituted during martial law often caused such events to conclude in a stampede of drag queens racing to get back indoors by the stroke of midnight.[80] Still wearing their frocks, the queens scaled walls or ran at full speed to dodge police officers enforcing the curfew. Despite being played for laughs, the terror that grips the beleaguered queer people in Brocka's film registers their susceptibility to masculinist violence, including the kinds inflicted by the state.

In the film's penultimate scene, Coring invokes present social conditions in a manner that may or may not have been designed to come across as politically significant to the film's original audience. During Coring's turn at the question-and-answer portion of the beauty pageant, the host asks him if "you have ever been ashamed of your sexuality?" In his touching response, Coring says that despite being "well-behaved" and "law-abiding," "to this day" ("*hanggang ngayon*") and "here" ("*dito sa atin*"), he is still unable to find respite from homophobia. Nadres's screenplay indicates—in English—that Coring should deliver the monologue "as if he is addressing the whole society."[81] The directions in Nadres's script confirm the idea that the deixis "here" extends beyond Coring's working-class neighborhood. Brocka telegraphs the idea of Coring speaking his truth to "the whole society" by alternating between solo shots of the drag queen's stirring delivery and reaction shots of the large crowd listening intently.

Coring's invocation of time ("to this day") and place ("here [in our society]") is ambiguous enough to be taken as a reference to prevailing conditions under martial law. During the Marcos regime, cross-dressers, gay men, and other queer persons felt vulnerable both because of and despite their public visibility. Katherine Ellison relates, for example, that when the state hosted international conferences and wanted to rid the capital of eyesores, authorities rounded up gay men and detained them on ships, presumably until the foreign guests left.[82] Not all queer persons were severely marginalized, however. Although working-class gays like Coring and his friends suffered the indignities described above, some of their upper-class counterparts achieved prominence as couturiers and hairdressers to Imelda Marcos or as glamorous fixtures in discos patronized by Manila's elite.[83]

Like *Gold Plated*, *My Father* opened to resounding commercial success. The film reportedly earned 4.8 million pesos, more than doubling its unusually high 2 million-peso budget.[84] Journalists and reviewers wrote approvingly of Dolphy's serio-comic approach to playing gay characters, even as one reporter noted that the actor had a difficult time adjusting to Brocka's method of directing actors.[85] A reviewer gave Dolphy—then already the "King of Comedy" and the highest paid actor at 800,000 pesos a movie—[86] full credit for his "most corrosive [sic] and impressive performance as a transvestite."[87] The same reviewer also commended "Brocka's realistic treatment of the life and problems of homosexuals." Other reviewers were simply unimpressed. Dormiendo, who praised *Gold Plated*, faulted *My Father* on several counts. Unsympathetic to the film's gay identity politics, he complained about Brocka's depictions of the "activities of inverts [*alanganin*], such as their flirtations, pageants, transvestite fashion shows, and many other things that are ostensibly superfluous."[88] Apart from scoffing at the film's politics of gay visibility, he also disapproved of Coring's plea for viewers to seek to "understand his fellow transvestites," asking: "What kind of sympathy is Dolphy asking—more fashion shows for transvestites? While truly amusing, they do not deepen and broaden our understanding of the third sex."[89] Dormiendo's objections point to the commonality of effeminophobia and "heterocentrist squeamishness"[90] even among gay or gay-friendly critics.

Despite some negative assessments, the film's reputation has only improved in the decades since its release. In an article from 1995, Noel Vera describes *My Father* as a landmark in Dolphy's long career, a "film or role worthy of his talents."[91] Vera's praise counters the view of some critics that Dolphy only produced caricatures of gay characters.[92] Similarly, in a 2008 essay on Philippine gay cinema, Ronald Batyan credits the film for its "comic and poignant exploration of a lower class *bakla*."[93]

ALWAYS CHANGING, ALWAYS MOVING

Always Changing, Always Moving (*Palipat-lipat, papalit-palit*) is the most critically neglected of Brocka's queer movies. Its producers and entertainment journalists alternately positioned it as a thoughtful film about relationships and as a "sex comedy."[94] Interestingly enough, much of the publicity for the film in Brocka's archive makes no mention of its homosexual content.[95] Presumably, this was because the producers hoped to attract a broad audience. One of the few articles that acknowledged the gay subject matter simply noted in passing that Mark Gil, one of the film's two leading men, "plays the role of a homosexual who falls in love with [fellow actor] Christopher [De Leon]."[96]

The depiction of this queer protagonist is one of the film's most distinctive aspects. Indeed, so uncommon was its approach to portraying gayness that one of the reporters who helped publicize the film appears to have entirely missed its significance. After noting that Gil portrayed a "homosexual musical director," the writer quotes the actor as saying the following: "I just want to portray an 'untypical' gay character, not the usual swishy *manicurista* [beautician] type of gay."[97] The writer failed to appreciate that the film codes the "untypical" and not-swishy gay character as a male bisexual, a figure seldom represented in Philippine cinema. Although an inconsistently "straight-acting" widowed queer man had recently appeared as the protagonist of a Filipino film—namely Danny Zialcita's sex comedy *Mahinhin vs. Mahinhin* (*Nelly vs. Nelly*, 1981)—the film's makers had painted that character and the narrative in broad strokes. *Always Changing*, in addition to featuring a more rounded bisexual character, employs various narrative and visual elements in a creditable representation of bisexual eroticism.

Ostensibly drawn from "real-life models" by writer Bibeth Orteza (who also happens to be an actress famous for playing tomboys), *Always Changing* tracks an unusual love triangle between a married couple and a "homosexual" man.[98] All three protagonists are upwardly mobile professionals in the entertainment industry. The leading lady, Carissa (Dina Bonnevie), produces a soap opera for network television. Unlike the typically conservative Filipina movie heroine, she is as a sexually "liberated" woman. She practically lives with fiancée Chuck (Christopher De Leon), a "director of production" and one of her superiors at the network, for a year and a half before their marriage. Chuck also breaks the mold of romantic leads. He insists on having casual sex with other partners after tying the knot with Carissa. Most of the time he trysts with ex-girlfriend Betsy (Martha Sevilla), a public affairs correspondent in the same organization. Gil's character, David, is the film's third protagonist. He is Carissa's one-time suitor and a musical composer frequently hired by the network.

Carissa tries to come to terms with Chuck's infidelity but realizes she cannot tolerate it, especially because she often sees him and Betsy together at their workplace. She asks for a trial separation within a year of their nuptials. She then begins spending a lot of time with David. Although noticeably still infatuated with her former suitor, Carissa pretends that she is only interested in his friendship. Chuck suspects them of having an affair but keeps mum about it. When he finally raises the issue with David, he does so timidly. He merely asks David to verify Carissa's assertion that they cannot be lovers because he is "*kwan*" ("umm . . ." or "what's it?"). David uses the term "*bakla*" to describe his sexuality to Chuck, most probably to keep things simple. To Carissa, however, David confides that he is in a long-distance relationship with "a Spanish girlfriend in Barcelona" but that he also likes being with men. He later introduces Carissa to his uncouth working-class lover Tommy (Rez Cortex), who later describes himself to her as a "masseur." Given his erotic relationships, David's orientation is more accurately labeled not as *bakla* but as *silahis*, a term that "loosely translates into 'bisexual'"

FIGURE 7.6. David (Mark Gil) offers his moral support and a spare bedroom to Carissa (Dina Bonnevie) during her trial separation from her husband. *Always Changing, Always Moving.* Courtesy of Mario and Cesar Hernando.

but is more ambiguous than the Western concept.[99] While the film explores the erotic modes of being known as *silahis* and *bisexuality* quite extensively, neither words figure in the dialogue.

Representing Bisexuality

The film's reticence in naming *silahis* as the sexual orientation of its leading gay character brings into relief the problem of figuring bisexuality on film. Patricia White uses the term "representability" to denote, among other things, the constraints and possibilities of making nonnormative sexualities legible on film even when they are not explicitly portrayed or named as such.[100] Among the things that complicate the representability of bisexuality is its resistance to what Alexander Doty describes as the logic of "gender binarism." The latter refers to the culturally ingrained "binary opposition of male and female or the homo and hetero."[101] The task of representing the figure of the "straight-acting" male bisexual was fraught as well in Philippine culture and film of the 1980s, because both continued to use effeminacy as the index of male homosexuality.

Furthermore, antipathy toward bisexuals has negatively impacted their cultural visibility. As Tan noted in the 1990s, the sexual ambiguity of the *silahis* troubles the Filipino schema of sexual identity, calling into question the "existing norms not just of 'heterosexuality' but also of 'homosexuality'" in that society.[102] Writing a decade later, Neil Garcia reports that some "out" homosexuals, especially those from the lower classes, regard the *silahis* as something of a "bourgeois coward" who "is merely acting masculinely in order to avoid the stigma attendant upon the effeminate identity."[103] He adds that some heterosexuals also dislike *silahis* people, seeing them as opportunists who suppress their "natural" gay effeminacy to attract straight males and females. The contempt for male bisexuals is evident in a sex column published in a widely circulated women's magazine in 1982, a year before the release of Brocka's film. In that column, the writer asks rhetorically what else to call a bisexual, and then enumerates the following alternatives: sexual opportunist, pseudo-homosexual, gay, queer, and *bakla*.[104]

Although there was a well-developed repertoire of visual clichés for representing male effeminacy and female masculinity in Philippine cinema during the 1980s, the same was not true of male bisexuality. In keeping with popular conceptions of *silahis* behavior, actor Mark Gil largely plays David as a "straight-acting" male. Now and then, however, he affects a slight effeminacy. In one of the film's uneventful moments, he flicks his wrist while smoking at a disco, evoking the stereotype of the limp-wristed homosexual. David's effeminacy also surfaces when he speaks with Carissa about his romantic problems in a softer, higher-pitched voice and behaves like a stereotypical nelly. The term *"pusong babae"* (female heart) is a euphemism for the *bakla*, a figure that Philippine society traditionally regards as a "male body with a female heart."[105] David reveals himself as *"pusong babae"* during such unguarded moments, in part to satisfy another one of the most familiar terms of gay representability in a Filipino movie.

The alternately intense and tender way in which David looks at certain men also signals his inconspicuous queerness. Indeed, as D. A. Miller reminds us, "perhaps the most salient index to male homosexuality, socially speaking consists in how a man looks at other men."[106] The film offers a less conventional portrayal of the sexuality of David's lover Tommy. He is gruff and hypermasculine—almost thug-like—except when sharing tender moments with David. He caters to a male clientele as a sex worker but, on occasion, seems comfortable being with women as well. He even makes sexual advances at Carissa while having a spat with her, but it is unclear if he actually desires her or is just being hostile. While Tommy and David project remarkably different sexual subjectivities (one conforms to the stereotypes of the lower-class "macho gay" or rough trade and the other represents the petit-bourgeois male "who swings both ways"), the film implicitly codes both characters as *silahis* because of their avowed sexual preference and traditional manly behavior. As Tan underscores in his study of Filipino bisexuals, conventional masculinity is the crux of being *silahis*. He writes: "In many cases, we will have men who have had sex only with men and who would be classified as 'homosexual' in a Western framework and yet be *silahis* in the Philippines simply because they do not fit into the stereotype of an effeminate male."[107] Due to self-censorship, the film never shows the two men making love or even kissing. However, the film acknowledges their sexual relationship in lines of dialogue and a handful of scenes where David entertains Tommy at his apartment and is shown in his bedroom.

Apart from the characters of David and Tommy, *Always Changing* offers other figurations of nonbinary modes of erotic being to suggest bisexuality. Counterintuitively, these figurations involve Chuck and Carissa. In reading the inscriptions of bisexuality into the words and images of these ostensibly heterosexual characters, it is useful to bear in mind Richardson's insight on why bisexuality is difficult to grasp for those accustomed to binary notions of sexual subjectivity. He writes that bisexuality represents a "liberating, dynamic state of unfixity" that "not only signifies instability in the subject's sexual identification but also questions the sexual subjectivity of others."[108] In *Always Changing*, the cinematic inscription of bisexuality involves implicitly "questioning" the sexual subjectivity of the straight-identified couple with whom the queer protagonist interacts. Reading against as well as along the grain of Brocka's film, I suggest that its most salient representation of bisexuality and sexual fluidity lies in the figuration of Chuck and Carissa's wayward desires for other partners and especially their apparent (and shared) infatuation with David. In other words, *Always Changing* counters its reticence in visualizing the bisexual male character's sexual doings through a subtle but consistent focus on the "straight" couple's bisexual yearnings.

How then do the film's narrative and visuals represent the straight-identified Chuck's bisexual desires? Chuck's interactions with David betray an unusual fascination for someone he has reason to despise. Indeed, he responds most curiously to the threat of sexual competition that David poses. Considering all the time Carissa spends in David's company, it only takes Chuck a single conversation with each of the two to allay his suspicions of an affair. More strangely, Chuck pals around with David even before he clears the air with him. He might be going easy on David because he is curious to learn the secret behind the self-identified *bakla's* chemistry with his wife. That said, Chuck and David's relationship is also neither simply competitive nor mercenary. Indeed, Chuck is remarkably tender with David when they are alone. Although the former is less affectionate in the presence of others, their mutual attraction is strong enough that their coworkers occasionally joke about them being lovers. Moreover, he occasionally teases David about his gayness and willingly figures with him in homoerotic situations. In one instance, he gets drunk with David and their coworker Noel (Richard Romualdez) at David's apartment. Chuck asks to use David's restroom after downing too many beers, and the host offers to help him get there. The former seizes the opportunity to flirt with David. Using inebriation as an excuse, Chuck stares intently at David before smiling and quipping mischievously: "No, I don't want to take your offer. I can pull the zipper down by myself." The teasing visibly frustrates David.

In another situation that shifts from homosocial to strongly homoerotic, Chuck takes David to a beer garden with female strippers. Noticing David's discomfort at the venue, Chuck offers to repair to a bar with male strippers. Upon arriving at the gay bar, Chuck makes a fuss of his boredom and, echoing David's earlier remarks at the beer garden, tells him watching naked men is "just not my thing." As if to compensate for his exposure to gayness, Chuck asks David to transfer to a non-gay venue but spends the rest of the night dancing with a female patron, leaving David by his lonesome. Adding insult to injury, Chuck takes the woman back to David's apartment and has sex with her in his bedroom. To drown out his sorrows and the couple's bedroom noises, David plays a doleful tune on the piano. At some point that same evening, he enters the bathroom and slits his wrists. The brief depiction of the suicide—which was wholly excised from the film's home video version—quickly cuts to a scene of Chuck watching over David at the hospital.

To my mind, Chuck orchestrated the evening's provocations to savor the homoerotic tension between him and David, as well as to expose the latter's infatuation with him. Chuck's noisy lovemaking on David's bed was a sadistic act of homoeroticism that happened to spin out of control and unwittingly pushed the depressive bisexual to attempt suicide. Chuck may have even unconsciously intended it as an overture to intimacy in the future, introducing a routine of getting drunk, repairing to David's place, talking salaciously, and flirting with him.

When David wakes up at the hospital with Chuck by his bedside, the latter nervously says, "I hope you didn't do that [cut yourself] for me." David absolves his friend of any responsibility for the suicide attempt, but Chuck's nervous smile and silence indicates that he knows better.

I venture that the film offers another inconspicuous figuration of bisexuality in Carissa's fascination with her queer ex-suitor and the homoerotic bond he forms with her husband. As Chris Straayer reminds us, in homoerotic situations in mainstream cinema, the presence of an opposite-sex figure often "induce[s] corrective heterosexuality."[109] At times Carissa's presence defuses the homoeroticism between Chuck and David but she also engages in trenchant efforts to defeat such "corrective heterosexuality." The film hints at Carissa's perverse desires by drawing a parallel between her obsession with her queer ex-suitor and Chuck's fascination with him. The parallelism begins when Carissa reencounters David several years after the end of their courtship. They reunite by chance while waiting outside Chuck's office. Carissa gets impatient and barges into the room with David in tow, finding Chuck leisurely conversing with Betsy. The incident—and Chuck's subsequent admission of his affair with their coworker—deeply wounds Carissa. In a series of moves that recall René Girard's concept of mimetic desire, the scorned

FIGURE 7.7. Carissa (Dina Bonnevie, center) renews her friendship with former suitor David (Mark Gil, left) in response to her husband Chuck's (Christopher De Leon, right) infidelity. *Always Changing, Always Moving*. Courtesy of Mario and Cesar Hernando.

wife mimics her husband by reuniting with an old flame (namely, David). According to Girard, "we borrow the desires of those we admire" and those proximate to us with whom we might also share a place in the "social hierarchy."[110] The desire for the same object creates a rivalry in which one party turns their competitor not only into an enemy but also into a model for fulfilling their yearnings. Carissa mimics Chuck's desire for adulterous lovers. She creates a pseudo-love triangle involving her, her husband, and David, either in an attempt to win Chuck back or push him further away from her. Carissa's entanglement with them is also reminiscent of Eve Kosofsky Sedgwick's account of triangulation. Drawing on Girard's insight into erotic rivalries, Sedgwick writes that the two men involved in a triangle with a woman often figure in a continuum of homosocial bonding and homosexual desire.[111] And the nature of that bond "is as intense and potent as the bond that links either of the rivals to the [female] beloved."[112] Indeed, there are several episodes in Brocka's film when Chuck's fascination with David surpasses his interest in Carissa.

The perverse triad—partly imagined and partly real—takes on a life of its own when Chuck subconsciously re-creates a scenario in David's apartment that previously had involved David, Carissa, and Tommy. The parallel scenarios are of

Chuck taking the woman he picked up at the disco to David's bedroom while the latter was waiting outside and, previous to that, of David taking Tommy into his bedroom while Carissa was stewing with jealousy in the next room. Chuck did not witness or even know of this latter scenario, but mimics it anyway, as though subconsciously compelled by the logic of Carissa's desire for symmetry in their erotic pursuits.

Carissa and David never have sexual intercourse during her separation from Chuck, but their relationship is not simply platonic. For want of a better term, "quasi-romantic" describes their bond due to their emotional intimacy and physical closeness. Moreover, their relationship may also be described as bisexual because it involves an economy of desire between a straight-identified woman and a non-straight man. Apart from flirting with David, Carissa also seems to relish the homoeroticism between her husband and their bisexual friend. She feigns to hate but actually encourages the sexual tension between the men. At one point during their separation, she demands sex from Chuck even though she was also being emotionally intimate with David (by crashing at his apartment, buying him clothes, and meddling in his personal affairs). She then proceeds to tell David about her tryst with Chuck at a lovers' motel, repelling or arousing him with talk of having a "full tank" courtesy of her estranged husband. The salacious remarks and the erotic fantasies they might trigger are part of the bisexual eroticism that links the three characters to each another. I use the term *eroticism* even in the absence of sexual contact for, as Nick Davis usefully points out, "sexuality of any kind should not be privatized as a bedroom-only concern or colonized strictly in the genitals."[113]

I do not wish to oversell the progressive aspects of the film's depiction of bisexuality. As I have mentioned above, the couple never explicitly admits to their attraction to David. More problematically, within the film's moral economy, David's suicide attempt symbolically pays for the "sin" of his and the couple's sexual transgressions. The film additionally depicts a hierarchy of sexual agency that favors men over women, for Carissa never has sex with David or with other men. She also does not express a desire for intimacy with Betsy or another woman, thus making her sexual subjectivity appear somewhat less complex than Chuck's.

The film ends on an apparently conservative note by reuniting the straight-identified couple after demonstrating the perils of entertaining their perverse desires. While recovering at the hospital, David counsels Chuck to reclaim his wife. Invoking the film's title, he tells Chuck that homosexuals are doomed to be "always changing, always moving" in search of the affection and stability that define his relationship with Carissa. Chuck rushes to Carissa's side, begging her to take him back. At first she demurs, recalling his chauvinism and infidelity. She softens up on their next meeting, however, literally allowing him back into her bed. Chuck invokes David's name while cuddling her, thanking him for his role in getting them back together. Although the couple's reunion sweeps away the melancholia of David's suicide attempt rather too quickly, a humorous episode near the film's conclusion reiterates the narrative's efforts to disrupt the moralistic binary opposition between blissful heterosexual unions and tormented gay singlehood. The brief scene shows Chuck paying David an unannounced visit and finding their ostensibly straight coworker Noel leaving the bedroom. Noel takes his unexpected "outing" in stride, hamming up a display of effeminate behavior to diffuse the awkwardness of the situation.

Two things are worth noting about the film's resolution. First, the understated scripting of the couple's reconciliation lacks the conventional exuberance of similar moments in popular romances. The conclusion affirms but stops short of exalting heterosexual monogamy, which is consistent with the film's depiction of the powerful forces and longings that drive couples apart. Chuck and Carissa's happiness at their reunion is not so overwhelming as to dwarf or negate their enjoyment of the time they each spent desiring or being desired by David. As Chuck admits, David's friendship—i.e., his participation in the couple's prolonged respite from monogamy—may have helped save the marriage. Second, David's words to Chuck at the hospital regarding the loneliness of gay singlehood are moralistic clichés that he tellingly never heeds. Although David consistently says that he hates being single, he picks men who are unlikely to settle down with him, such as the opportunistic Tommy (whom he describes at some point as a "hustler") or the newly uncloseted Noel (who appears without him in the final scene). David's reluctance to seek viable partners might be his way of embracing what Jack Halberstam describes as the "contingency of queer relations."[114] The bisexual protagonist's unexamined attachment to the romance of monogamy might make him loath to admit his actual preference for "always changing, always moving" between lovers.

Simulating a Bisexual Gaze

Brocka's film compensates for its reticence in visualizing same-sex and bisexual romance by featuring semi-nudity of both sexes as well as by simulating what might be called a bisexual or queer spectatorial viewing position. In an article titled "Happy Days Are Here Again," entertainment journalist Oscar Miranda gushes that *Always Changing* "is full of scenes that offer a feast to the eyes."[115] Aptly enough, he does not specify the sexual orientations he thinks would benefit from the film's surplus of eroticized visual pleasure.

The film is replete with scenes of the three leads and other characters in dishabille. They include heterosexual romps in motels, sexy displays of male and female bodies on a beach, brief shots of male and female strippers, and solo images of a half-naked character getting dressed. By aggregating visual attractions that appeal to various sexual orientations, the film arguably caters to and also shapes polymorphous erotic desires among its spectators.

Carol Cover famously theorizes the workings of a bisexual viewing position in the consumption of a subgenre of horror movies. She characterizes the "final girl"—the lone survivor in gruesome slasher movies—as a figure that engenders a shifting, gender-crossing process of identification from moviegoers. Clover suggests that the predominantly male viewers of horror films alternately identify with the final girl's (feminized) suffering as the would-be victim and also with her (masculinized) agency as the retaliating fighter who outwits the killer. The final girl thus often functions as a stand-in for the genre's typical male teen spectator.[116] Linda Williams argues that the viewers of melodramas and other genres that appeal to primal emotions also experience something of the "bisexual oscillation" Clover describes among horror film viewers.[117] Spectators of melodrama may, for instance, simultaneously feel one with the character of the moralizing priest and also with the fallen woman he chastises. The reason, Williams notes, is that "identification is neither fixed nor entirely passive" and that "subject-positions that appear to be constructed by each of the genres are not as gender-linked or gender-fixed as has often been supposed."[118]

Admittedly, much of the scenes of male and female semi-nudity in *Always Changing* occurs in the context of heterosexual romance between Chuck and either Betsy or Carissa, but some scenes stand out for their intimations of the married couple's queer desires and for inviting spectators to appreciate both same and opposite-sex bodies shown onscreen. For instance, one scene depicts Carissa frolicking on the beach with David. She sports a revealing one-piece bathing suit, while David wears black swimming briefs. Apart from showcasing the beauty of actors Bonnevie and Gil, the scene simulates bisexual eroticism by depicting a straight-identified woman's sexual attraction to her queer male friend.

The film's construction of a bisexual or queer viewing position extends as well to scenes that feature De Leon in solo moments of semi-nudity. De Leon's lithe body and mestizo features exemplify the Filipino ideal of *"magandang lalaki"* (beautiful man) as opposed to the other prized models of male attractiveness like macho men or *"brusko"* (brusque and rugged) guys. Filipinos typically refrain from associating the word *"maganda"* (beautiful) with masculinity, except when paired with *"lalaki"* (man). *"Magandang lalaki"* are feminized because of their delicate features (a high-bridged nose, fair or bronzed skin, small lips) and they are implicitly considered objects of visual pleasure not only for queers and women but straight-identified males as well. The figure of the "beautiful man" thus appeals to ambiguously homoerotic or queer desires.

The film capitalizes on De Leon's visual appeal to various sexual orientations and desires by featuring him in skimpy attire. On several occasions, including the film's title sequence, he sports wet white swimming briefs at the beach. In one such scene, he rises out of the water and sprints toward Bonnevie (and the camera). The long take ends with his crotch at the center of the frame. In another "beefcake" moment, he leisurely puts on socks and chats with Bonnevie while half-naked, giving viewers ample time to admire him in white underwear. Straayer observes that mainstream depictions of queerness often "support heterosexual desire at the narrative level and challenge it at a more ambiguous visual level where other desires [such as queer ones] are suggested."[119] In Brocka's film, the scenes featuring the three leads either all together or in male-female pairs alternately exemplify and upend that dynamic. At some of those moments, the film invites viewers to desire characters who are implicitly *silahis*, if not also to imagine what it might feel like to desire as a *silahis*.

Self-Reflexivity and Queer Representability

I have so far avoided discussing the significance of the protagonists' involvement in the television industry and, more specifically, in creating (televisual) melodrama. This self-consciousness is foregrounded at the film's beginning, in the scene immediately following the title sequence. The episode shows Carissa working behind the camera in a soap opera, taping a scene of two female characters quarreling hysterically. The scene and others that depict the making of a soap opera comprise an extended commentary on the problem of representing non-normative intimate relations in popular entertainment. Throughout the film, Carissa pitches story ideas that mirror her personal affairs to her bosses. A woman described by her mother as too "modern"—that is, too sexually permissive—for her own good, Carissa's relationships fall outside the norms of the morally conservative society in which she lives. Her first pitch to Chuck is for a new show about a couple in a "live-in" relationship. It is clear that the narrative draws inspiration from their premarital arrangements. Chuck rejects the idea, telling Carissa that it will only "freak out people like [her] mother" if it even passes censorship. In a seemingly random but pointed jab at the censors, Chuck reminds her that the state's gatekeepers are far stricter with domestic programs than with foreign ones. As for Carissa's second proposal—a show about a "feuding married couple"—it too does not pass muster. Chuck rejects the pitch without bothering to remind her that the story also resembles their life. Her third story idea, which she proposes to her coworker Noel after Chuck takes a leave from his job, imagines how the "leading lady and her gay friend might end up together." Noel warns her that the network bosses have already expressed alarm over her previous proposals, implying that an even more risqué storyline about homosexuality was out of the question.

These self-reflexive depictions of the process of creating TV melodrama examine the fraught relationship between the sexual liberalism of content creators such as Carissa and the strictures that governed representations of sexuality during the Marcos era. By suppressing Carissa's narratives of sexual permissiveness, Chuck and Noel instinctively align their interests with those of the censors. Their practice of self-censorship indexes the banal repressiveness of the authoritarian state. It portrays the regulation of the media as a mechanism of governmentality that has already been deeply internalized by artists. Conversely, the film's self-reflexive portrayals of censorship also testify to the unfreedom of citizens whose intimate relations are judged, by proxy of their media representations, as illicit and immoral. Insofar as perverse relations are sometimes characterized as queer even when they involve straight-identified persons, the network's censorship of Carissa's fictionalized scenarios also self-consciously depicts the proscription of queerness in the mass media.[120] It is fitting and also ironic that Brocka filmed the scenes set at the TV network in a government-owned TV station and that the Ministry of Information appears in the film's acknowledgments.

Luckily for Brocka's film, an unexpected and short-lived relaxation of censorship standards following the lifting of martial law in the early 1980s permitted the film to be shown with few, if any, mandatory deletions.[121] That said, the racy content may have only been allowed because they stayed clear of gay love scenes.

With its small publicity budget and deviation from Brocka's usual repertoire of commercial tearjerkers and social melodramas, *Always Changing* was mostly ignored by entertainment reporters and reviewers. A few critics based in academia, however, recognized the film's rare and innovative figuration of queerness. Wilfredo Alberca described *Always Changing* as "another successful attempt at presenting homosexuality not in a faggoty, fairy-like, frivolous fashion . . . but in a low-key, masculine-looking, and sympathy-drawing manner."[122] (Note the unexamined effeminophobia of the otherwise queer-friendly critic.) Manunuri ng Pelikulang Pilipino, an association of film critics and academics, honored Gil with a best supporting actor trophy.

CONCLUSION

Brocka produced landmark gay and queer movies, but he was not the first to represent male same-sex desire on Philippine screens. Although unlikely, it might have even been the case that his first venture, *Gold Plated*, offered less explicit depictions of gay male eroticism than films made around the same time. While most of those comparable movies no longer exist, publicity materials and reviews lend insight into their content. A press release for *On The Fifth Floor* (*Sa fifth floor*, Ely Ramos Jr., 1971) describes an "emotion-packed drama" about a cross-dressed male (or transgender woman) and a younger man involved in a "strange relationship."[123] A film review indicates that another drama, *Avenida Boy* (Emmanuel H. Borlaza, 1971), features the popular actress Rita Gomez in the role of a male-to-female "sex-transform."[124] Around the same time, a human interest article reports on the life and career of an actual male-to-female transgender woman named Liza Amor. She obtained gender confirmation surgery in Denmark, worked at cabarets in Thailand, and "performed sexy roles" in the films *Flesh to Flesh* (*Laman sa laman*, Lauro Pacheco, 1970) and *Temptation* (*Tukso*, Romy Espiritu, 1971).[125] Finally, *Horny* (*Hayok*), a soft-core pornographic film I mentioned earlier, reportedly includes a scene in which actor "Lito [Legaspi] made love to Stella Suarez while pretending that she was Tito Galla."[126]

Brocka populated his movies with sympathetic and often rounded queer protagonists. True to their roots in melodrama, these characters yearned to escape the crushing pressure of social marginalization, harbored fantasies of ideal partners and guiltless sex, and waxed melancholic for a better world for queer persons. Some of them managed to find happiness, however imperfect, while others ended their lives.

In the spirit of making depictions of same-sex desire legible and also palatable to a mass audience, the director's work trafficked in some well-worn and problematic tropes. Some of the provocative audiovisual elements of Brocka's work are undercut by the moralistic predilections of their narratives, just like other melodramas and queer movies in the commercial mainstream. Moreover, the gender politics of a four-decade-old oeuvre, including its notions of gender fluidity, may not meet the standards of some of today's critics. None of these reasons diminish the importance of Brocka's cultural productions or the urgency of studying them. As Halberstam reminds us, one of the goals of a queer critique is to seek "alternatives to the inevitable and seemingly organic models we use for marking progress and achievement."[127] Even as I have endeavored to stress the insurgent energies and forwardly oriented queer eroticism of Brocka's work, I have also tried not to lose sight of what Heather Love describes as the stubborn "backwardness" of queer artifacts and texts.[128] Love correctly warns against the tendency of scholars to propose unabashedly redemptive interpretations of queer cultural productions, for such readings may undermine or efface "the painful and traumatic dimensions of these texts."[129] As I have suggested in this chapter, generous but clear-eyed assessments of Brocka's films should account for the daunting historical constraints he and his collaborators faced and not just the opportunities they missed.

I have attempted to track how Brocka's melodramas reflected some developments in queer visibility and identity politics during the Marcos regime. Counterintuitively enough, the frank homosexual content of *Gold Plated*, made prior to martial law, gave way to tamer portrayals in the director's later work. Stricter censorship and the commercial imperatives of the entertainment industry caused this retrogression. Fortunately, the virulent homophobia that animated the criticism of *Gold Plated* subsided in the late 1970s. By 1978, when *My Father, My Mother* was released, the popular discourse on homosexuality in the Philippines reflected a begrudging recognition of the dignity of gay men. For instance, women's magazines ran largely sympathetic human interest stories about gay nightclubs and male sex workers. One of those stories rather flatteringly described gay bars as "not unlike the grand central station of the gay liberation movement."[130] In the early 1980s, when *Always Changing, Always Moving* reached cinemas, the same women's magazines noted with alarm that Philippine television, film, and theater were suffering from a "virtual invasion" by gay directors and writers.[131] However, alongside such residual homophobia and in some of the same magazines, one finds advice columns urging parents of queer children to seek "counseling assistance to accept the reality of something that cannot be changed."[132] The commercial or critical success of Brocka's queer movies meant that they were able to contribute to the struggle against such homophobic attitudes in no insignificant way.

I have attempted throughout this book to show what the filmmaker's work teaches us about the relation between politics and art. In this chapter, I have extended that project by modifying the terms of cinema politics to include sexuality and gender. I have found that in Brocka's queer melodramas, the issues in representing nonnormative sexuality both parallel and diverge from those of antiauthoritarian politics. Despite their central focus on personal struggles and relationships, the director's films arguably implicated the authoritarian regime in their accounts of the lives of queer people. Indeed, as I mentioned earlier, the figure of the perverse patriarch, who would later become Marcos's shadow in Brocka's more overtly political films, first emerges in the director's work in *Gold Plated*. That said, if the director's "gay-themed" oeuvre seems to have been much less concerned with political issues than one might expect, it might be because queer cultural productions are sometimes wisely indifferent to the matters that most strongly preoccupy the nation-state. Moreover, it could be said that depictions of homophobic prejudice and self-loathing always already register the antipathy of state and society, albeit in the abstraction of tumultuous emotions and intolerable personal crises that some critics and scholars hesitate to read as political.

Coda

Three Non-endings

I

One of the most underappreciated achievements of Brocka's career was his 1989 film *Macho Dancer*. A critic for the *New York Times* called it "a soft-core sex film masquerading as a political statement."[1] A Filipino reviewer dismissed it as a "picaresque soap opera" with "lewd and lurid macho dancing sequences."[2] The critiques, which focused on production values and reeked of unexamined homophobia, missed some of the most vital aspects of the filmmaker's effort.

For Brocka, *Macho Dancer* was not just a mercenary attempt to cash in on the Philippines' reputation for gay sex tourism. In interviews, he described the film as his long-awaited "dream" project and a "message picture," if admittedly not a "masterpiece."[3] The film's producer and publicist, Boy C. DeGuia, rightly noted that it tackles social issues such as "male prostitution, [and] police brutality."[4] A press release amplified DeGuia's message about the film's intent, pitching *Macho Dancer* as Brocka's return to "social commentary" following a period of "indulging the whims of the public with a series of commercial films."[5] The article went on to compare *Macho Dancer* to the director's earlier prestige pictures, including *Manila in the Claws of Light* (*Maynila: Sa mga kuko ng liwanag*, 1975) and *My Own Country: Gripping the Knife's Edge* (*Bayan ko: Kapit sa patalim*, 1984). As I shall explain later, the reference to *Manila*, which many regard as the director's magnum opus, may sound counterintuitive but it is well justified.

Brocka understood that he had to operate once again as an independent filmmaker if he wanted to finally get *Macho Dancer* made after ten years of conceiving it.[6] He revisited the filmmaking model he had used in *Weighed but Found Wanting*

FIGURE 8.1. Lino Brocka (top) directs Allan Paule (bottom) on the set of *Macho Dancer*. Courtesy of Danilo Brocka/CCP Library.

(*Tinimbang ka ngunit kulang*, 1974) and *Manila*, except for their price tags. Instead of making a lavish prestige film, he and his independent producers opted for a modestly budgeted outing. Brocka filled the major and minor roles of *Macho Dancer* with newcomers, character actors, and stage players, adding the rising starlet Jaclyn Jose to round out the cast. He partnered with a leading studio and distributor to bring the small movie to mainstream theaters. As with his earlier passion projects, Brocka used his earnings from commercial endeavors to cover some of the film's negative costs. Those money-making ventures include the execrable musical drama *God Is Sleeping* (*Natutulog pa ang Diyos*, 1988), and television commercials for products like Royal Tru-Orange soft drink. He struggled, as he had in the past, to raise enough money to complete his project. A journalist reported in May 1988 that Brocka had already "finished editing the entire movie" but was still scrounging around for the 100,000 pesos he needed for "music and sound effects."[7] Several months later, an article noted that the director needed "some ₱600,000 more for post-production work and promotions."[8]

Brocka did not initially plan on taking on so much of the financing. Indeed, he had hoped to raise it from investors. Speculating on the existence of a market in the West for gay films about the third world, he sent a copy of the story idea for *Macho Dancer* to his friend David Overbey, a Canadian writer and film programmer based at that time in France. Overbey was enthusiastic about the film's prospects and predicted that if it were to be budgeted at "200,000 and 300,000 dollars . . . such money could be made back from the gay audience alone in North America."[9] He tried to secure an investment from the Canadian film outfit that had retained him as a consultant, but was unsuccessful. In the meantime, Brocka started making the film. Overbey eventually managed to help his friend, if only by arranging for the film's premiere at the high-visibility Festival of Festivals in Toronto and covering the cost of subtitling.

To strengthen *Macho Dancer's* appeal to its prospective foreign gay audience, Brocka added scenes of nudity and male-male eroticism, including an explicit depiction of group masturbation. Brocka prepared a tamer "Philippine version" with the racy scenes drastically shortened or omitted.[10] The soundness of Brocka's approach was confirmed with the film's warm reception at its Toronto debut. The Philippine consul general reported that Brocka's movie played to capacity (of "over 1,500") and that the director received several rounds of applause from viewers of "sophistication," among them "a Ph.D. and professor of cinema critique at the University of Toronto." Aquino's chief censor had tasked the diplomat with providing information that could form the basis of legal action against Brocka and the film.[11] The consul would have none of it, and used his report instead to educate the censor on film appreciation and the value of free speech. He wrote: "I am of course ashamed of the realities portrayed in the film, which realities I think can not be denied. However, I am able to situate those realities in the context of the Philippines of 59 million people, who can not all be prostitutes exploited by crime bosses.... It is my opinion that the Filipino people and the Philippine government did not get condemnation but sympathy for the problems that they are facing, which though not in the same level and degree, exist in modern countries including Canada."[12]

After its screening in Toronto, *Macho Dancer* found distributors and viewers in other countries. Most notably, it made enough in its US release to jump-start the operations of Strand Releasing, a firm that would later become a leading distributor of queer independent and world cinema.

Brocka understood that owing to *Macho Dancer's* gay content, its domestic run would probably draw "a mature, and possibly very limited, [target] audience."[13] He appealed to this demographic by turning to the same aggressive publicity and marketing efforts he had used previously for his commercial films. For instance, he encouraged leading man Allan Paule to respond to gossip columns about his alleged relationship with a sugar daddy, if only to keep people talking about the film.[14] Brocka also filed a lawsuit against an entertainment reporter who claimed that he forced "his stars to do some kinky sexual moves on the set."[15] By engaging the rumor mill instead of ignoring it, he fueled the circulation of even more salacious print and broadcast stories. Brocka also cannily raised expectations about the film's sexual explicitness by noting that the film was eventually "passed without cuts" after he pushed back—as always—against the censors. Moreover, he reassured domestic audiences that "the local version is only slightly different from that [more explicit] one shown in film festivals abroad."[16]

When Aquino's chief censor Manuel Morato began causing trouble for the film as expected, Brocka countered by touting its international success. He also sought to turn public sentiment against the censor by telling reporters of how the self-righteous guardian of public morality improperly delayed the film's release,[17] slapped a previously nonexistent rating on it, and then pressured the distributor to pull the movie out of theaters. The shortened domestic run (only four days according to the director)[18] may have been too brief to serve as an index of the project's viability in the Philippines, but *Macho Dancer's* impressive showing abroad confirmed that Brocka no longer had to make pricey, high-minded prestige films to break new ground in local filmmaking and reach an international audience. The cheaper and demotic form of exploitation cinema—albeit with the distinction of having a sociopolitical bent—would serve him just as well.

Macho Dancer updates *Manila's* scenario of a provincial émigré's corruption and disillusionment in the big city. Pol (Paule), a denizen of a town outside a US military base, relocates to Manila to work as an exotic dancer following the departure of his American sugar daddy. He lands at a gay bar in the red-light district and develops a close friendship with his coworker Noel (Daniel Fernando). The latter teaches him dance moves as well as the ins and outs of city life. During his spare time, Noel invites Pol to tag along as he goes searching for a sister who might have fallen into white slavery. Viewers familiar with the plot of *Manila* might be wise to the fact that Pol and Noel are composites of Julio Madiaga, the protagonist of the earlier film. Moreover, Noel's sister is reminiscent of *Manila's* heroine Ligaya, who was also a victim of forced prostitution in a Chinatown brothel. *Macho Dancer* uses these appropriated characters and plot elements to create a rejoinder to *Manila's* account of poverty and exploitation in the Philippine capital. At the same time, *Macho Dancer* remakes *Manila* into a queer melodrama, expanding a sequence from the 1975 film into a feature-length narrative that is set after the fall of the dictatorship.

In addition to its social critique, *Macho Dancer* espouses a far more progressive version of gay identity politics than Brocka did in his previous films. Unknown to many, one of the key scenes in *Macho Dancer* is actually a reimagining of a moment of homophobia that was excised from *Manila* after the film's domestic release. The deleted portion shows Bobby, the man who persuades the protagonist Julio to try sex work, stealing a kiss from him. Julio rejects the advance, punching Bobby in the face and then cutting him off for good. In *Macho Dancer*, the reconfigured scene shows Noel suddenly kissing Pol on the lips in a moment of sadness and distress. The kindness of the protagonist's response was not lost on a female critic. She described it as follows: "It is an electrifying moment. Pol is surprised, but he does not draw back. He is a [straight-identified] man, but he is also a friend."[19] Brocka's reparative gesture is quite moving. Wiser and gutsier after more than two decades of making films about queer experiences, the director seized the opportunity to turn an instance of anti-gay prejudice from his earlier work into its virtual opposite. Pol cannot bear to push Noel away because he cares deeply for him. Moreover, the protagonist's occupation as a sex worker has not only made him more tolerant of homosexuality but also reeducated his erotic desires and habits of expressing affection.

Macho Dancer's liberal stance on same-sex relations was a few steps ahead of gender politics in the Philippines but reflective of prevailing attitudes in the West. Brocka's strategy of advancing a progressive gender politics to change the sensibilities of audiences at home while meeting the expectations of those abroad represented yet another innovation that emerged from the film.

In sum, *Macho Dancer* combined three key elements in its model of transcultural filmmaking. They include advancing a sociopolitical critique, working at a scale of production appropriate to the film's modest target audience, and incorporating elements that might enhance the project's cross-cultural appeal. This model, in which those features functioned in both local and transnational circuits, aided Philippine cinema's transculturation in the years come. Indeed, except for Filipino art films that are mainly foreign funded, much of the independent films exported to festivals and theaters abroad seem to incorporate some of the strategic elements and attractions of *Macho Dancer*.

II

Brocka's longtime association with "slum movies" and his confrontations with the Marcos regime may have obscured the full breadth of his sociopolitical vision. The filmmaker tackled some of the most pressing social issues of his time in both commercial and prestige efforts. For instance, his romantic thriller *PX* (1982) explored neo-imperial relations between the United States and the Philippines in a narrative set outside a US military base. *Oca* (1990), his seven-minute contribution to the international anthology film *How Are The Kids?* portrays child labor in the fishing industry and implicates Japanese firms in the exploitation and death of Filipino children.[20] Filmed with a cast of nonprofessional actors from a fishing village, its galvanizing combination of melodrama and raw naturalism is reminiscent of Italian neorealism and especially Pier Paolo Pasolini's most incendiary work.

Later in his career, Brocka became increasingly concerned with the social consequences of the large-scale exportation of Filipino labor. As I mentioned in chapter 4, *Such Pain, Brother Eddie* (1986) featured a protagonist who seeks his fortune in the Middle East but falls prey to illegal recruiters and comes home to find his family in shambles. With the film, the director demonstrated his appreciation of a profoundly transformative issue that was not yet well understood. Brocka related in a 1989 interview that he was considering three more projects about the subject. He said: "I have an offer to do a movie about migrant workers in Italy with [actress] Gina (Alajar). A group of Filipino businessmen in Canada wants me to make a movie about the plight of the mail order brides there. Such horrible, horrible stories I've heard. I also have an offer to do a movie about the Japayuki (Filipinas who go to Japan to work as entertainers but end up as prostitutes. But, I'll have to tackle the attitude of the Philippine embassy officials in Tokyo [if I decide to make the film])."[21] Although none of the three projects saw the light of day, other directors made films on those very subjects in the years following Brocka's demise. For instance, national outrage over the death of a nightclub hostess in Fukushima led to the making of *Maricris Sioson: Japayuki* (Joey Romero, 1993), one of the first mainstream features about Filipina entertainers in Japan. As for melodramas about Filipino workers in Italy, one would not make it to theaters until 2004, with Olivia Lamasan's *Milan*.

Brocka had still more plans to tackle other social issues. He reported working at one point on a project about land reform, Corazon Aquino's signature campaign issue and what would later become the great missed opportunity of her presidency. He was also on his way to realizing a long-held dream of bringing national hero José Rizal's nineteenth-century anti-colonial novels to the screen. The monumental projects were in addition to a modern-day adaptation of Rizal's *Noli me tangere*, which he was scheduled to begin filming just days after his fatal accident.

Two unrealized projects would have brought an even more pronounced transnational dimension to the director's cinema politics. In the late 1980s, Brocka was in talks to make a film about the experience of Filipino emigres in the United States. The project was to be an adaptation of *Scent of Apples,* Bienvenido Santos's celebrated story about the Filipino American diaspora.[22] He would have been a suitable director for that film, having lived for several years in the San Francisco Bay Area, which was known for its large population of Filipino expatriates. Another transnational project was much further along. He had already signed a contract to direct his first international picture in Zimbabwe before the studio, Columbia Pictures, pulled the plug. The film, called *The Basement,* was to be a biopic of the South African boxer Arthur Mayisela.[23] The French and British-financed project would have allowed the director to bring his understanding of social injustice under authoritarianism to a narrative about black oppression under apartheid.

III

Above Everything Else (*Sa kabila ng lahat,* 1991) was Brocka's last political film. He was unable to move forward with *Miserere nobis,* the second installment (after *Orapronobis,* 1989) in a projected trilogy of films about human rights during and after Marcosian rule. However, the director's engagement in activism left such a strong impact on him that politics seemed to cling to various aspects of his subsequent commercial efforts. His final work, *Sparkle in the Dark* (*Kislap sa dilim,* 1991), follows the harrowing aftermath of a woman's gang rape by three men in the presence of her husband. Unable to deal with the guilt of failing to protect his wife, the husband retreats into a depressive state. A male friend of the couple lends his support, only to be unfairly accused of coming between the spouses. In a shocking turn of events—one which film critic Nestor Torre found incomprehensible—the jealous husband forces himself on his wife after she repeatedly excuses herself from sex.[24] While the marital rape appears to have occurred in a fit of jealousy, it also reads as the husband's unconscious attempt to compensate for his emasculation during the assault on his wife. Through the heinous act, he retroactively transforms himself from a helpless spouse into one of her (powerful) assailants.

The brutal scene in which thugs attack the husband and wife recalls the emblematic scene of violence that I have been calling a "Marcosian moment." At such moments, acts of brutality evoke the trauma of state violence in the authoritarian Philippines. Interestingly, it seems possible that Brocka did not even direct the "Marcosian moment" in *Sparkle,* because a few sequences remained unfilmed before his death.[25] If that were the case, it would appear that his longtime actor Christopher De Leon or assistant director Bey Vito, who reportedly took over filming, did not have any trouble executing the familiar scenario in their mentor's stead.

Despite its lowbrow origins, the narrative of *Sparkle*—adapted from a *komiks* or serial graphic novella—arguably lends itself to a political reading. Brocka's long-

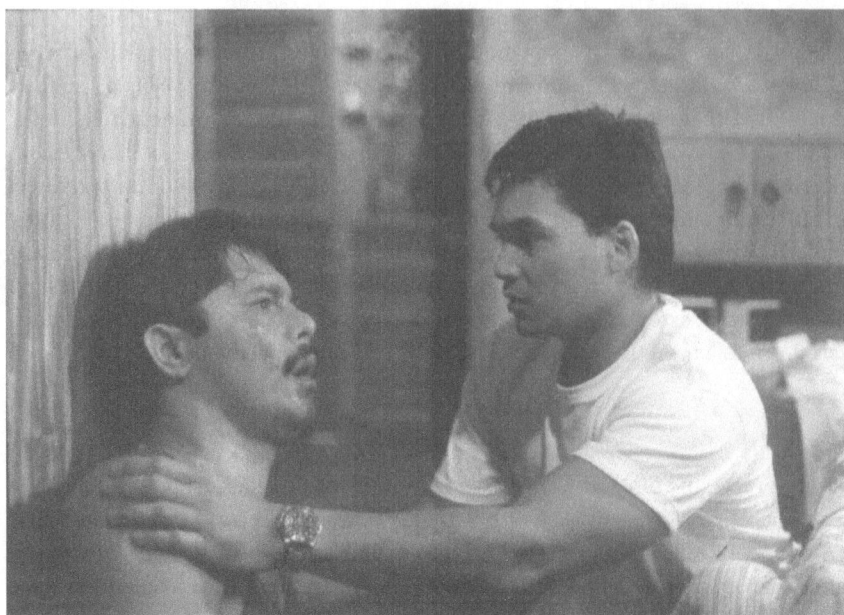

FIGURE 8.2. Dick (Gabby Concepcion, right) tends to his friend Nitoy (Christopher De Leon, left) after armed men brutalize the latter and his wife. *Sparkle in the Dark*. Courtesy of Danilo Brocka/CCP Library.

time interest in sociopolitical signification suggests the aptness of such an interpretive approach. Apart from the film's "Marcosian moment," the protagonists' turbulent emotional life following the attack—their unbearable guilt and trauma, their ugly recriminations, and their misdirected reprisals—are strangely evocative of the affective milieu of national politics after authoritarianism. President Aquino's critics blamed some of her failure to heal the nation's wounds on her unchecked vindictiveness, as seen, for instance, in her decision to tear down the Marcos regime's accomplishments as well as her predilection for shutting out allies like Brocka over both minor and principled disagreements.

I venture that Brocka's filmmaking practice indelibly changed Philippine cinema by supercharging Filipino melodrama with sociopolitical valences and teaching Filipino moviegoers to appreciate a regular dose of political discourse in their popular entertainment. Film and literature scholars have used Mikhail Bakhtin's term "genre memory" to describe, among other things, the familiar narratives, historical resonances, and sociopolitical meanings that accrue over time in popular genres.[26] I imagine that Brocka's films have left their share of traces on the genre memory of the Filipino melodrama and the nation's mainstream cinema more broadly. His martial law–era films—and those of other directors inspired by his example—enhanced Philippine cinema's sensitivity for registering politics. His oeuvre activated popular cinema's many signs, features, and conventions as luminous fields of sociopolitical signification. The results seem to have persisted long after Brocka's death. Indeed, even in the twenty-first century, sociopolitical subplots are quite prevalent both in commercial movies as well as the vast majority of independent films from the Philippines. For instance, contemporary romances take up such important social issues as labor migration, Filipino American transnational belonging, and the Communist Party's stance toward gay couples. Even when the depictions of sociopolitical concerns seem half-baked or perfunctory, the mere fact that they are now thought to be one of the basic features of popular cinema is remarkable enough. This mundane politicization of mass entertainment is the legacy of a struggle to save and cultivate democracy through cinema. Indeed, the ubiquity of political figurations has become a hallmark of Philippine movies. It is a tribute to Brocka, to martial law melodramas, and to the vibrant film culture and cinema politics of the era.

NOTES

PREFACE

1. Isagani Cruz, *Movie Times* (Manila: National Book Store, 1984), 279.
2. Nestor Torre, "Obsession," in *The Urian Anthology, 1980–1989*, ed. Nicanor Tiongson (Manila: A. P. Tuviera, 2001), 159.
3. Jacques Fieschi, "Violences," *Cinématographe*, April 1982, 17.
4. Bienvenido Lumbera, "The Philippine Film, 1961–1992," in *Re-viewing Filipino Cinema* (Manila: Anvil, 2011), 24.
5. "Film Prod. Funding, Nat'l Cinema Center Eyed for Philippines," *Variety*, February 25, 1981, 41.
6. David A. Rosenberg, ed., *Marcos and Martial Law in the Philippines* (Ithaca, NY: Cornell University Press, 1979), 44.
7. Emmanuel S. de Dios, "The Erosion of the Dictatorship," in *Dictatorship and Revolution: Roots of People's Power*, ed. Aurora Javate de Dios, Petronilo Daroy, and Lorna Kalaw-Tirol (Manila: Conspectus Foundation, 1988), 78.
8. Rigoberto Tiglao, "Consolidation of the Dictatorship," in *Dictatorship and Revolution: Roots of People's Power*, ed. Aurora Javate de Dios, Petronilo Daroy, and Lorna Kalaw-Tirol (Manila: Conspectus Foundation, 1988), 41.
9. Albert F. Celoza, *Ferdinand Marcos and the Philippines: The Political Economy of Authoritarianism* (Westport, CT: Greenwood, 1997), 47.
10. Rosenberg, *Marcos and Martial Law in the Philippines*, 21.
11. Celoza, *Ferdinand Marcos and the Philippines*, 65.
12. G. Luis Igaya, "The Political Economy of the Philippine Democratic Transition," in *Transitions to Democracy in East and Southeast Asia*, ed. Kristina N. Gaerlan (Quezon City: Institute for Popular Democracy, 1999), 18.
13. Lumbera, "The Philippine Film, 1961–1992," 23.

14. John Lent, *The Asian Film Industry* (Austin: University of Texas Press, 1990), 176.
15. "Marcos Ups Penalties for 'Subversive' Films in Philippines Decree," *Variety*, August 25, 1976, 32.
16. Lumbera, "The Philippine Film, 1961–1992," 23.
17. D.D., "Censors Okay 'Init' Film," *Philippines Daily Express*, February 2, 1979.
18. "Filipino Censorship a Model for Control over Pic Content," *Variety*, May 17, 1978, 427.
19. Aaron Pines, "New, Meatier Censor Body Is Formed Post-Fest in Manila," *Variety*, February 23, 1983, 41.
20. Todd McCarthy, "Philippines Lets '*Jaguar*' out of Cage for Cannes, Nowhere Else," *Daily Variety*, April 7, 1980.
21. "Far East: Despite Beefs, Filipino Pix Biz Is Booming, Cinemas Spring Up," *Variety*, May 11, 1977, 441.
22. Joel David, *The National Pastime: Contemporary Philippine Cinema* (Pasig: Anvil, 1990), 5.
23. Jessie B. Garcia, "New Wave in Tagalog Movies," *Focus Philippines*, November 30, 1974, 13.
24. Emmanuel A. Reyes, *Notes on Philippine Cinema* (Manila: De La Salle University Press, 1989), 100.
25. Nestor Torre, "Classics of the Filipino Film," *CCP Encyclopedia of Philippine Art* (Manila: Cultural Center of the Philippines, 1994), 55.
26. Ramon Magsaysay Award Foundation, *Ramon Magsaysay Award: Journalism, Literature & Creative Communication Arts 1985: Lino Brocka* (Manila: Ramon Magsaysay Award Foundation, 1990), 11.
27. Edmund Sicam, "The First Critic of Every Film Should Be the Director Himself," *Manila Chronicle*, December 20, 1987.
28. Jose A. Quirino, "The Unsinkable Lino Brocka," *Focus Philippines*, June 28, 1975.
29. Ishko Lopez, "Filmclips," *Asia-Philippines Leader*, November 26, 1971, 53.
30. Butch Francisco, "Lino Brocka: The Craft and Business of Television," in *Lino Brocka: The Artist and His Times*, ed. Mario A. Hernando (Manila: Cultural Center of the Philippines, 1993), 49.
31. Benjamin Pimentel, *UG: An Underground Tale* (Manila: Anvil, 2006), 22.
32. William Chapman, *Inside the Philippine Revolution* (New York: W. W. Norton, 1987), 12.
33. Robert L. Youngblood, *Marcos against the Church: Economic Development and Political Repression in the Philippines* (Ithaca, NY: Cornell University Press, 1990), 17.
34. Lewis E. Gleeck, *President Marcos and the Philippine Political Culture* (Manila: L. E. Gleeck, 1987), 70.
35. Ricardo Lo, "A, Ewan, Baska kina direk pa rin ako [I'm Standing by My Director]," *Weekly Graphic*, December 1, 1971.
36. Paula Carolina Malay, "Farewell, Lino," *Sunday Times Magazine*, June 2, 1991, Clippings on Lino Brocka, MOWELFUND Film Institute.
37. Ramon Magsaysay Award Foundation, *Ramon Magsaysay Award 1985: Lino Brocka*, 24.
38. "Brocka & Cervantes Freed from Prison," *Variety*, February 20, 1985, 3.

39. Mario A. Hernando, "Lino Brocka: Director in Control Blending Popular Entertainment, Realism and Social Comment," in *Lino Brocka: The Artist and His Times*, ed. Mario A. Hernando (Manila: Cultural Center of the Philippines, 1993), 41.

40. Alain Badiou, *Cinema*, trans. Susan Spitzer (Malden, MA: Polity Press, 2013), 45.

41. Badiou, *Cinema*, 10.

42. Michel Ciment, "Entretien avec Lino Brocka," *Positif*, no. 231 (1980): 27.

43. Jacques Rancière, *The Intervals of Cinema*, trans. John Howe (London: Verso, 2014), 13.

44. Rancière, *The Intervals of Cinema*, 103.

45. Martin O'Shaughnessy, *The New Face of Political Cinema: Commitment in French Film since 1995* (New York: Berghahn Books, 2008); Mike Wayne, *Political Film: The Dialectics of Third Cinema* (London: Pluto Press, 2001).

46. Gilles Deleuze, *Cinema 2: The Time-Image* (Minneapolis: University of Minnesota Press, 1989), 216.

47. Linda Williams, *Playing the Race Card: Melodramas of Black and White from Uncle Tom to O. J. Simpson* (Princeton, NJ: Princeton University Press, 2001), 11.

48. Michael Walker, "Melodrama and American Cinema," *Movie* 29/30 (Summer 1982): 16.

49. Ravi Vasudevan, "Addressing the Spectator of a 'Third World' National Cinema: The Bombay 'Social' Film of the 1940s and 1950s," in *Film and Theory: An Anthology*, ed. Robert Stam and Toby Miller (Malden, MA: Blackwell, 2000), 382.

50. Christine Gledhill, "Between Melodrama and Realism: Anthony Asquith's *Underground* and King Vidor's *The Crowd*," in *Classical Hollywood Narrative: The Paradigm Wars*, ed. Jane M. Gaines (Durham, NC: Duke University Press, 1992), 131.

51. Williams, *Playing the Race Card*, 15.

52. Williams, *Playing the Race Card*, 307.

53. Elisabeth Anker, "Left Melodrama," *Contemporary Political Theory* 11, no. 2 (May 2012): 131.

54. Anker, "Left Melodrama," 142.

55. Anker, "Left Melodrama," 131.

56. Cruz, *Movie Times*, 290.

57. Clodualdo Del Mundo Jr., "*Kapit sa patalim* and *Orapronobis*: Stories of Our Country and Brocka's Melodramatic Strategy: A Review of *Kapit sa patalim* and *Orapronobis*," in *Lino Brocka: The Artist and His Times*, ed. Mario A. Hernando (Manila: Cultural Center of the Philippines, 1993), 189.

58. Guillermo C. de Vega, *Film and Freedom: Movie Censorship in the Philippines* (Manila: Guillermo de Vega, 1975), 104.

59. Bonnie Honig, *Antigone, Interrupted* (New York: Cambridge University Press, 2013), 69.

60. Jacques Rancière, *The Emancipated Spectator* (London: Verso, 2011), 74.

61. Rancière, *The Emancipated Spectator*, 103.

62. Rancière, *The Emancipated Spectator*, 105.

63. Lino Brocka, "The State of the Film Industry," in *The Politics of Culture: The Philippine Experience*, ed. Nicanor G. Tiongson (Manila: PETA, 1984), 51.

64. Rolando B. Tolentino, *Contestable Nation-Space: Cinema, Cultural Politics, and Transnationalism in the Marcos-Brocka Philippines* (Quezon City: University of the Philippines Press, 2014); Talitha Espiritu, *Passionate Revolutions: The Media and the Rise and Fall of the Marcos Regime* (Athens: Ohio University Press, 2017); Arminda V. Santiago, "The Struggle of the Oppressed: Lino Brocka and the New Cinema of the Philippines" (master's thesis, University of North Texas, 1993).

65. Bienvenido Lumbera, "Philippine Film: A Brief History (1989)," in *Re-viewing Filipino Cinema* (Manila: Anvil, 2011), 15.

66. Paterno Esmaquel II, "Duterte Donor Imee Marcos Not in His SOCE," *Rappler*, October 11, 2016, http://www.rappler.com/nation/politics/elections/2016/148841-duterte-imee-marcos-campaign-contributor-soce.

67. Amnesty International, "Philippines: Duterte's 100 Days of Carnage," October 7, 2016, https://www.amnesty.org/en/latest/news/2016/10/philippines-dutertes-hundred-days-of-carnage/.

68. Rachel A. G. Reyes, "Counting the Killings: 20,000 and Rising," *The Manila Times*, April 24, 2018, https://www.manilatimes.net/counting-the-killings-20000-and-rising/394576/.

69. Alfred W. McCoy, "Dark Legacy: Human Rights under the Marcos Dictatorship," in *Memory, Truth Telling, and the Pursuit of Justice: A Conference on the Legacies of the Marcos Dictatorship* (Quezon City: Office of Research and Publications, 2001), 131.

70. Nash Jenkins, "Philippines: Duterte Threatens 'Martial Law' In War on Drugs," *Time*, August 9, 2016, http://time.com/4446169/duterte-philippines-martial-law-drugs/.

71. Maila Ager, "Congress Has Power to Tackle Martial Law in Joint Session," *Inquirer.net*, June 1, 2017, http://newsinfo.inquirer.net/901727/congress-has-mandate-to-tackle-martial-law-in-joint-session-says-nene-pimentel.

72. Vernise Tantuco, "Brillante Mendoza on SONA 2016 Criticism: 'Let's Limit It to the Craft,'" *Rappler*, July 27, 2016, http://www.rappler.com/entertainment/news/141120-sona-2016-director-brillante-mendoza-criticism-propaganda-comparison.

CHAPTER 1. THE COUNTRY AND THE CITY

1. Manuel Caoili, *The Origins of Metropolitan Manila: A Social and Political Analysis* (Quezon City: University of the Philippines Press, 1999), 140.

2. Raymond Bonner, *Waltzing with a Dictator* (New York: Random House, 1987), 78.

3. Petronilo Daroy, "On the Eve of Dictatorship and Revolution," in *Dictatorship and Revolution: Roots of People's Power*, ed. Aurora Javate de Dios, Petronilo Daroy, and Lorna Kalaw-Tirol (Manila: Conspectus Foundation, 1988), 7.

4. Joey Martinez, "Lino Brocka: The 34-Carat Director," 1974, 38, Clippings, Lino O. Brocka Collection (hereafter LOBC).

5. Ricardo Lee, "Batubato sa langit ang tamaa'y harang [Sticks and Stones]," *Asia Philippines Leader*, April 10, 1971, 43; Ishko Lopez, "Filmclips," *Asia-Philippines Leader*, August 25, 1972, 16.

6. Richie Benavides, "Lino Brocka: Self-Critic," August 26, 1972, 15, Clippings, LOBC.

7. Martinez, "The 34-Carat Director."

8. Fanny A. Garcia, "Lino Brocka: Direktor para sa mga Pilipino [Directing for Filipinos]," *Sagisag*, July 1975, 46.
9. Nelia Tan, "Sa pagbabalik ni direktor Lino Brocka, alin-aling bagay ang titimbangin? [Brocka's Comeback: What Matters Will He Weigh?]," *Pilipino Express*, February 27, 1974, 9.
10. Martinez, "The 34-Carat Director."
11. "With Cine Manila Here, Can A-1 Films Be Far Behind?," *Times Journal*, February 4, 1974.
12. "With Cine Manila Here."
13. Tan, "Brocka's Comeback."
14. Billy Balbastro, "At Long Last, an Intelligent Movie," *Home Life*, June 1974, 31.
15. Martinez, "The 34-Carat Director."
16. Tan, "Brocka's Comeback," 9.
17. John G. Cawleti, *Adventure, Mystery, and Romance: Formula Stories as Art and Popular Culture* (Chicago: University of Chicago Press, 1976), 260.
18. Cawleti, *Adventure, Mystery, and Romance*, 261.
19. Doreen Fernandez, *Panitikan: An Essay on Philippine Literature* (Manila: Cultural Center of the Philippines, 1989), 17.
20. Soledad S. Reyes, *From Darna to Zsazsa Zaturnnah: Desire and Fantasy* (Pasig City: Anvil, 2009), 255.
21. Epifanio San Juan, *Rizal in Our Time: Essays in Interpretation* (Manila: Anvil, 2011), xi.
22. Noel Vera, "'Tinimbang' Judged Today," in *Critic After Dark: A Review of Philippine Cinema* (Singapore: BigO Books, 2005), 186.
23. San Juan, *Rizal in Our Time*, 104.
24. Joe Quirino, "Brocka's Rejoinder," *Times Journal*, January 23, 1976, 8.
25. San Juan, *Rizal in Our Time*, 15.
26. San Juan, *Rizal in Our Time*, 103.
27. San Juan, *Rizal in Our Time*, 14.
28. Fredric Jameson, *The Geopolitical Aesthetic: Cinema and Space in the World System* (Bloomington: Indiana University Press, 1995), 3.
29. Mario O'Hara, "Screenplay of *Tinimbang ka ngunit kulang*" (n.d.), Scripts, LOBC. The script calls for some of the dialogue at the wake "to be improvised on set by the director and actors for a natural and boisterous cacophony" ("magi-improvise na lang on the set ang director at ang mga artista para lumabas na natural at maingay, sabay-sabay, walang kawawaan"); see page 12. The seduction at the bowling hall, minus the line about the curfew, is found on pages 30–31.
30. Albert F. Celoza, *Ferdinand Marcos and the Philippines: The Political Economy of Authoritarianism* (Westport, CT: Greenwood, 1997), 41.
31. David A. Rosenberg, ed., *Marcos and Martial Law in the Philippines* (Ithaca, NY: Cornell University Press, 1979), 35.
32. G. N. Zaragoza, "Lino, Kuala and Wonder Vi," *Philippine Collegian*, July 8, 1974.
33. O'Hara, "*Tinimbang ka ngunit kulang* Screenplay," 50–51.
34. Luis Francia, "Brocka: From Bang to Fizzle," in *Memories of Overdevelopment: Reviews and Essays of Two Decades* (Pasig City: Anvil Publishing, 1998), 36.

35. Hamid Naficy, "The Americanization and Indigenization of Lino Brocka through Cinema: An Interview," *Framework*, no. 38 (1992): 141–42.

36. Jose F. Lacaba, *Emmanuel Lacaba: Salvaged Poems* (Manila: Salinlahi Publishing House, 1986), 133.

37. Lacaba, *Emmanuel Lacaba*, 15.

38. Vicente Rafael, "Patronage, Pornography, and Youth: Ideology and Spectatorship during the Early Marcos Years," in *White Love and Other Events in Filipino History* (Quezon City: Ateneo De Manila University Press, 2000), 150.

39. Lino Brocka, "Pasasalamat [Gratitude]: Newspaper Advertisement for '*Tinimbang ka ngunit kulang*,'" June 21, 1974, Clippings, LOBC.

40. Jose A. Quirino, "The Unsinkable Lino Brocka," *Focus Philippines*, June 28, 1975, 46.

41. CineManila, "*Tinimbang ka ngunit kulang*" (Marketing Brochure, n.d.), Scripts, LOBC.

42. Quirino, "The Unsinkable Lino Brocka," 46.

43. Amelia Lapeña-Bonifacio, *Sepang Loca and Others* (Quezon City: University of the Philippines Press, 1981), 101–2, 131–49.

44. Quirino, "The Unsinkable Lino Brocka," 47.

45. Quirino, "The Unsinkable Lino Brocka," 47.

46. Balbastro, "At Long Last," 31.

47. Jesselynn L. Garcia, "A Plea, an Accusation," n.d., Clippings, LOBC.

48. Jorge Arago, "Lino Brocka's '*Tinimbang ka*,'" n.d., Clippings, LOBC. A review in *Variety* appears to have lifted much of its content from Arago's review. See Anon., "Review of *Tinimbang ka nguni't kulang*," *Variety*, July 17, 1974, 18.

49. Jessie B. Garcia, "Social Realism in Filipino Movies," *Philippine Graphic*, August 18, 1971, 31.

50. Jessie B. Garcia, "New Wave in Tagalog Movies," *Focus Philippines*, November 30, 1974, 41.

51. Francia, "Brocka: From Bang to Fizzle," 34.

52. Francia, "Brocka: From Bang to Fizzle," 35.

53. David Bordwell and Kristin Thompson, *Film Art: An Introduction*, tenth edition (New York, N.Y: McGraw-Hill Education, 2012), 59.

54. Balbastro, "At Long Last," 31.

55. Garcia, "A Plea, an Accusation."

56. Justino M. Dormiendo, "Brocka's Breakthroughs," *Philippines Sunday Express*, June 13, 1976, 28.

57. Jerry Sussman, "Lino Brocka on Film," December 19, 1975, Clippings, LOBC.

58. Arago, "Lino Brocka's 'Tinimbang Ka.'"

59. Charles Tesson, "The Cult of the Image in Lino," in *Lino Brocka: The Artist and His Times*, ed. Mario A. Hernando, trans. Ma. Teresa Manuel (Manila: Cultural Center of the Philippines, 1993), 160.

60. Gina Marchetti, "Four Hundred Years in a Convent; Fifty in Hollywood: Sexual Identity and Dissent in Contemporary Philippine Cinema," *East-West Film Journal* 2 (June 1988): 38.

61. Marchetti, "Four Hundred Years in a Convent," 38.

62. Marchetti, "Four Hundred Years in a Convent," 38.
63. Jeremy Tambling, *Allegory* (New York: Routledge, 2009), 119.
64. CineManila, "They're Raving! So Will You!" Newspaper Advertisement for *Tinimbang ka ngunit kulang* (*Times Journal*, June 1, 1974), Clippings, LOBC.
65. Chelo R. Banal, "Brocka: Earth, Wind and Fire," *Philippine Panorama*, August 10, 1975, 17.
66. Zaragoza, "Lino, Kuala and Wonder Vi," 6.
67. Zaragoza, "Lino, Kuala and Wonder Vi," 6.
68. Clodualdo del Mundo Jr., "Preface," in *Maynila . . . 'Merika, Alyas Raha Matanda: Tatlong dulang pampelikula [Three screenplays]* (Manila: De La Salle University Press, 1992), 2.
69. Flor Caagusan, "Interview with Mike De Leon," *Diliman Review*, October 1983, 48.
70. Email from Curtis Tsui, producer for the Criterion Collection, quoting Mike De Leon's response to a query from José Capino, March 13, 2018.
71. Ferdinand Marcos, *Notes on the New Society of the Philippines* (Manila: Marcos Foundation, 1973), 102.
72. Clodualdo del Mundo Jr., "Maynila . . . *Isang pelikulang Filipino* [A Filipino film]," Blu-ray, special feature in *Two Films by Lino Brocka* (London: British Film Institute, 2017).
73. Michael Pinches, "Modernisation and the Quest for Modernity: Architectural Form, Squatter Settlements and the New Society in Manila," in *Cultural Identity and Urban Change in Southeast Asia: Interpretative Essays*, ed. William Stewart Logan and Marc Askew (Geelong, Victoria: Deakin University Press, 1994), 17.
74. Raymond Williams, *The Country and the City* (New York: Oxford University Press, 1973), 239.
75. Gavin Shatkin, "Planning to Forget: Informal Settlements as 'Forgotten Places' in Globalising Metro Manila," in *Globalisation and the Politics of Forgetting*, ed. Yong-Sook Lee and Brenda S. A. Yeoh (New York: Routledge, 2006), 176.
76. Marcos, *Notes on the New Society*, 57.
77. Caoili, *Origins of Metropolitan Manila*, 75.
78. Imelda Romualdez Marcos, "City of Man," in *The Ideas of Imelda Romualdez Marcos*, ed. Ileana Maramag, vol. I (Manila: National Media Production Center, 1978), 258.
79. Shatkin, "Planning to Forget," 184.
80. Marcos, "City of Man," 261.
81. Pinches, "Modernisation," 31.
82. Pinches, Modernisation," 31.
83. Caoili, *Origins of Metropolitan Manila*, 150.
84. Marcos, "City of Man," 259.
85. Caoili, *Origins of Metropolitan Manila*, 69.
86. Caoili, *Origins of Metropolitan Manila*, 1.
87. André Bazin, *André Bazin and Italian Neorealism*, ed. Bert Cardullo (London: Bloomsbury, 2011), 187.
88. Bazin, *André Bazin and Italian Neorealism*, 6.
89. Bazin, *André Bazin and Italian Neorealism*, 48.
90. Bazin, *André Bazin and Italian Neorealism*, 171.

91. Patrick Flores, "The Slum and the Town: Reassessing the Brocka Paradigm in Philippine Progressive Cinema," *Diliman Review* 39, no. 4 (1992): 45–52. Those invested in ferreting out poverty porn from ostensibly more ethical representations of poverty are often unmindful of the fraught cultural politics behind making such problematic distinctions, including the privileging of the critics' judgment above those of filmmakers and viewers, and the implicit bias against exploitation movies and films that are well received at international festivals, both of which are most likely to get slapped with the pejorative label.

92. Cristina del Carmen, "Lino Brocka: The Director Is Also a Star," *WHO*, April 10, 1982, 26.

93. Ronald Constantino, "Explosive Scene ni Brocka sa 'Maynila' [Brocka's Explosive Scene]," n.d., Clippings, LOBC.

94. Email from Curtis Tsui quoting Mike De Leon's response.

95. Marquita Doassans and Nef Diffusion, "*Manille dans les griffes du neon*" (Press kit, ca 1982), 7, Scripts, LOBC.

96. Email from Curtis Tsui, producer for the Criterion Collection, about scenes excised from *Manila*, February 21, 2018.

97. Joel David, "Thinking Straight: Queer Imaging in Lino Brocka's *Maynila* (1975)," *Plaridel* 9, no. 2 (August 2012): 27; Lito Zulueta, "Macho Dancer: A More Cynical Brocka," *Manila Chronicle*, January 25, 1989, 9.

98. Clodualdo del Mundo Jr., "Production Script of *Maynila: Sa mga kuko ng liwanag*" (n.d.), 77, Scripts, LOBC.

99. Zulueta, "Macho Dancer: A More Cynical Brocka"; David, "Thinking Straight," 29.

100. Mac Alejandre, "Brocka Refutes Criticisms," *Sunday Times*, July 23, 1989, Clippings.

101. Ronald Wintrobe, *The Political Economy of Dictatorship* (New York: Cambridge University Press, 1998), 55.

102. Email from Curtis Tsui about scenes excised from *Manila*.

103. Caagusan, "Interview with Mike De Leon," 52.

104. "'*Maynila: Sa mga kuko ng liwanag*' Reshown," n.d., Clippings, LOBC.

105. Rose Hilario, "The Trail Brocka Blazes," *Philippines Daily Express?*, August 14, 1975, Clippings, LOBC.

106. Box office data for old films is hard to find in the Philippines. *Manila*'s screenwriter, Clodualdo del Mundo Jr. recalls in an email correspondence that he saw many theaters filled to capacity during the film's opening.

107. "Filipino Dialect Pics Exceed All Imports in Home Market," *Variety*, May 14, 1975. The article cites a $50–$100,000 range in the budget of Filipino movies. The US dollar-Philippine peso exchange rate that year was officially recorded at 1:7.5, but was 1:8.5 in the black market.

108. Caagusan, "Interview with Mike De Leon," 49.

109. Ma. Socorro Garcia Roque, "Goodbye to Fantasyland," n.d., Clippings, LOBC.

110. Cristina Pantoja-Hidalgo, "Pros and Cons on the Best Local Film," *Times Journal*, July 21, 1975, 15.

111. Mario A. Hernando, "*Maynila*: Brocka's Best," in *The Urian Anthology, 1970–1979*, ed. Nicanor G. Tiongson (Manila: M. L. Morato, 1983), 213.

112. Culture Staff, "Many Facets of a Film," *Philippine Collegian*, July 30, 1975, 7.
113. M. R. Avena, "Where '*Maynila*' Fails," *Philippine Panorama*, August 10, 1979, 17–18.
114. Thomas Schatz, *Hollywood Genres: Formulas, Filmmaking, and The Studio System* (Boston, MA: McGraw-Hill, 1981), 23; Elsaesser, "Tales of Sound and Fury: Observations on the Family Melodrama," 53.
115. José Rizal, *Noli me tangere (Touch Me Not)*, trans. Harold Augenbraum (New York: Penguin, 2006), 169–70.
116. Rizal, *Noli me tangere*, 93.
117. Rizal, *Noli me tangere*, 97.
118. Justino M. Dormiendo, "Mula sa eskapismo tungo sa realismo [From Escapism to Realism]," *Sagisag*, August 1975, 54.
119. "A Brief on *Sa mga kuko ng liwanag* (Or Why *Maynila* Should Ever Be Masculine)," in *Sa mga kuko ng liwanag*, by Edgardo M. Reyes (Quezon City: C & E Publishing, 2007), xxiv.
120. Roque, "Goodbye to Fantasyland."
121. Culture Staff, "Many Facets of a Film," 7.
122. Culture Staff, "Many Facets of a Film," 7.
123. Culture Staff, "Many Facets of a Film," 7.
124. Agustin L. Sotto, "Interview with Lino Brocka on *Maynila: Sa mga kuko ng liwanag*," in *Lino Brocka: The Artist and His Times*, ed. Mario A. Hernando (Manila: Cultural Center of the Philippines, 1993), 226.
125. Caroline S. Hau, *Necessary Fictions: Philippine Literature and the Nation, 1946–1980* (Quezon City: Ateneo de Manila Univ. Press, 2000), 165.
126. Caroline S. Hau, "Conditions of Visibility: Resignifying the 'Chinese'/'Filipino' in *Mano po* and *Crying Ladies*," *Philippine Studies* 53, no. 4 (2005): 521.
127. Amy Chua, *World on Fire* (New York: Doubleday, 2003), 2–5; "A Brief," xxii.
128. Marchetti, "Four Hundred Years in a Convent," 34.
129. Hernando, "*Maynila*: Brocka's Best," 212.
130. Hernando, "*Maynila*: Brocka's Best," 212.
131. Bienvenido Lumbera, "Review of *Maynila: Sa mga kuko ng liwanag* (Cinema Artists Productions)," in *Lino Brocka: The Artist and His Times*, ed. Mario A. Hernando (Manila: Cultural Center of the Philippines, 1993), 115.
132. Bienvenido Lumbera, "Ang problema ng *Maynila: Sa mga kuko ng liwanag* [The Problem with *Maynila*]," in *Re-Viewing Filipino Cinema* (Mandaluyong City: Anvil, 2011), 169.
133. Sotto, "Interview with Lino Brocka on *Maynila*," 223.
134. Lumbera, "The Problem with *Maynila*," 168–69.
135. Lumbera, "The Problem with *Maynila*," 169.
136. The film's production script identifies the Japanese firms advertised in two of the neon billboards, substituting them for the illuminated sign for the City University of Manila specified in Reyes's novel. The script also suggests titles of English songs heard during particular scenes.
137. Pinches, "Modernisation," 28, 26.
138. Fredric Jameson, *Signatures of the Visible* (New York: Routledge, 2013), 54.

139. Friedrich Engels, *The Condition of the Working Class in England*, ed. David McLellan and Florence Kelley (Oxford: Oxford University Press, 1999), xvii.

140. John G. Cawelti, *Adventure, Mystery, and Romance: Formula Stories as Art and Popular Culture* (Chicago: University of Chicago Press, 1976), 262.

141. Cawelti, *Adventure, Mystery, and Romance*, 261.

142. Cawelti, *Adventure, Mystery, and Romance*, 264.

143. Cawelti, *Adventure, Mystery, and Romance*, 266.

144. Lumbera, "The Problem with *Maynila*," 170.

145. Mario E. Bautista, "The Essential Brocka Part II: Filmmaker," *Philippines Daily Express*, September 1978.

CHAPTER 2. "A THOROUGHLY DIFFERENT KIND OF MOTHER"

1. Mary Ann Doane, *The Desire to Desire: The Woman's Film of the 1940s* (Bloomington: Indiana University Press, 1987), 73.

2. Noel Vera, *Critic after Dark: A Review of Philippine Cinema* (Singapore: BigO Books, 2005), 189.

3. E. Ann Kaplan, *Motherhood and Representation: The Mother in Popular Culture and Melodrama* (New York: Routledge, 1992), 115.

4. Emmanuel A. Reyes, "The World on Her Shoulders: Women in Melodrama," in *Notes on Philippine Cinema* (Manila: De La Salle University Press, 1989), 44.

5. Rolando B. Tolentino, "Inangbayan, the Mother-Nation, in Lino Brocka's *Bayan ko: Kapit sa patalim* and *Orapronobis*," *Screen* 37, no. 4 (1996): 368–88.

6. Marsha Kinder, *Blood Cinema: The Reconstruction of National Identity in Spain* (Berkeley: University of California Press, 1993), 198.

7. Kinder, *Blood Cinema*, 199.

8. Kinder, *Blood Cinema*, 225.

9. Barbara Creed, "The Position of Women in Hollywood Melodramas," *Australian Journal of Screen Theory* 4 (1978): 27.

10. Michael Walker, "Melodrama and American Cinema," *Movie* 29/30 (Summer 1982): 18.

11. Franz Samelson, "The Authoritarian Character from Berlin to Berkeley and Beyond: The Odyssey of a Problem," in *Strength and Weakness: The Authoritarian Personality Today*, ed. William F. Stone, Gerda Lederer, and Richard Christie (New York: Springer-Verlag, 1993), 28.

12. Samelson, "The Authoritarian Character," 35.

13. Theodor W. Adorno et al., *The Authoritarian Personality*, abridged edition (New York: Norton, 1982), 259, and 356. I owe this summation to Samelson, cited above.

14. Samelson, "The Authoritarian Character," 25.

15. Katherine W. Ellison, *Imelda, Steel Butterfly of the Philippines* (New York: McGraw-Hill, 1988), 118.

16. "Naiibang Papel Kay Mona Lisa [A Different Role]," n.d., Clippings, LOBC.

17. Agustin L. Sotto, "Interview with Lino Brocka on *Insiang*," in *Lino Brocka: The Artist and His Times*, ed. Mario A. Hernando (Manila: Cultural Center of the Philippines, 1993), 227.

18. F. Landa Jocano, *Slum as a Way of Life* (Quezon City: Punlad Research House, 2002), 113.
19. Kinder, *Blood Cinema*, 202.
20. Adorno et al., *The Authoritarian Personality*, 346–85.
21. Ronald Wintrobe, *The Political Economy of Dictatorship* (New York: Cambridge University Press, 1998), 15.
22. Adorno et al., *The Authoritarian Personality*, 363.
23. Belen T. G. Medina, *The Filipino Family*, third edition (Quezon City: University of the Philippines Press, 2015), 229.
24. Sotto, "Interview with Lino Brocka on *Insiang*," 228.
25. Mario O'Hara, "*Insiang* Teleplay" (n.d.), 6, Scripts, LOBC.
26. O'Hara, "*Insiang* Teleplay," 16.
27. Linda Williams, "'Something Else Besides a Mother: *Stella Dallas* and the Maternal Melodrama," in *Issues in Feminist Film Criticism*, ed. Patricia Erens (Bloomington: Indiana University Press, 1990), 158.
28. Sotto, "Interview with Lino Brocka on *Insiang*," 227.
29. Mario O'Hara, "Synopsis of *Insiang*, 2nd of 2" (n.d.), 2, Scripts, LOBC.
30. O'Hara, "*Insiang* Teleplay," 17. The Filipino dialogue reads: "Hindi, inay. Hindi ko siya minahal kahit kailan. Kinasusuklaman ko siya. Nagpalit lamang tayo ng lugar, inay. Ngayon, nakaganti na ako."
31. Mario O'Hara, "Synopsis of *Insiang*, 1st of 2" (n.d.), 3, Scripts, LOBC.
32. Chelo R. Banal, "Take Four," *Philippine Panorama*, December 26, 1976, 26.
33. Adorno et al., *The Authoritarian Personality*, 364.
34. "Filipino Censorship a Model for Control Over Pic Content," *Variety*, May 17, 1978, 427.
35. Pablo Tariman, "The Small, Big World of Lino Brocka," n.d., Clippings, LOBC. The quotation on the country's "true image" comes from Brocka's paraphrase, which Tariman reports.
36. André Bazin, *André Bazin and Italian Neorealism*, ed. Bert Cardullo (London: Bloomsbury, 2011), 27.
37. Jo-Ann Q. Maglipon, "Brocka, Imelda, Imee . . . and Other Vanities," *Manila Times*, May 24, 1986.
38. Mario O'Hara, "*Insiang* Teleplay" (n.d.), 2, Scripts, LOBC.
39. "Tri-Dimensional Effect of 'Insiang,'" *Philippines Daily Express*, December 29, 1976.
40. Maglipon, "Brocka, Imelda, Imee . . . and Other Vanities."
41. Cristina del Carmen, "Lino Brocka: The Director Is Also a Star," *WHO*, April 10, 1982, 27.
42. del Carmen, "Lino Brocka: The Director Is Also a Star," 26.
43. "Imee Heads Sponsors of 'Insiang' Premiere," *Philippines Evening Express*, December 20, 1976.
44. "Sapang Palay Is Example of Resettlement as a Continuing Task of Rehabilitation," *Philippines Daily Express*, December 21, 1976, 33.
45. "Brocka Creates 'Insiang,'" *Times Journal*, December 22, 1976.
46. Michael Pinches, "Modernisation and the Quest for Modernity: Architectural Form, Squatter Settlements and the New Society in Manila," in *Cultural Identity and Urban*

Change in Southeast Asia: Interpretative Essays, ed. William Stewart Logan and Marc Askew (Geelong, Victoria: Deakin University Press, 1994), 31.

47. Pinches, "Modernisation and the Quest for Modernity," 27.
48. Mario O'Hara, "Synopsis of *Insiang*, 2nd of 2" (n.d.), 2, Scripts, LOBC.
49. "Top Cinematographer behind *'Insiang'* Camera," *Evening Post*, December 15, 1976.
50. Chelo R. Banal, "Take Four," *Philippine Panorama*, December 26, 1976, 26.
51. Mel Tobias, "Rare Ruby of the Philippines," *Screen International*, May 23, 1978.
52. Tobias, "Rare Ruby of the Philippines."
53. Diego C. Cagahastian, "Umuunlad na ang panlasa ng masa [The mass audience has gotten more sophisticated]," *Pilipino Express*, January 7, 1977.
54. GAC, "Ang *'Insiang'* ang maituturing na pinakamalaking pagsubok . . . [The Greatest Challenge . . .]," n.d., Clippings, LOBC.
55. Ethel C. Causapin, "Lino Brocka's *'Insiang'* Touches on the Psychology of Slum Living," n.d., Clippings, LOBC.
56. Zenaida LaTorre, "Show-Buzz," n.d., Clippings, LOBC.
57. Billy R. Balbastro, "Studio Whispers," *Evening Post*, December 30, 1976, Clippings, LOBC.
58. Pio de Castro III, "A Monument to the Human Spirit," *Times Journal*, December 24, 1976.
59. J. M. de M., "*Insiang*," *La Croix*, November 9, 1978.
60. Kieron Corless and Chris Darke, *Cannes: Inside the World's Premier Film Festival* (London: Faber & Faber, 2007), 153.
61. Ricardo F. Lo, "Brocka; 'On the Threshold of an International Career,'" *Expressweek*, April 20, 1978.
62. Michel Marmin, "Une ame de femme," *Le Figaro*, December 6, 1978.
63. François Maurin, "Bonjour Philippines," *L' Humanité*, December 15, 1978.
64. Michel Peréz, "*Insiang*, de Lino Brocka: Un Terrain Culturel Inconnu," *Le Matin*, December 6, 1978.
65. Albert Cervoni, "A l'opposé," *France Nouvelle*, December 18, 1978.
66. Joshka Schidlow, "*Insiang*: Des vauriens pathétiques dans les taudis philippins," *Télérama*, November 8, 1978, 102.
67. M.P., "I pour *Insiang*," *Le Matin*, May 25, 1978; Schidlow, "*Insiang*: Des vauriens pathétiques."
68. Maurin, "Bonjour Philippines."
69. Robert Chazal, "*Insiang*: Neo-realisme philippin," *France-Soir*, December 6, 1978.
70. Samuel Lachize, "Neo-realisme philippin," *L'Humanité-Dimanche*, November 1, 1978.
71. A.F., "Le premier film philippin," *Rouge*, May 27, 1978.
72. Maurin, "Bonjour Philippines."
73. Peréz, "*Insiang*, de Lino Brocka"; "En vedette," *Nouvel Observateur*, November 6, 1978; Jean-Luc Douin, "Entretien avec le réalisateur Lino Brocka," *Télérama*, November 8, 1978; Eugène Guillevic, "Un racine du tiers-monde," *Les Nouvelles Littéraires*, December 14, 1978; Paulo Antonio Paranagua, "Paris, capitale du provincialisme européocentrique," *Libération*, December 20, 1978.

74. F. F., "Capsule Review of *Insiang*," *L'Express*, November 18, 1978, 17.
75. M. Dumas, "Review of *Insiang*," *Le Quotidien de Paris*, May 21, 1978.
76. "Review of *Insiang*," *Le Canard Enchaîné*, December 13, 1978.
77. Albert F. Celoza, *Ferdinand Marcos and the Philippines: The Political Economy of Authoritarianism* (Westport, CT: Greenwood, 1997), 61.
78. "Review of *Insiang*"; "Violent," *Le Point*, December 2, 1978.
79. Lachize, "Neo-realisme philippin."
80. Andrea Walsh, *Women's Film and Female Experience, 1940-1950* (New York: Praeger, 1984), 112.
81. Mary Ann Doane, *The Desire to Desire: The Woman's Film of the 1940s* (Bloomington: Indiana University Press, 1987), 81.
82. Christian Viviani, "Who Is without Sin? The Maternal Melodrama in American Film, 1930–39," in *Home Is Where the Heart Is: Studies in Melodrama and the Woman's Film*, ed. Christine Gledhill (London: British Film Institute, 1987), 96.
83. Milan W. Svolik, *The Politics of Authoritarian Rule* (Cambridge: Cambridge University Press, 2012), 198.
84. Ronald Wintrobe, *The Political Economy of Dictatorship* (New York: Cambridge University Press, 1998), 4.
85. Ricardo Lee, "Screenplay of *Cain at Abel*" (n.d.), 1, Scripts, LOBC.
86. Theodor W. Adorno et al., *The Authoritarian Personality*, abridged edition (New York: Norton, 1982), 59.
87. Adorno et al., *The Authoritarian Personality*, 361.
88. Adorno et al., *The Authoritarian Personality*, 259.
89. Franz Samelson, "The Authoritarian Character from Berlin to Berkeley and Beyond: The Odyssey of a Problem," in *Strength and Weakness: The Authoritarian Personality Today*, ed. William F. Stone, Gerda Lederer, and Richard Christie (New York: Springer-Verlag, 1993), 128.
90. Raymond Bonner, *Waltzing with a Dictator* (New York: Random House, 1987), 369.
91. Lee, "Screenplay of *Cain at Abel*," 29.
92. Ricardo Lee, "Story Outline for *Cain at Abel*" (n.d.), 5, Scripts, LOBC.
93. William Chapman, *Inside the Philippine Revolution* (New York: W. W. Norton, 1987), 11.
94. Cine Suerte Productions, "Press Kit for *Cain at Abel*" (ca 1982), Cinémathèque de Toulouse, France.
95. Vicente Rafael, "Patronage, Pornography, and Youth: Ideology and Spectatorship during the Early Marcos Years," in *White Love and Other Events in Filipino History* (Quezon City: Ateneo De Manila University Press, 2000), 160; William Chapman, *Inside the Philippine Revolution* (New York: W. W. Norton, 1987), 192.
96. Rigoberto Tiglao, "Consolidation of the Dictatorship," in *Dictatorship and Revolution: Roots of People's Power*, ed. Aurora Javate de Dios, Petronilo Daroy, and Lorna Kalaw-Tirol (Manila: Conspectus Foundation, 1988), 57.
97. Kathleen Weekley, *The Communist Party of the Philippines, 1968–1993: A Story of Its Theory and Practice* (Quezon City: University of the Philippines Press, 2001), 72.
98. Ferdinand Marcos, *Notes on the New Society of the Philippines* (Manila: Marcos Foundation, 1973), i.

99. Marcos, *Notes on the New Society of the Philippines*, v.

100. William C. Rempel, *Delusions of a Dictator: The Mind of Marcos as Revealed in His Secret Diaries* (Boston: Little, Brown, 1993), 49.

101. Rempel, *Delusions of a Dictator*, 58.

102. Marcos, *Notes on the New Society*, 12.

103. Marcos, *Notes on the New Society*, 35.

104. Marcos, *Notes on the New Society*, 33.

105. Mike Wayne, *Political Film: The Dialectics of Third Cinema* (London: Pluto Press, 2001), 70.

106. Lee, "Story Outline for *Cain at Abel*," 8.

107. Ched P. Gonzales, "Welcome, Cine Suerte and the Best of Luck!," *Movie Specials*, May 13, 1982, Clippings, LOBC.

108. The descriptors *serious* and *important* occur respectively in Zenaida LaTorre, "Mula kay Lino Brocka, isang pambihirang proyekto [From Brocka, an Exceptional Project]," *Jingle Extra Hot*, November 4, 1982 and Boy C. DeGuia, "Bakit iba ang shooting ni Brocka? [Why Are Brocka's Shoots Different?]," *Weekly Gem*, June 8, 1982.

109. RM, "'Cain at Abel': Panlaban Ni Brocka [Brocka's Ace]," *Pogi*, September 29, 1982.

110. Cristina Gomez, "Mabago na naman kaya ni Lino Brocka ang takbo ng industriya ngayon? [Can Brocka Still Change the Industry?]," *Bulaklak*, June 7, 1982.

111. The reviewer's phrase, originally in Tagalog, is "ang rebolusyonaryong kapatid ni Zita." See LaTorre, "Mula kay Lino Brocka."

112. Isagani Cruz, *Movie Times* (Manila: National Book Store, 1984), 296.

113. Alfred A. Yuson, "*Batch '81*' and '*Cain at Abel*' Get High Marks from Film Ratings Board," *Philippines Daily Express*, October 25, 1982.

114. "'*Cain at Abel*': 1st FRB Tax Rebate Awardee," *The Manila Evening Post*, November 27, 1982.

115. "Dominant" is Pina's characterization in Zenaida LaTorre, "Mona Lisa in Action," *Jingle Extra Hot*, September 9, 1992. The descriptors "tough, intimidating" appear in Boy C. De Guia, "Kulay Showbiz [Showbiz Colors]," *Movie Specials*, June 3, 1982. The term "viciousness" occurs in Cruz, *Movie Times*, 293. Pina's "irascible" and "unmotherly attitude" is noted in Lawrence delos Trinos, "Review of *Cain at Abel*," *Star!*, n.d., Clippings, LOBC.

116. On Pina as cause of "great misery," see De Guia, "Kulay Showbiz [Showbiz Colors]." On her being "heard-hearted," see LaTorre, "Mona Lisa in Action."

117. Crispina Martinez-Belen, "Celebrity World," *Bulletin Today*, January 30, 1979; D.D., "Censors Okay '*Init*' Film," *Philippines Daily Express*, February 2, 1979.

118. D.D., "Censors Warn Movie Makers," *Philippines Evening Express*, January 19, 1979.

119. The words meant to be spoken as "Ester's face crumbles into a contorted picture of livid rage and disbelief" were: "Paano, ano'ng—ano ito? Nanaaang! Ano'ng ginawa n'yo sa akin?" ["But what's this? Mother! What have you done to me?"]. See Jose Y. Dalisay Jr., "Screenplay of *Ina ka ng anak mo*" (August 15, 1979), 36, Scripts, LOBC.

120. Cruz, *Movie Times*, 265.

121. Mario E. Bautista, "'*Ina ka ng anak mo*': Tunggalian ng dalawang magaling [Duelling Greats]," *Jingle Extra Hot*, January 4, 1980.

122. Jim Morrell, "Aid to the Philippines: Who Benefits?," in *The Philippines Reader: A History of Colonialism, Neocolonialism, Dictatorship, and Resistance*, ed. Daniel B. Schirmer and Stephen Rosskamm Shalom (Boston: South End Press, 1987), 258.

123. Ariel Ureta and Pyng Urbano, "Insiang: The Screen's Loveliest Face! [Comic Strip]," *Unkonwn*, June 1997, Clippings, LOBC.

124. Board of Investments, *Philippine Progress* (Manila: Board of Investments, 1971), 8.

125. Dalisay, "Screenplay of *Ina ka ng anak mo*," 16.

126. "Nora, Lolita Clash," *Times Journal*, November 8, 1979.

127. Boy C. De Guia, "Bakit maraming 'kiyeme' sa mga titulo ng pelikula? [Why Fuss about Movie Titles?]," *Modern Romance & True Confessions*, November 23, 1979.

128. Edilberto Noblejas and Interim Board of Censors for Motion Pictures, "Letter to Letty Fariñas," August 24, 1979, Scripts, LOBC.

129. Domingo Landicho, "Dalawang mahalagang pelikula [Two Important Films]," January 6, 1980, Clippings, LOBC.

130. "Lolita Delineates Complex Role in '*Ina ka . . . ,*'" *Philippines Daily Express*, December 10, 1979.

131. Ros H. Matienzo, "The 1979 Metro Manila Film Festival: An 'Overview,'" *Jingle Extra Hot*, January 21, 1980.

132. Boy C. De Guia, "Pelikulang Lolita-Nora, tatapatan ng Charito-Vilma! [Lolita-Nora vs. Charito-Vilma Films]," n.d., Clippings, LOBC.

133. Marsha Kinder, *Blood Cinema: The Reconstruction of National Identity in Spain* (Berkeley: University of California Press, 1993), 234.

134. Geoffrey Nowell-Smith, "Minnelli and Melodrama," in *Movies and Methods: An Anthology*, ed. Bill Nichols (Berkeley: University of California Press, 1985), 193.

135. Amber Jacobs, *On Matricide: Myth, Psychoanalysis, and the Law of the Mother* (New York: Columbia University Press, 2007), 47.

136. Jacobs, *On Matricide*, 62.

137. Bonnie Honig, *Antigone, Interrupted* (New York: Cambridge University Press, 2013), 79.

138. Honig, *Antigone, Interrupted*, 53.

CHAPTER 3. THE MELODRAMATICS OF CRIME

1. Andrew Sarris, "Cannes: A Last Hurrah," *Village Voice*, May 26, 1980, 49.

2. Jo-Ann Q. Maglipon, "Brocka's Battles," in *Lino Brocka: The Artist and His Times*, ed. Mario A. Hernando (Manila: Cultural Center of the Philippines, 1993), 125.

3. James Naremore, *More Than Night: Film Noir in Its Contexts*, 2nd ed. (Berkeley: University of California Press, 2008), 284.

4. Naremore, *More Than Night*, 37.

5. Naremore, *More Than Night*, 277.

6. Foster Hirsch, *The Dark Side of the Screen: Film Noir* (New York: Da Capo, 2001), 2.

7. Robert Porifirio, "No Way Out: Existential Motifs in the Film Noir," in *Film Noir: Reader*, ed. Alain Silver and James Ursini (Pompton Plains, NJ: Limelight Ed., 1996), 81.

8. Dana Polan, "College Course File: Film Noir," *Journal of Film and Video* 37, no. 2 (Spring 1985): 85.

9. Paul Arthur, "Murder's Tongue: Identity, Death, and the City in Film Noir," in *Violence and American Cinema*, ed. J. David Slocum (New York: Routledge, 2000), 158.

10. Carlos Clarens, *Crime Movies* (New York: Da Capo, 1980), 298.

11. Domietta Torlasco, *The Time of the Crime: Phenomenology, Psychoanalysis, Italian Film* (Stanford, CA: Stanford University Press, 2008), 9.

12. Thomas Leitch, *Crime Films* (New York: Cambridge University Press, 2002), 306.

13. Charles J. Maland, "'Film Gris': Crime, Critique and Cold War Culture in 1951," *Film Criticism* 26, no. 3 (2002): 22.

14. Janet Staiger, "Film Noir as Male Melodrama: The Politics of Film Genre Labeling," in *The Shifting Definitions of Genre: Essays on Labeling Films, Television Shows and Media*, ed. Lincoln Geraghty and Mark Jancovich (Jefferson, NC: McFarland, 2008), 71.

15. Elizabeth Cowie, "Women in Film Noir," in *Shades of Noir: A Reader*, ed. Joan Copjec (London: Verso, 1993), 129.

16. Steve Neale, "Melo Talk: On the Meaning and Use of the Term 'Melodrama' in the American Trade Press," *Velvet Light Trap* 32 (Fall 1993): 69.

17. Sarah Casey Benyahia, *Crime* (London: Routledge, 2012), 121.

18. Raymond Durgnat, "Paint It Black: The Family Tree of the Film Noir," in *Film Noir: Reader*, ed. Alain Silver and James Ursini (Pompton Plains, NJ: Limelight Ed., 1996), 37.

19. Albert F. Celoza, *Ferdinand Marcos and the Philippines: The Political Economy of Authoritarianism* (Westport, CT: Greenwood, 1997), 62.

20. Paula Rabinowitz, *Black and White and Noir* (New York: Columbia University Press, 2002), 12.

21. Rabinowitz, *Black and White and Noir*, 18.

22. Kirsten Moana Thompson, *Crime Films: Investigating the Scene* (London: Wallflower Press, 2007), 6.

23. Jack Shadoian, *Dreams and Dead Ends: The American Gangster/Crime Film* (Cambridge, MA: The MIT Press, 1979), 6.

24. Arun Vasudev and Philip Cheah, "Lino Brocka On His Own Terms," in *Asian Film Journeys: Selection from Cinemaya*, ed. Latika Padgaonkar and Rashmi Doraiswamy (New Delhi: Wisdom Tree Publishers, 2011), 318.

25. A French critic wrote about a "subtextual homosexuality" (*homosexualité occulte*) in Brocka's films. See Jacques Fieschi, "Violences," *Cinématographe*, April 1982, 17.

26. Durgnat, "Paint It Black," 48.

27. Paul Arthur, "The Gun in the Briefcase; or, The Inscription of Class in Film Noir," in *The Hidden Foundation: Cinema and the Question of Class*, ed. David E. James and Rick Berg (Minneapolis: University of Minnesota Press, 1996), 105.

28. Michael Walker, "Introduction," in *The Movie Book of Film Noir*, ed. Ian Cameron (London: Continuum, 1992), 23.

29. David A. Rosenberg, ed., *Marcos and Martial Law in the Philippines* (Ithaca, NY: Cornell University Press, 1979), 263.

30. Amy Wendling, "Second Nature: Gender in Marx's *Grundrisse*," in *In Marx's Laboratory: Critical Interpretations of the Grundrisse*, ed. Riccardo Bellofiore, Guido Starosta, and Peter D. Thomas (London: Brill, 2013), 367.

31. Robert Stam, *Reflexivity in Film and Literature: From Don Quixote to Jean-Luc Godard* (New York: Columbia University Press, 1992), 209.

32. Christine Gledhill, "Between Melodrama and Realism: Anthony Asquith's *Underground* and King Vidor's *The Crowd*," in *Classical Hollywood Narrative: The Paradigm Wars*, ed. Jane M. Gaines (Durham, NC: Duke University Press, 1992), 164.

33. Nick Joaquin, "The Boy Who Wanted to Become 'Society,'" in *Reportage on Crime: Thirteen Horror Happenings That Hit the Headlines* (Pasig City: Anvil, 2009), 17.

34. Joaquin, "The Boy Who Wanted," 53.

35. Joaquin, The Boy Who Wanted," 52.

36. Joaquin, The Boy Who Wanted," 55.

37. Michel Ciment, "Entretien avec Lino Brocka," *Positif*, no. 231 (1980): 27.

38. Ferdinand Marcos, *Notes on the New Society of the Philippines* (Manila: Marcos Foundation, 1973), 47.

39. Marcos, *Notes on the New Society*, 95.

40. Marcos, *Notes on the New Society*, 83, 57.

41. Marcos, *Notes on the New Society*, 59.

42. Marcos, *Notes on the New Society*, 94.

43. Marcos, *Notes on the New Society*, 150.

44. James K. Boyce, *The Political Economy of Growth and Impoverishment in the Marcos Era* (Manila: Ateneo de Manila University Press, 1993), xiii.

45. Boyce, *The Political Economy of Growth*, 43.

46. Boyce, *The Political Economy of Growth*, 44.

47. Boyce, *The Political Economy of Growth*, 291.

48. Jo-Ann Q. Maglipon, "Brocka, Imelda, Imee . . . and Other Vanities," *Manila Times*, May 24, 1986.

49. Vasudev and Cheah, "Lino Brocka on His Own Terms," 318.

50. Ciment, "Entretien avec Lino Brocka," 27.

51. Ciment, "Entretien avec Lino Brocka," 27.

52. Ciment, "Entretien avec Lino Brocka," 27.

53. Max Tessier, "*Jaguar*," *Image et son/Revue du cinéma*, no. 376 (October 1982): 50.

54. Gene Moskowitz, "*Jaguar*," *Variety*, May 21, 1980, 22.

55. Michel Ciment, "Tempêtes venues d'Asie," *L'Express*, May 16, 1980.

56. Fieschi, "Violences."

57. Ciment, "Entretien avec Lino Brocka," 29.

58. Guillermo C. de Vega, *Film and Freedom: Movie Censorship in the Philippines* (Manila: Guillermo de Vega, 1975), 36.

59. James Goodwin, *Eisenstein, Cinema, and History* (Urbana: University of Illinois Press, 1993), 63–75.

60. Christian Espiritu, "Review of *Jaguar*," *Philippine Sunday Express*, September 9, 1979, 22.

61. Todd McCarthy, "Philippines Lets 'Jaguar' Out of Cage for Cannes, Nowhere Else," *Daily Variety*, April 7, 1980.

62. Pierre Rissient, interview by José B. Capino, July 12, 2017.

63. Jay Scott, "*Jaguar's* Shadowed World Is Stark and Compelling," *Globe and Mail*, May 15, 1980.

64. Ian Stocks, "Philippine Cinema: Lino Brocka," *Cinema Papers* 29 (1980): 338.
65. Luis Francia, "Philippine Cinema: The Struggle against Repression," in *Film & Politics in the Third World*, ed. John Downing (New York: Praeger, 1987), 213.
66. Marsha Kinder, *Blood Cinema: The Reconstruction of National Identity in Spain* (Berkeley: University of California Press, 1993), 29.
67. Durgnat, "Paint It Black," 40.
68. Edward Dimendberg, *Film Noir and the Spaces of Modernity* (Cambridge, MA: Harvard University Press, 2004), 119.
69. Dimendberg, *Film Noir and the Spaces of Modernity*, 197.
70. Dimendberg, *Film Noir and the Spaces of Modernity*, 17.
71. Dimendberg, *Film Noir and the Spaces of Modernity*, 199.
72. Ciment, "Entretien Avec Lino Brocka," 29.
73. Mario E. Bautista, "Phillip's Search for Stardom," *Weekend*, August 10, 1979, 11.
74. Alain Garsault, "Slum Triptych: The Struggle for Dignity," in *Lino Brocka: The Artist and His Times*, ed. Mario A. Hernando, trans. Paula Carolina Malay (Manila: Cultural Center of the Philippines, 1993), 180.
75. Dimendberg, *Film Noir and the Spaces of Modernity*, 114.
76. Wheeler Winston Dixon, *Film Noir and the Cinema of Paranoia* (Edinburgh: Edinburgh University Press, 2009), 1.
77. Rigoberto Tiglao, "Consolidation of the Dictatorship," in *Dictatorship and Revolution: Roots of People's Power*, ed. Aurora Javate de Dios, Petronilo Daroy, and Lorna Kalaw-Tirol (Manila: Conspectus Foundation, 1988), 54.
78. Alfred W. McCoy, "Dark Legacy: Human Rights under the Marcos Dictatorship," in *Memory, Truth Telling, and the Pursuit of Justice: A Conference on the Legacies of the Marcos Dictatorship* (Quezon City: Office of Research and Publications, 2001), 132.
79. William Chapman, *Inside the Philippine Revolution* (New York: W. W. Norton, 1987), 170.
80. Ferdinand C. Llanes, *Tibak Rising: Activism in the Days of Martial Law* (Mandaluyong City: Anvil, 2012), 188.
81. Agustin L. Sotto, "Interview with Lino Brocka on *Jaguar*," in *Lino Brocka: The Artist and His Times*, ed. Nicanor G. Tiongson (Manila: Cultural Center of the Philippines, 1993), 233.
82. Naremore, *More Than Night*, 20.
83. Jose F. Lacaba and Ricardo Lee, "Story Outline for *Jaguar* 2nd of 2" (n.d.), Scripts, LOBC.
84. Ciment, "Entretien avec Lino Brocka," 28.
85. Isagani Cruz, "*Jaguar*," *TV Times*, September 16, 1979, 9.
86. Jose F. Lacaba, interview by José B. Capino, April 22, 2016.
87. Jose F. Lacaba and Ricardo Lee, "Story Outline for *Jaguar* 1st of 2" (n.d.), Scripts, LOBC.
88. Robert L. Youngblood, *Marcos against the Church: Economic Development and Political Repression in the Philippines* (Ithaca, NY: Cornell University Press, 1990), 112.
89. Lacaba and Lee, "Story Outline for *Jaguar* 1st of 2."
90. Youngblood, *Marcos against the Church*, 112.

91. Chapman, *Inside the Philippine Revolution*, 126.
92. Maglipon, "Brocka's Battles," 125.
93. Chapman, *Inside the Philippine Revolution*, 126.
94. Jose F. Lacaba and Ricardo Lee, "Sequence Treatment for *Jaguar*, Third Draft" (December 16, 1978), 7, Scripts, LOBC.
95. Francisco Nemenzo, "From Autocracy to Elite Democracy," in *Dictatorship and Revolution: Roots of People's Power*, ed. Aurora Javate de Dios, Petronilo Daroy, and Lorna Kalaw-Tirol (Manila: Conspectus Foundation, 1988), 237.
96. Nick Davis paraphrases Gilles Deleuze's gloss on the term *virtual* to invoke, among other things, "what is potentially 'in' an image without being directly perceptible." I appropriate the term here to reference deleted or alternate scenarios. See *The Desiring-Image: Gilles Deleuze and Contemporary Queer Cinema* (New York: Oxford University Press, 2013).
97. Cowie, "Women in Film Noir," 141.
98. Espiritu, "Review of *Jaguar*," 22.
99. Sotto, "Interview with Lino Brocka on *Jaguar*," 232.
100. Mario E. Bautista, "Jaguar: Phillip's Final Test," *Philippines Daily Express*, September 10, 1979, 23.
101. François Cuel, Jean-Claude Bonnet, and Michel Celemenski, "Entretiens avec Lino Brocka," *Cinématographe*, April 1982, 7.
102. Joël Magny, "*Jaguar*," *Cinéma*, October 1982, 85.
103. Davis, *The Desiring-Image*, 178.
104. Cuel, Bonnet, and Celemenski, "Entretiens avec Lino Brocka," 8.
105. Vasudev and Cheah, "Lino Brocka on His Own Terms," 327.
106. Isagani Cruz, *Movie Times* (Manila: National Book Store, 1984), 275–76.
107. Agustin L. Sotto, "Lino Brocka: The International Director," in *Lino Brocka: The Artist and His Times*, ed. Mario A. Hernando (Manila: Cultural Center of the Philippines, 1993), 115.
108. Sarah Projansky, *Watching Rape: Film and Television in Postfeminist Culture* (New York: New York University Press, 2001), 60.
109. Amnesty International, *Report of an Amnesty International Mission to the Republic of the Philippines, 22 November–5 December 1975* (London: Amnesty International Publications, 1977), 198.
110. Amnesty International, *Report of an Amnesty International Mission*, 23.
111. Amnesty International, *Report of an Amnesty International Mission*, 83.
112. Llanes, *Tibak Rising*, 46.
113. Amnesty International, *Torture in the Eighties: An Amnesty International Report* (London: Amnesty International Publications, 1984), 199.
114. Amnesty International, *Report of an Amnesty International Mission*, 28.
115. Amnesty International, *Report of an Amnesty International Mission*, 86.
116. Amnesty International, *Report of an Amnesty International Mission*, 51.
117. Amnesty International, *Report of an Amnesty International Mission*, 47.
118. McCoy, "Dark Legacy," 134.
119. McCoy, "Dark Legacy," 133.
120. McCoy, "Dark Legacy," 135.

121. Jose F. Lacaba, "Remembering Martial Law," *Ka Pete* (blog), September 21, 2008, https://kapetesapatalim.blogspot.com/2008/09/remembering-martial-law.html.

122. Richard Allen, "Pesaro 1," *Framework*, Autumn 1983, 74.

123. Jose F. Lacaba, "Screenplay of *Angela markado*" (n.d.), 13, Scripts, LOBC.

124. Lacaba, "Screenplay of *Angela markado*," 14.

125. Rabinowitz, *Black & White and Noir*, 74.

126. Peter Brooks, *The Melodramatic Imagination: Balzac, Henry James, Melodrama, and the Mode of Excess* (New Haven, CT: Yale University Press, 1995), 38.

127. Paul Willemen, "*Angela markado*," in *The BFI Companion to Crime*, ed. Phil Hardy (London: Cassell, 1997), 34.

128. Boyce, *The Political Economy of Growth*, 225.

129. Katherine W. Ellison, *Imelda, Steel Butterfly of the Philippines* (New York: McGraw-Hill, 1988), 224.

130. Benyahia, *Crime*, 113.

131. Vasudev and Cheah, "Lino Brocka on His Own Terms," 327.

132. Cruz, *Movie Times*, 276.

133. Jose F. Lacaba, "*Angela markado*: Synopsis of the Story" (n.d.), 13, Scripts, LOBC.

134. Clarens, *Crime Movies*, 294.

135. Jean-Pierre Berthomé, "Le festival des trois continents," *Positif*, March 1984; Louis Marcorelles, "Lino Brocka couronné, Xie Jin honoré," *Le Monde*, December 2, 1983.

136. Hubert Niogret, "Pesaro 83," *Positif*, September 1983.

137. Pete Jundan, "Sulyap sa kamera [Peek into the Camera]," *The Reflector*, December 2, 1980.

138. Rico Alegre, "Review of *Angela markado*," *Modern Romances & True Confessions*, October 27, 1980, 29.

139. Marcos, *Notes on the New Society*, v.

140. Chapman, *Inside the Philippine Revolution*, 132.

141. Chapman, *Inside the Philippine Revolution*, 117.

142. Emmanuel S. de Dios, "The Erosion of the Dictatorship," in *Dictatorship and Revolution: Roots of People's Power*, ed. Aurora Javate de Dios, Petronilo Daroy, and Lorna Kalaw-Tirol (Manila: Conspectus Foundation, 1988), 72–73.

143. Lee Stull, "President Marcos Announces Changes to Martial Law [Confidential, Cable, 13106]" (ProQuest LLC, August 22, 1977), The Philippines: U.S. Policy during the Marcos Years, 1965–1986, Digital National Security Archive, http://gateway.proquest.com/openurl?url_ver=Z39.88-2004&res_dat=xri:dnsa&rft_dat=xri:dnsa:article:CPH01006.

144. Celoza, *Ferdinand Marcos and the Philippines*, 62.

145. Raymond Bonner, *Waltzing with a Dictator* (New York: Random House, 1987), 301.

146. Ileana Maramag, *The Marcos Years: Achievements under the New Society* (Manila: Office of Media Affairs, 1981), 100.

147. Bonner, *Waltzing with a Dictator*, 121.

148. Maramag, *The Marcos Years*, 105.

149. National Census and Statistics Office, *Philippine Yearbook 1981* (Manila: National Economic Development Authority, 1981), 93.

150. Maramag, *The Marcos Years*, 105.

CHAPTER 4. TALES OF UNRELENTING MISFORTUNES

1. Ronald Wintrobe, *The Political Economy of Dictatorship* (New York: Cambridge University Press, 1998), 17.
2. Wintrobe, *The Political Economy of Dictatorship*, 32.
3. Milan W. Svolik, *The Politics of Authoritarian Rule* (Cambridge: Cambridge University Press, 2012), 12.
4. Wintrobe, *The Political Economy of Dictatorship*, 101.
5. Emmanuel S. de Dios, ed., *An Analysis of the Philippine Economic Crisis: A Workshop Report* (Quezon City: University of the Philippines Press, 1984), 2.
6. James K. Boyce, *The Political Economy of Growth and Impoverishment in the Marcos Era* (Manila: Ateneo de Manila University Press, 1993), 10.
7. Boyce, *The Political Economy of Growth*, 320.
8. Robin Broad, *Unequal Alliance: The World Bank, the International Monetary Fund, and the Philippines* (Berkeley: University of California Press, 1988), 218.
9. de Dios, *Philippine Economic Crisis*, 49.
10. Boyce, *The Political Economy of Growth*, 280.
11. de Dios, *Philippine Economic Crisis*.
12. Emmanuel S. de Dios, "The Erosion of the Dictatorship," in *Dictatorship and Revolution: Roots of People's Power*, ed. Aurora Javate de Dios, Petronilo Daroy, and Lorna Kalaw-Tirol (Manila: Conspectus Foundation, 1988), 110.
13. The source material is not identified in the credits or publicity, but I suspect it is this: Aida Sevilla Mendoza, "The Woman Who Had Two Husbands," in *More Unforgettable Legal Stories* (Quezon City: Alemar-Phoenix Publishing House, 1978), 14–29.
14. David Harvey, *Seventeen Contradictions and the End of Capitalism* (New York: Oxford University Press, 2014), 182.
15. de Dios, *Philippine Economic Crisis*, 21.
16. Val Vidad, "May kabit si Vilma Santos [Vilma Santos Has a Lover]," *Jingle Extra Hot*, May 18, 1984.
17. Peter Brooks, *The Melodramatic Imagination: Balzac, Henry James, Melodrama, and the Mode of Excess* (New Haven, CT: Yale University Press, 1995), 38.
18. Brooks, *The Melodramatic Imagination*, 31.
19. Friedrich Engels, *The Origin of the Family, Private Property, and the State* (London: Penguin Classics, 2010), 92.
20. Engels, *The Origin of the Family*, 106.
21. Engels, *The Origin of the Family*, 106.
22. Engels, *The Origin of the Family*, 105.
23. Mario E. Bautista, "Vilma Santos Times Two," *Movie Flash*, May 31, 1984, 32.
24. Anselle Belluso, "Iba't-ibang sabi-sabi tungkol sa pelikulang may sinasabi! [Rumors about a meaningful film]," *Jingle Extra Hot*, May 18, 1984.
25. "Untitled Magazine Clipping on 'Adultery,'" *Sensation*, n.d., Clippings, LOBC.
26. "Vilma, Phillip Paired Once More in 'Adultery,'" *Bulletin Today*, January 20, 1984.
27. Lou Samareno, "Maling-mali si Vilma! [Vilma was wrong!]," *Movie Flash*, May 31, 1984.
28. Hermie Francisco, "Eddie Garcia Is the New 'Comedian'!," *Modern Romance & True Confessions*, June 4, 1984.

29. Cristina Gomez, "Mas maganda ang '*Adultery*' kaysa sa marami kong nakaraang pelikula!-Vilma Santos ['*Adultery*' is better than my previous films]," *Bulaklak*, n.d., Clippings, LOBC.

30. Rico Alegre, "Phillip Salvador: A Sensitive and Politically Aware Actor," *Jingle Extra Hot*, n.d., Clippings, LOBC.

31. "Busy Lino," *Movie Flash*, May 31, 1984.

32. N. Julio Cinko, "Mother Lily: Producer of the (Martial Law) Years," *Movie Flash*, June 21, 1984.

33. Ricardo Lo, "The Team to Beat: Phillip & Vilma," *Mr. & Ms.*, June 26, 1984, 44.

34. Oskar Salazar, "Philippines," in *International Film Guide.*, ed. Peter Cowie (London: Tantivy, 1981), 265.

35. Cinko, "Mother Lily: Producer of the (Martial Law) Years."

36. "Film Ratings Board Reviews" (Film Ratings Board, ca 1984), Moving Pictures Reviews, 1982–1989, CCP Library.

37. Danny Villanueva, "'*Napakasakit kuya Eddie*' Soon a Movie," *Movie Flash*, May 2, 1985, 2.

38. M. L. Celestial, "Aga and Janice (Again)," *Woman's Home Companion*, August 2, 1985.

39. "Coming Soon ... '*Napakasakit, kuya Eddie*,'" *Sensation*, September 10, 1985.

40. Jose Javier Reyes, "Screenplay of *Napakasakit, kuya Eddie*" (n.d.), 63, Scripts, LOBC.

41. Broad, *Unequal Alliance*, 223.

42. Boyce, *The Political Economy of Growth*, 38.

43. Jose Javier Reyes, "*Napakasakit, kuya Eddie* Screenplay." Reyes did not respond to my request to examine the copy of the script held at De La Salle University Library.

44. Emmanuel S. de Dios and Paul D. Hutchcroft, "Political Economy," in *The Philippine Economy: Development, Policies, and Challenges*, ed. A. M Balisacan and Hal Hill (Quezon City: Ateneo De Manila University Press, 2006), 49.

45. Broad, *Unequal Alliance*, 223.

46. de Dios, *Philippine Economic Crisis*, 17.

47. Jose Javier Reyes, "*Napakasakit, kuya Eddie* Screenplay," 53.

48. Union of Democratic Filipinos, *People's War in the Philippines* (Manila, 1975), 8.

49. Joanna Page, *Crisis and Capitalism in Contemporary Argentine Cinema* (Durham, NC: Duke University Press, 2009), 4.

50. Page, *Crisis and Capitalism*, 75.

51. Engels, *The Origin of the Family*, 105.

52. Daniel Gerould and Noel Carroll, "The Moral Ecology of Melodrama: The Family Plot and *Magnificent Obssession*," in *Melodrama* (New York: New York Literary Forum, 1980), 198.

53. Christine Gledhill, *Home Is Where the Heart Is: Studies in Melodrama and the Woman's Film* (London: British Film Institute, 1987), 21.

54. Robyn Magalit Rodriguez, *Migrants for Export: How the Philippine State Brokers Labor to the World* (Minneapolis: University of Minnesota Press, 2010), 80.

55. Anna Romina Guevarra, *Marketing Dreams, Manufacturing Heroes: The Transnational Labor Brokering of Filipino Workers* (New Brunswick, NJ: Rutgers University Press, 2009), 22.

56. de Dios, *Philippine Economic Crisis*, 52.

57. Guevarra, *Marketing Dreams*, 34.

58. Rodriguez, *Migrants for Export*, 83.

59. Pauline Gardiner Barber, "Contradictions of Class and Consumption When the Commodity Is Labour," *Anthropologica* 46, no. 2 (2004): 205.

60. David Harvey, "Globalization and the 'Spatial Fix,'" *Geographische Revue*, no. 2 (2001): 25.

61. Harvey, *Seventeen Contradictions and the End of Capitalism*, 153.

62. David Harvey, *Spaces of Capital: Towards a Critical Geography* (New York: Taylor & Francis, 2001), 94.

63. Harvey *Spaces of Capital*, 305.

64. James A. Tyner, *The Philippines: Mobilities, Identities, Globalization* (New York: Routledge, 2010), 7.

65. Gayatri C. Spivak, "Teaching for the Times," in *The Decolonization of Imagination: Culture, Knowledge, and Power*, ed. Jan Nederveen Pieterse and Bhikhu Parekh (London: Zed Books, 1995), 194.

66. Jose Javier Reyes, "*Napakasakit, kuya Eddie* Screenplay," 78.

67. Lino Brocka, "The State of the Film Industry," in *The Politics of Culture: The Philippine Experience*, ed. Nicanor G. Tiongson (Manila: PETA, 1984), 50.

68. Jose Javier Reyes, "*Napakasakit, kuya Eddie* Screenplay," 55.

69. Raul Regalado, "Out of Focus," *National Midweek*, April 16, 1986. This and subsequent quotations are drawn from the same one-page review.

70. Regalado, "Out of Focus."

71. "Coming Soon . . . '*Napakasakit, kuya Eddie.*'"

72. Ramon Teodoro, "Nawala na ba ang box-office appeal ni Lino Brocka? [Has Brocka's Box Office Appeal Waned?]," *The New Record*, January 18, 1986.

73. Daniel Gerould, "The Americanization of Melodrama," in *American Melodrama*, ed. Daniel Gerould (New York: Performing Arts Journal Publications, 1983), 27.

74. de Dios and Hutchcroft, "Political Economy," 50.

75. Barbara Geddes, "What Do We Know about Democratization after Twenty Years?," *Annual Review of Political Science* 2, no. 1 (June 1999): 138.

CHAPTER 5. MEN IN REVOLT

1. Maria Serena I. Diokno, "Unity and Struggle," in *Dictatorship and Revolution: Roots of People's Power*, ed. Aurora Javate de Dios, Petronilo Daroy, and Lorna Kalaw-Tirol (Manila: Conspectus Foundation, 1988), 145.

2. Robert L. Youngblood, *Marcos against the Church: Economic Development and Political Repression in the Phillipines* (Ithaca, NY: Cornell University Press, 1990), 146.

3. P. N. Abinales and Donna J. Amoroso, *State and Society in the Philippines* (Lanham, MD: Rowman & Littlefield, 2005), 207.

4. James K. Boyce, *The Political Economy of Growth and Impoverishment in the Marcos Era* (Manila: Ateneo de Manila University Press, 1993), 14.

5. Oskar Salazar, "Film Industry Hit by Philippine Economy," *Hollywood Reporter*, December 4, 1984, 7.

6. William C. Rempel, *Delusions of a Dictator: The Mind of Marcos as Revealed in His Secret Diaries* (Boston: Little, Brown, 1993), 194; Katherine W. Ellison, *Imelda, Steel Butterfly of the Philippines* (New York: McGraw-Hill, 1988), 216.

7. Alfred W. McCoy, *An Anarchy of Families: State and Family in the Philippines* (Madison: University of Wisconsin Press, 2009), 259.

8. Julie Ney, "Only One Oppressor," *Village Voice*, November 15, 1983, 109.

9. Ronald Constantino, "Brocka–De Leon Crusade," *Tempo*, February 10, 1983.

10. Marietta Giron, "Many Filipino Industry Changes; Some Fear a 'Nationalization,'" *Variety*, May 26, 1982, 39.

11. Marietta Giron, "Anti-Censor Tirade Ruffles 1st Filipino Film Acad Awards," *Variety*, May 18, 1983, 35.

12. "Resolution for the Abolition of the PCO" (Abolish the PCO, Restore the Writ Movement, n.d.), Correspondences, LOBC.

13. Cristina del Carmen, "Lino Brocka: Rebel Artist," *WHO*, August 24, 1983.

14. John Wilson, "Moviegoing in Manila," *Washington Post*, February 16, 1986, F9.

15. Diokno, "Unity and Struggle," 164.

16. Oskar Salazar, "Philippine Moviegoers Return to Theatres," *Hollywood Reporter*, March 20, 1984.

17. Eric Gamalinda, "Politics and Screenwriting," September 2, 1984, Clippings, LOBC.

18. Cristina del Carmen, "Impeach Katigbak?," *WHO*, April 6, 1983.

19. Mario Dumaual, "Vilma's Year," *Malaya*, n.d., Clippings, LOBC.

20. Gilles Deleuze, *Cinema 2: The Time-Image* (Minneapolis: University of Minnesota Press, 1989), 217.

21. Patricia Pisters, *The Matrix of Visual Culture: Working with Deleuze in Film Theory* (Stanford, CA: Stanford University Press, 2003), 177; Deleuze, *Cinema 2*, 219.

22. Laura U. Marks, "A Deleuzian Politics of Hybrid Cinema," *Screen* 35, no. 3 (Autumn 1994): 261.

23. D. N. Rodowick, *Gilles Deleuze's Time Machine* (Durham, NC: Duke University Press, 1997), 152.

24. Deleuze, *Cinema 2*, 1989, 224.

25. Deleuze, *Cinema 2*, 222.

26. Deleuze, *Cinema 2*, 219.

27. Deleuze, *Cinema 2*, 220.

28. András Bálint Kovács, *Screening Modernism: European Art Cinema, 1950–1980* (Chicago: University of Chicago Press, 2007), 141.

29. Nick Davis, *The Desiring-Image: Gilles Deleuze and Contemporary Queer Cinema* (New York: Oxford University Press, 2013), 26.

30. Gilles Deleuze, "Literature and Life," trans. Daniel W. Smith and Michael A. Greco, *Critical Inquiry*, no. 23 (Winter 1997): 229.

31. Deleuze, *Cinema 2*, 1989, 217.

32. Fonds Festival International du Film de Cannes, "Festival de Cannes 1984 Programme" (Catalogue, n.d.), La Cinémathèque Française, Paris.

33. Eric Gamalinda, "Brocka in 6 Takes," *National Midweek*, December 18, 1985.

34. Jose F. Lacaba, "A Strike," *Asia-Philippines Leader*, May 26, 1972, 8, 32–33; Jose Carreon, "Hostages or Hosts?," *Asia-Philippines Leader*, December 3, 1971, 10–11, 48.

35. Rolando B. Tolentino, "Inangbayan, the Mother-Nation, in Lino Brocka's *Bayan ko: Kapit sa patalim* and *Orapronobis*," *Screen* 37, no. 4 (1996): 368–88; Damiana L. Eugenio, *Philippine Folk Literature: The Proverbs* (Quezon City: University of the Philippines Press, 1992), 340.

36. Agustin L. Sotto, "Interview with Jose F. Lacaba on *Kapit sa patalim*," in *The Urian Anthology, 1980–1989*, ed. Nicanor G. Tiongson (Manila: A. P. Tuviera, 2001), 320.

37. Wylie Sypher, "Aesthetic of Revolution: Marxist Melodrama," in *Tragedy: Vision and Form*, ed. Robert W. Corrigan (New York: Harper & Row, 1981), 219.

38. Michael Walker, "Introduction," in *The Movie Book of Film Noir*, ed. Ian Cameron (London: Continuum, 1992), 16.

39. Raymond Bonner, *Waltzing with a Dictator* (New York: Random House, 1987), 278.

40. Michel Foucault, *The History of Sexuality: An Introduction*, trans. Robert Hurley (New York: Vintage Books, 1988), 141.

41. Rigoberto Tiglao, "Consolidation of the Dictatorship," in *Dictatorship and Revolution: Roots of People's Power*, ed. Aurora Javate de Dios, Petronilo Daroy, and Lorna Kalaw-Tirol (Manila: Conspectus Foundation, 1988), 30.

42. Ferdinand C. Llanes, *Tibak Rising: Activism in the Days of Martial Law* (Mandaluyong City: Anvil, 2012), 113.

43. Susan F. Quimpo, "Globe Steel," in *Tibak Rising: Activism in the Days of Martial Law*, ed. Ferdinand C. Llanes (Mandaluyong City: Anvil, 2012), 113.

44. Jose F. Lacaba, "Screenplay for *Kapit sa patalim*" (January 17, 1984), 132, Scripts, LOBC.

45. Jose F. Lacaba, "Sequence Treatment for *Kapit sa patalim*" (June 23, 1982), 7–8, Scripts, LOBC.

46. Lacaba, "Screenplay for *Kapit sa patalim*," 132.

47. Sypher, "Aesthetic of Revolution: Marxist Melodrama," 217.

48. Joel David notes several other instances of self-reflexivity in Brocka's films in Joel David, *Fields of Vision: Critical Applications in Recent Philippine Cinema* (Ateneo de Manila University Press, 1995), 21.

49. Francisco Nemenzo, "From Autocracy to Elite Democracy," in *Dictatorship and Revolution: Roots of People's Power*, ed. Aurora Javate de Dios, Petronilo Daroy, and Lorna Kalaw-Tirol (Manila: Conspectus Foundation, 1988), 237.

50. Nemenzo, "From Autocracy to Elite Democracy," 237.

51. Ferdinand C. Llanes, "Rise of Olalia as Unity Chair against Marcosian Fascism," in *Tibak Rising: Activism in the Days of Martial Law*, ed. Ferdinand C. Llanes (Mandaluyong City: Anvil, 2012), 197.

52. Ted O. Lopez, "'Buklod' to Bukluran: Unionism Reborn," in *Tibak Rising: Activism in the Days of Martial Law*, ed. Ferdinand C. Llanes (Mandaluyong City: Anvil, 2012), 192.

53. William Chapman, *Inside the Philippine Revolution* (New York: W. W. Norton, 1987), 229.

54. Chapman, *Inside the Philippine Revolution*, 231.

55. Sotto, "Interview with Jose F. Lacaba on *Kapit sa patalim*," 327.

56. Lacaba confirmed that the notes are in his handwriting during an interview at his home on April 22, 2016.

57. Lacaba, "Sequence Treatment for *Kapit sa patalim*," 1.

58. Lacaba, "Sequence Treatment," 22.
59. David Overbey and Marquita Doassans, "'Bayan ko: Kapit sa patalim' Press Kit" (Malaya and Stephan Films, n.d.), 7, La Cinémathèque Française, Paris.
60. Deleuze, *Cinema 2*, 222.
61. Deleuze, *Cinema 2*, 216.
62. Deleuze, *Cinema 2*, 224.
63. Milan W. Svolik, *The Politics of Authoritarian Rule* (Cambridge: Cambridge University Press, 2012), 131.
64. Barbara Geddes, "What Do We Know about Democratization after Twenty Years?," *Annual Review of Political Science* 2, no. 1 (June 1999): 135.
65. Mark R. Thompson, *The Anti-Marcos Struggle* (New Haven, CT: Yale University Press, 1995), 1.
66. Pierre Rissient, interview by José B. Capino, July 12, 2017.
67. Fonds Festival International du Film de Cannes, "Cannes 1984 Programme," 3.
68. Overbey and Doassans, "'Bayan ko: Kapit sa patalim' Press Kit."
69. Sotto, "Interview with Jose F. Lacaba on *Kapit sa patalim*," 61.
70. Sotto, "Interview with Jose F. Lacaba," 62.
71. Nigel Andrews, *Financial Times*, May 29, 1984.
72. Derek Malcolm, *The Guardian*, May 24, 1984.
73. James Leahy, "*Bayan ko: Kapit Sa patalim* (Bayan Ko: My Own Country)," *Monthly Film Bulletin* 52, no. 616 (1985): 147.
74. Gilles Horvilleur, "*Bayan ko*," *Cinématographe*, no. 106 (1985): 48.
75. Colette-Marie Renard, "*Bayan ko*," *Cinéma 72*, no. 313 (1985): 41.
76. Michel Sineux, "*Bayan ko*: Comme la vie," *Positif*, no. 288 (1985): 64.
77. Jay Scott, "A Panoramic Landscape of the Underside of Manila," *Globe and Mail*, July 13, 1985.
78. F.F., "Un Philippin semi-clandestin," *L'Express*, May 18, 1984, Revue de presse film—*Bayan ko: Kapit sa patalim*, Cinémathèque Française; Michel Peréz, "*Bayan ko*," *Le Matin*, May 18, 1984; Claude Sartirano, "*Bayan ko*," *L' Humanité-Dimanche*, May 21, 1986.
79. Leahy, "*Bayan ko*," 147.
80. Rita Festin, "Lino Brocka's Latest Battle with the Censors," *Malaya*, November 18, 1984.
81. "Philippine Release Blocked by Censor, Cause of Picketing," *Variety*, January 9, 1985.
82. Nestor Cuartero, "Brocka, Lacaba Answer Censors," *Tempo*, January 7, 1985.
83. "Supreme Court of the Philippines Decision on *Gonzalez v Katigbak*," July 22, 1985, http://www.lawphil.net/judjuris/juri1985/jul1985/gr_l69500_1985.html.
84. Jose F. Lacaba, "Kapritso [Caprice]," *Mr. & Ms.*, November 27, 1984.
85. Jo-Ann Q. Maglipon, "Brocka's Battles," in *Lino Brocka: The Artist and His Times*, ed. Mario A. Hernando (Manila: Cultural Center of the Philippines, 1993), 119–249.
86. Cristina P. del Carmen-Pastor, "'Kapit' vs Katigbak Part II," *Balita*, November 24, 1984.
87. London Press Service, "British Film Award for Brocka," *Malaya*, December 18, 1984; Virginia Dignam, "Support Needed to Free Director Brocka from Jail," *Morning Star*, March 29, 1985.

88. Mario E. Bautista, "Laban ni Lino [Lino's Fight]," *People's Journal*, December 19, 1984.

89. "Philippine Release Blocked by Censor, Cause of Picketing."

90. Joseph Yap, "'Bayan ko' vs Censors . . . Ang harana sa init ng araw ['My Own Country' versus the Censors . . . The Serenade under the Hot Sun]," *Kislap Magasin*, December 10, 1984.

91. Mario V. Dumaual, "Censors Softening up on 'Bayan Ko': Release Eyed," *Malaya*, December 18, 1984.

92. Christi-Anne Castro, *Musical Renderings of the Philippine Nation* (Oxford: Oxford University Press, 2011), 179.

93. Cuartero, "Brocka, Lacaba Answer Censors."

94. Cuartero, "Brocka, Lacaba Answer Censors."

95. Rico E. Alegre, "Lino Brocka: Lalong tumatapang at wala pa ring takot hanggang ngayon! [Braver and Still Fearless!]," *Kontrobersyal*, n.d., Clippings, LOBC.

96. Danny T. Vibas, "No Wish to Turn Politician," *WE Forum*, April 25, 1985.

97. Mario V. Dumaual, "Brocka Still Won," *Malaya*, July 25, 1985.

98. "BRMPT Allows Showing of '*Bayan ko*' without Cuts," *Philippines Daily Express*, January 21, 1985.

99. Jo-Ann Q. Maglipon, "Brocka, Cervantes in Jail: Smelly, Sleepless Nights," *WE Forum*, n.d., Clippings, LOBC.

100. Danny T. Vibas, "Brocka Reports on People's Protest," *WE Forum*, September 27, 1985.

101. SA, "Brocka, Cervantes: Pinalaya na ni FM [Brocka, Cervantes: Freed by FM]," *Taliba*, February 14, 1985.

102. Luciano E. Soriano, "Lino Brocka Kalibre 45 [Lino Brocka 45 Caliber]," *Moviestar*, April 10, 1985.

103. Alegre, "Braver and Still Fearless."

104. Vibas, "Brocka Reports on People's Protest."

105. Pierre Rissient, "Letter to Gilly Hodson," February 27, 1985, Correspondences, LOBC; "Britons Turn Out to Back Lino Brocka," *Variety*, March 27, 1985.

106. Danny T. Vibas, "Brocka, Cervantes and Company: Free but Not Really!" *Variety [Philippines]*, March 9, 1985, Clippings, LOBC.

107. Michael Macintyre, "Bayan ko Pilipinas," *Arena* (British Broadcasting Corporation, March 4, 1987), British Film Institute.

108. Dumaual, "Brocka Still Won."

109. Conrad Galang, "Balik-komersiyal movies [Back to Commercial Movies]," *Balita*, January 3, 1986.

110. Luciano E. Soriano, "Kumapit sa patalim si Phillip Salvador para kay Gina Alajar [Phillip Salvador Gripped the Knife's Edge for Gina Alajar]," August 2, 1984, Clippings, LOBC.

111. Deedee Siytangco, "Review of '*Bayan ko: Kapit sa patalim*,'" *Bulletin Today*, July 15, 1984.

112. Emmanuel A. Reyes, "Review of *Bayan ko*," in *Notes on Philippine Cinema* (Manila: De La Salle University Press, 1989), 113.

113. Reyes, "Review of *Bayan ko*," 114.
114. Reyes, "Review of *Bayan ko*," 115.
115. Sotto, "Interview with Jose F. Lacaba on *Kapit sa patalim*," 327.
116. Rodowick, *Gilles Deleuze's Time Machine*, 155.
117. Soriano, "Phillip Salvador Gripped," 35.
118. Siytangco, "Review of '*Bayan ko: Kapit sa patalim*.'"
119. Maglipon, "Brocka's Battles."
120. Nap C. Alip, "Latest love ni Aga [Aga's Latest Love]," *Balita*, May 5, 1985.
121. Mar F. Cornes, "Brocka's New Favorite," *PM News in Action*, March 16, 1985; Billy Balbastro, "Will Aga Starrer Wait until Brocka's Back from Bicutan?," *Times Journal*, February 3, 1985; Rod Samson, "Lumalaban kapag tama [Fights When Needed]," *Times Journal*, June 13, 1985.
122. Hamid Naficy, "The Americanization and Indigenization of Lino Brocka through Cinema: An Interview," *Framework*, no. 38 (1992): 141.
123. Vir Mateo, "Maging another Christopher De Leon kaya si Aga Mulach sa kamay ni Brocka? [Will Brocka Turn Aga Mulach into the Next Christopher De Leon?]," *Superstar Komiks*, March 18, 1985.
124. "Tinimbang ang Miguelito [Weighing Miguelito]," *Movie Flash*, April 18, 1985.
125. Deleuze, *Cinema 2*, 218.
126. Pam Cook, *Screening the Past: Memory and Nostalgia in Cinema* (London: Routledge, 2004), 79.
127. Ricardo F. Lo, "Nida, Liza Potential Acting Awardees," *Philippines Daily Express*, June 5, 1985.
128. Bonner, *Waltzing with a Dictator*, 132.
129. Geddes, "What Do We Know," 130.
130. Geddes, "What Do We Know," 139.
131. Svolik, *The Politics of Authoritarian Rule*, 57.
132. Svolik, *The Politics of Authoritarian Rule*, 56.
133. Samson, "Lumalaban kapag tama [Fights When Needed]."
134. Billy Balbastro, "Brocka vs. Board: Producers Worried?" *Times Journal*, June 12, 1985.
135. Geddes, "What Do We Know?," 130.
136. Ernie Pecho, "Lino Brocka's Heart and Mind Very Much at Work in *Miguelito*," *Times Journal*, June 1, 1985.
137. Ricardo F. Lo, "Lino Brocka: From Bold to Bold," *Philippine Daily Inquirer*, July 26, 1985.
138. Butch Francisco, "A Power House Cast in a Movie to Watch," *Malaya*, June 3, 1985.
139. Mario E. Bautista, "Review of *Miguelito*," in *The Urian Anthology, 1980–1989*, ed. Nicanor G. Tiongson (Manila: A. P. Tuviera, 2001), 220.
140. "Beth Bautista Proves Lino Brocka Right," June 13, 1985, Clippings, LOBC.
141. Teddy Hayden Lim, "Aga Mulach: A Revelation," *PM News in Action*, April 1, 1985; "Brocka Directs Aga," *Bulletin Today*, March 30, 1985.
142. Jo-Ann Q. Maglipon, "A Mouthful for the Critics," *Manila Chronicle*, July 11, 1986, 16.

143. Clodualdo del Mundo Jr., "*Kapit sa patalim and Orapronobis*: Stories of Our Country and Brocka's Melodramatic Strategy: A Review of *Kapit sa patalim* and *Orapronobis*," in *Lino Brocka: The Artist and His Times*, ed. Mario A. Hernando (Manila: Cultural Center of the Philippines, 1993), 89.

144. Francisco, "A Power House Cast in a Movie to Watch."

145. John Wilson, "Moviegoing in Manila," *Washington Post*, February 16, 1986, F8.

CHAPTER 6. A DIRTY AFFAIR

1. "The Uncompromising Lino Brocka," *WE Forum*, n.d., Clippings, LOBC.

2. Agence France Presse, "Brocka Hits Aquino Gov't While in Cannes," *Malaya*, May 24, 1989.

3. Gretchen Casper, "From Confrontation to Conciliation: The Philippine Path Toward Democratic Consolidation," in *Pathways to Democracy: The Political Economy of Democratic Transitions*, ed. James Frank Hollifield and Calvin C. Jillson (New York: Routledge, 2014), 156–57.

4. Jane Hutchison, "Class and State Power in the Philippines," in *Southeast Asia in the 1990s*, ed. Kevin Hewison, Richard Robison, and Garry Rodan (Sydney: Allen and Unwin, 1993), 193.

5. Eva-Lotta Hedman and John Sidel, *Philippine Politics and Society in the Twentieth Century: Colonial Legacies, Post-Colonial Trajectories* (London: Routledge, 2000), 36.

6. Barbara Geddes, "What Do We Know about Democratization after Twenty Years?," *Annual Review of Political Science* 2, no. 1 (June 1999): 131, 134.

7. Gretchen Casper, *Fragile Democracies: The Legacies of Authoritarian Rule* (Pittsburgh: University of Pittsburgh Press, 1995).

8. Jay Scott, "*Jaguar's* Shadowed World Is Stark and Compelling," *Globe and Mail*, May 15, 1980.

9. Linda Williams, *Playing the Race Card: Melodramas of Black and White from Uncle Tom to O. J. Simpson* (Princeton, NJ : Princeton University Press, 2001), 307.

10. Ravi Vasudevan, *The Melodramatic Public: Film Form and Spectatorship in Indian Cinema* (New York: Palgrave Macmillan, 2011), 18.

11. Bonnie Honig, *Antigone, Interrupted* (New York: Cambridge University Press, 2013), 78.

12. Vasudevan, *The Melodramatic Public*, 25.

13. Elisabeth Anker, "Left Melodrama," *Contemporary Political Theory* 11, no. 2 (May 2012): 142.

14. Star Elamparo, "The Film and the Furor," *National Midweek*, September 27, 1989.

15. Tinna B. Mauricio, "Lino Brocka: Controversial Megman," *Starweek*, July 30, 1989.

16. Elamparo, "The Film and the Furor."

17. Sheila Coronel, "Brocka Film Focuses on the Underside," *Manila Times*, July 17, 1989.

18. Ernie Pecho, "Brocka's Orapronobis to Be Shown Uncensored," *Philippine Daily Globe*, July 25, 1989; Jo-Ann Q. Maglipon, "Brocka's Battles," in *Lino Brocka: The Artist and His Times*, ed. Mario A. Hernando (Manila: Cultural Center of the Philippines, 1993), 141.

19. Pecho, "Brocka's Orapronobis to Be Shown Uncensored."

20. Maglipon, "Brocka's Battles," 142.
21. Coronel, "Brocka Film Focuses on the Underside."
22. Maglipon, "Brocka's Battles," 141.
23. Janet Fine, "Brocka Fights Filipino Pressure," *Hollywood Reporter*, October 31, 1989.
24. Margie T. Logarta, "There's a Lot of Risk When You Make a Movie Like '*Orapronobis*,'" *Manila Chronicle*, July 9, 1989.
25. Isah V. Red, "Brocka Clears Air on '*Les insoumis*,'" *Manila Chronicle*, July 24, 1989.
26. Jose F. Lacaba, "'*Orapronobis*': A Clarification," *Philippine Daily Inquirer*, n.d., Clippings, LOBC.
27. Logarta, "There's a Lot of Risk."
28. Elamparo, "The Film and the Furor."
29. Lacaba, "'*Orapronobis*': A Clarification."
30. Sheila S. Coronel, *Coups, Cults and Cannibals: Chronicles of a Troubled Decade, 1982–1992* (Manila: Anvil, 1993), 112.
31. *Philippines: Unlawful Killings by Military and Paramilitary Forces* (London: Amnesty International Publications, 1988), 11.
32. David Wurfel, *Filipino Politics: Development and Decay* (Ithaca, NY: Cornell University Press, 1988), 311.
33. "Brocka Complains of Harassment," *Manila Chronicle*, May 27, 1989.
34. Dan Connell, "Apocalypse Again, the Philippines: America's Next Secret War," *Spin*, September 1987, 44.
35. Merlinda Manalo, "Morato Denies Censoring New Film of Brocka," *Philippine Daily Globe*, May 17, 1989; Chris Chase, "Marcos Is Gone, but Fear Still Reigns in Philippines," *Manhattan Daily News*, October 18, 1989.
36. Wurfel, *Filipino Politics*, 316.
37. Hubert Niogret and Paul Louis Thirard, "Lino Brocka," *Positif*, nos. 341–342 (1989): 2–6.
38. Wurfel, *Filipino Politics*, 19.
39. Danièle Parra, "Entretien avec Lino Brocka: Mon film le plus politique," *Revue du Cinéma*, no. 451 (1989): 41.
40. Len, "*Les insoumis*," *Variety*, June 14, 1989, 23.
41. Alain Badiou, *Cinema*, trans. Susan Spitzer (Malden, MA: Polity Press, 2013), 9.
42. Badiou, *Cinema*, 19.
43. Lacaba, "'*Orapronobis*': A Clarification."
44. Len, "*Les insoumis*."
45. Joel David, *The National Pastime: Contemporary Philippine Cinema* (Pasig: Anvil, 1990), 187.
46. Randy S. David, "Orapronobis," *Diyaryo Filipino*, October 24, 1989.
47. Richard Corliss, "Sex, Lies, Action!," *Time (Asian Edition)*, June 5, 1989, 53.
48. Raphaël Bassan, "*Les insoumis*: Un cinéma de l'urgence," *Revue du Cinéma*, no. 451 (August 1989): 39.
49. Anselm Jungeblodt, "Fight for Us," *Film-Dienst* 45, no. 6 (March 17, 1992): 33.
50. Coronel, "Brocka Film Focuses on the Underside."
51. John J. Michalczyk, *Costa-Gavras* (Philadelphia: Art Alliance Press, 1984), 11, 50.

52. Michalczyk, *Costa-Gavras*, 46.
53. Badiou, *Cinema*, 10.
54. Karl Schoonover, *Brutal Vision: The Neorealist Body in Postwar Italian Cinema* (Minneapolis: University of Minnesota Press, 2012), 109.
55. Schoonover, *Brutal Vision*, xxviii.
56. Schoonover, *Brutal Vision*, xxx.
57. Schoonover, *Brutal Vision*, xvii.
58. Schoonover, *Brutal Vision*, 110.
59. Schoonover, *Brutal Vision*, xxx.
60. "UP Film Center Venue ng '*Ora*. . .'?," *Diyaryo Filipino*, August 7, 1989, Clippings, LOBC.
61. Jim Libiran, "*Orapronobis*, dapat ipalabas," *Sensation*, November 7, 1989.
62. Belinda Olivares-Cunanan, "Brocka Depicts Pinoys as Cannibals," *Philippine Daily Inquirer*, July 11, 1989.
63. Belinda Olivares-Cunanan, "Pinays Abroad Losing Jobs," *Philippine Daily Inquirer*, July 19, 1989.
64. Frank Mallo, "Brocka's Cory Tirade Draws Angry Reactions," *People's Journal Tonight*, May 18, 1989, Clippings, LOBC.
65. Cynthia Sycip, "Marcos Money Eyed behind Brocka's Anti-Cory Movie," *People's Journal Tonight*, June 12, 1989.
66. Jose F. Lacaba, "*Oraprobnobis* II: The 'Dear Bel' Letter," *National Midweek*, November 15, 1989.
67. Jim C. Naval, "Reds—Welcome to Showbiz!," *Bongga*, August 31, 1989.
68. Pecho, "Brocka's *Oraprobnobis* to Be Shown Uncensored."
69. Manuel L. Morato, "Brocka's Delusions," *Philippine Star*, May 19, 1989, Clippings, LOBC.
70. Logarta, "There's a Lot of Risk."
71. Mario A. Hernando, "'Oraprobnobis' Not Qualified—Morato," *Malaya*, January 4, 1990.
72. Mario A. Hernando, "No Theater for Masterwork?," *Malaya*, October 25, 1989.
73. "Press Kit for *Fight for Us*" (Pathé, 1989).
74. Candy Quimpo, "The Vigilantes," *Asia Magazine*, August 7, 1988, 16.
75. Coco Fusco, "Brocka Promises," *The Village Voice*, October 17, 1989.
76. William Chapman, *Inside the Philippine Revolution* (New York: W. W. Norton, 1987), 17.
77. Tom Lutz, "Men's Tears and the Roles of Melodrama," in *Boys Don't Cry? Rethinking Narratives of Masculinity and Emotion in the U.S.*, ed. Milette Shamir and Jennifer Travis (New York: Columbia University Press, 2012), 186.
78. David, "*Oraprobnobis*."
79. William Chapman, *Inside the Philippine Revolution* (New York: W. W. Norton, 1987), 244.
80. Nathan Gilbert Quimpo, *Contested Democracy and the Left in the Philippines after Marcos* (New Haven: Yale University Southeast Asia Studies, 2008), 77.
81. Chapman, *Inside the Philippine Revolution*, 1987, 168.

82. Red, "Brocka Clears Air on 'Les insoumis.'"

83. In the 1970s, members of the Filipino Left held different visions of the means and ends of radical social change. Some of those differences, especially with respect to Communism, are discussed in Benjamin Pimentel, *UG: An Underground Tale* (Manila: Anvil, 2006), 45–46.

84. Todd McCarthy, "Pictures: Top Filipino Helmer Brocka Set To Lens English-Lingo Pic For Col," *Variety*, April 29, 1987.

85. Mario E. Bautista, "Walang pakialam ang producer [The Producer Did Not Interfere]," *Tempo*, May 16, 1990.

86. William C. Rempel, *Delusions of a Dictator: The Mind of Marcos as Revealed in His Secret Diaries* (Boston: Little, Brown, 1993), 23.

87. Hermie Rotea, *Marcos' Lovey Dovie* (Los Angeles: Liberty Publishing, 1983), 122.

88. Walden F. Bello and John Gershman, "Democratization and Stabilization in the Philippines," *Critical Sociology* 17, no. 1 (1990): 45.

89. Katherine W. Ellison, *Imelda, Steel Butterfly of the Philippines* (New York: McGraw-Hill, 1988), 135.

90. Ellison, *Imelda*, 135.

91. Ferdinand Marcos, *Notes on the New Society of the Philippines* (Manila: Marcos Foundation, 1973), v.

92. Marcos, *Notes on the New Society*, 33.

93. James Hamilton-Paterson, *America's Boy: The Marcoses and the Philippines* (New York: Henry Holt and Company, 1999), 265.

94. Rotea, *Marcos' Lovey Dovie*, 138.

95. Rempel, *Delusions of a Dictator*, 92.

96. Joel David, "'Head Held High,'" *National Midweek*, June 20, 1990, 28.

97. Ann Douglas, *The Feminization of American Culture* (New York: Macmillan, 1996), 12.

98. Douglas, *The Feminization of American Culture*, 12.

99. Alain Badiou, *Cinema*, trans. Susan Spitzer (Malden, MA: Polity Press, 2013), 3.

100. Gretchen Casper, "From Confrontation to Conciliation: The Philippine Path toward Democratic Consolidation," in *Pathways to Democracy: The Political Economy of Democratic Transitions*, ed. James Frank Hollifield and Calvin C. Jillson (New York: Routledge, 2014), 155.

101. Bello and Gershman, "Democratization and Stabilization in the Philippines," 147.

102. Rod Samson, "Nagsama muli: Sining, komersyo," *Bongga*, May 25, 1990.

103. Bibsy M. Carballo, "Ten Minutes of Lino Brocka," *Metro Times*, May 28, 1990.

104. Nestor U. Torre, "Political Limbo and Personal Hell," *Philippine Daily Inquirer*, May 20, 1990.

105. David, "'Head Held High.'"

106. Luis Francia, "Three Reviews," in *Memories of Overdevelopment: Reviews and Essays of Two Decades* (Mandaluyong City: Anvil, 1998), 87.

107. Nestor U. Torre, "Political Limbo and Personal Hell," May 20, 1990.

108. Isah V. Red, "Sudsy Politics," *Sunday Standard*, June 10, 1990.

109. John T. Sidel, *Capital, Coercion, and Crime: Bossism in the Philippines* (Stanford, CA: Stanford University Press, 1999), 146.

110. Sidel, *Capital, Coercion, and Crime*, 146.
111. Bello and Gershman, "Democratization and Stabilization in the Philippines," 48.
112. Sidel, *Capital, Coercion, and Crime*, 121.
113. Sidel, *Capital, Coercion, and Crime*, 11.
114. G. Luis Igaya, "The Political Economy of the Philippine Democratic Transition," in *Transitions to Democracy in East and Southeast Asia*, ed. Kristina N. Gaerlan (Quezon City: Institute for Popular Democracy, 1999), 37–38.
115. Jeffrey M. Riedinger, *Agrarian Reform in the Philippines: Democratic Transitions and Redistributive Reform* (Stanford, CA: Stanford University Press, 1995), 211.
116. Jose F. Lacaba, "Lino Brocka's Last Shooting Day," *Kapetesapatalim* (blog), May 24, 2009, accessed September 14, 2015, http://kapetesapatalim.blogspot.com/2009/05/lino-brockas-last-shooting-day.html.
117. Mario A. Hernando, "*Sa kabila ng lahat*: Bleak, Disturbing," in *The Urian Anthology, 1990–1999*, ed. Nicanor G. Tiongson (Quezon City: University of the Philippines Press, 2010), 160–61.
118. Hernando, "*Sa kabila ng lahat*: Bleak."
119. "Brocka's '*Sa kabila ng lahat*' Chosen Best Film by Young Critics," *Philippine Times Journal*, January 26, 1992.
120. Grace Javier Alfonso, "*Sa kabila ng lahat*: Brocka's Success within a Compromise," in *Lino Brocka: The Artist and His Times*, ed. Mario A. Hernando (Manila: Cultural Center of the Philippines, 1993), 199.
121. Alfonso, "*Sa kabila ng lahat*: Brocka's Success," 201.
122. Jacques Rancière, *The Intervals of Cinema*, trans. John Howe (London: Verso, 2014), 105.
123. Mike Wayne, *Political Film: The Dialectics of Third Cinema* (London: Pluto Press, 2001), 33.
124. Wayne, *Political Film*, 9.
125. Wayne, *Political Film*, 125.
126. Wayne, *Political Film*, 1.
127. Wayne, *Political Film*, 124.
128. David, "'Head Held High.'"

CHAPTER 7. PICTURING "A FAGGOT'S DILEMMA"

1. Jacques Fieschi, "Violences," *Cinématographe*, April 1982, 17.
2. Eve Kosofsky Sedgwick, *Between Men: English Literature and Male Homosocial Desire* (New York: Columbia University Press, 1985), 208.
3. Board of Censors for Motion Pictures, *Guidelines on Film and Television Production and Exhibition* (Manila: National Media Production Center, 1975), 2.
4. Guillermo C. de Vega, *Film and Freedom: Movie Censorship in the Philippines* (Manila: Guillermo de Vega, 1975), 57.
5. Karl Schoonover and Rosalind Galt, *Queer Cinema in the World* (Durham, NC: Duke University Press, 2016), 9.

6. Eve Kosofsky Sedgwick and Annamarie Jagose, "Queer and Now," in *The Routledge Queer Studies Reader*, ed. Donald E. Hall (New York: Routledge, 2013), 8–9.

7. "Patawarin mo po sila! [Please Forgive Them]," *Asia-Philippines Leader*, November 12, 1971.

8. Joel David, "Thinking Straight: Queer Imaging in Lino Brocka's *Maynila* (1975)," *Plaridel* 9, no. 2 (August 2012): 21.

9. David, "Thinking Straight," 35.

10. John Champagne, *Italian Masculinity as Queer Melodrama: Caravaggio, Puccini, Contemporary Cinema* (New York: Palgrave, 2015), 149.

11. Champagne *Italian Masculinity*, 147.

12. Daniel Gerould, "The Americanization of Melodrama," in *American Melodrama*, ed. Daniel Gerould (New York: Performing Arts Journal Publications, 1983), 8.

13. "'Brocka Presents' Tackles Controversial Subject Matters," *The Daily Tribune*, May 18, 1979.

14. Jarius Bondoc, "'Brocka Presents': And More of Brocka's Frustrations," *TV Times*, June 17, 1979, 19.

15. Judith Halberstam, *The Queer Art of Failure* (Durham, NC: Duke University Press, 2011), 11–12.

16. J. Neil Garcia, *Philippine Gay Culture: Binabae to Bakla, Silahis to MSM*, 2nd ed. (Quezon City: University of the Philippines Press, 2008), 74.

17. Leopoldo Cacnio, "A Different Breed of 'Bomba,'" *Philippine Graphic*, February 17, 1971.

18. Vito Russo, *The Celluloid Closet: Homosexuality in the Movies* (New York: Harper & Row, 1987), 146.

19. Niall Richardson, *The Queer Cinema of Derek Jarman: Critical and Cultural Readings* (London: I. B. Tauris, 2008), 48.

20. Cacnio, "A Different Breed of 'Bomba,'" 38.

21. Lino Brocka, "Screenplay of *Tubog sa ginto*" (n.d.), 10, Scripts, LOBC.

22. Russo, *The Celluloid Closet*, 294.

23. Harry Benshoff and Sean Griffin, *Queer Images: A History of Gay and Lesbian Film in America* (Lanham, MD: Rowman & Littlefield, 2006), 148–49.

24. Vega, *Film and Freedom*, 38.

25. Board of Censors for Motion Pictures, "Guidelines on Film and Television Production and Exhibition" (Manila: National Media Production Center, 1975), 28.

26. Brocka, "*Tubog sa ginto* Screenplay," 21.

27. Brocka, "*Tubog sa ginto* Screenplay," 26.

28. Board of Censors for Motion Pictures, *Guidelines on Film and Television Production and Exhibition*, 27–29.

29. Brocka, "*Tubog sa ginto* Screenplay," 28.

30. Vega, *Film and Freedom*, 23, 60.

31. Nestor U. Torre, "Pelikula, The Year in Philippine Movies," *Fookien Times Yearbook*, 1971.

32. "Jay Ilagan: Sa '*Tubog*' abangan [Jay Ilagan: Watch Him in 'Tubog']," *Pilipino Star*, January 17, 1971.

33. "Bakit hindi itinanghal ang *Tubog sa ginto* [Why Was *Tubog sa ginto* Not Exhibited?]," *Hiwaga Komiks*, January 9, 1971, 8.
34. Amelita Reysio-Cruz, "Talented Actor-Director Joins the 'Bomba' Wave," *Philippine Panorama*, January 17, 1971, 15.
35. Julie Y. Daza, "Brocka's 'Bomba,'" *Mirror*, February 4, 1971.
36. Cacnio, "A Different Breed of 'Bomba.'"
37. Clodualdo del Mundo Jr., "Review of *Tubog sa ginto*," in *The Urian Anthology, 1970–1979*, ed. Nicanor G. Tiongson (Manila: M. L. Morato, 1983), 200.
38. del Mundo Jr., "Review of *Tubog sa ginto*," 200.
39. Lee Edelman, *Homographesis: Essays in Gay Literary and Cultural Theory* (New York: Routledge, 1993), 187.
40. Edelman, *Homographesis*, 173.
41. Raymond Bonner, *Waltzing with a Dictator* (New York: Random House, 1987), 78.
42. James K. Boyce, *The Political Economy of Growth and Impoverishment in the Marcos Era* (Manila: Ateneo de Manila University Press, 1993), 249.
43. Petronilo Daroy, "On the Eve of Dictatorship and Revolution," in *Dictatorship and Revolution: Roots of People's Power*, ed. Aurora Javate de Dios, Petronilo Daroy, and Lorna Kalaw-Tirol (Manila: Conspectus Foundation, 1988), 9.
44. Primitivo Mijares, *The Conjugal Dictatorship of Ferdinand and Imelda Marcos* (San Francisco: Union Square Publications, 1976), 22.
45. Manuel Caoili, *The Origins of Metropolitan Manila: A Social and Political Analysis* (Quezon City: University of the Philippines Press, 1999), 136.
46. Brocka, "*Tubog sa ginto* Screenplay," 17.
47. Schoonover and Galt, *Queer Cinema in the World*, 290–93.
48. The version transmitted on the Philippine cable channel Cinema One is largely similar to the cut uploaded to YouTube and sold on pirate DVDs in that country.
49. Lino Brocka, *Tubog sa ginto*, VHS (Century Video, n.d.). The Worldcat database lists Manila and Cerritos, CA as places of publications for other tapes released by Century. The reference copy I used is courtesy of Jojo De Vera.
50. Brocka, "*Tubog sa ginto* Screenplay," 27.
51. Parker Tyler, *Screening the Sexes: Homosexuality in the Movies* (New York: Da Capo Press, 1993), 301.
52. The following articles note, respectively, that the film "made money" and was a "top-grosser at the box office": Cleo Cruz, "Uncle Mars Talks about Lino Brocka," n.d., Clippings, LOBC; Verushka, "That Man, Brocka," *Pilipino Reporter*, May 30, 1971.
53. Ricardo Lee, "Sandosenang komiks at isang interbyu [A Dozen Comic Books In One Interview]," *Asia-Philippines Leader*, December 3, 1971, 42.
54. Cacnio, "A Different Breed of 'Bomba.'"
55. Justino M. Dormiendo, "Brocka's Breakthroughs," *Philippines Sunday Express*, June 13, 1976, 28.
56. Board of Censors for Motion Pictures, *Guidelines on Film and Television Production and Exhibition*, 2.
57. Zenaida LaTorre, "The Last Word," *Klasiks Magazine Romance*, May 5, 1978.

58. Richard Dyer, *Now You See It: Studies on Lesbian and Gay Film* (London; New York: Routledge, 1990), 228.

59. "'*Ang tatay kong nanay*' Begins Where '*Hanggang dito . . .*' Ends—Brocka," *The Times Journal*, May 15, 1988, Clippings, LOBC.

60. Richard Dyer, *Gays and Film* (London: BFI, 1980), 35–36.

61. Tyler, *Screening the Sexes*, 55.

62. Edelman, *Homographesis*, 156.

63. Dyer, *Now You See It*, 230.

64. Garcia, *Philippine Gay Culture*, 91.

65. Linda Williams, *Playing the Race Card: Melodramas of Black and White from Uncle Tom to O. J. Simpson* (Princeton, NJ : Princeton University Press, 2001), 99.

66. Sara Ahmed, "Queer Feelings," in *The Routledge Queer Studies Reader*, ed. Donald E. Hall (London: Routledge, 2013), 423.

67. Orlando Nadres, "Screenplay of *Ang tatay kong nanay*" (1978), 65, Scripts, LOBC.

68. Tom Lutz, "Men's Tears and the Roles of Melodrama," in *Boys Don't Cry?: Rethinking Narratives of Masculinity and Emotion in the U.S.*, ed. Milette Shamir and Jennifer Travis (New York: Columbia University Press, 2012), 186.

69. Ahmed, "Queer Feelings," 429.

70. Robin Wood, "Responsibilities of a Gay Film Critic," in *Out in Culture : Gay, Lesbian, and Queer Essays on Popular Culture*, ed. Corey Creekmur and Alexander Doty (Durham, NC: Duke University Press, 1995), 14.

71. Lee Edelman, *No Future: Queer Theory and the Death Drive* (Durham, NC: Duke University Press Books, 2004), 57.

72. E. Ann Kaplan, *Motherhood and Representation: The Mother in Popular Culture and Melodrama* (New York: Routledge, 1992), 80.

73. Chelo R. Banal, "Don't Send in Just Any Clown, It's Got to Be Dolphy," *Philippine Panorama*, July 23, 1978.

74. Ernie Pecho, "Sa shooting ni Brocka [At Brocka's Filming]," n.d., Clippings, LOBC.

75. Rod Samson, "Dolphy, Niño and Brocka in One Package," *Kislap Magasin*, June 1, 1978.

76. Champagne, *Italian Masculinity*, 167.

77. Nadres, "*Ang tatay kong nanay* Screenplay," 7.

78. Nadres, "*Ang tatay kong nanay* Screenplay," 87.

79. Katherine W. Ellison, *Imelda, Steel Butterfly of the Philippines* (New York: McGraw-Hill, 1988), 127.

80. Ferdinand Lopez, "Spectacular Spaces, Spaces of Spectacle: Philippine Gay Beauty Pageants and the Aesthetics of Otherness in the Martial Law Period" (10th International Conference on Philippine Studies, Silliman University, Dumaguete City, 2016).

81. Nadres, "*Ang tatay kong nanay* Screenplay," 94.

82. Ellison, *Imelda, Steel Butterfly*, 95.

83. Michael L. Tan, "Survival through Pluralism: Emerging Gay Communities in the Philippines," in *Gay and Lesbian Asia: Culture, Identity, Community*, ed. Gerard Sullivan and Peter A. Jackson (New York: Routledge, 2011), 123.

84. Gerry A. Camacho, "Meet Jesus Yu," *Weekly Topstar*, May 26, 1978, Clippings 1979.

85. Gerry A. Camacho, "Dolphy at Lino Brocka: Hindi kaya mahirapan sa isa't isa? [Will Dolphy and Lino Brocka Get Along?]," *Movie Specials*, May 14, 1978.

86. Baby K. Jimenez, "Dolphy at Niño: Wala bang sapawan sa kanilang pelikula? [Did Dolphy and Niño Try to Outdo Each Other?]," *Kislap Magasin*, June 15, 1978; "At ngayon ... Dolphy at Niño sa pelikula ni Brocka [And Now ... Dolphy and Niño in Brocka's Film]," *Weekly Superstar*, May 1, 1978, Clippings, LOBC.

87. Banal, "Don't Send in Just Any Clown, It's Got to Be Dolphy."

88. Justino M. Dormiendo, "Sa bitag ng komersiyalismo [The Trap of Commercialism]," *Sagisag*, June 1978.

89. Dormiendo, "Sa bitag ng komersiyalismo."

90. Richardson, *The Queer Cinema of Derek Jarman*, 48.

91. Noel Vera, *Critic After Dark : A Review of Philippine Cinema* (Singapore: BigO Books, 2005), 132.

92. Such criticism does not account for the actor's skill or the fact that his performance may have been informed by his affection for his openly gay brother and fellow actor Georgie Quizon. "Ex-CCP Top Official Opposed Dolphy's National Artist Award, Says Guidote-Alvarez," *Philippine Daily Inquirer*, July 5, 2012, https://entertainment.inquirer.net/47941/ex-ccp-president-opposed-dolphy%E2%80%99s-national-artist-award-says-guidote-alvarez.

93. Ronald Baytan, "Bading na Bading: Evolving Identities in Philippine Cinema," in *AsiaPacifiQueer: Rethinking Genders and Sexualities*, ed. Fran Martin et al. (Urbana: University of Illinois Press, 2008), 183.

94. "Brocka Film," *Times Journal*, January 18, 1982.

95. Boy C. De Guia, "Christopher: Brocka na, Bernal pa!," *Weekly Movie Specials*, January 21, 1982.

96. "Si Dina Bonnevie ay naging asawa ni Christopher De Leon [Dina Bonnevie Plays Christopher De Leon's Spouse]," *Pilipino Express*, May 28, 1982.

97. Ricardo F. Lo, "Bibeth's 'obra maestra' [Bibeth's Masterpiece]," *Philippines Daily Express*, May 29, 1982.

98. Lo, "Bibeth's 'obra maestra.'"

99. Michael Tan, "Silahis: Looking for the Missing Filipino Bisexual Male," in *Bisexualities and AIDS: International Perspectives*, ed. Peter Aggleton (London: Taylor & Francis, 1996), 207.

100. Patricia White, *Uninvited: Classical Hollywood Cinema and Lesbian Representability* (Bloomington: Indiana University Press, 1999), 12.

101. Alexander Doty, *Making Things Perfectly Queer: Interpreting Mass Culture* (Minneapolis: University of Minnesota Press, 1993), xv.

102. Tan, "Silahis," 207.

103. Garcia, *Philippine Gay Culture*, 134.

104. Greg Laconsay, "Are Baklas Really Effeminate?," *WHO*, August 11, 1982.

105. Martin F. Manalansan IV, *Global Divas: Filipino Gay Men in the Diaspora* (Durham, NC: Duke University Press, 2003), 25.

106. Quoted in Edelman, *Homographesis*, 200.

107. Tan, "Silahis," 219.

108. Richardson, *The Queer Cinema of Derek Jarman*, 28.

109. Chris Straayer, *Deviant Eyes, Deviant Bodies* (New York: Columbia University Press, 1996), 19.

110. René Girard, "Mimetic Desire in the Underground: Feodor Dostoevsky," in *Mimesis and Theory: Essays on Literature and Criticism, 1953–2005*, ed. Robert Doran (Stanford, CA: Stanford University Press, 2011), 247–48.

111. Sedgwick, *Between Men*, 1.

112. Sedgwick, 21.

113. Nick Davis, *The Desiring-Image: Gilles Deleuze and Contemporary Queer Cinema* (New York: Oxford University Press, 2013), 171.

114. Halberstam, *The Queer Art of Failure*, 74.

115. Oscar Miranda, "Narito na naman ang masasayang araw [Happy Days Are Here Again]," n.d., Clippings, LOBC.

116. Carol J. Clover, *Men, Women, and Chain Saws: Gender in the Modern Horror Film* (Princeton, NJ: Princeton University Press, 1993), 51.

117. Linda Williams, "Film Bodies: Gender, Genre, and Excess," in *Film and Theory: An Anthology*, ed. Toby Miller and Robert Stam (Malden, MA: Wiley, 2000), 215.

118. Williams, "Film Bodies," 215.

119. Straayer, *Deviant Eyes, Deviant Bodies*, 54.

120. Harry M. Benshoff and Sean Griffin, *Queer Cinema: The Film Reader* (New York: Routledge, 2004), 3; Nikki Sullivan, *A Critical Introduction to Queer Theory* (New York: New York University Press, 2003), 44.

121. Miranda, "Happy Days."

122. Wilfredo L. Alberca, "Brocka Makes Another Successful Attempt at Presenting Homosexuality," *Times Journal*, 1982, James Dela Rosa Collection, *Pelikula ATBP* (blog) https://pelikulaatbp.blogspot.com/2017/01/film-review-palipat-lipat-papalit-palit.html.

123. "Photograph from *Sa fifth floor* with a Caption Clipped from *The Daily Mirror*," February 20, 1971, Rizal Library Special Collections, Ateneo de Manila University.

124. Behn Cervantes, "*Avenida Boy*: Must Be Taken with a Grain of Salt," *Asia-Philippines Leader*, n.d., Clippings, LOBC.

125. Alfredo Marquez and Liza Amor, "From Gayboy to Woman: A Sad and Painful Trail," *Weekly Nation*, n.d., Clippings, LOBC.

126. Cacnio, "A Different Breed of 'Bomba.'"

127. Halberstam, *The Queer Art of Failure*, 70.

128. Heather Love, *Feeling Backward: Loss and the Politics of Queer History* (Cambridge, MA: Harvard University Press, 2009), 7.

129. Love, *Feeling Backward*, 4.

130. Fred Reyes, "Where the Gays Are," *Philippine Panorama*, August 6, 1978, 47.

131. "Homosexual Artists," *WHO*, July 21, 1982, 32.

132. Gregorio Moral and Rustica Moral, "Accepting Homosexuality," *Mr. & Ms.*, May 25, 1982, 49.

CODA

1. Caryn James, "Mingling Sex and Politics In a Gay Bar in Manila," *New York Times*, March 16, 1990, C12.

2. Mars Cavestany, "Brocka, a Disappointment in His Film, 'Macho Dancer,'" *The Journal*, January 16, 1989, 15.

3. Melissa Contreras, "Life in the Sleazy Lane," *Manila Chronicle Weekend Guide*, March 5, 1988, 15.

4. Boy C. De Guia, "Brocka Wins in Berlin Filmfest," *News Today*, April 20, 1988, 6.

5. "Brocka Returns to Film Commentary," *Malaya*, January 12, 1989.

6. "*Macho Dancer*: Brocka's Dream Movie," *Manila Standard*, January 16, 1989, 15.

7. Dodo Dee, "Brocka Directs TV Commercial," *Manila Chronicle*, May 13, 1988.

8. Ricardo Lo, "Lino Brocka: 'Stop the Fascist,'" *Starweek Newsmagazine*, August 27, 1988.

9. David Overbey, "Letter from David Overbey to Lino Brocka," February 11, 1987, Correspondences, LOBC.

10. "*Macho Dancer*: Brocka's Dream Movie."

11. Raul Manglapus, "Telex to the Philippine Consul General in Toronto from the Secretary of Foreign Affairs," September 16, 1988, Correspondences, LOBC.

12. Juan Ona, "Letter from the Philippine Consul General in Toronto to Secretary of Foreign Affairs Raul Manglapus Regarding *Macho Dancer*," September 29, 1988, Correspondences, LOBC.

13. Contreras, "Life in the Sleazy Lane."

14. Melanie Manlogon, "Interview: Alan Paule," *Midweek*, April 13, 1988, 22.

15. Contreras, "Life in the Sleazy Lane," 15.

16. "*Macho Dancer*: Brocka's Dream Movie."

17. Ian Victoriano, "Much Ado Over 'Macho Dancer,'" *Midweek*, January 18, 1989, 20.

18. Margie T. Logarta, "There's a Lot of Risk When You Make a Movie Like '*Orapronobis*,'" *Manila Chronicle*, July 9, 1989, 16.

19. Elvira Mata, "Disappointing for a Brocka," *Philippine Daily Globe*, January 8, 1989.

20. "Brocka, Imbitado sa UN [Invited to the UN]," *Bongga*, November 2, 1990.

21. Logarta, "There's a Lot of Risk."

22. Ernie Pecho, "Brocka Now a World Class Director," *Philippine Daily Globe*, November 25, 1988.

23. "International News: Brocka to Direct Belbo's *Basement*," *Screen International*, May 27, 1989.

24. Nestor Torre, "Rape and Marital Rape," *Philippine Daily Inquirer*, July 2, 1991.

25. Boy C. De Guia, "Death and Lino Brocka," *Philippine Graphic*, June 10, 1991.

26. Robert Burgoyne, *Film Nation: Hollywood Looks at U.S. History* (Minneapolis: University of Minnesota Press, 1997), 13.

INDEX

Above Everything Else (*Sa kabila ng lahat*, Brocka, 1991), xxiv, 191–95, 243; reception, 195, 196; storyline, 192–94
Adorno, Theodor, 44, 45, 47
Adultery: Aida Macaraeg Case No. 7892 (Brocka, 1984), 110–17, 126; censorship of, 117; reception, 117, 126; storyline, xxii, 109–14, 117
Ahmed, Sara, 217, 218
Alberca, Wilfredo, 234
Alfonso, Grace, 195
allegories, 11, 76; of anti-authoritarian resistance, 139, 141; in Brocka's films, 2, 21–22, 107, 132; political, 4, 21–22, 39, 85. *See also* Marcos, Ferdinand, allegories of; Marcos, Ferdinand, regime of, allegories of; Marcos, Imelda, allegories of; *and under individual film titles*
Allen, Richard, 101, 104
Always Changing, Always Moving (*Palipat-lipat, papalit-palit,* Brocka), 223–34; bisexuality in, 224–33; censorship of, 227, 233–34; reception, 234; storyline, xxiv, 224–25, 227–31, 233
Amor, Liza, 234–35
Andreotti Law of 1949 (Italy), 51
Andrews, Nigel, 146
Angela, the Marked One (*Angela markado,* Brocka, 1980), 77, 97–106; allegories in, 97; censorship of, 97, 102, 104, 105; violence depicted, 98–103, 104–5

Anker, Elizabeth, xviii–xix
Antonio, Lamberto, *Insiang* screenplay by, 49
Aquino, Begnino "Ninoy," Jr., 153, 154, 182; assassination, xv, xxii, 73, 128–30, 133, 138–39, 142, 183–84
Aquino, Corazon "Cory," presidency of, xxiii, 153, 161, 171, 178, 180; corruption in family, 191–92; disagreements with Brocka, 177, 244; fight against communism, 167, 193; reform programs, 162, 242
Arago, Jorge, 19, 21
Arthur, Paul, 79
Aunor, Nora, *Bona* producer, xi
authoritarianism, xii, 1–41, 162–63, 165, 166, 209, 212; capitalism and, 136–39; melodramas of, xvi, xx, 44, 62, 72, 195; parental, 66, 68, 72; patriarchy and, xx, 7, 13–18, 71, 133; personalist, 58–59, 156; politics of, xii–xiii, 46, 55; preserving, 108, 123; protests against, 139, 141, 159–60, 180; resurgence of, xxiv–xxv; symptoms of, 45, 209, 222; violence under, 81, 98–103, 107, 138, 184, 243. *See also* Marcos, Ferdinand, regime of; repression; *and under individual film titles*
autocracy/autocrats, 18, 50, 108; paranoia of, 46, 47, 57–58; patriarchal, 43–44, 97; violence of, 59, 81, 222. *See also* Marcos, Ferdinand, regime of

287

288   INDEX

Avena, M. R., 35–36
Avenida Boy (Borlaza, 1971), 234

Badiou, Alain, xvi, xvii, 171, 173, 187
Bakhtin, Mikhail, 244
Balbastro, Billy, 19, 54
Baltazar, Conrado, cinematographer: for *Angela*, 97; for *Insiang*, 51; for *Jaguar*, 90
Barbero, Carmelo, 51
Barrio Captain Tales (*Kabesang Tales*, Dumol, 1975), 5
Bassan. Raphäel, 172
Batac, Joe, *Weighed but Found Wanting* cinematographer, 4
Batch '81 (Mike De Leon, 1982), 66
Battleship Potemkin, The (Eisenstein, 1915), 86
Batyan, Ronald, 223
Bautista, Mario, 68, 95, 116, 158, 187, 190
Bazin, André, 29
Beams, Dovie, affair with Ferdinand Marcos, xxiv, 115, 182, 185, 191
Bello, Walden, 183, 188–89, 192
Belluso, Anselle, 116
Belmont, Vera, 133
Benjamin, Walter, 22
Bicycle Thieves (De Sica, 1948), 55
Big Clock, The (Farrow, 1948), 90–91
bisexuality, xxiv, 79, 224–33
Blood of the Condor (Sanjines, 1969), 146
Body and Soul (Rossen, 1947), 76
bomba films, 203, 207
Bona (Brocka, 1980), xi–xiii, 87, 198
Bonifacio, Amelia Lapena, lawsuit against *Weighed but Found Wanting*, 19
Bonner, Raymond, 106, 136
Boorman, John, 87
Bordwell, David, 21
Bound by the Heavens (*Pinagbuklod ng langit*, Marcos biopic, 1969), 155
Boyce, James K., 84, 108
"Boy Who Wanted to Become 'Society,' The" (Nick Joaquin writing as Quijano de Manila), 83
Breathless (*À bout de souffle*, Godard, 1960), 54
Bride Wore Black, The (Truffaut, 1968), 97, 101
Broad, Robin, 119
Brocka, Lino, xx, 148, 243; allegories in films of, 2, 21–22, 107, 132; biographical information, xiv–xv, 204, 211, 212; Constitutional Commission delegate, 161, 163–64, 197; death of, xv, 195; European following, 54–55; political activism of, 129–31, 143, 157–58, 159–60, 243; sociopolitical critiques by, 7, 20, 21–22, 35–36, 171, 181. *See also individual films*
Bronze Model (*Modelong tanso*, Santiago), 71
Brooks, Peter, 103, 113

Cain and Abel (*Cain at Abel*, Brocka, 1982), 56–66; allegories in, 65; censorship of, 65, 66; hostile mother figure, xxii, 58, 60, 66, 71; political themes, 60–61, 65–66; reception, 42, 65–66; storyline, 56–63, 64–65
Calida, Franco, 167
Canby, Vincent, 178
Cannes International Film Festival, Brocka's films shown at: *Bona*, xi–xii; *Insiang*, 50, 54, 198; *Jaguar*, 74, 86–87, 97, 145; *My Own Country*, 145–46, 148; *Oraproobis*, 161, 164, 174, 176
Cannon Group (production company), 164, 176
Caoili, Manuel, 29
Caparas, Carlo, 101
capitalism, 34, 37, 38, 39, 120–21, 123; authoritarianism and, 136–39; crony, 127, 193
Carballo, Bibsy, 190
Carrie (De Palma, 1976), 67
Carunungan, Celso Al, 22
Casper, Gretchen, 162
Caught in the Act (Brocka, 1981), 77, 107
Cawleti, John G., 4, 39–40
censorship, xiii, xiv, xv, 2, 43, 129, 133, 198–99, 240. *See also* Film Ratings Board (FRB); *and under individual film titles*
Cervantes, Behn, arrest of, 148
Chain of Love (*Cadena de amor*, Brocka, 1971), 3
Champagne, John, 199
Chapman, William, 88, 92, 140
Cherry Blossoms (Brocka, 1972), 3
Chinese people, prejudice against, 33, 36–37, 119, 134
Christmas Carol, A (Dickens), 91
Ciment, Michel, 85
cinema, Philippine: Brocka's remaking of, 3, 40–41; peak years, xiii–xiv; transcultural/transnational nature of, 3, 54–56, 132, 173–74, 241, 242–43. *See also* commercial films; independent films; melodramas; prestige films
Cinema Artists (production company), 23
CineManila (production company), 3, 19, 41, 54
cinema politics, 93, 160, 236; anti-authoritarian, 160, 199, 200; Brocka's, xvi–xvii, xviii, xxiv, 26, 133, 174, 195–97, 242–43; censorship and, 4, 72; neorealism a feature of, 9; social problem films, xiv, 41. *See also* political

melodramas; politics; sociopolitical critiques
Clarence, Carlos, 104
class(es), xviii, 9, 29, 81–82, 189; conflict between, 83, 84, 88; inequities between, 27, 38–39; mobility of, 77, 79, 83, 91. *See also* working class
class melodramas, 77–84
Cobra (Cosmatos, 1986), 167
commercial films, xiv, 40–41, 75, 158–59, 235, 245; Brocka's, xv, xxiv, 54, 130–31, 157, 162, 196, 237, 240, 242
communism/communists, 92, 140–41, 167, 170, 176, 183–84, 245, 278n83; fighting against, xxii, 63, 105, 138, 162, 169, 193. *See also* Marxism; socialism
Condition of the Working Class in England, The (Engels), 39, 114
Connery, Sean, 87
Coppola, Francis Ford, 148
Corliss, Richard, 172–73, 174
Coronel, Sheila, 172–73
corporealism, 173–74, 177. *See also* neorealism, Italian; realism
Costa-Gavras, Constantin, films of, xvi, 173
Cover, Carol, 232
Cowie, Elizabeth, 76, 94
crime melodramas. *See* film noir
Cruz, Isagani, xix, 65–66, 90, 97, 104
Cruz, M. N., 19
curfew, xxii, 12–14, 44, 77, 106, 222. *See also* martial law

Dalisay, Jose Y., Jr., *Whore of a Mother* screenplay, 69, 260n119
David, Joel, 171–72, 185, 190, 197, 199
David, Randolf, 36, 172, 179
Davis, Nick, 230
Dawn of A New Day (*Ang bagong umaga*, Gerardo De Leon, 1952), 20
Daza, Julie Yap, 207–8
Death Wish [Winner, 1974], 101
De Belen, Janice, 126
De Castro, Pio, III, 54
De Dios, Emmanuel, 108, 110, 119
DeGuia, Boy C., *Macho Dancer* producer and publicist, 237
De Leon, Christopher, 243
De Leon, Gerardo, 5, 20
De Leon, Mike, 23, 129, 133; *Manila in the Claws of Light* cinematographer, 29, 30, 31, 35; *Sister Stella L.*, 130, 131
Deleuze, Gilles, xvii, 131, 132, 133, 143, 153

Del Mundo, Clodualdo, Jr., xix, 208; *Manila in the Claws of Light* screenplay, 23, 24, 159
DeSica, Victor, 20
dictatorship. *See* Marcos, Ferdinand, regime of
Dimaranan, Mariani, 166
Dimendberg, Edward, 87, 88
Diokno, Serena, 130
Dirty Affair, A (*Gumapang ka sa lusak*, Brocka), 180–91; communists in, 183–84; intertextuality in, 184, 186–91; political themes, 181, 185–91; reception, 190–91, 196; storyline, xxiii–xxiv, 181–85, 187–89
Doane, Mary Ann, 42
Dodes'ka-den (Kurosawa, 1970), 55
Dormiendo, Gino, 19–20, 21, 35, 36, 213, 223
Doty, Alexander, 225
Dumas, M., 55
Durgnat, Raymond, 76, 79, 87
Duterte, Rodrigo, xxiv–xxv, 177–78
Dyer, Richard, 214, 215

economy, crisis in 1980s, xviii, xxii–xxiii, 73, 108–27, 128, 208–9. *See also* poverty, Marcos-era
Edelman, Lee, 208, 218
effeminophobia, 215, 220, 223, 234. *See also* homophobia
El filibusterismo (Rizal), 6, 27, 38
Ellison, Katherine, 184, 222
Epistola, Nieves, 35, 36
eroticism: bisexual, 224–33; gay male, 79, 203–8, 219–20, 234–35, 239
Espiritu, Christian, 86
exploitation films, xiv, 78, 104–5, 159, 164, 190, 196, 240, 254n91. *See also* sexploitation films

family melodramas, xviii, xxii–xxiii, 108–27, 212, 220; *Adultery: Aida Macaraeg Case No. 7892*, 110–17; *My Father, My Mother*, 214, 215–19, 220; *Such Pain, Brother Eddie*, 117–26
Fariñas, Leticia, *Whore of a Mother* story outline, 69, 70
Favali, Tullio, 166
Fernandez, Rudy, 133
Fieschi, Jacques, xi–xii, 85, 198, 199
film noir, xxii, 74–107; *Angela, the Marked One*, 97–106; class themes, 77, 79, 80, 87–88; elements of, 75–77; female characters, 94–97; *Jaguar*, 74–97; *My Own Country*, 145; political themes, 76, 77, 90, 94, 97; sexual themes, 79, 80; slums as settings for, 86–90

INDEX

Film Ratings Board (FRB), 66, 117, 158. *See also* censorship
First Quarter Storm, 1–2
Flesh to Flesh (*Laman sa laman,* Pacheco, 1970), 234–35
Francia, Luis H., 20, 178, 190
Francisco, Butch, 158, 159
Franco, Francisco, regime of, 43, 87
Free the Artist Movement (aka Concerned Artists of the Philippines (CAP)), 129, 147
Fusco, Coco, 178

Galman, Rolando, 182
Galt, Rosalind, 199, 209
Garcia, Jesselynn L., 19, 20, 21
Garcia, Neil, 202, 217, 226
Garcia Roque, Maria Socorro, 35
Garsault, Alain, 88
Geddes, Barbara, 127, 156
gender. *See* politics, gender
Gershman, John, 183, 192
Girard, René, 228–29
Gledhill, Christine, 122
God Is Sleeping (*Natutulog pa ang Diyos,* Brocka, 1988), 239
Gold Plated (*Tubog sa ginto,* Brocka, 1971), 200–214; censorship of, 203, 205–6, 209–14; homosexual themes, xxiv, 3, 203–14, 234, 235, 236; political themes, 209–14; reception, 213; storyline, 201–3
Gonzalez, Jose Antonio, 133
Great Gatsby, The (Fitzgerald), 83
Guillevic, Eugène, 55

Halberstam, Jack, 231, 235
Harvey, David, 123
Hau, Caroline S., 36–37
Heat Wave (*Init,* Brocka, 1979), 66–67
Hernando, Mario, 35, 37–38, 195
Hollywood melodramas, xvii, xix, 19, 131, 132
homelessness, 27–30. *See also* squatters/squatting
homophobia, 199, 206, 207–8, 217, 222, 235–37. *See also* effeminophobia
homosexuality/homosexuals. *See* eroticism, gay male; politics, gay identity; queer melodramas; *and under individual film titles*
Honig, Bonnie, xix, 73
Horkheimer, Max, 44
Horny (*Hayok,* Abalos, 1970), 203, 235
"Hostages or Hosts" (Carreon), 133

hostile mothers, xxi–xxii, 42–46, 56–60, 66–67, 71, 72–73
How Are the Kids? (international anthology film), 242
human rights: films about, 162, 167, 173, 177–78, 243; Marcos era violations, xiii, xxiii, 162, 176
human trafficking, 30–33, 38. *See also* prostitution
Hutchcroft, Paul, 119

I for Icarus (Verneuil, 1979), 130
Imitation of Life (Sirk, 1959), 43
independent films, 40, 118, 200, 241, 245
informal settlements/settlers. *See* slums; squatters/squatting
Insiang (Brocka, 1976), 44–56; authoritarianism in, 45, 47, 50, 55–56; censorship of, 49–51, 55; French theatrical release, 54–56; hostile mother figure in, 42, 45, 55–56, 72; Oresteian script, 72–73; political themes, 50–53; reception, 53–56; slum settings in, 50–53, 54; storyline, xxi–xxii, 44–50
International Monetary Fund (IMF), loans from, 26, 109
In the Blink of an Eye (*Kisapmata,* Mike de Leon, 1981), 43
In the Claws of Light (*Sa mga kuko ng liwanag,* Edgardo M. Reyes), 23, 27, 36, 38, 39, 130
In the Realm of the Senses (Oshima, 1976), 67
I Spit on Your Grave (Zarchi, 1978), 101

Jacobs, Amber, 72–73
Jaguar (Brocka, 1979), xxii, 74–97, 106, 107; censorship of, 75, 84–86, 93, 95, 96, 97; class melodrama in, 77–84, 92; *A Dirty Affair* a continuation of, 187–89; slum settings, 74, 77–78, 86–90, 91–92, 94–95; sociopolitical critiques in, 81, 82, 85, 90–97; storyline, 74, 77–82, 91–93, 94–95
Jameson, Fredric, 11, 39
Jocano, F. Landa, 45
Johnny Belinda (Jean Negulesco, 1948), 19
Jungeblodt, Anselm, 172

Kalaw-Katigbak, Maria, 146, 147, 160, 176
Kinder, Marsha, 43, 72
Kurosawa, Akira, influence of, 55

Lacaba, Emmanuel, 17
Lacaba, Jose F., 133, 180, 196; *Angela* screenplay, 77, 102; *Jaguar* screenplay, 77, 90, 91, 93, 102; *My Own Country* screenplay, 138, 141, 142–43,

147, 149; *Orapronobis* screenplay, 163–64, 166, 171, 177; tortured during Marcos regime, 100–101, 102
Lacap, Rody, *Orapronobis* cinematography, 171
LaTorre, Zenaida, 65
Leahy, James, 146
Lee, Ricardo, 196; *Jaguar* screenplay, 77, 90, 93, 102
Lizaso, Nick, 176
Lo, Ricardo, 117, 158
Local Government Code of 1991, 193
Lopez, Ferdinand, 222
Lorenzo, William, 195
Los olvidados (Buñuel, 1950), 55
Love, Heather, 235
Lucas, George, 148
Lumbera, Bienvenido, xii, 38, 39, 40
Lutz, Tom, 218
LVN Pictures (movie studio), 23

Macho Dancer (Brocka, 1989), xxiv, 176, 237–41
Maglipon, Jo-Ann, 51, 52
Magny, Joël, 95, 96
Maharlika (1970), 182
Making Love (Hiller, 1982), 205
Malaya Films, 133
male melodramas, xxiii, 73, 76, 179, 218
Manero, Norberto, Jr., 166
Manila, 28, 107, 221–22; beautification program, 28–29, 38, 51, 53, 78, 87. *See also* slums, in Manila
Manila in the Claws of Light (*Maynila: Sa mga kuko ng liwanag*, Brocka, 1975), xxi, 1–2, 22–39, 239; allegories in, 24, 25, 33, 39; authoritarianism in, 23–24, 33–35; censorship of, 23, 34, 38; homosexual themes, 30–31, 36, 198, 199, 241; noir elements, 77; political themes, 37–39, 141–42; as prestige film, 237, 239; realism in, 35, 36; reception, 34–39, 40; sociopolitical critiques, xxi, 23–33, 39; storyline, 1–2, 24–25, 30–31, 31–32, 33, 40; update to, 240–41; violence in, 33–34
Marchetti, Gina, 21–22, 37
Marcos, Ferdinand, 83, 128, 153, 154, 194; affair with Dovie Beams, xxiv, 115, 182, 185, 191; allegories of, xxi–xxii, 18, 56, 71, 73, 92–93, 155–56, 236; on the "old society," 23–24; posters of, 12, 13; reelection, 1–2, 55, 208–9; *Weighed but Found Wanting* references to, 4, 21
Marcos, Ferdinand, regime of, 18, 69, 73, 95–97, 103; allegories of, xii, 7, 22, 43, 105, 115, 133;

biopolitics of, 136–37; crime rate under, 84, 106–7; *Dirty Affair*'s post mortem on, 186–91; economic policies, 26, 27; history, 33–34; homosexuals vulnerable during, 222–23; labor export program, 123–26, 141, 242; as New Society, 13, 83–84, 86; normalization period, 77, 106; organized labor suppression, 137–45; overthrow of, xvi, 117, 144, 161–62, 166, 174, 178, 188; police state during, 88–90, 97; politics of, 5, 51; protests against, 47, 54, 60, 63–65, 128–30, 133, 139–45, 150, 153, 208; social and living conditions under, 55, 68–69, 70, 77, 97, 136–37, 208; torture during, xxii, 100–101, 105, 168, 190; violence during, 61–62, 62–63, 154, 155. *See also* censorship; economy, crisis in the 1980s; martial law; poverty, Marcos-era
Marcos, Imee, xxiv, xxv, 29, 52–53, 66
Marcos, Imelda, 23, 44, 53, 86, 128, 184, 194, 222; allegories of, 92–93, 146, 155, 180, 182; Brocka's tirades against, 129, 148; dislike of *Jaguar*, 75, 84, 85; Manila beautification program, 28–29, 38, 51, 53, 78, 87
Marcosian moments, xviii, 107; in *Angela*, 100–101; in *A Dirty Affair*, 184; in *Jaguar*, 81; in *Manila*, 33–34; in *Miguelito*, 154; in *My Own Country*, 138; in *Orapronobis*, 166, 168, 174; in *Sparkle in the Dark*, 243–44
Maricris Sioson: Japayuki (Romero, 1993), 242
Marks, Laura U., 131
martial law, 8, 38, 95, 107; declaration of, xiii, xxx, 27, 137; early years of, 5, 221–22; ending, xxii, 74–107, 234; justifying, 63, 83–84, 105, 184–85; protests against, 71, 222; violence associated with, 65, 101. *See also* curfew
martial law melodramas, xi–xiii, xxii, 1–41, 133, 166
Marxism, 82, 92, 110, 196. *See also* communism/communists; socialism
maternal melodramas, xxi–xxii, 42–73, 106; *Cain and Abel*, 56–66; *Heat Wave*, 66–67; *Insiang*, 44–56; *My Father, My Mother*, 215, 219; *Whore of a Mother*, 66–71
McCoy, Alfred, 88, 100
Medina, Belen, 47
melodramas, xvii–xx, 39, 64, 76, 160, 232; didacticism of, 26–27; Oedipal issues, 13, 14, 43, 153–54, 163; political themes, xix–xx, 22; television, 233–34; tropes of, 16, 103, 113, 134, 185, 202; visuals in, 35, 36. *See also individual types of melodramas*
Mendoza, Briliante, xxv

Mendoza, Estelito, 147–48
'Merika (Portes, 1984), 123
Midnight Cowboy (1969), 31
Miguelito: The Rebellious Child (*Miguelito: Ang Batang rebelde*, Brocka, 1985), 150–59; allegories in, 18, 151–56; autocracy in, 154, 155–59; censorship of, 157; political themes, 132–33, 150, 155–59, 162; reception, 126, 157, 158–59, 159–60; storyline, xxiii, 150–56, 157
Milan (Lamasan, 2004), 242
Miller, D. A., 226
Miranda, Oscar, 231
Missing (Costa-Gavras, 1982), 173
Miss X (Portes, 1980), 123
Morato, Manuel, Jr., 176, 239–40
Moskowitz, Gene, 85
Mother Courage and Her Children (Brecht), 52
Mother Dear (Brocka, 1982), xix
Mulach, Cheng, 126, 150
My Father, My Mother (*Ang tatay kong nanay*, Brocka, 1978), 214–23; homosexual themes, 235; political themes, 220–23; reception, 223; storyline, xxiv, 214–18, 219–20
My Own Country: Gripping the Knife's Edge (*Bayan ko: Kapit sa patalim*, Brocka, 1984), 133–50, 237; censorship of, 138, 146–48, 149, 176–77; political themes, 66, 132, 146, 149–50, 153, 162; reception, 146, 148, 149–50, 159–60; storyline, xxiii, 134–36, 137–39, 141;
"My Own Country" ("Bayang ko", song), 133, 139, 141

Nadres, Orlando, *My Father, My Mother* screenplay by, 214, 217, 219, 222
Naremore, James, 75–76
National Democratic Front, 140–41. *See also* communism/communists
Neale, Steve, 76
Nelly vs. Nelly (*Mahinhin vs. Mahinhin*, Zialcita, 1981), 224
Nemenzo, Francisco, 93
neorealism, Italian, 20, 29–30, 55, 146, 173, 242. *See also* corporealism; realism
New Teacher, The (*Ang bagong maestra*, Gerardo De Leon, 1953), 20
Nights of Cabiria (Fellini, 1957), 29
Niogret, Hubert, 105
Nofuente, Valerio, 36
Noli me tangere (Rizal), 2–3, 4, 242; allegories in, 13, 24, 36–37; influence on *Weighed but Found Wanting*, 5–6, 7, 8–9, 13–14, 16, 22;

melodrama of, 35–36; sociopolitical critiques, 38, 39
Now (Brocka, 1971), 3

Oca (Brocka, 1990), 242
O'Hara, Mario, screenplays by: *Insiang*, 49–50, 51; *Weighed but Found Wanting*, 4, 251n29
"Old Selo" ("Tata Selo," Sicat, 1962), 5
Olivares-Cunanan, Belinda, 175–76
On the Fifth Floor (*Sa fifth floor*, Ramos Jr., 1971), 234
Oraprobonis (*Fight for Us/Les insoumis*, Brocka, 1989), 163–80; allegories in, 165, 166; censorship of, 174–76; documentary material, 171–72; political themes, 168, 169–71; reception, 171–72, 175–76, 178; storyline, 164–70, 178–80; vigilantism, xxiii, 163–77; violence, 172–78, 179
Orteza, Bibeth, 224
O'Shaughnessy, Martin, xvii
Overbey, David, 145, 239
Ozu, Yasujiro Ozu, influence of, 55

Page, Joanna, 121
Pantoja-Hidalgo, Cristina, 35
Paper Boats on a Sea of Fire (*Bangkang papel sa dagat ng apoy*, Edgardo M. Reyes, 1979), 130
Pasolini, Pier Paolo, 242
patriarchy, 22, 40–41, 48, 114, 189; authoritarianism and, xx, 7, 13–18, 71, 133; autocratic, 43–44, 97; hostile mother as substitute for, xxi, 58–60, 66–67, 71; protests against, 208, 212
Pecho, Ernie, 157–58
Perez Jacob, Ava, 36
Pinches, Michael, 53
police state. *See* martial law; surveillance
political melodramas, xix–xx, xxiii–xiv, 128–97; *Above Everything Else*, 191–95; *A Dirty Affair*, 180–91; *Miguelito*, 150–59; *My Own Country*, 133–50; *Oraprobonis*, 163–80
politics: of affirmation, 214; of authoritarianism, xii–xiii, 15, 46, 55; in Brocka's melodramas, xvi, xviii, xx; cultural, 51, 173, 254n91; in film noir, 76, 77, 90, 94, 97; gangster-politicians, 192–93; gay identity, 209–14, 215, 217, 223, 241; gender, xii–xiii, 65–66, 72–73, 199–200, 215–18, 225, 235, 241; identity, 36, 235; Marcos regime's, 5, 51; Philippine, 143, 144, 189, 190, 191–93; Rizal's treatment of, 35. *See also* cinema politics; sociopolitical critiques; *and*

the term political themes *under individual film titles*
poverty, Marcos-era, 34, 90, 114, 127; depicting, 29, 35, 86, 87, 254n91. *See also* economy, crisis in 1980s; Marcos, Ferdinand, regime of, economic policies; slums
prestige films, xiv, 19, 23, 41, 54, 75, 132; Brocka's, xv, 54, 131, 158–59, 196, 237, 240, 242
Projansky, Sarah, 98
prostitution, 22, 25, 66, 131, 207, 210, 237, 242. *See also* human trafficking
protesters/protests, 73, 105, 222; against authoritarianism, 139, 141, 159–60, 180; graffiti, 1–2, 24, 33; youthful, xv, 47, 154, 212. *See also* Marcos, Ferdinand, regime of, protests against
Prowler, The (Losey, 1951), 74, 76
PX (Brocka, 1982), 242

queer melodramas, xxiv, 2–3, 198–241; *Always Changing, Always Moving*, 223–34; *Gold Plated*, 200–214; *Macho Dancer*, 176, 237–41; *My Father, My Mother*, 214–23
Quest for Fire (Annaud, 1981), 133
Quijano, Rebecca, 139
Quimpo, Susan F., 138

Rabinovitz, Paula, 77, 103
Ramirez, Sonny, 175
Rancière, Jacques, xvi–xvii, xix–xx, 195
rape, scenes of, 47, 95, 99, 243
rape-revenge films, xxii, 98, 101–5
Ravelo, Mars, 200–201, 203, 213
realism, xvii–xviii, 20, 76. *See also* corporealism; neorealism, Italian
Rebel without a Cause (Ray), 16, 150
Red, Isah, 191
Regalado, Raul, 125
Regal Films (production company), 130
Rempel, William, 63–64
Renard, Collette-Marie, 146
Reportage on Crime (Joaquin), 86, 90
repression, 21, 46, 47, 63, 154, 159; mechanisms of, xiii, xxii; of organized labor, 137–45; social, 13, 76. *See also* authoritarianism
revenge, 72–73, 93. *See also* rape-revenge films
Reyes, Emmanuel, 149, 157
Reyes, Jose Javier, scripts by: *Adultery*, 110; *Such Pain, Brother Eddie*, 125
Reyes, Soledad, 5
Richardson, Niall, 203, 227
Rimas, Jerico, 118
Rissient, Pierre, 54, 87, 145, 148

Rizal, José, xxi, 131. *See also El filibusterismo* (Rizal); *Noli me tangere* (Rizal)
Rodowick, D. N., 131
Russo, Vito, 203

Salas, Rodolfo, 183
salvaging. *See* violence, salvaging as form of
Samelson, Franz, 44
San Juan, Epifanio, Jr., 7, 11
Sarris, Andrew, 74, 75
Scent of Apples (Santos), 243
Schoonover, Karl, 173–74, 199, 209
Scott, Jay, 146
Sedgwick, Eve Kosofsky, 229
Sepang Ioca (1957), 19
Sevilla Mendoza, Aida, 110
sexploitation films, 203, 207. *See also* exploitation films
sexuality. *See* bisexuality; prostitution
shantytowns. *See* slums
Shatkin, Gavin, 26
Sidel, John T., 191, 193
Signed, Lino Brocka (Blackwood, 1987), 204, 211, 212
Sin, Jaime Cardinal, 169
Sineux, Michel, 146
Sirk, Douglas, 207
Siytangco, Deedee, 149
slums: in Brocka's films, xi, 242; in Manila, xxii, 35, 45, 46, 77–78. *See also* squatters/squatting; *and under individual film titles*
socialism, 150, 178, 180, 196. *See also* communism/communists; Marxism
social melodramas, xiv, xv, xxi, 1–41, 132, 199; *Manila in the Claws of Light*, 23–39; *Weighed but Found Wanting*, 5–22
sociopolitical critiques: in *Above Everything Else*, 191; Brocka's, xiv, xv, xvi, xviii, 132, 195, 242, 244; in film noir, 76, 77; in maternal melodramas, 43–44; in Philippine films, xiii, 245; in Rizal's novels, xxi, 24, 39. *See also* cinema politics; human rights, films about; political melodramas; politics
Soriano, Luciano, 149
Sotto, Agustin, 97, 145
Sound of Music, The (Wise, 1965), 42, 201
Spain, Philippines' relationship to, 2–3, 4, 43
Sparkle in the Dark (*Kislap sa dilim*, Brocka, 1991), 243–44
Spivak, Gayatri, 123
squatters/squatting, 27–30, 50–52, 53, 92, 93, 94. *See also* slums

Stam, Robert, 82–83
State of Siege (Costa-Gavras, 1972), 173
Straayer, Chris, 228, 233
Strand Releasing (film distributor), 240
strikes, 93, 137–45, 148
Such Pain, Brother Eddie (Napakasakit, kuya Eddie, Brocka, 1986*)*, 109–10, 117–26; censorship, 125; Filipino overseas workers, 117–18, 123–26, 242; reception, 117, 118, 125–26; sociopolitical critique, 123, 29
surveillance, xxii, 15, 77, 88–89, 97
Sussman, Jerry, 21
Svolik, Milan, 58, 108, 156

Tadtad (religious cult), 163–64
Tan, Nelia, 226–27
Task Force Detainees of the Philippines, 166
Taxi Driver (Scorsese, 1976), 75, 76
Temptation (Tukso, Espiritu, 1971), 235
Tessier, Max, 85
Tesson, Charles, 21
That's All for Now and Many Thanks (Hanggang dito na lamang at maraming salamat, Nadres, 1974), 217
Third Cinema, xvi, 131, 146, 196
Thompson, Kristen Moana, 21, 77
Thompson, Mark R., 145
Three, Two, One (Tatlo, Dalawa, Isa, Brocka, 1974), 29
Tiong Tan, Ruby, 54
Torre, Nestor, 190, 191, 243
torture. *See* violence, torture
Tyler, Parker, 212, 215

United States, Philippines' relationship to, xv, 55, 109, 133, 141, 167, 169, 208, 242

Vasudevan, Ravi, xvii
Vera, Noel, 7, 42, 223
Victim (Dearden, 1961), 201
Vidal, Ricardo Cardinal, 167
vigilantism, xxiii, 93, 105, 162, 184
violence: of autocracy, 22, 59, 81; patriarchal, 72–73; political, 169–70, 184, 222; salvaging as form of, 61–62, 155, 168; state-sponsored, xxii, xxv, 60, 105, 138, 172–78; torture, 77, 98–103, 104–5. *See also* authoritarianism, violence during; Marcos, Ferdinand, regime of, violence under; vigilantism; *and under individual film titles*
Visit, The (Duerrenmatt), 158
Vito, Bey, *Sparkle in the Dark* assistant director, 243
Viva Films (movie studio), 164, 176, 181

Walker, Michael, xvii, 80
Wanted: Perfect Mother (Brocka, 1970), 3, 42, 200–201
Wayne, Mike, xvii, 196
Weighed but Found Wanting (Tinimbang ka ngunit kulang, Brocka), xxi, 5–22, 237, 239; allegories in, 4, 7, 18, 21–22; authoritarianism in, 11–18; censorship of, 4, 21; homosexual themes, 198; martial law, 4, 11–14, 21; *Miguelito* a remake of, 150; Oedipal issues, 13–18; reception, 18–22; sexuality in, 8, 14–15, 21; sociopolitical critique, 4, 7–11, 16–18, 20, 21; storyline, 6–7, 8–11, 11–12, 14, 15–17, 251n29
Wendling, Amy, 81
White, Patricia, 225
White Slavery (Brocka), 126
Whore of a Mother (Ina ka ng anak mo, Brocka, 1979), 42, 66–71; censorship of, 70; Oresteian script, 72–73; political themes, 67; reception, 70–71; storyline, xxii, 67–68, 69, 260n119
Wildflower (Ligaw na bulaklak, 1976), 43
Willemen, Paul, 103
Williams, Linda, xvii, xviii, 217, 232
Williams, Raymond, 25
Wintrobe, Ronald, 46, 58, 108
Wood, Robin, 218
working class, 25–27, 34, 35, 55, 80–81, 83–84; Engels's book on, 39, 114
World Bank, loans from, 26, 109
Written by Destiny (Iginuhit ng tadhana, 1965), 155
Wurfel, David, 169

Youngblood, Robert, 91–92
You're No Longer a Child, Sally (Hindi ka na bata, Sally, Brocka), 200

Z (Costa-Gavras, 1969), 173
Zabat, Fiel, *Insiang* production designer, 51

Founded in 1893,
UNIVERSITY OF CALIFORNIA PRESS
publishes bold, progressive books and journals
on topics in the arts, humanities, social sciences,
and natural sciences—with a focus on social
justice issues—that inspire thought and action
among readers worldwide.

The UC PRESS FOUNDATION
raises funds to uphold the press's vital role
as an independent, nonprofit publisher, and
receives philanthropic support from a wide
range of individuals and institutions—and from
committed readers like you. To learn more, visit
ucpress.edu/supportus.

www.ingramcontent.com/pod-product-compliance
Lightning Source LLC
Chambersburg PA
CBHW020942230426
43666CB00005B/126